Subverting Masculinity

GENUS:
Gender in Modern Culture

1

Russell West (Magdeburg)
Jennifer Yee (Newcastle-upon-Tyne)
Frank Lay (Cologne)

Amsterdam – Atlanta, GA 2000

Subverting Masculinity
Hegemonic and Alternative Versions of Masculinity in Contemporary Culture

Edited by
Russell West
and
Frank Lay

The paper on which this book is printed meets the requirements of "ISO 9706:1994, Information and documentation - Paper for documents - Requirements for permanence".

ISBN: 90-420-1234-X
©Editions Rodopi B.V., Amsterdam - Atlanta, GA 2000
Printed in The Netherlands

CONTENTS

Men, the Market and Models of Masculinity in Contemporary Culture: Introduction

Russell West

A man (or so one assumes) leans against the bar in a chic café, legs slightly crossed, both hands toying with a ballpoint pen, conversing with a figure who is just out of sight on the right hand side of the photo. The man appears to be somewhere between thirty and forty, has cropped hair and a receding hairline, and is regarding his interlocutor with an slightly ironic smile. He wears a knee-length skirt with matching jacket and a modish black top. He is pictured in a black and white advertisement for the fashion firm Oui Woman in the German women's magazine *Brigitte*. The caption of the advertisement reads "Mode für das starke Geschlecht" – *Fashion for the stronger sex* (*Brigitte* 1999: 65).

The advertisement undoubtedly seeks to provoke, orchestrating the collision of ostensibly incommensurable qualities: masculinity and femininity, male chic and women's fashion, strength and weakness. Clearly the advertisement is aimed at a very specific audience, the readers of the women's magazine *Brigitte*. It is unlikely to shock them; rather, one suspects, this drag pose is seen as quite amusing, even intriguing, a catchy variation on the normal gendered state of affairs. Far more, the advertisement flatters the modern self-assertive and upwardly-mobile members of the "stronger sex" while allowing them to retain signifiers of essentialised femininity. The slogan suggests that women who purchase articles from this fashion house will be able to appear in public with the brash self-confidence normally reserved for males – a self-confidence materially linked to Oui Woman by the metonymic association of costume with self-assertive masculinity.

Let us take the pun at face value, however, thereby trying to read the advertisement against the grain – against the grain because the photo is emphatically *not* designed, one knows instinctively, to be consumed by male readers. For the slogan "fashion for the stronger sex", when addressed to men, could only be understood as a deeply corrosive irony. There are several reasons for this. First, the tangible, visually performed suggestion that a skirt could be appropriate attire for a man directly undermines one element of the predominantly visual demarcation of masculine and feminine gender upon which European masculinity at least is predicated: to don a dress, within our culture, cannot but soften masculinity, turning a man into a member of "the weaker sex". Secondly, even more problematic is perhaps the cumulative message of image and text together, namely, the combination of this man's easy, slightly ironic manner, and the attribution of the label "the stronger sex". This fusion of smile and label produces two principal connotations with vertiginous implications: on the one hand, the photo, with its naturalist realism, patently offers a plausible subject position the male viewer could himself take up, thus gaining an appelative function and proposing imitation of the figure with whom a degree of identification is possible, if only latently so – for such identification would most likely be instantly foreclosed by most male viewers. On the other hand, the ensemble suggests that wearing a dress is in no way problematic, does not threaten a "real man" in his masculinity, and that any male overtaken by an indefinable malaise when gazing at this photo is in some way prone to gender fragility – a recognition which, one could surmise, would equally need to be converted immediately into rejection or bland indifference in order not to be thought through in all its consequences. The photo suggests in tangible visual form to what extent masculine gender is produced by processes of performativity whose reiterated character elides but cannot exclude alternatives. Reading the photo with an eye to its larger implications also suggests to what extent such performativity is imbricated in a wide range of social and economic practices which make subversion of hegemonic forms of masculinity a much less accessible option than we often like to acknowledge.

I stumbled upon the Oui Woman drag advertisement during the preparation of this volume, and, intrigued by an image which eminently seemed to embody the "subversion of masculinity" foregrounded in the volume's proposed title, I enquired with the fashion house about gaining permission to use the photo for the cover. The reader will of course have already noticed that the photo I have described is *not* on the cover of this collection: unsurprisingly, I was firmly told that the photo rights could on no account be ceded, as the company would not be in a position to know whether it could sanction the contents of the book. Obviously Oui Woman's use of such images of men is motivated by the creation of profitable margins on the sales of fashion items, and not by the desire to explore the cultural significance of contemporary versions of masculinity. Yet what was quite compelling was the vehemence with which the enquiry about photo rights was refused, and the justification given for the refusal. Even if it was no more than a convenient pretext, the rejection apparently reposed upon anxiety about control of a controversial image of masculinity, and in particular, about the commentary upon that image contained in a text it might have accompanied. Oui Woman's advertising image unleashes the disparate semiotic forces underlying the construction of gender, with the intent of channelling them in carefully controlled directions. The powerful and potentially explosive contradictions set free by the slogan "Fashion for the stronger sex" are rigidly policed so as not to be supplemented by other texts which might modify the meaning of the image-text ensemble, potentially opening up a range of meanings latently present in such an ensemble but not intended by the advertisers.

I suggest that the refusal of Oui Woman to cede rights to this photo, albeit motivated by quite pragmatic desire to restrict the distribution of a potent advertising image to a selected market, is also in some way symptomatic of the current state of instability of definitions of gender within Western culture. This photo clearly mobilises a deeply disturbing image of masculinity as a mutable, nebulous entity, capable of being travestied by the simple assumption of a set of clothes. The photo utilises an extremely provocative gesture of gender subversion, indeed, one which erodes the very foundations of masculinity, only to carefully recuperate it for reasons of profit. This recuperation is achieved partly by the specific connotations it contains for female viewers (an affirmation of essential feminine values) and partly by its restriction to that specific group of addressees. The distribution of the photo works to stabilise the boundaries of a market – a feminine market whose dissolution the photo nevertheless implicitly flirts with. Indeed, it is only because the constitutive masculine/feminine gender division is so deeply anchored in everyday reality that its erasure can be so effectively – and presumably lucratively – toyed with.

This brief episode centred around the Oui Woman drag advertisement encapsulates some of the paradoxes and contradictions of contemporary shifts and rifts in culturally determined articulations of masculine gender. The opposition between hegemonic and alternative versions of masculinity contained in the title of this volume should not be taken as implying a bipolar field of conflict between monolithic gender configurations: far more, the "subverting" present in the title seeks to evoke localised, uneven processes serving various interests not always compatible with each other nor recuperable within a single economic, political or social programme. This collection of essays aims to map the contours of the new and often ambivalent configurations of masculinity in modern culture, configurations which increasingly defy easy categorisation, or can only be located at the paradoxical interstices of several seemingly contradictory discourses: thus, in the example given above, the apparently subversive mobilisation of images of an ambivalent masculinity are harnessed within the heterogeneous field of visual advertising, fashion discourses and notions of gender identity for purposes which are anything but emancipatory. As Robert Connell observes, "[t]he idea that we live at the moment when a traditional male sex role is softening is as drastically inadequate as the idea that a true, natural masculinity is being recovered" (Connell 1995: 199). This opening anecdote is not offered merely as a gratuitous illustration of the inextricably tangled knots of hegemonic and alternative versions of masculinity, but precisely because it exemplifies the novel configurations of gender out of which this collection arises. For the development of untoward alliances between the market and new discourses of masculinity shares the same context of historical development as the emergent discourses of gender studies, and more specifically, men's studies, to which the present collection sees itself as a contribution.

Gillian Rose has accused male discourse of frequently eliding its context of enunciation, thereby implicitly making a claim towards placelessness and thus universal validity – whereas in fact, every discourse arises out of a situation which both gives it its relevance and marks the limits of its truth claims (Rose 1993: 7-8). Similarly, Luce Irigaray has typified masculine discourse as that which refuses to acknowledge its debts, thus eliding the network of relations within which any enunciation can be made (Irigaray 1982). Giacobazzi, in his work on Gadamer's hermeneutics, has pointed out that the discovery of the limits, and thereby of the situatedness of one's knowledge, constitutes the only possible starting point for the modification of that knowledge (Giacobazzi 1998). In the light of these critiques, I hope, by declaring some of the discursive starting-points for the enquiries contained in this volume, to manifest some debts incurred and mark out some of the locations (even in the quite specific geographical sense of the ways gender-theory and men's studies in particular travels [see Connell 1999: 13-15; August 1994: xi-xii; Said 1998]) from which the contributors to the volume speak. The following introductory remarks are thus intended partly as a clarification of the context in which new discourses of masculinity have begun to emerge and thus, at the same time, of the immediate history of the new field of men's studies in which this collection is situated; at the same time, these remarks constitute an acknowledgement of our indebtedness to prior theoreticians in the field of gender studies. The place of this book, and the location of a critical men's studies which the essays it contains attempt to explore, is between novel versions of masculinity, the increasing subversion of hitherto hegemonic masculinities, and recuperation of these subversions for a traditional project of gender domination: the domination of women, the domination of the natural environment, and the domination internal to masculinity itself and relations between men.

The starting point for a critical men's studies was the questioning of the universal character of masculinity, an interrogation famously initiated by Simon de Beauvoir in her *Second Sex*, when she dismantled the Norm/Deviation, Neutral/Marked, Self/Other, Masculine/Feminine isomorphism at the heart of patriarchal thought and practice, by questioning the ostensibly neutral or unproblematic character of masculinity: "Un homme n'aurait pas idée d'écrire un livre sur la situation singulière qu'occupent dans l'humanité les mâles. [...] Un homme ne commence jamais par se poser comme un individu d'un certain sexe: qu'il soit homme, cela va de soi" (de Beauvoir 1996 [1949]: I 14). In a provocative gesture which refuses the self-evidence of masculine being, Freud's epithet for women as the "dark continent" has been reversed and outbidded by Formaini in her book on *Men: The Darker Continent* (Formaini 1990); likewise, Rutherford has recast Freud's "What do women want?" into the more disturbing and perplexed "What do men want?" (Rutherford 1988: 25). The specificity and highly problematic character of masculinity as a complex of discursive and extra-discursive practices has increasingly become the focus of pragmatic attempts to deal with social conflict, with Schnack and Neutzling for example discovering that it is boys, and not girls, who display the most prominent problems with academic achievement and social integration, leading the authors to suggest that contradictions in the models of masculinity available to young boys set them under considerable pressure (Schnack/Neutzling 1990: 127-163). The suggestion that masculinity is problematic, and therefore not a natural given, allows it to become a specific focus of theoretical study, and implicitly, a field for discursive interventions (Easthope 1987:1). Not only at the level of published theoretisation, but also in the domain of everyday critical reflection, masculinity as the conjunction of a specific mode of experience, set of practices and of constitutive discourses has taken on the status of a distinct and problematic entity or focus of attention (see Christian 1994). "Given these circumstances [...]", observes Connell, "we should not be surprised to find among the men of the rich countries a widespread awareness of change in gender arrangements" (Connell 1995: 201).

Thus the emergence of a substantial number of men concerned to think critically about their own gender practice and that of the patriarchal society of which they are a part has gone hand in hand with the emergence of a considerable body of theoretical work and the establishment of a controversial niche in higher education known as men's studies. Following on early theories of sex role models which tended to leave unquestioned the stereotypical attributes of masculinity and femininity (Connell 1995: 21-27), more recent gender theorisations drawing upon the insights of poststructuralist theories have stressed the "fabrication" of masculinity (Falconnet/Lefaucheur 1977) as a discursive construct embedded in non-discursive practices. The invisibility of male bodies in public discourse and sociological theory lamented by Ramsay Burt, apparently contradicted by the clear visibility of men's bodies in public life, has increasingly been cast into question by recent gender theory (Burt 1995: 13; Mishkind et.al. 1987: 41). Mieke Bal has stressed the extent to which the innate sense of an embodied masculine or feminine identity is produced within a complex set of discursive, social and bodily mechanisms: "the relation between the individual subject and the culturally normative images is bodily without being 'innate' or anatomically determined. [...] the issue is *feeling*: how the subject *feels* his or her position in space. What we call 'feeling is the threshold between body and subjectivity." Language , in particular the deictic operations of such culturally loaded words such as "I", "you", "here", "my", is locked into the "proprioceptivity": "the sensation of the self within the body"; but "this proprioceptive basis for deixis comprehends more than words alone. It comprises the muscular system as well as the space around the body, the space in which it 'fits' like within a skin" (Bal 1997: 214-215). Connell has remarked that the hallmark of masculinity, at the most intimate level of "the physical sense of maleness", "is distinctly to occupy space, to have a physical presence in the world"; such bodily experience is not given, but constructed through, for instance, sporting activities, which teach a certain intra- and intercorporeal mode of bodily functioning, contributing to the "somatisation" of social relations (Connell 1983: 19; Bourdieu 1998: 29) These theoretical explorations have gone hand in hand with the overcoming of the frequent foreclosure of men's own bodily experience, and the inability to give voice to the intimate texturisation of masculine bodily experience. Such bodily modes of experience are in turn constructed within a family history which been carefully examined within the context of feminist psychoanalysis and its attention to the relationships between boys and their mothers and fathers (Chodorow 1978; Dinnerstein 1978; Frosh 1994). The construction of individual masculine subjectivities and patterns of behaviour cannot however be examined out of the context of the larger social framework of patriarchy. There has been considerable theoretical work done upon masculinity as the "gender of oppression" (Hearn 1987) and masculinity and power (Brittan 1989, Connell 1987), and particularly upon the defence of masculine privilege through the direct use of physical violence directed at women, gay men or children (Horsfall 1991; Myslik 1996; Connell 1987: 12-13; Kaufmann 1987: 15-23). These are some of the most disturbing aspects of the hegemony of masculine power in our society, and ones which have led individual men or groups of men to think critically about the configurations of masculinity in which they participate.

The distancing tactic involved in stepping back from masculinity-as-a-given to masculinity-as-a-construct is accompanied by a similar use of a meta-level of reflection to move from the plane of practices to the plane of the discourses which transmit, mediate, legitimate or buttress those practices of masculinity. Both these tactics within critical reflection upon masculinity are not evidence of a retreat from the dilemmas of everyday existence within gendered relationships so much as an attempt at political intervention at the level of the production of gender practices as well as at the level of the *results* of those productive mechanisms, though both discursive mediation and material practices would appear to merit, indeed, demand political intervention on the part of dissenting men. The relations between the symbolic/cultural domain and the material domain of masculine domination need to be brought to light in order to gain a better

understanding of the ways in which patriarchy is made to
evident (Bourdieu 1998: 7, 9). Thus recent scholarship has
discourses of masculinity in history (Roper/Tosh 1991;
literature (Schwenger 1984; Middleton 1992; Nyman 1997;
philosophy (Lloyd 1984, Seidler 1994), or in the particularly convoluted
nexus of racial oppression and gender oppression in the US and the UK, in
which black masculinity appears both and oppressed and oppressive (Segal
1990: 168-204; Alexander 2000). (Similar complexities have been analysed
in the context of Latino masculinity [Leak 1999]). These studies undertake
the investigation of the "self-evident" ideologies of masculinity which
support the reproduction of gendered relations of production in society (see
Althusser 1976). The task of the present volume is to contribute to the
mapping of contemporary relationships between material practice of
patriarchy and cultural practices which encode and legitimise the
configurations of modern masculinity and its transformations.

Yet the history of configurations of masculinity, and in conjunction with
that, the history of men's studies, continues to evolve in complex and often
perplexing ways. The inroads of feminism in various Western countries,
coupled with structural transformations of Western capitalism, as industry-
based economies have increasingly made the transition to information- and
service-based economies, appear to have produced a widespread crisis of
masculine identity with the onset of high unemployment in previously
male-dominated industrial sectors, and the increased participation of
women in the professions and information sectors. It was a sense of crisis
of masculinity, which, as also became clear, by no means implied the
demise of masculine power, which triggered interrogation of the nature of
masculine identity from the 1970s on, as Kobena Mercer pointed out in a
broad retrospective in 1990: "identity only becomes an issue when it is in
crisis, when something assumed to be fixed, coherent and stable is
displaced by the experience of doubt and uncertainty" (Mercer 1990: 43).
Men's responses to the challenge of feminism in the 1970s, in many cases
involving a combination of political activism, a critical gaze upon personal
relationships and attempts to change the dynamics of those relationships,
and accompanied by reflection upon the social, psychological and political
aspects of masculinity, are documented for instance in the British anti-
sexist men's journal *Achilles Heel* (for a selection of articles see Seidler
1991). However, such politicised activism and reflection appeared to fall
off from the mid-1980s onwards: Jonathon Rutherford gives 1982, when
Achilles Heel ceased publishing, as a watershed date (Rutherford 1988: 40-
41). (That said, it would seem that such anti-sexist activism remains a
potent if minority stream in radical gender politics. Both *Achilles Heel* and
men's groups were alive and well in the 1990s; my own participation in a
men's group in Cardiff from 1995 to 1997 was the result of a contact
obtained from a list of addresses published in the revived *Achilles Heel*).

The emergence of the "soft" masculinities of "New Men" (Rutherford 1988: 32-36) were followed by a return to Jungian mythologies of Ur-masculinity (Bly 1990, Tacey 1997). In the wake of these socio-discursive movements came a much-proclaimed "backlash" said to be clamping down since the 1980s on women's new-found economic and professional independence (Faludi 1992). Reactionary men's lobbies stressed the oppression of men and "the 'forgotten' problem of discrimination suffered by white males as a result of affirmative action quotas and preferential treatment of women and minorities in hiring, promotion and educational opportunities" (Yúdice 1995; August 1994: 223). More recently, reaction has taken the form of a resurgence of "bad-boy" cultural forms or notions of "Retributive Man" (Rutherford 1988: 28). Simultaneously, the production of "soft masculinities", despite a swing back to "hardness" in some social and cultural sectors, appears to have taken root on the market with an increased commodification of the male body, in the form of a noticeable growth in the male health, cosmetics and fashion industries, rebutting claims made for the drab continuity of the public appearance of men made as late as the mid-1980s (Coward 1984: 29-30). Paradoxically, however, the market co-optation of a new awareness of the embodiment of masculinity appears to sit quite comfortably alongside "unreformed" aspects of masculinity such as macho conquest, sexist stereotypes and the cult of the mastery of personal and public space encapsulated in body-building. Such paradoxical combinations are exemplified in the rash of successful male style magazines such as *GM*, *Arena* and *Men's Health* (see Mort 1996: Part 1), which often appear in several American, British and European editions, thus testifying to a trend which straddles the Western cultures, even when local variations can be found. What is emerging here is the equivalent for gender-configurations of what Habermas has called "the new perplexity" ("die neue Unübersichtlichkeit") (Habermas 1996). Emblematic of this perplexity, in the area of masculinity theory, are attempts to reconcile apparently incompatible approaches to masculinity such as Bly's mythopoetics with the political analyses of the anti-sexist men's movement, a quixotic task undertaken for instance by Vic Seidler (Seidler 1997).

However, this nexus of postindustrial, postcolonial and postmodern phenomena has also been accompanied in gender studies by a radical questioning of the very basis of previous explorations of gender practices in society. Exemplary for this radical interrogation is the work of Judith Butler, which has questioned the very constitutive terms of gender debates, the binary oppositions masculine/feminine and sex/gender (Butler 1990; Butler 1993). This dissolution of the central terms of gender debates might well appear to sabotage the very feasibility of achieving real political change within gender relationships when the constitutive terms of the debate are jettisoned. How to constitute an anti-sexist masculinity, for instance, when masculinity itself, as a mere linguistic or social construct, is disqualified as a term of analysis? As Peter Middleton has observed, "once made the subject of reflection upon itself, gender deconstructs almost all the founding concepts upon which theories of language, culture and self are based. Gender is a much more radically destabilising concept than most men theorists have recognised" (Middleton 1992: 159). In place of these binary terms, Butler suggests the notion of performativity, which transpires to be no less useful as an instrument for the critical scrutiny of practices of patriarchy, as Laura Levine suggests, in remarking "that men are only men in the performance of their masculinity (or, put more frighteningly, they are not men except in the performance, the constant re-enactment of their masculinity)" (Levine 1994: 7). Performance and insecurity-driven repetition have also been identified as one of the mechanisms underlying aggressive contemporary defences of hegemonic masculinities (Connell 1995: 83-86). Similarly, the binary paradigm which verses patriarchy against anti-sexist men is replaced by theoreticians such as Connell through the more flexible terms of hegemonic, subordinated, complicit and marginalised masculinities. Connell opts for an array of masculine "gender projects", dispersed localised strategies involving varying degrees and forms of resistance to or compliance with hegemonic masculinity (Connell 1995: 71-81). Is Connell's new analytical apparatus evidence of perplexity, or an accurate index of the fragmentation of the field of gender and in particularity of masculine genders? Certainly it would appear that we urgently need a new "cognitive mapping" of postmodern gender, to pilfer Jameson's response to the perplexing alliances of technology, culture and global capitalism in the postmodern age (Jameson 1992: 51). It will be clear that the essays in this collection almost without exception operate within the dissolution of earlier simpler oppositions of patriarchy and dissent, showing how complex the imbrications of masculinity, gender subversion, neo-liberal market forces and globalised social transformations have become in the contemporary age.

Not only the perplexing new configurations of masculine gender practices at the beginning of the millennium but also the continued association of masculinity and power make it exceedingly difficult to undertake such a project of critique with any degree of integrity. In Alice Jardine and Paul Smith's 1987 collection entitled *Men in Feminism*, Stephen Heath concluded that the relation of men to feminism was an impossible one (Heath 1987: 1). Similarly, Connell is doubtless correct in drawing attention to the daunting difficulties entailed by the crucial element of auto-reflexivity in men's studies, for such reflection about masculine power involves speaking against one's own interests as a man (Connell 1995: 7, 203). Joseph Boone has argued for the possibilities opened up by a collaboration between men and feminist theory, one that acknowledged male critics' debts to feminism while being careful not to appropriate or annexe the institutional and theoretical territory mapped out by feminist women (Boone 1990: 12). On an avowedly subjective plane, and without hesitating to draw attention to the symptomatic value of the inarticulate language he uses, Jonathon Rutherford acknowledges both the necessity and difficulty of "respond[ing] to a sexual politics that was extremely critical of me, but also offered me a sense of myself and something that I wanted" (Rutherford 1988: 22). Clearly, for both subjective and political reasons, analyses of the functioning of masculinity must be undertaken, whatever axiological pitfalls the cultural critic may have watch out for and negotiate in the process. Indeed, it is only through the process of undertaking such analyses that these theoretical aporias can be implicitly addressed. This volume includes contributions by women and men critics, thereby suggesting that analyses of hegemonic and subversive versions of masculinity in contemporary culture can be carried out from within a wide range of institutional, theoretical and gender affiliations without prejudicing their validity. The programme of political intervention pursued by the individual contributors to this volume may be quite different from one another, a variation which is surely reflected in their respective papers.

What the contributions do have in common, despite the healthy heterogeneity of their approach and of the objects of their analyses, is the conviction of the potent agency of gender discourses in the constitution of gender practices, and by extension, the agency of analyses of gender in the transformation of gender practices. In notable interviews with Deleuze and Fontana, Foucault suggested that the principal role of analyses of discursive configurations was to provide knowledge for political action, to map out and lay bare workings of discourse (Foucault 1972/1977 and 1977). But such analyses are themselves discursive interventions which take effect within their context of production, be it in the mediated form of teaching, discussions which stimulate the participants' critical awareness, or in the banal context of everyday domestic existence or issue-oriented political activity. As Annamarie Jagose points out, there can be no simple opposition of theory and practice, knowledge and action (Jagose 1996: 110-11). Many of the contributors to this volume teach in higher education institutions, a context in which gender theorisation directly engages provokes or with young people's reflection upon everyday experience of gender arrangements. In a society which has all but lost contact with earlier religious, oral or spectacle traditions (with the exception, perhaps, of spectator sport), cultural values are transmitted almost exclusively by textual means – whether printed (fiction, popular magazines, newspapers), visual (advertising, television, film), or digital and electronic (popular music, the Internet). It is these cultural modes which transmit, legitimise, reinforce, perpetuate or conversely, inflect, question, or contest the material practices of masculinity and the reproduction of patriarchal power. In turn, analytical discursive interventions, of which a publication such as the present volume is one form, however broad or narrow the possible radius of their effects – something that can hardly be measured – engage with those same discourses of masculinity, across the cultural forms which they take as their object of meditation, thus also participating in a field of power and its contestation. Theoretical interventions need to be seen as possible positions to be taken up within a broad and complex spectrum of discursive modes of figuration and refiguration of masculinity. Within a large variety of text types, from literary fiction through films to popular magazines, gender theory is one specific site, a specific mode of intervention within a dispersed, disparate but interlocking and over-determined field of cultural production (see Jameson 1981: 23-58). Clear evidence of the capacity of newer analyses of masculinity to engage with the discourses underpinning masculine power and assuring its reproduction is to be found in the ferocity with which critical approaches to masculinity are combated within some circles. One commentator condemns academic work which "uncritically" takes on board a "radical feminist perspective" guided by a "narrowly politicized" approach to gender in turn leading to a "reductive view" of cultural phenomena; such analyses "[lack] any positive concept of masculinity and [deal] in oversimplifications of Marxist-feminist doctrine" to produce the "spectacle of a male critic, having internalised a misandric [sic] mythology of male evil, relentlessly flagellating himself and other men" (August 1994: 371, 151). Against such perversions, the writer praises attempts "to transcend stereotypes of males and to present them as human beings in all their complexity and contradictions, with their triumphs and failures given equitable treatment" (August 1994: xiii). Clearly this agenda privileges a non-politicised "liberal" approach to the study of masculinities which elides the social processes and collective mechanisms characterised by the interlocking of culture, power and economics, and reduces heterogeneity and tension to the level of individual personal idiosyncrasy. The violence of the language used here to discredit critical analyses of masculinities belies the ostensibly liberal and apolitical character of this neo-conservative programme, and betrays the scope of the discursive power struggle at stake.

Such reactions are inevitable because critical analyses of masculinities question the strategic privilege of invisibility – one of the most effective forms of hegemony (Foucault 1976: 113) – unquestionability and self-evidence, and lay bare the representational tactics which legitimise and thus contribute to the perpetuation of masculine privilege. Admittedly, critical men's studies can equally be accused of shoring up of male power in the academy by posing as a competitor to women's studies, and attempting to usurp upon the niche thus opened up for women in the academy. Here the political responsibility accepted by anti-sexist men appears as a cynical attempt to commandeer a trendy theoretical bandwagon (see Braidotti 1987). Such criticisms must be taken seriously by the proponents of men's studies. It is of course not unproblematic that this volume on masculinity, edited by two male academics, inaugurates a new series on representations of gender in modern culture. It would be hypocritical to deny that research on gender is often intimately involved with institutional and professional stakes. It would be even more naive to pretend to be ignorant of the charge of recuperation of feminist institutional terrain which could potentially be levelled at us as the editors of this volume. Yet the inevitable and inextricable entanglement of "baser" institutional imperatives and more "progressive" political agendas, while needing to be acknowledged and confronted (both by men and women, whether studying masculinity or femininity), cannot serve as a rationale for *not* exploring the contradictory configurations of contemporary representations of gender. Significantly, the manifold possibilities of academic recuperation of a critical discourse and its capacity for subversion accurately reflect the ambiguous function of new discourses of masculinity in a wider social context, and thus place a further burden of responsibility upon those women and men who pursue the discipline of critical gender studies, to continue to reflect about ongoing ways of resisting such recuperation. Thus the pursuit of critical insights into the configurations of lived masculinities at the beginning of the twenty-first century needs to be reflected upon within the parameters, respectively, of theoretical debates, institutional contexts, cultural and representational projects, various sexual practices and orientations, market forces and commitment to political struggles for change, both in the private and public spheres. This task is attempted by the contributors of the present volume in three domains dedicated to film, literature and diverse cultural forms respectively.

It is film's combination of visual, textual and performance discourses which makes it such a potent encoding of gender patterns, but at the same time, lays such patterns open to subversion, be it only briefly. The subversion and often the recuperation of hegemonic representations of masculinity in film are discussed in the first part of the present collection. Elisabeth Krimmer examines a number of recent films foregrounding the female impersonator, *Mrs Doubtfire* (1993), *To Wong Foo: Thanks for Everything, Julie Newmar* (1995) and *Just Like a Woman* (1995), to show that male transvestitism in cinema is symptomatic of a crisis in masculinity and a concomitant sentiment of the necessity of a radical transformation of the traditional shape of manhood. At the same time, she detects in such movies not only an appropriation of attributes of femininity which facilitates the marginalisation of women themselves, but also the reinforcement of a "display culture" which simultaneously signals the subjection of men to a consumerist gaze. In similar vein, my article on *Crocodile Dundee* (1986) highlights the importance of film as a public discourse with immense power to determine discourses of gender. *Crocodile Dundee* figures national identity in terms of gender in order to articulate the problematic relationship of Australia to the United States, but at the same time, steering around the perils of gender indeterminacy to recuperate masculine weakness for the mediatised commodification of cultural and gender difference. Buttressed by discourses of national identity, hegemonic masculinity can be seen to co-opt challenges to its dominance by agile adaptation to a new regime of gender discourses. In a reading of a number of recent American films, *Pulp Fiction* (1994), *The Doom Generation* (1995), *American Generation X* (1998) and *The Fifth Element* (1997) Stefan Brandt suggests that as traditional concepts of "masculinity" and "femininity" are eroded, a novel signifier of masculine ambiguity has emerged in public discourse, both as a symptom and a putative resolution of this widely felt ambivalence. His contribution ends with the query as to whether the taboo upon homosexual desire, symbolically located in the corporeal site of the anus, appears in the most recent Hollywood productions also to be susceptible of negotiation by the discourses of mainstream cinema, perhaps with more radical consequences for discourses of masculinity those of masculine ambivalence, all too easily co-opted by the market. Barry Levinson's *Disclosure* (1994) is interpreted by Neil Badmington as symptomatic of the "backlash" against the inroads of American feminism diagnosed by Faludi (Faludi 1992); the film yearns for the good old days of patriarchy before feminism threatened male self-respect and job security. The unavowed, and unavowable subtext of the film, however, suggests Badmington, is the way in which the power structures of patriarchy preys upon its own representatives, posing a far greater threat to their well-being than that of self-assertive women. The film's undermining of its own project epitomises the limitations of patriarchal domination, but also sketches out possibilities for questioning hegemonic forms of masculinity.

The second part of the collection examines representations of masculinity in contemporary literature. Irving Welsh, in Stefan Herbrechter's article, is shown placing the contemporary crisis of masculinity in the larger context of the turbulent social transformations of post-Thatcherite Britain. Welsh's recent novel *Filth* (1998) portrays the utter bankruptcy of traditional working-class masculinity. Both postmodern social reality, in which social values have been destroyed by the paternalism of conservative politics, and contemporary family life, in the form of dysfunctional paternal relationships, are portrayed as inherently pathological in this bleak picture of gender as a social phenomenon. Madalena Gonzalez argues that Salman Rushdie's work, exemplified in her essay by a reading of *The Moor's Last Sigh* (1995), undermines the patriarchal structures of Indian society past and present, colonial and postcolonial. Rushdie's character Moor is an embodiment of the indeterminacy of masculine gender understood not as essence but as a parodic copy which abolishes the very notion of an original. By virtue of its celebration of a "carnival of indeterminacy", Rushdie's fiction attacks the very bases upon which the patriarchal order founds the discourses naturalising and thereby legitimising its hegemony. The prominence of popular contemporary fiction in these readings shows to what extent literary approaches to the contestation of hegemonic masculinity continue to possess agency, despite the fact that literature no longer occupies a dominant position in the cultural sphere. At the same time, it would appear that literary texts, as cultural atrefacts less easily assimilated to the market regime of visual commodification than film or fashion for example, may sometimes resist being co-opted by the consumerism which pervades other forms of gender indeterminacy. This is not always the case, however. Monika Müller discusses the conflict of roles attributed to the protagonists of Paul Auster's *New York Trilogy* (1985). On the one hand, the main characters of the three novels, all of them writers of detective fiction, strive to acquire the hyper-masculine traits of their invented sleuths by blending the respective identities of writer and private investigator; yet at the same time, the perilous proximity of the writer's profession to feminised domestic occupations and the corrosive effect of self-reflexive engagement with language threaten to undermine the masculine identity of the writing subject itself. Auster's trilogy, according to Müller, is marked by a deep anxiety about the capacity of men to fulfil their traditional bread-winner role and at the same time an anxiety about the writer's work with language, leading to a disjunction between these two tasks. A single protagonist in the trilogy successfully reconciles these two roles, thereby, however, merely reinforcing the hegemonic image of the male as breadwinner. A somewhat different cultural complex, characterised by a similar ambivalence however, is described by Peter Middleton in his analysis of a literary form increasingly marginalised from today's public sphere, that of poetry. Middleton traces the postwar ascendancy of fatherhood poetry, a literary phenomenon until now little explored, finding in the plethora of poetry about paternal figures more than a mere fad. Rather, he suggests, the filiative lyric represents a desire to re-establish masculine control over the ways in which the present is generated, or perhaps engendered by history, itself understood as a patriarchal linearity; it is accompanied by a strong tendency to marginalise the figure of the mother. In this perspective, poetical attacks on paternal power and domination may merely the obverse of an appropriation of the very discourse of phallic dominance being rejected, producing a complicit embrace between apparent subversion and the perpetuation of hegemony – an embrace only genuinely eluded by *parodic* poetic forms.

The third and final section of the collection encompasses diverse or mixed cultural forms. Here the readings of contemporary culture undertaken by the contributors embrace the broadest and most varied stretches of the cultural landscape of today's English-speaking world.

Eleanor Hogan argues that the recent rash of popular press attention to fatherhood and filitation in Australia is one symptom of the profoundly conservative character of the "men's movement", with its claims for men's disadvantaged status and its attempts to regain monopoly of the public sphere by representing the feminist movement as obsolete, predatory and family-eroding. In these new public discourses of a refounded masculinity, propagated by the lifestyle pages of the Sunday magazines, fathers are urged to dedicate themselves to the work of fathering so as to offer their sons positive masculine role-models – and also, according to Hogan's analysis, so as to reinforce social discipline through the policing of families as diagnosed by Foucault and Donzelot. This in turn serves the middle-class interests of the readers of such lifestyle magazines, who, reassured that their sons are being brought up as governable subjects, must not query the broader imbrications of social inequality and juvenile delinquent masculinity. Rainer Emig's article analyses the gender-categorical perplexities arising out of the conflicts between the increasing implication of masculinity in style, in consumerism, in market-driven desire, and the ongoing power of binary oppositions. Heterosexuality, Emig argues, having created its homosexual Other in service of its own self-constitution, is intimately related to that Other. Thus hegemonic heterosexual masculinity is of its very nature crisis-ridden – a state of affairs which is laid bare when, under the pressure of market forces, the excluded, peripheral Other comes to occupy the cultural centre, with disturbing results not only for hegemonic masculine identity, but also for the ostensibly deviant homosexual fringe. Emig identifies the contemporary inroads of fashion and lifestyle as the vehicle of such blurring of constitutive boundaries, going on to analyse with great precision such affluence-dominated trends through their mass-cultural dramatisation in late 1990s British "gay" television series like *Queer as Folk*, a series which resolutely employed sexual transgression as a marketing ploy. Emig then transfers this increasing blurring of straight/gay boundaries to that of hegemonic and subversive masculinities, and finally, to masculinity itself – leading, he suggests, perhaps to some sort of liberation or, less progressively, to an existence defined by undifferentiated consumerism and its simulacra. In a contribution on discourses of masculinity in contemporary popular music, Frank Lay reads the music industry, with its complex interactions of auditory, visual, sensory, textual and performative codes, for manifestations of shifts in gender consciousness, and in particular, discourses of masculinity. In music, of all the mixed cultural forms examined here, the overdetermination of codes is perhaps at its most instense. In the music industry, the imbrication of various domains of economic enterprise are also at their densest, making the relations of gender hegemony and subversion exceedingly difficult to untangle. Building upon an analysis of developments in contemporary popular music over the past few decades, Lay examines the various ways in which models of masculinity have been deployed in the male-dominated world of popular music, revealing the manner in which much of the difuse perplexity regarding transformations of masculinity is crystallised in the lyrics of musicians such as Joe Jackson, Randy Newman and Beck. Ruth Mayer looks at three White male figures in Africa – Edgar Rice Burrough's Tarzan, Hemingway's figure Macomber, and Clint Eastwood playing a film maker in *White Hunter, Black Heart* – to survey a broad span of twentieth-century representations of Western masculinity against the backdrop of Africa. Mayer highlights the autotelic character of white masculinity in Africa, its predominantly performative, rather than utilitarian, aspects in the figure of Tarzan. In Hemingway's Macomber, the ostentatious performance of masculinity is replaced by an interiorised sensual identification with the continent which is nonetheless equally dependent upon using Africa to stage its self-authorisation. In contemporary filmic texts such as *White Hunter, Black Heart* the action-based identification of masculinity with Africa is at once performed and deconstructed, self-reflexively scrutinising the entire trope of exploiting Africa as a scenario for rehearsals of White manliness. Action cedes to acting, in a sleight of hand which both undermines and simultaneously reifies and rescues the masquerades of masculinity. What is stressed most strongly in all the contributions of the final section is an aspect of masculinity present in muted form in part one and two: that of capitalism's capacity to co-opt all apparent threats to its dominance, including those of transformed gender configurations. The diversification of versions of masculinity appears all too often not as a genuine challenge to hegemonic masculinity, but as fetishised differentiation which channels possible challenges to gender hegemony into mere consumption.

The contributions in this volume map out the ongoing relevance of gender politics in contemporary culture. Parallel to this perspective, they also raise the disturbing spectacle of increasingly unclear distinctions between hegemonic and subversive versions of masculinity in the various artistic forms which structure contemporary cultural production. It is more and more clear that the splintering of versions of masculinity to be witnessed today in Western societies does not necessarily signify the end of male hegemony, although it may signal the bankruptcy of certain hitherto monolithic forms of masculine habitus and their images. Rather, relatively stable regimes of gender representation appear to have been replaced by a wider spectrum of varieties of masculine "lifestyles" taken up by the media and the market, to produce new and immensely flexible forms consumerised gender hegemony. At first glance the title of this volume, with its opposition of hegemony and subversion, might implicitly appear to assume a progressive political programme predicated upon the possibility of clear delineation between two forms of representation and the social structures thus signified. But the essays in the volume demonstrate that the subversion of traditional images of masculinity may itself be susceptible of assimilation by new hegemonic configurations of masculinity, thereby potentially short-circuiting agendas for progressive politics. There is thus no clearly marked front-line between hegemonic and subversive versions of masculinity, but rather, a complex and hybrid field of gender practices and representational practices where specific local struggles constitute foci for strategies whose character is not hegemonic or subversive in some essential fashion, but rather arises out of the issues involved and the coalitions of the groups working together (see Foucault 1972: 9-10/1977: 216-217). Such struggles may range from the banal but ubiquitous question of the division of household tasks (see for instance, *Le Monde* 2000) to fraught issues around patterns of fatherhood and child custody, the presence of gays and women in the military, same-sex marriages and adoption rights, the availability of the abortive pill or the representation of women in political institutions, to mention only a few current debates. The regimes of representation which pervade and determine such debates and the texture of their corresponding everyday lived experiences are not stable, but rather immensely fluid and volatile, demanding that the participants in such debates and struggles constantly renew the work of analysis of global and specific representations of gender in contemporary society. The present collection of essays on representations of masculinity in contemporary culture aims to contribute to that ongoing work of critical analysis.

My thanks to my co-editor Frank Lay for stimulating and productive conversations which were influential particularly in the writing of the final sections of this essay.

Works cited

Alexander, Claire 2000. "Black masculinity" in Kwesi Owusu (ed.). *Black British Culture and Society: A Text Reader*. London: Routledge, 373-384.

Althusser, Louis 1976. "Idéologie et appareils idéologiques d'Etat" in *Positions*. Paris: Éditions sociales, 79-137.

August, Eugene R. 1994. *The New Men's Studies: A Selected and Annotated Interdisciplinary Biography*. 2nd ed. Englewood, Col.: Libraries Unlimited.

Bal, Mieke 1997, "Space, Incorporated" in E. Hess-Lüttich (ed.). *Signs and Space, Zeichen und Raum: An International Conference on the Semiotics of Space and Culture in Amsterdam*. Tübingen: Gunter Narr, 1997, 199-223.

de Beauvoir, Simone 1996 [1949]. *Le Deuxième sexe*. Paris: Gallimard/Folio. 2 vols.

Bly, Robert 1990. *Iron John: A Book about Men*. Shaftsbury, Dorset/Rockport, Mass.: Element.

Boone, Joseph A. 1990. "Of Me(n) and Feminism: Who(se) Is the Sex that Writes?" in Joseph A. Boone, and Michael Cadden (eds). *Engendering Men: The Question of Male Feminist Criticism*. New York: Routledge. 11-25.

Bourdieu, Pierre 1998. *La Domination masculine*. Paris: Seuil/Liber.
Braidotti, Rosi 1987. "Envy: or With Your Brains and My Looks" in Alice Jardine and Paul Smith (eds.). *Men in Feminism*. New York: Methuen, 233-241.
Brandt, Stefan Leonhard 1997. *Männerblicke: Zur Konstruktion von 'Männlichkeit' in der Literatur und Kultur der amerikanischen Jahrhundertwende*. Stuttgart: M&P, 1997
Brigitte 1999. 19 (8 September 1999).
Brittan, Arthur 1989. *Masculinity and Power*. Oxford: Basil Blackwell.
Burt, Ramsay 1995. *The Male Dancer: Bodies, Spectacle, Sexualities*. London: Routledge.
Butler, Judith 1990. *Gender Trouble: Feminism and the Subversion of Identity*. New York: Routledge.
────── 1993. *Bodies that Matter: On the Discursive Limits of "Sex"*. New York: Routledge.
Chodorow, Nancy 1978. *The Reproduction of Mothering: Psychoanalysis and the Sociology of Gender*. London: University of California Press.
Christian, Harry 1994. *The Making of Anti-Sexist Men*. London: Routledge.
Connell, Robert W. 1983. *Which way is up? Essays on sex, class and culture*. Sydney: George Allen and Unwin.
────── 1987. *Gender and Power: Society, the person and sexual politics*. Cambridge: Polity Press.
────── 1995. *Masculinities*. Sydney: Allen and Unwin.
────── 1999. *Der gemachte Mann: Konstruktion und Krise von Männlichkeiten*. Trans. Christian Stahl. Opladen: Leske + Budrich.
Coward, Rosalind 1984. *Female Desire*. London: Paladin.
Dinnerstein, Dorothy 1978. *The Rocking of the Cradle and the Ruling of the World*. London: The Women's Press.
Easthope, Anthony 1987. *What A Man's Gotta Do: The Masculine Myth in Popular Culture*. London: Methuen.
Falconnet, Georges and Nadine Lefauchcur 1977. *La Fabrication des mâles*. Paris: Seuil/Points.
Faludi, Susan 1992. *Backlash: The Undeclared War against American Women*. New York: Anchor Doubleday.
Formaini, Heather 1990. *Men: The Darker Continent*. London: Mandarin.
Foucault, Michel 1972. "Les intellectuels et le pouvoir. Entretien Michel Foucault-Gilles Deleuze". *L'Arc* 49 (1972), 3-10.
────── 1976. *Histoire de la sexualité, 1: La Volonté de savoir*. Paris: Gallimard.
────── 1977. "Intellectuals and Power" in Donald F. Bouchard (ed.). *Language, Counter-Memory, Practice: Selected Essays and Interviews*. Ithaca: Cornell University Press, 205-217.
────── 1977. "Vérité et pouvoir. Entretien avec M. Fontana", *L'Arc* 70 (1977), 16-20.
Frosh, Stephen 1994. *Sexual Difference: Masculinity and Psychoanalysis*. London: Routledge.
Giacobazzi, Cesare 1998. "Gadamer in Neapel. Wie wahr ist ein erfundener Lebenslauf?" in Bernd Thum and Thomas Keller (eds.). *Interkulturelle Lebensläufe*. Tübingen: Stauffenberg, 235-250.
Habermas, Jürgen 1996. *Die Neue Unübersichtlichkeit (Kleine Politische Svhriften V)*. Frankfurt/Main: Suhrkamp.
Hearn, Jeff 1987. *The Gender of Oppression: Men, Masculinity and the Critique of Marxism*. Brighton: Wheatsheaf.
Heath, Stephen 1987. "Male Feminism" in Alice Jardine and Paul Smith (eds.). *Men in Feminism*. New York: Methuen, 1-25.

Horsfall, Jan 1991. *The Presence of the Past: Male Violence in the Family.* Sydney: Allen and Unwin.

Irigaray, Luce 1982. *Passions élémentaires.* Paris: Minuit.

Jagose, Annamarie 1996. *Queer Theory: An Introduction.* New York: New York University Press.

Jameson, Fredric 1981. *The Political Unconscious: Narrative as a Socially Symbolic Act.* London: Methuen.

Jameson, Fredric 1992. *Postmodernism, or, The Cultural Logic of Late Capitalism.* London/New York: Verso.

Kaufmann, Michael 1987. "The Construction of Masculinity and the Triad of Men's Violence" in Michael Kaufmann (ed.). *Beyond Patriarchy.* Toronto: Oxford University Press, 1-29.

Leak, Jeffrey B. 1999. "American and European Masculinity: A Transatlantic Dialogue" (Review Essay). *American Quarterly* 51: 1 (March 1999), 195-211.

Le Monde 2000, "Famille: les 'nouveaux pères' ont disparu", 17211 (27 May 2000), 1, 11.

Levine, Laura 1994. *Men in Women's Clothing: Anti-theatricality and Effeminization 1579-1642.* Cambridge: Cambridge University Press.

Lloyd, Genevieve 1984. *The Man of Reason: "Male" and "Female" in Western Philosophy.* London: Methuen.

Mercer, Kobena 1990. "Welcome to the Jungle: Identity and Diversity in Postmodern Politics" in Jonathon Rutherford (ed.). *Identity, Community, Culture, Difference.* London: Lawrence and Wishart, 43-71.

Mort, Frank 1996. *Cultures of Consumption: Masculinities and Social Space in late Twentieth-Century Britain.* London: Routledge.

Middleton, Peter 1992. *The Inward Gaze: Masculinity and Subjectivity in Modern Culture.* London: Routledge.

Mishkind, Marc E., et. al. 1987. "The Embodiment of Masculinity: Cultural, Psychological and Behavioral Dimensions" in Michael S. Kimmel (ed.). *Changing Men: New Directions in Research on Men and Masculinity.* Newbury Park, CA: Sage, 37-52.

Myslik, Wayne D. 1996. "Renegotiating the Social/Sexual Identities of Places: Gay Communities as safe havens or sites of resistance?" in Nancy Duncan (ed.). *BodySpace: Destabilizing the Geographies of Gender and Sexuality.* London: Routledge, 156-169.

Nyman, Jopi 1997. *Men Alone: Masculinity, Individualism, and Hard-Boiled Fiction.* Amsterdam/Atlanta: Rodopi.

Roper, Michael and John Tosh 1991. *Manful Assertions: Masculinities in Britain since 1800.* London: Routledge.

Rose, Gillian 1993. *Feminism and Geography: The Limits of Geographical Knowledge.* Oxford: Polity Press.

Rutherford, Jonathon 1988. "Who's That Man?" in Rowena Chapman and Mike Rutherford (eds.). *Male Order: Unwrapping Masculinity.* London: Lawrence and Wishart, 21-67.

Said, Edward W. 1998. "Traveling Theory" in Rainer Gahnal (ed.). *Imported: A Reading Seminar. Semiotext(e)* #18 – 6, 3 (1988), 157-181.

Schnack, Dieter and Rainer Neutzling 1990. *Kleine Helden in Not: Jungen auf der Suche nach Männlichkeit.* Reinbek: Rowohlt.

Schwenger, Peter 1984. *Phallic Critiques: Masculinity and Twentieth-Century Literature.* London: Routledge and Kegan Paul.

Segal, Lynne 1990. *Slow Motion: Changing Masculinities, Changing Men*. London: Virago.

Seidler, Victor J. (ed.) 1991. *The Achilles Heel Reader: Men, Sexual Politics and Socialism*. London: Routledge.

Seidler, Victor J. 1994. *Unreasonable Men: Masculinity and Social Theory*. London: Routledge.

———— 1997. *Man Enough: Embodying Masculinities*. London: Sage.

Tacey, David 1997. *Remaking Men: Jung, Sprituality and Social Change*. London: Routledge.

Tosh, John 1999. *A Man's Place: Masculinity and the Middle-Class Home in Victorian England*. New Haven: Yale University Press.

Yúdice, George 1995. "What's a Straight Man to Do?" in Maurice Berger, Brian Wallis and Simon Watson (eds.). *Constructing Masculinity*. New York: Routledge, 267-283.

Part I:

Cinema

Nobody Wants to Be A Man Anymore? Cross-Dressing in American Movies of the 90's

Elisabeth Krimmer

Celluloid Transvestism

No aficionado of American mainstream cinema could have missed the abundance of female impersonators appearing in feature films during the past two decades. While female-to-male cross-dressing has become a rarity, male-to-female transvestism now dominates the screen. In films such as *Tootsie* (1982), *Mrs. Doubtfire* (1993), *Priscilla, Queen of the Desert* (1993), *To Wong Foo, Thanks for Everything, Julie Newmar* (1995), *The Crying Game* (1992), *Just Like a Woman* (1995), and *The Birdcage* (1996), female impersonators have attracted audiences by reworking our culture's obsession with gender roles.

Although the preponderance of male-to-female cross-dressing in today's movies is an incontrovertible fact, interpretations of this phenomenon are multiple and contradictory. Some critics maintain that male impersonation has almost dropped from today's screen because women now wear the pants in everyday life (Bell-Metereau 1993: 2). Such critics argue that "the decrease in male impersonation and the increase in female impersonation coincide with an apparent rise in prestige for women within society" (Bell-Metereau 1993: 3). Others see the flood of female impersonation as indicative of a growing awareness of the deficiencies of current hegemonic definitions of masculinity and hence as an expression of the need to redefine and reform masculinity by incorporating character traits that are generally coded as feminine. Indeed, numerous male-to-female cross-dressers emerge from their transvestite experience as new men who have faced the shortcomings of masculine rationality and have grown to be emotionally developed and socially competent characters.

While such instances of individual growth might be welcomed on a personal level, we should be wary of consumerism's power to co-opt images of deviance and rebellion for the fortification (via modernization) of hegemonic definitions of masculinity. The celebration of the individual man's path to self-perfection not only fails to address questions of social and institutional change, it is also liable to reproduce the current gender hierarchy. Critics such as Abigail Solomon-Godeau have drawn attention to what could be described as a "colonization of femininity." To Solomon-Godeau, the new "feminized" man does not necessarily constitute a refutation of the patriarchal law and order. Rather, the incorporation of femininity may be read as the "logical extension of the 'real' historical event of women's expulsion from the public sphere." The male-to-female cross-dresser may be no more than "a cultural fantasy in which the feminine can be conjured away altogether [...] only to be reinscribed and recuperated within a masculine representation" (Solomon-Godeau 1995: 72).

By analyzing some of the recent feature films that thematize cross-dressing, I hope to shed light on the question of whether female impersonation can initiate and contribute to the liberation of both genders or whether it serves to reify hegemonic definitions of masculinity. I will also investigate whether the redefinition of manhood enacted in these films addresses the social and economic problems which face today's men or whether it deflects our attention away from what could be described as the real crisis of masculinity. In order to answer these questions I will first review the current research on masculinity. Based on this framework, I will analyze several movies with male-to-female cross-dressers (*Mrs. Doubtfire*, *To Wong Foo*, *Just Like a Woman*) which I will then contrast with an interpretation of one movie with a female-to-male cross-dresser (*The Associate*, 1996).

Manhood in Crisis

In recent years the American book market has been swamped with new publications on men and masculinity. While the authors of these studies are often affiliated with different interest groups and therefore pursue very different agendas, their assessment of the status of manhood is surprisingly unanimous. In almost all these texts, masculinity emerges as a concept under siege. Modern manhood, so it seems, is in a state of crisis (cf. Berger 1995: 70; Connell 1995: 207 ff; Faludi 1999: 6). The uniformity of this general diagnosis, however, is undermined by the authors' widely differing views on the precise nature of this crisis. Some maintain that the rise of feminism led to the disenfranchisement of men. They think that the white male is now the most discriminated-against minority, and attempt to restore a masculinity that – so they claim – has been damaged by recent social developments. Others, such as R. W. Connell, point out that men's privileged position of power is as yet untouched. The average income of men still exceeds that of women by far, and men still "virtually monopolize the elite levels of corporate and state power" (Connell 1995: 226). Thus, Connell concludes, it is not the material and institutional structures of patriarchy itself that are crumbling. Rather, it is the legitimization of patriarchy that has come under attack.

Patriarchal structures have been exposed not only by feminist critics but also by male advocates of Black and gay rights. The growing awareness that the definition of masculinity is subject to historical, social and ethnic variations is the result of the same conceptual framework which also allows us to account for the oppression of male minorities who do not conform to the current hegemonic definition of masculinity. Numerous attempts to de-essentialize gender (cf. Butler 1990) have made it possible to realize that masculinity is not always about men and that definitions of manhood are not actually a description of a status quo but rather provide a standard and norm to which men must aspire. Consequently, as Gilmore pointed out, if manhood is conceived of as an accomplishment, i.e., as a state that does not unfold naturally but that is achieved through performance, then manhood correlates directly with male role stress (Gilmore 1990: 221).

Susan Faludi's book *Stiffed: The Betrayal of the American Man* provides a far-reaching and insightful analysis of the phenomenon of male role stress. Faludi draws attention to the social, historical, and economic changes that have given rise to the wide-spread perception of masculinity in crisis. Rather than limiting her investigation to the psychological make-up of individuals, Faludi locates the origin of the manhood crisis in the rise of new corporate structures and the emergence of what she calls a display culture, a culture that is "constructed around celebrity and image, glamour and entertainment, marketing and consumerism" (35). Faludi theorizes that, although post World War II definitions of masculinity emphasizing the role of the male breadwinner persist into the 90s, new impersonal, corporate forms of domination – and mass lay-offs in their wake – have made it impossible for many men to live up to this ideal.

But it is not only the corporate betrayal of the American worker that undermines men's traditional self-definition. Faludi perceives a far more fundamental societal revolution that has resulted in the pre-eminence of representation and appearance over production and substance. Interestingly, this cultural revolution is intertwined with gender definitions. As representation and appearance are traditionally associated with the feminine realm, women are now perceived to have a competitive advantage in this new ornamental culture.

While it cannot be denied that ornamental culture is detrimental to both women's and men's identities, it is important to realize that the concept of femininity is more easily compatible with the new ethic which idealizes glamour, the creation of an image, and personal celebrity. Display culture is bound to limit women's personal growth but it is not diametrically opposed to their gender identity. Men, on the other hand, cannot comply with the requirements of ornamental culture without acting against the demands of traditional manhood. Thus Faludi's surprising conclusion, "men of the late twentieth century are falling into a status oddly similar to that of women at mid-century" (39).

Evidence for the "feminization" of men brought about by their subjection to the dictates of a display culture are numerous. Recently, critics have noticed a significant change in the portrayal of men by both the fashion and the movie industries. Susan Bordo has analyzed the way in which fashion advertisements of recent years have pioneered a depiction of men that consciously presents them as the object of the (homosexual or female) sexual gaze (Bordo 1999: 177). Solomon-Godeau claims that poses and facial expressions that were previously reserved for the iconography of femininity can now be seen on male models. In his analysis of male action heroes in mainstream Hollywood movies, Paul Smith has demonstrated how the voyeuristic admiration of the male hero is based on the eroticization of his body, which in turn depends on the objectification of that body (Smith 1995: 81). The objectification of the male body, however, is synonymous with its feminization. Clearly, consumerism and the media have now reached men: male bodies are now being made available for sexual fantasy and aesthetic admiration (cf. Bordo 1999: 215).

Given this background, any investigation of cross-dressing as an assumption of a female persona needs to take into account the far more persistent feminization of men by a culture that focuses on appearance, glamour and celebrity. Furthermore, any such investigation must also address how feature films with male-to-female transvestites portray the potentially emasculating structure of corporate America. For it is only by shedding light on these emasculating and feminizing social and economic tendencies that we can properly assess whether celluloid transvestites reinscribe or transgress against hegemonic definitions of gender.

Mrs. Doubtfire (1993)

In the Robin Williams-vehicle *Mrs. Doubtfire* (1993) the newly divorced actor Daniel Hillard undergoes a serious crisis. Hillard, who has just lost his job, is devastated by the impending separation from his wife and children. A judge awards sole custody of the children to his wife Miranda because Hillard has neither an apartment of his own nor a source of regular income. Motivated by his deep love for his children and aided by his homosexual brother, Hillard puts on make-up and women's clothing and pretends to be Mrs. Doubtfire, a sixty-year-old housekeeper and nanny. As Mrs. Doubtfire, Hillard accepts a job with his ex-wife in order to be able to see his children. Formerly irresponsible and unreliable, the cross-dressed Hillard is transformed into a disciplined and empathic person. His transformation is so beneficial to the family that, when the judge again deprives him of the company of his children because of his transvestite escapades, Hillard's wife Miranda readmits him into the family circle as babysitter.

It does not take more than the first few minutes of the movie to establish Daniel Hillard as the prototypical example of a man who falls short of the requirements of both male breadwinner and responsible parent. Hillard has no apartment, no job, and no money. But, even worse than that, he also has no visibility. In a culture that emphasizes display and image, Daniel Hillards's professional life as a voice actor erases his bodily presence. Hillard's own self vanishes as his disembodied voice gives life to various animated comic strip characters. Hillard's attempt to assert himself and to stand up for his convictions by insisting on a child-friendly interpretation of one of the animated stories results in the loss of his job. Clearly, Hillard's professional activity is emasculating in a dual sense: it renders Hillard invisible as a man both by obliterating his body and by denying him the right to define his own role.

Hillard's professional malaise is contrasted with the vocational accomplishments of his wife Miranda. Miranda is highly successful in her career as an architect and is the main provider of the Hillard family. Given these circumstances it might appear as though a reversal of the traditional roles might offer a solution to the family problems. Daniel as a house-husband and loving father with no professional ambitions could be the ideal complement to his work-oriented wife. This, however, is an option that *Mrs. Doubtfire* does not pursue. We might therefore wonder why a movie whose plot is based on the feminization of its protagonist refuses to explore a resolution that requires a much lesser degree of emasculinization than the one presented. In other words, we might ask if Hillard's corporeal transformation into a woman is meant to blot out the traces of a far more threatening feminization that plays itself out in the cultural, social, and economic realm.

Initially, a reassignment of family roles is prevented by Daniel's spontaneous, childlike behavior which, at the beginning of the movie, culminates in his hurly-burly birthday party for his son. Daniel's irresponsibility as a parent is proven as the loud party music and the grazing sheep and other animal attractions that he brings to his home disturb his neighbors and provoke the intervention of the police. But is it really Daniel's lack of discipline and his Peter-Pan-syndrome that prevent him from becoming a house-husband? Clearly, this obstacle is removed as the persona of Mrs. Doubtfire functions as the catalyst that reverses Daniel's arrested development and turns him into a mature caretaker. As Mrs. Doubtfire, Daniel learns how to cook and sew, how to keep a house spotless and how to supervise homework. But in spite of his newly won maturity, the reformed Daniel is not invited to reenter his home.

It is at this point that we understand that – no matter what sartorial delight we derive from Robin William's cross-dressing, no matter how exuberant and appealing his performance may be – a true role reversal was never intended. On the contrary, Daniel's transformation into the perfect housekeeper and his assumption of a female persona are the precise reasons why he is not awarded custody of his children. Responding to his transvestite escapades, the judge suggests psychological treatment. Thus,

Daniel Hillard is blocked in by a threefold predicament. He fails as a man because the emasculating demands of his job prevent him from fully developing his masculinity. But he also cannot prevail as a woman because the institutions of the law and his wife's desire for a masculine man (see below) collaborate in the rejection of his "feminized" self and make it unacceptable for him to take refuge in the female realm of domesticity. It is not surprising that, in *Mrs. Doubtfire*, this dilemma can be solved only by the hero's adjustment to the demands of a display culture.

Miranda Hillard's choice of lover demonstrates that a male housewife is not what she has in mind. Miranda's new beau Stu Dunmeyer, played by Pierce Brosnan, is rich, successful, and handsome. Stu's masculinity is enhanced by his wealth, and his good looks guarantee success in an ornamental culture. Appropriately, Stu Dunmeyer is played by the actor who, only one year later, as the new James Bond, came to symbolize the compatibility of masculinity, ornamentality, and consumerism through his seductive advertisements for watches, cars and other male necessities. Thus, while Stu Dunmeyer embodies the new male cultural icon who combines buying power with celebrity appeal, Daniel Hillard is America's new John Doe, a guy who can neither hold a job nor take care of his family. The fact that Hillard is portrayed as loving and caring, while Dunmeyer's character development vanishes behind the display of his status symbols and his beautiful body, cannot turn the tables in this uneven fight. Nor can Hillard's numerous tricks and clandestine subversion of Dunmeyer's superiority provide any more than vicarious pleasure for a spectator who shares Hillard's predicament.

That the movie itself is uncomfortable with Hillard's growing feminization is demonstrated by the interjection of numerous episodes designed to highlight Hillard's masculinity. When a cross-dressed Hillard defends himself successfully against a mugger, when he proves his staying power by drinking large quantities of alcohol and shows his hairy knees under his frock, Hillard's underlying masculinity is emphasized.

Daniel Hilliard's own resistance to his total feminization, along with the legal and sexual rejection of his "female" self by his environment, prevent him from becoming a male housekeeper and confront him with the task of proving himself outside of the domestic realm. Consequently, it is only because Daniel – alias Mrs. Doubtfire – establishes a national reputation as the host of a TV show for children that Miranda changes her mind about him. As a TV celebrity, Daniel Hillard has finally succeeded in conforming to the demands of a display culture. His victory, however, provides little cause for celebration because it ties Daniel to his female alter ego and thus inadvertently exposes the uncanny truth that celebrity culture, although it is the only way for Daniel to secure his masculine authority, is bought at the price of objectification and feminization of its proponents. That Daniel is now allowed to visit his children as himself attests to his successful incorporation of desirable "female" character traits. But the fact that he can only be professionally successful in the persona of Mrs. Doubtfire demonstrates that society has no room for men like Daniel.

Daniel Hillard falls prey to the dilemma inherent in an ornamental culture as his own identity disappears behind his female mask. If being in the spotlight is the only viable option, there is no victory possible. Men must choose between two unlivable positions: "you either retreated from the lens and were deemed an invisible man or you moved toward the light and saw your identity vanish in its blaze" (Faludi 1999: 580). In *Mrs. Doubtfire*, it is women and ornamental men like Stu Dunmeyer who call the shots while the average guys, the Daniel Hillards of this world, are left in limbo.

To Wong Foo: Thanks for Everything, Julie Newmar (1995)

In *To Wong Foo: Thanks for Everything, Julie Newmar*, three New York drag queens, the white Vida Boheme (Patrick Swayze), the black Noxeema Jackson (Wesley Snipes), and the Hispanic Chi Chi Rodriguez (John Leguizamo), embark on a journey to Hollywood to take part in the "Drag Queen of America" contest. After an unsavory adventure with a policeman, their stylish but unreliable car breaks down and the three are forced to spend some time in the god-forsaken Midwestern town of Snydersville. This involuntary visit proves to be a transformative experience for everybody involved as the transvestites teach the Snydersville women to stand up for themselves and to live their dreams.

In *To Wong Foo* the theme of a glamorous existence in an ornamental culture is foregrounded from the start. To begin with, the drag queens themselves are defined by their attention to style and display. A drag queen, so Noxeema Jackson tells us, is "a gay man with way too much fashion sense for his gender." It is only consistent that the action of the movie is set in motion by the drag queens' journey to Hollywood, the very epitome of a display culture. In Hollywood, the three protagonists will participate in a national drag queen contest, an event that ranks its contestants according to their mastery of style and fashion and that sees fit to bestow on its winner the much desired "moment in the spotlight" – the pinnacle of Chi Chi Rodriguez' aspirations. Appropriately enough, the transvestites' role model and the guardian angel of their journey is Julie Newmar, a Hollywood actress and dancer, best known for her roles as the first Catwoman and as Stupefying Jones in *Li'l Abner* (a woman so beautiful that she turns men to stone).

However, glamour and fashion do not remain limited to the realm of the transvestites. The transformation of Snyderville's women is itself a matter of style, a gigantic make-over whose cosmetic and sartorial allure cross over into the world of social and emotional relations. The transvestites'

"Operation Decorator Storm" turns their dumpy hotel room into an exotic night club lounge and the drab and ugly townswomen into dazzling fashion queens. Noxeema performs a miracle when she manages to have a conversation with an old lady who was considered deaf and had not spoken in years. Tellingly, the topic of the conversation is Hollywood movies.

The positive repercussions of this sartorial rebellion and its concomitant Hollywood luster are not to be underestimated. The transvestites not only bring life and love to Snydersville, they also effect some degree of racial reconciliation not only in their own group but also in Snydersville where a white townswoman and a black man discover their affection for each other. But in spite of these achievements, the purpose of this dressed-up revolution remains rather vague, and its long-term effects are highly questionable. The liberating message contained in lipsticks, frills and feather boas is necessarily undercut by the omission of any economic dimension. Throughout the entire movie, the characters' everyday work life drops completely from our field of vision. The spectators never learn how the three drag queens or most of the townswomen make a living. Rather, they come to assume that, in some magical way, glamour takes care of its own.

Doubts regarding the range and efficacy of the transvestite revolution are further underscored by the fact that the most crucial change that the drag queens bring about, namely the containment of male violence in the village, is effected by a recourse to masculine strength, not by improvements of design and outfit. When Vida Boheme defends herself against the crude sexual attention of a white policeman and protects her battered host from the violent attacks of her husband, and when Noxeema Jackson teaches the local thugs how to properly greet and respect a lady by grabbing their leader by the balls, it is the male body and its strength that save the day. Everything comes down to Vida's succinct answer to the battering Virgil's claim that some ladies need to be hit: "Some men need to be hit back."

In her fascinating study of cross-dressing, Marjorie Garber claims that transvestism is an enabling fantasy that marks a space of desire (Garber 1993: 6, 75). Garber draws attention to the political energy contained in a reversal of gender roles and to cross-dressing's challenge to easy notions of binarity (Garber 1993: 159, 10). Clearly, there are shadows and hints of this in *To Wong Foo*. While the transformation of Snydersville attests to the political potential of transvestism, the femininity of the drag queens destabilizes the gender dichotomy. But just as Snydersville's transformation is limited by the absence of economic references, so is the de-essentialization of gender halted by the movie's growing emphasis on the male body. In the opening scenes the femininity of the drag queens' scantily clothed bodies is emphasized through soft lighting that brings out the suppleness of their movements. But as the movie progresses, references to their superior physical (masculine) strength proliferate until, in the end, their gender is relocated in the body by naming the Adam's apple as an infallible indication of a person's masculinity. Thus, any initial questions as to whether the greater visibility and organizational strength of male-to-females is a sign of female, not of male power (cf. Garber 1993: 51), must be answered in the negative. Rather, the cross-dressing episode serves to reinforce the power of the male hero as he emerges triumphant from the encounter with the feminine. Paradoxically, it is the ability to absorb femininity without the risk of becoming feminized that becomes the ultimate test of high-octane masculinity (cf. Silveira Cyrino 1998: 208-210).

In many ways, *To Wong Foo* offers glimpses of the liberating potential of cross-dressing. Its message of racial reconciliation as well as its efforts to redefine glamour by naming ethical progress as its obligatory complement promise to undermine the subjugation to a celebrity culture. However, the limits of this subversion are evident in Noxeema's final statement that she will "make Hollywood wherever I'm at." Rather than refusing to submit to the "Hollywood imperative", Noxeema reconfirms its universal stronghold. Consequently, *To Wong Foo* does not end with the party in the liberated Snydersville but with Chi Chi's victory in the "Drag Queen of America" contest in Hollywood. It need hardly be pointed out that the two quintessential losers of the movie, the white policeman and the battering husband Virgil, are also the single two characters who lack every photogenic quality and hence prove unfit as the object of the spotlight. By villainizing and expelling those men who cannot adapt themselves to a display culture, *To Wong Foo* forfeits every chance of offering a solution to the threats that plague modern masculinity. It is the glamourized, i.e. feminized male who wins the day.

Just Like a Woman (1995)

The 1995 movie *Just Like a Woman* is one of the rare examples of a film that does not embed female impersonation in some form of a progress narrative – i.e., the protagonist has to cross-dress in order to escape persecution, to get a job etc. – but that actually addresses the problems that come with real-life transvestism. The movie's protagonist, Gerald Tilton (Adrian Pasdar), is a broker in Mergers and Acquisitions who happens to like dressing up in women's clothing. When his wife unexpectedly returns from a trip, she finds female underwear in the apartment and demands a divorce. Gerald rents a room from the recently divorced, middle-aged Monica (Julie Walters), who is taken in by his charm. Monica accepts her tenant's other self, Geraldine, and starts going out with Gerald/ine. Everything seems to be going fine until the cross-dressed Gerald is caught for speeding and has to show his driver's license, whereupon he is arrested and taken to the police. His boss Miles uses the incident as an excuse to fire him. But everything ends well as Geraldine exposes the corrupt nature of a deal that Miles had planned. S/he is accepted back into the business world and finds private happiness with Monica.

With great political sensitivity, *Just Like a Woman* speaks of the everyday humiliations and dangers to which a male-to-female transvestite is exposed in a Western society. It portrays the taunting and violent reactions of friends, colleagues, and strangers, the threat to marriage and career, and the omnipresent fear of being "read", of having to show one's driver's license, of being exposed and shamed. But as it does so, it also paints an extraordinarily sympathetic picture of Gerald/Geraldine, the cross-dressing executive. Partly, this is achieved by setting Gerald in stark contrast to his highly masculine but also highly corrupt and insensitive boss Miles. Miles, whose business philosophy is summarized in his pet phrase "grab them by the balls, their hearts and minds will follow", is characterized by his ignorance of and lack of respect for other cultures, his unethical business practices, and his general macho attitude. Gerald's androgynous masculinity, on the other hand, is closely connected to his cultural empathy. It is his fluent Japanese as well as his ability to understand and work with people from other cultures that are essential to his professional success. Gerald is fun, smart, creative, competent and, most importantly of all, capable of true love and companionship. Clearly, it is the man who is in touch with his "feminine" side who wins the hearts of the spectator. It is of interest to note that Gerald's partner C. J., a reliable friend and ethical businessman, is also shown "cross-dressed": he is wearing a traditional Scottish kilt at a company party.

While Gerald truly appreciates and displays character traits that are generally coded as feminine, his lover Monica cannot lay claim to a similar androgyny. Monica, in many ways, is a very traditional woman. She makes a living by taking in lodgers, by cooking for them, cleaning for them, and by listening to their worries and concerns. Aside from the management of her household, Monica has no professional skills. While Gerald branches out into the feminine domain, Monica stays put in the traditional female realm. Unsurprisingly, the only women present at the final show-down business meeting are Geraldine, an utterly overwhelmed Monica, and a female translator.

Just Like a Woman is the *Bildungsroman* of a male-to-female transvestite. Just like in the traditional *Bildungsroman*, it is the man who develops into a more integrated self whereas his female partner does not experience any form of personal growth (cf. MacLeod 1998). She remains what she always was: loving and understanding. It is because of this bias that *Just Like a Woman* effectively reproduces the traditional gender hierarchy that its overt message seems to reject.

Thus, on one level, *Just Like a Woman* is a powerful plea for individuality and tolerance and against rigid gender norms. On this level, the transvestite Gerald does indeed describe a space of desire, namely the desire for a better masculinity. And a better masculinity is defined as one that incorporates feminine traits. In this sense, *Just Like a Woman* undertakes a reevaluation of traditional gender definitions. It contains a eulogy to femininity in that "feminine" qualities are depicted as much more suitable for the success of business transactions and for finding fulfillment in personal relationships. However, since the androgyny of the male hero is not complemented by a similar expansion on Monica's part, *Just Like a Woman* is liable to be charged with a colonization of the feminine. It is only if the emotionally and socially competent male is complemented by the rationally and professionally successful woman that a true role reversal can be said to have taken effect.

The Associate (1996)

The Associate is one of the rare instances of female-to-male impersonation in American movies of the last two decades. Laurel, played by Whoopi Goldberg, is a highly talented Wall Street broker who, in spite of her untiring and excellent work, has to watch helplessly as her mediocre male colleagues harvest all promotions. Frustrated by the injustice of such treatment, Laurel decides to open her own firm. After numerous unsuccessful attempts to win clients, she invents a white male partner, whom she calls Cutty. Subsequently, Laurel attributes all her ideas to him while she herself claims to be his "assistant". But while Laurel's business thrives, the phantasmagoria of her elusive male partner is increasingly difficult to maintain and Laurel finds herself the victim of her own creation. After the failure of several "attacks" on Cutty's life, Laurel asserts herself by revealing publicly that she herself is the brain behind Cutty's success.

The Associate offers a comical yet unrelenting critique of the continuing discrimination of women and racial minorities in the upper echelons of the business world. As Sally, an under-appreciated assistant at Laurel's first firm, points out: "The women's movement hasn't made it to Wall Street." This message is driven home as the spectator watches the highly motivated and brilliant Laurel being passed over in favor of her good-for-nothing colleague Frank. Frank, who endears himself to his clients by taking them to a strip bar, sneakily manages to get credit for Laurel's hard work and to steal her long overdue promotion from her. After some prompting from Sally, Laurel realizes that, because of her gender and race, her work will never find the recognition of her male superiors and she decides to fashion a male boss of her own liking.

In earlier works of fiction, whether novels or films, female-to-male cross-dressing enabled women to experience a sense of freedom that was previously unknown to them. Notwithstanding some poetic license, such descriptions of an expanded sphere of agency accurately reflected the socio-historical realities of previous centuries. In the 18th, 19th and even early 20th centuries, cross-dressed women often used their disguise to enter the masculine realm of the military. Numerous female cross-dressers fought in battles during the French Revolution, the German Wars of Liberation, the American Civil War and the Russian Revolution (Wheelwright 1989; Dekker/van de Pol 1989; Bullough & Bullough 1993; Petersen 1987; Schmidt-Linsenhoff 1989; Noel 1912). During the 18th and early 19th centuries, women assumed male clothing in order to travel (Gilbert 1932, Dekker/van de Pol 1989). But we also know of less harmless occupations, such as cross-dressed pirates (Anne Bonny and Mary Read) and thieves (e.g., Julie Blasius, the female companion of the German robber Schinderhannes, cf. Küther 1976: 85). As different as these examples might seem, for all these women cross-dressing opened up a new sphere of action and a new life full of adventure and excitement which, in turn, inspired fictional works that depict cross-dressed women as powerful agents. This tradition of the adventurous female-to-male cross-dresser continued into our century. Bell-Metereau claims that, "during the first half-century of film, male imitation seemed a worthwhile exchange, for what the woman lost in expressiveness, she gained in mobility and freedom to enter the forbidden male realm" (Bell-Metereau 1993: 236).

Given this history, it is even more surprising that in *The Associate* cross-dressing is no longer portrayed as a liberating experience but rather prolongs the enslavement of the heroine. Initially, Laurel seems to profit from her invention of a male boss. Gradually, however, her new situation proves to be an uncanny repetition of her old predicament, as Laurel does all the work while Cutty gets all the credit. Not one of Laurel's clients shows any interest in her other than as a channel to Cutty. This injustice culminates when a male business partner advises Cutty, i.e. the cross-dressed Laurel, to put the blame for his subpoena on Laurel and then fire her. For the remainder of the movie, Laurel devotes all her energy to getting rid of the specter that she has conjured up. Clearly, in *The Associate*, cross-dressing is no solution. It can only perpetuate the injustice that it is meant to fight. It is only by publicly exposing the mechanisms that excluded her that Laurel finally achieves a viable position.

In *The Associate*, male businessmen such as Frank are not subjected to the feminization that an ornamental culture brings about. Rather, the power of patriarchy proves unshakeable due to its hard-core economic foundation. At first glance, it might seem as though Wall Street in *The Associate* remained completely unaffected by the emasculating influence of a display culture. At second glance, however, we realize that the persona of Cutty is both the incorporation of the omnipotence of a masculine celebrity character as well as the revelation of its hollowness. From the start, Cutty has all the media attention and presence in the national consciousness that Laurel could only dream of. He is the object of numerous newspaper articles and television shows. Cutty owes his power and influence to a combination of the right array of status symbols – including a Mercedes and the stuffed head of a rhinoceros – the right gender, and the right race. But while the myth of Cutty can function without requiring actual competency on Cutty's part, it cannot function without a male body to go with his persona. It is Cutty's incorporeality that brings about a crisis. The absence of an actual body that goes with the myth of his persona makes it impossible for Laurel to kill Cutty, while it allows Frank to appropriate his image and present himself as Cutty's new partner. Consequently, Laurel's final speech is an indictment of a culture that focuses its attention on images rather than on substance: "Image is a funny thing: underneath the right image could be the wrong one. And underneath the wrong image could be the right person."

In this sense, *The Associate* is a plea not to overestimate image and celebrity but to go back to substance and competence. Interestingly, *The Associate* is not only one of the rare examples of female-to-male transvestism, it is also one of the rare instances of a narrative that finds no advantage in the appropriation of the trappings of the other gender.

Conclusion

For the last two decades, popular movies have been marked by the peculiar absence of male impersonation while male-to-female cross-dressing has proliferated. This imbalance is brought about by two mutually dependent social developments. Firstly, the lack of female-to-male transvestites, as well as a close reading of the rare depictions of such cross-dressing, demonstrate that appropriating the clothes of the male gender no longer holds the promise of freedom and agency that it had for centuries. If we encounter male impersonation in movies of the last two decades, it is in period pieces, such as *Impromptu* (1990) or *Yentl* (1983), or films which focus on the victimization of the female transvestite, such as *Boys Don't Cry* (1999).

The flood of female impersonators, on the other hand, speaks to several different social and cultural needs. It attests to a growing appreciation for qualities that are traditionally coded as feminine, and expresses the belief that masculinity needs to be refined and corrected by the incorporation of feminine character traits. However, as such stories of growth all too often focus their attention on the male protagonist, they easily combine the reevaluation of femininity with the erasure of women. As one critic states, "when 'female' qualities – softness, sensitivity, passivity – were exalted in the post-Brando hero and in the rock/anti-war ethic of the counter-culture, it did not bring about a corresponding exaltation of woman, but, on the contrary, a diminution of her role as the new movie hero appropriated her qualities without losing his place at the center of the stage" (Bell-Metereau 1993: 235).

Though appreciation of feminine qualities is openly expressed, another constellation, namely the supposed competitive advantage of femininity in today's display culture, forms the unspoken, though ever-present subtext of these stories. In the ever fiercer competition of today's consumer and celebrity culture, masculinity can only prevail if it succeeds in incorporating female glamour (*To Wong Foo*) or if it is compatible with an ornamental culture because of its accoutrements of beauty and wealth (Stu Dunmeyer alias Pierce Brosnan). However, lurking behind these success stories is the uncanny realization that in order to be on TV, a man needs to be a TV. It is only if we acknowledge the full impact of this connection between masculinity and glamor that we come to understand the frightening implications of today's consumer and media culture. For while we had long suspected that the end of patriarchy is not the same as women's emancipation, we now realize that the end of patriarchy does not even herald the liberation of men.

Works Cited

Bell-Metereau, Rebecca 1993. *Hollywood Androgyny*. New York: Columbia University Press.

Berger, Maurice, Wallis, Brian, and Simon Watson (eds.) 1995. *Constructing Masculinity*. New York: Routledge.

Bordo, Susan 1999. *The Male Body: A New Look at Men in Public and Private*. New York: Farrar, Straus and Giroux.

Bullough, Vern L. and Bonnie Bullough 1993. *Cross-Dressing, Sex, and Gender*. Philadelphia: University of Pennsylvania Press.

Butler, Judith 1990. *Gender Trouble: Feminism and the Subversion of Identity*. New York: Routledge.

Connell, R.W. 1995. *Masculinities: Knowledge, Power, and Social Change*. Berkeley: University of California Press.

Dekker, Rudolf M. and Lotte C. van de Pol 1989. *The Tradition of Female Transvestism in Early Modern Europe*. New York: St. Martin's Press.

Faludi, Susan 1999. *Stiffed: The Betrayal of the American Man*. New York: William Morrow and Company.

Garber, Marjorie 1993. *Vested Interests: Cross-Dressing and Cultural Anxiety*. New York: Harper Perennial.

Gilbert, O.P. 1932. *Women in Men's Guise*. London: Jarrold & Sons.

Gilmore, David D. 1990. *Manhood in the Making: Cultural Concepts of Masculinity*. New Haven: Yale University Press.

Küther, Carsten 1976. *Räuber und Gauner in Deutschland: Das organisierte Bandenwesen im 18. und frühen 19. Jahrhundert*. Göttingen: Vandenhoeck & Ruprecht.

Noel, Major z.D. 1912. *Die deutschen Heldinnen in den Kriegsjahren 1807-1815*. Berlin: Julius Köppen.

MacLeod, Catriona 1998. *Embodying Ambiguity: Androgyny and Aesthetics from Winckelmann to Keller*. Wayne State University Press.

Mosse, George L. 1996. *The Image of Man: The Creation of Modern Masculinity*. New York: Oxford University Press.

Petersen, Susanne 1987. *Marktweiber und Amazonen: Frauen in der Französischen Revolution. Dokumente, Kommentare, Bilder*. Köln: Pahl-Rugenstein.

Schmidt-Linsenhoff, Viktoria (ed.) 1989. *Sklavin oder Bürgerin? Französische Revolution und neue Weiblichkeit 1760-1830*. Frankfurt am Main: Jonas.

Silveira Cyrino, Monica 1998. "Heroes in D(u)ress: Transvestism and Power in the Myths of Heracles and Achilles." *Arethusa* 31 (1998), 207-241.

Smith, Paul 1995. "Eastward Bound" in Maurice Berger, Brian Wallis and Simon Watson (eds.). *Constructing Masculinity*. New York: Routledge, 77-97.

Solomon-Godeau, Abigail 1995. "Male Trouble" in Maurice Berger, Brian Wallis and Simon Watson (eds.). *Constructing Masculinity*. New York: Routledge, 69-76.

Wheelwright, Julie 1989. *Amazons and Military Maids: Women Who Dressed as Men in the Pursuit of Life, Liberty, and Happiness*. London: Pandora.

"This is a Man's Country": Masculinity and Australian National Identity in *Crocodile Dundee*

Russell West

National Identity, Masculinity and Film

In 1994 the Australian brewery Foster's launched an advertising campaign marketing Foster's Lager ("Australia's Famous Beer") with the title "How to Speak Australian". All the advertising clips in the series featured stereotypical images of Australia and Australians so as to present this mark of beer and its consumption as a way of participating, albeit from afar, in that Antipodean lifestyle. The campaign was originally introduced onto the US market, and was subsequently extended for use on markets throughout Europe, Asia, the Middle East and Pacific (Foster's 1999). The aim of the advertising series was to facilitate the extension of this already dominant brand of Australian beer on world-wide markets by associating it with particular notions of the Australian character. Significantly, such notions were from the outset connected with quite distinct representations of masculinity and femininity.

One of the earliest and most striking clips in the "How to Speak Australian" series featured two scenes in an outback pub. In the first scene, two brawny Australians are sitting at the bar. One of them, at the far end of the bar, picks up a boomerang and sends it looping through the air to the other end of the bar where his mate is sitting. The boomerang hits the second bloke on the back of the head; he reaches up and switches the channel of the television anchored in the wall, to a programme showing a game of Australian Rules football. A subtitle appears at the bottom of the frame: "Remote Control". The second scene shows the pub from outside. The Western-style saloon doors suddenly swing open as a man comes flying through them to land on his face in the dirt outside. Equally abruptly, a tall and attractive woman steps through the doors, flinging the ejected fellow's Akubra bush hat after him. Again, a subtitle appears at the bottom of the screen: "No". The clip finishes with a view of a bottle of Foster's Lager, and the inscription: "Australian for Beer: Foster's Lager – Australia's Famous Beer".

The advertising series focuses on the transmission of the Foster's image across the world, in the forms of "translation" of exotic Australian practices ostensibly in need of explanation to a puzzled overseas public. These translative operations culminate in an image of the alcoholic beverage, itself an iconic translation of "Australian for Beer" – Foster's Lager, for those who have not already got the message. The humorous *distance* between image and explanation underlines the *difference* which apparently contributes to the market success of Foster's: it is the very fact of its difficult translatability which makes it desirable as a metonym of the inaccessible and thus mysteriously beckoning southern continent. Both the form and the content of the mute vignettes figures this process of translation, foregrounding culture as communication.

Equally important to the working of the clips is the notion that Australian culture is characterised by particular modes of communication between men and women. The distance and difference figured in the advertising clip clearly constitutes the gender identity of Australian masculinity. The wordless communication of the two men at the bar, borne by the boomerang's lazy arc, is a figure of the silence of men and between men, which, appropriately, needs to be translated into verbal form for the rest of humanity. In the second clip, the women's "No", expressed in equally wordless form, suggests the exhaustion of verbal means of refusal. Only her final recourse to physical violence can get the message across. Thus what the clip transmits to the world are images of a raw, masculine outback society in which language appears almost to have withered away. The function of translation in this context is to compensate for the gendered absence of speech – but also enshrine it and glorify that mute ruggedness.

The gendered images of communication in the outback in the context of a Foster's advertising campaign were partly derived from a massively successful predecessor in which the Foster's logo was also prominently visible. In the openings scenes of Peter Faiman's 1986 film *Crocodile Dundee*, featuring Paul Hogan (as Mick "Crocodile" Dundee) and Linda Kozlowski (as American journalist Sue Charlton), a typical outback pub is also the scene of sub-verbal masculine communication, rough humour and physical violence as one drinker attempts to make a pass at Sue. Here too a brash outback woman appears in the person of Ida the barmaid, and a hat is also tossed out the door as a senseless kangaroo-hunter is carried away after being knocked out by Mick Dundee. In alluding to the opening scenes of the *Crocodile Dundee* the Foster's advertising clip acknowledges its debts to the earlier text whose world-wide success paved the way for the subsequent international reach and explicit cross-cultural orientation of the advertising campaign. Interestingly, the film's phenomenal success also arose out of audience familiarity with Hogan from even earlier advertising clips run by the Australian Tourist Commission in the US (Crofts 1992: 217). Given this continuity, the advertising clip can be seen to draw attention to the prominence of gender features in the film's propagation of images of Australia. In this article I wish to explore the ways in which *Crocodile Dundee* structures its pictures of Australian national identity in gender terms.

It is precisely the success of *Crocodile Dundee* which makes it worth examining in more detail, for it appears to have had a long-lasting effect on the manner in which Australia is perceived all around the world. *Crocodile Dundee* was the most successful Australian film to date, the most successful film internationally in its year of release and the most successful foreign film ever on the US market, staying in the American cinemas for weeks on end and making $174.6 million in its American release (Morris 1988: 242; O'Regan 1996: 83). Given the durability of the impression made by the film and its remarkable global resonance, it would appear that there is some call for an analysis of the way in which a particularly potent image of the Australian nation has been presented in terms of masculine gender. In this article I will concentrate on three aspects in particular of this gendering of national identity, all of which are highlighted by the Foster's advertisement. The first aspect is that of the paring-down of speech. The laconic men of the pub are bearers of verbal reserve as one of the central characteristics of Australian masculinity as presented in *Crocodile Dundee*. Reserve, and its concomitant rhetorical figure of litotes, it transpires, is the instrument with the help of which masculinity is constructed in relation to but also in defiance of its constitutive Other. But this reserve is predicated upon a second aspect of the film highlighted by the advertisement, namely, that of the inextricable entanglement of masculinity with the Other in (ostensible) opposition to which it is constituted (whence the necessity of translation into verbal communication, thus furnishing the central motive of the advertisement). Thirdly, the relation of pub-scene and Foster's beer is one of chiastic inversion: whereas the *Crocodile Dundee* film scene takes place in an Australian country pub, with ubiquitous Foster's advertising posters constantly visible in the background of the frame as a marginal allusion, the Foster's advertising clips are framed by the "Australia's Famous Beer" slogan and logo and employ the pub scene as the background material which alludes to the film as intertextual predecessor. Chiasmus underlies the entire structure of *Crocodile Dundee* as the rhetorical turn which best figures the reciprocal imbrication of the respective components of a binary opposition. Translation, foregrounded by the Foster's advertising campaign, represents one striking chiastic relationship constantly thematised in the film: "walkabout" and "tucker" need to be translated for tourist Sue, whilst Mick is confronted with New York parlance when talking with the Italo-American taxi-driver and the Black drinking-companion in a down-town bar, and has to have the word (and the concept) "shrink" translated for him at a well-to-do NY reception. The culmination of this aspect of the film is the symmetrical exchange of the other nationality's respective greetings carried out by Mick and the New York hotel doorman: "Have a nice day" – "No worries, mate".

Language, and its various modes of deployment as expansive or restrictive, as imperial or modest, whether linked to power or powerlessness, whether co-operative or offensive ("bad language", for instance, is the pretext Mick gives for knocking out the obese kangaroo hunter in the Walkabout Creek pub during his inaugural foxtrot with Sue, and later, the new York pimp who interrupts his well-meaning though naive conversation with two prostitutes) constitutes the underlying tenor of the film. How masculinity is predicated upon language functions as a figure of fraught but unavoidable gender relationships is one of the principle problems addressed in *Crocodile Dundee*.

In turn, these interconnections of masculine gender and language, understood as a network of articulations of differences, are bound up in the constitution of national identity. The background to the gendered configurations of *Crocodile Dundee* is the history of Australian involvement with US foreign politics since Prime Minister John Curtin's historic announcement of December 1941, when the Australian government decided to relinquish its traditional loyalty to Britain and transfer its military allegiance to the US, perceived as a world power whose strategic interests in the Pacific area were more likely to be compatible those of Australia than far away, beleaguered Britain. Since the end of the Second World War, Australia has sealed a military pact with the US (ANZUS), and offered its support in Korea, Vietnam and the Gulf alongside the American forces. The fifty-year policy of military co-operation with the US was motivated by the confident expectation of reciprocated assistance in time of need. In 1999 this assumption was revealed to be fundamentally flawed when Australia, intervening in the East Timor crisis, received only lukewarm American support. At the same time, Australia found itself accused by Southeast Asian neighbours of mimicking the US as world-policeman, a situation not without a degree of comic irony as the action showed Australia's utter military unpreparedness for such a mission. What was particularly striking in the television reports on the Australian military presence in East Timor was the clearly gendered character of representations of the operation: shaven-headed Australian soldiers wearing wrap-around sunglasses struck nonchalant poses for the TV cameras, while the Australian commander in chief, Major-General Peter Cosgrove, was barely articulate, the chin-band of his slouch-hat (a crucial sartorial element in the ANZAC myth [Gilbert 1998: 191]) apparently preventing him from opening his mouth properly; here Australian militarism followed a American strategic example, modified by the unmistakable influence of contemporary commodified macho-genre, but also of laconic bush manhood (somewhat in the tradition of the famous photo of a slouch-hatted soldier carving the sardonic inscription "heaven" in the stucco wall of the Tobruk railway-station).

Not only military policy but also economic exchange with the US has also come to supplant the earlier primacy of trade with Britain, and US-Australian trade relations have also had their ups and down in the half-century since the war. What is notable about the post-war relations between Australia and the US is that this constitutive relationship is not embedded in a cultural tradition in the ways in which the relationship with Britain was, and to a certain extent, continues to be. The rich cultural inheritance which has for two centuries afforded a wide range of cultural icons and discourses of the British-Australian relationship, from the image of the colonial new chum (the naive and inexperienced British immigrant in the bush newly arrived from "the old country") or stereotypes of effete English aristocrats, to the rhetoric of cricket and affectionate "Pommie-bashing", is lacking for the more recent dependence on America (Rickard 1995: 218; White 1981: 79-81; see also Stratton/Ang 1998). This apparent cultural vacuum is all the more curious given the profound and widespread effects of American culture on Australian society, evinced in film, television, music and slang (Langer 1991: 30) – or even such everyday phenomena as the design of road signs. Symptomatic in this context, for instance, is the perplexity patently experienced by the prominent Australian art critic and historian Patrick McCaughey in finding a contemporary common denominator in the domain of culture in his introduction to a combined US-Australian exhibition of early colonial landscape painting in the two ex-British settler colonies (McCaughey 1998). Contemporary Australia still lacks a cultural framework within which the all-pervasive relationship with the US can be reflected and debated. It is possible that these difficulties in developing a public discourse of the history of Australian-American relations may have been entrenched by Australian eagerness *not* to remember the shameful Vietnam episode of the 1960s and early 1970s. Admittedly, there have been frequent thematisations of Americans in Australian in films from the fifth continent (O'Regan 1996: 52). *Crocodile Dundee* nonetheless represents a new departure, in that it actively approaches the profound and reciprocal interlocking of the two cultures from both directions at once. In the recent history of Australian films on popular national heroes abroad Jim Davidson provides an illuminating contrast between the Australian comic hero Bazza McKenzie at large in the UK in Bruce Bereford's 1972 film *The Adventures of Barry McKenzie*, and later avatars: "The idea worked because Australia and England were still close enough to be locked in some kind of dialogue, if not dialectic" (Davidson 1987: 123). *Crocodile Dundee* is notable as the most powerful recent attempt to give expression to the Australian-American relationship in its two-way functioning.

The effectiveness of *Crocodile Dundee*'s undertaking derives from the fact that the Australian-American relationship is articulated in terms of gender, the most familiar, everyday and deep-seated system of binary logic structuring representations of social existence. In 1974 the German performance artist Joseph Beuys staged a three-day action in New York entitled "I like America and America likes me", in which the European artist and a wild American coyote cautiously approached one another in a gradual process of reciprocal familiarisation (Tisdall 1988; Schneede 1994: 330-53). *Crocodile Dundee* undertakes a similar project, albeit in a rather more radical manner, with Sue's cry across the crowded subway station at the end of film, "I love you", being multiplied and relayed from person to person, so that it becomes the staging of a collective love affair, modelled along hegemonic heterosexual lines, spoken into existence by the film's own incantatory power. It is this aspect of the film which demands closer examination, thereby necessitating a reconsideration of national identity in conjunction with some recent innovations in film theory.

Recent developments in film theory have shifted the focus of gender interrogation from the female body on the screen, to the less discussed aspect of masculinity. In reviewing some recent writing on film Steven Cohan and Ina Rae Hark point out that: "In concentrating upon the female body as the primary stake of cinematic representation, [...] even the most acute and insightful of [the discussions following upon Laura Mulvey's essay on visual pleasure] have ignored the problem of masculinity which motivates that system. [...]" (Cohan/Hark 1993: 1). They go on to elucidate their position in the following terms:

> While we certainly do not minimize the importance of exposing the disadvantaged positioning of the female spectator and the women within the diegesis in Hollywood cinema, the scant attention paid to the spectacle of men ends up reinforcing the apparent effacement of the masculine as a social construction in American culture. The male's seeming exemption from visual representation may work very hard to preserve the cultural fiction that masculinity is not a social construction, but American movies have always served as one of the primary sites through which the culture, in the process of promulgating that fiction, has also exposed its workings as a mythology. The male image on the cinema screen is therefore as significant a representational stake as the female. (Cohan/Hark 1993: 2-3).

The following analysis assumes that the representation of gender, and in particular of masculinity, in the film possesses a crucial role in the formation of public consciousness and collective experiences of social life. This assumption in turn obliges one to ask the question of which forms of community the representation of gender in film may contribute to moulding. In general this question is not asked, the relevant social context being assumed as a given.

At the point at which the question of gender is linked to that of national identity, however, a further gap in research comes to light. In an apparently throwaway line in his classic work on the formation of national identity, Benedict Anderson writes that: "in the modern world everyone can, should, will 'have' a nationality, as he or she 'has' a gender" (Anderson 1991: 5). But the problem has rarely been addressed in its reverse form: does a nation have a gender? Several writers on the sociology of the nation comment that until recently, the literature on nationalism had been blind to issues of gender. As McClintock notes that: "Nationalism becomes [...] radically constitutive of people's identities through social contests that bare frequently violent and always gendered. Yet, if the invented nature of nationalism has found wide theoretical currency, explorations of the gendering of the national imagery have been conspicuously paltry" (McClintock 1995: 353). This imbalance has been righted in recent years, with some attention to the place of women in nationalist discourses and their utility for projects of national identity-construction. Nonetheless this literature has largely neglected to examine men as an equally constructed category (Yuval-Davies 1997: 1; Mayer 2000: 5). Here, for instance, Bryon, following Chantal Mouffe and Carole Pateman, argue that citizenship is a patriarchal and masculist category serving to exclude women (Brydon 1994: 25), and E. Ann Kaplan claims that the space of the nation is a male dominated space, discourses of nationalism confining women's role to the space of the home and co-opting them for reproductive functions within nationalist causes (Kaplan 1997: 45, 49-50). These theses are illuminating and helpful, but in the context of *Crocodile Dundee* it is worthwhile asking a prior question, namely, about the ways nationalism is *constructed* on the basis of gender characteristics. This direction of reflection is implicitly suggested for instance by Mayer's claim that: "Because nationalism, gender and sexuality are all socially and culturally constructed, they frequently play an important role in constructing one another – by invoking and helping to construct the 'us' versus 'them' distinction and the exclusion of the Other" (Mayer 2000: 1). Such a reversal of the terms of the causal link may then allow one to understand better how the construction of nation with the help of gender imagery in turn assists in the justification of sexual oppression in the name of nationalism. Exemplary in this respect is Dana Nelson, who identifies a historically constructed white fraternity which, regardless of social class, has claimed to represent "national manhood" in the United States (Nelson 1998). Mayer's conclusion just cited is particularly relevant for the case of film as an instance in which national identity is both constructed and gendered: "The nation is comprised of sexed subjects whose 'performativity' constructs not only their own gender identity but the identity of the entire nation as well" (Mayer 2000: 5). In what follows the question of performativity, in particular the forms of performativity evident in film, will be considered in the light of the agency of binary oppositions in constructing notions of male selfhood and of national selfhood.

Chiasmus and entwining in masculinity and national identity

Australia was created in 1901 by the Act of Federation which united the hitherto disparate British colonies on the Australian continent. Australia's conception as a modern nation-state thus coincided almost exactly with the First World War, which signalled both the end of the political importance of the large dynasties and the historical high-water mark of the nation-state (Anderson 1991: 85-86). Despite this auspicious beginning, Australian national identity has been marked from its inception by a high degree of instability, being caught up in a constant process of "re-invention" (White 1981). *Crocodile Dundee* would thus appear to participate in an ongoing project of national self-definition, and can be understood as an instance of what Tom O'Regan has called "national cinema". National cinema functions as a social bond, uniting and excluding diverse people, constituting an object of knowledge "which narratively and discursively connects Australia, society, the cinema, genre and various cultural differences", "representing Australia to itself" (O'Regan 1996: 10, 35). Significantly, Mick Dundee combines a number of well-known masculine personifications of Australia: the bushman, the larrikin outlaw, the digger abroad. But at the same time, there is something slightly antiquated about this notion of national cinema, particularly when looking at a film such as *Crocodile Dundee*. For it is virtually impossible to think about the nation-state today without placing it in an international, indeed global context which increasingly casts the concept of the nation into the shadow (Beck 1997). What is remarkable about the film is its project, based on the financial necessity of releasing the film simultaneously in the US and in Australia, and of addressing two publics, the Australian and the American, at the same time. Thus national identity is inherently situated in a relational context, rather than being assumed to be some sort of autonomous entity. This is reflected directly in the narrative structure of the film, which is divided into two equal halves set in the Australian outback and New York respectively, and balanced symmetrically by a chiastic construction: the American journalist Sue visits Mick Dundee in his outback homeland, and he accompanies her back to her home in the Big Apple. Tom O'Regan speaks of the pronounced tendency of some Australian films to effect "border-crossings" which then subject them to "productive mis-readings" (O'Regan 1996: 59; see also Crofts 1992). In *Crocodile Dundee*, such border-crossings are pre-programmed in a film which was designed from the outset to speak to quite disparate audiences, and whose very plot maps the history of a border transit. International border-crossing is the precondition of the film and the constitutive framework which its plot self-reflexively mimics.

The in-built border-crossing process is not, however, the result of a symmetrical relationship. At all levels the relationship between Australia and the US is an unequal one, as demonstrated by Australia's fawning to the US in matters of military assistance (epitomised in the Vietnam-era slogan "All the way with LBJ"), and the US refusal to reciprocate that assistance in the 1999 East Timor crisis, or a US proposal of 1998 that Australia should become the dumping ground for the world's nuclear waste. In the immediate context of the Australian film industry, Meaghan Morris has drawn attention to the funding cuts in government film subsidies which meant that Australian films had to gain pre-selling guarantees, preferably in the United States, in order to buttress investment at home (Morris 1988: 247-248). The film does little more than point, via a bold mise-en-abyme, to its own conditions of production, namely, the radical financial involvement of the Australian film industry with America. The small Australian media industry is not independent on the world market, so that the chiastic, two part structure of the film thus constitutes a loud expression of dependence of national selfhood on Otherness. In the interests of narcissism-driven box-office takings, both audiences had to be able to recognise themselves not only in the representations of their respective countries, but also in the "other" national site in the film. The ubiquitous pervasiveness of American elements in the Australian part of the film is similarly evidence of such cultural interlacing: from the Wild-West-saloon-fight to the very un-Australian tassles festooning Mick's leather waistcoat and cowboy boots, or from Mick's proclaiming himself as Fred Astair to the Country music overlaid upon tourist-industry panoramas of the natural beauty of Kakadu National Park. Later on, elements of the Australian environment are translated into the New York context, with Mick replacing his cowboy tassles with a snake-skin jacket, and echoing his "Out of the way dopey!" (originally addressed to the ponderous water buffalo blocking the outback track) for the benefit of a New York motorist driving on the "wrong" (right) side of the street. Similarly, the multicultural face of New York society, whether plebeian or upper-crust, mirrors a prominent aspect of contemporary Australian society which is otherwise elided by the exclusively outback setting of the Antipodean half of the film. These are all forms of chiasmus which declare a radical interdependence of Australian and American culture. O'Regan comments that: "this seeming dependence on 'other cinemas' and their norms, genres and so on – is actually one of the most fascinating aspects of Australian cinema, enabling it to speak so powerfully to local and international audiences alike in *Strictly Ballroom*, *Mad Max II (The Road Warrior)*, *My Brilliant Career* and *Crocodile Dundee*" (O'Regan 1996: 71).

All these instances of chiasmus, however, do not just figure radical dependence upon an opposed Other; they are also a way of masking that dependence, of presenting it as symmetrical and mirroring. The most prominent figure of mystificatory chiasmus in the film is that of a gender reversal. The traditional association of masculinity with power and femininity with powerlessness could not be allowed to remain intact in the film, for the simple reason that for the film to function for two audiences, the balance of power had to be equal. In contrast to the real historical situation of the thousands of Australian World War Two war-wives, where the journey was largely one way and where Australia figured in the exchange as the female partner, the film inverts the usual gender hierarchy, figuring Australia as the masculine Mick Dundee, and America as the female journalist Sue. In this manner, the film suggests an equilibrium between essential masculine and feminine attributes: America's power is toned down by virtue of its being incorporated in a woman (which accords with the iconic feminine figure of the statue of liberty, but also allows the blunt facts of American world dominance to be recast in the equally patent fact of women's restricted access to social and political power). Simply ignoring political realities is in no way an effective ideological strategy, and so the superior power of the US must be surreptitiously acknowledged, but in such a way as to mask the imbalance. This chiastic strategy affords the possibility of articulating whilst simultaneously disavowing America's status as a potent object of desire on the part of Australians (Sue is alternately desired by the kangaroo hunter in the walkabout Creek pub, by the crocodile, by Mick, by Wally). Thus, in the Australian section of the film, Mick is portrayed as sexist but deeply impressed by his American guest, while Sue is presented as the liberated, independent modern girl who is nonetheless incapable of defending herself in the bush. In the American section of the film, Mick is shown to be celebrated but finally defenceless before American wealth, newspaper editor Richard's priority as Sue's fiancé, and the violence of the pimps. In a nutshell, Sue is powerful by virtue of her derived power, but as a woman can be seduced by Mick.

This attempted compromise between the realities of geopolitical power imbalances, and the necessity to pander to viewers' nationalist-narcissistic sensibilities, both based upon chiasmus, tends however to produce major contradictions, particularly in the images of body which are proposed to the public. Benedict Anderson suggests that: "The nation is imagined as *limited* because even the largest of them, encompassing perhaps a billion living human beings, has finite, if elastic, boundaries, beyond which lie other nations. No nation imagines itself coterminous with mankind" (Anderson 1996: 5). On an individual scale, psychic identity is constructed upon the establishment of bodily limits (Sami-Ali 1982; Anzieu 1985), and this establishment of identity through the delineation of borders is particularly apposite as a figure for the formation of national identity. The perforation or fraying of the community's limits or the points where it is constituted or dissolves – for instance in the threshold moments of birth, initiation, marriage, or death – is a cause for much concern, particularly when the nation is figured as a gendered body, often feminine (see Douglas 1980; Turner 1982; Brotton 1996). The imagined vulnerability of Australia to invasion from the North has been a persistent trope in the nation's foreign policy discourse. Paradoxically, the presence of defenders against such an invasion, for instance that of American GIs in Australia during the Second World War, has also frequently been described, both in popular and historical accounts, as an "invasion", thus implying a threat to Australian femininity, with distinct overtones of rape (Gilbert 1998: 187-88). Yet the perforation of the national body is presumably even more disturbing when a national selfhood figured as *masculine*, and therefore as penetrating rather than as penetrable, is threatened from outside. Here it is worth mentioning the importance of the journey abroad as a rite of passage for Australian masculinity, the classic example being the ANZACs' campaigns overseas in the first half of the century, and the year overseas for the youth of the second half; as George Johnston famously wrote, the Australian male "has been obliged to look elsewhere for the great adventures, the necessary challenges to flesh and spirit. This is why his wars must be fought for other causes than his own – and often for strange one – and always in faraway places" (Johnston [1964] 1981: 271). That *Crocodile Dundee* re-enacts such a conquest narrative in the second half of the film, is perhaps indicative of a sense of needing to re-establish equilibrium following a traumatic symbolic experience of loss of (national) boundaries. For masculinity is predicated upon the erection of boundaries against Others, in particular against the mother and femininity in general, and equally, upon the refusal of the desire which inevitably accompanies a converse and equally constitutive identification with masculinity (Chodorow 1978; Dinnerstein 1987; Butler 1995). The undermining of such boundaries threatens the very constitution of masculinity, as has been shown in film studies by Silverman's work on the permeability of the margins of the masculine body which bring it close to femininity, and Krutnik's analyses of the instability of the ostensibly autonomous masculine self in the American detective film (Silverman 1992; Krutnik 1991).

Other symptoms of this vulnerability to invasion, intrusion or perforation are to be found in the film. Sue's friendly attempts at empathy for Mick are refused, taken as attempts to occupy Mick's home territory. In reflecting about his mauling by a crocodile, she says: "I reckon I know how you must have felt. Or how I would have felt if I was you." Mick scoffs: "You out here alone? A city girl like you? You wouldn't last five minutes out here love. This is a man's country." At which point, deeply offended and determined to set out her own through the bush towards the day's destination, she takes up the rifle he presents her for the case of an emergency. When Mick patronisingly tells her "That's the dangerous end", Sue fires a shot at his feet which barely misses penetrating his boot. Here feminine (near)-perforation of the masculine body is presented as a concomitant of feminine penetration of the masculised outback heart of Australian national identity. A similar risk of penetration of the male body is also presented in terms of a gendered relationship when Mick self-deprecatingly described his leg-wounds from the crocodile's attack as "just a love bite"; this predatory feminine intrusion into the body of the masculine incorporation of Australian identity will be almost immediately reversed into masculine pursuit of Sue, with the obese kangaroo hunter in the pub "just want[ing] to get a bite" and the crocodile also directing its attentions to the American journalist a short while later. The perforation of the masculine body is such a threat because it erases the very borders upon which the gendering of that body is predicated.

It is here that the major contradiction produced by the chiasmus-structure of the film, and its intertwining of masculinity and femininity, emerges. If is on the basis of self-differentiation that masculine gender is formed, and upon the maintenance of a limit between the two genders that the stability of masculinity is upheld, then gender chiasmus represents a perilous and fraught process. A precedent for this aspect of *Crocodile Dundee* can be found in the films of Anthony Mann, where the recurring motif of a chiastic love/hate rapport of the charming "villain" and the near-psychotic "hero" dramatises the danger of the masculine hero becoming his enemy – to whom, moreover, he is often related by blood (Willemen 1981). Gender chiasmus represents a "catastrophe" for identity in the sense of René Thom's catastrophe theory, the point at which a coherent mathematical structure meets another structure and undergoes a radical structural transformation (Petitot-Cocorda 1983; see also Thom 1983). Whence Mick's oath as the plane takes off from Australian soil for New York, and his nervous negotiation of the escalator at JFK Airport, with its critical point of transition, its visual, mechanical tectonic-plate-like divide between two cultures and the respective realms of two genders. The end of the escalator figures a brutal fine-toothed maw which will mince up anyone getting caught in its embrace, a pair of metal jaws which signals once again the vulnerability of the masculine body (as it now enters "feminine" US territory). The chiastic structure which brings together Australia/America and masculinity/femininity threatens to rip open the closure of the masculine persona. In bringing masculinity and femininity into close contact, and even more, exchanging their various attributes in a chiastic inversion, the film threatens to undo its very constitutive terms, and to destroy the masculinity with which the Australian nation is endowed. (It is worth asking whether such a chiastic inversion and concomitant blending would have the same results for feminine identity: the answer may be negative [see in particular Irigaray 1984, 1990 and 1992]). Significantly, the encounter with the toothed escalator is accompanied by an even more ambiguous, but utterly banal phenomenon: as Mick dithers in front of the tectonic intersection, a young woman moves past him, virtually ignoring him (a dramatisation of the feared dissolution of a genderless, and thus non-differentiated self) but for a fleeting, disinterested glance (the feared catastrophe as absolute anticlimax).

These possibilities, however, can barely be articulated by the film's gender topographies. Within the political project of *Crocodile Dundee*, the two sides of the gendered equation must inevitably bonded to each other with a distribution of strength and weakness which implicitly questions the gender divide. Explicitly, however, this blurring of gender power must be controlled and recuperated; the strategy of levelling cannot be allowed to question the very schema used to portray power and its equalisation.

Silence, Reserve and Litotes

One way this fraying of the boundaries of masculine identity can be forestalled is by strategies of reserve, understatement or silence. When Sue's point-blank rifle-shot barely misses Mick's foot, his only response is a sort of startled high-pitched grunt. The speechlessness produced by her sudden departure from stereotypical feminine behaviour is in part evidence of Mick's abrupt disarray – but also, the sign of a very effective system of defence. "I hope you're not going to be the strong silent type", Sue says as she sets out to interview Mick Dundee – to which he replies that he is his own favourite topic of conversation. But *Crocodile Dundee* emphasises Australian masculinity as a form of reserve involving minimal speech, minimal action, minimal violence, reserved energy – what Meaghan Morris refers to as the film's " 'masculine' refusal of overkill, hyperbole, and hysteria as principles of action" (Morris 1988: 252). This is all part of the Australian male stereotype of laconic speech, dry understatement and economy of action. Mick's reactions to the excessive violence of the kangaroo hunters is to employ the object of their terror (the kangaroo itself) to scare away the intruders; in the same way, the American male with its overblown rhetoric and false elegance, connoting forms of effeminacy (Richard with his Italian and italianate posturing and elegant words, the pimp with his exaggerated Latino sarcasm) are silenced with one carefully measured blow. Thus the film presents Australia in understated terms, making no claims to be a powerful nation. In so doing, the film attenuates the power of Australian masculinity (or masculine Australia) in accord with the realities of geopolitical power, while accommodating that attenuation to a national stereotype of low-keyed masculinity, whose very strength is evinced, paradoxically, in the absence of force. This masculinity operates according to the rhetorical figure of restraint, that of litotes, which reins in excessive emotion by ironic negation. Mick Dundee is a past-master of this laconic form. Typically, rather than admiring the palatial hotel suite Sue has reserved for him in New York, Mick's dry response is: "It's a bit rough, but I'll manage." Popular wisdom has it that the Australian vernacular is characterised by opening one's mouth as little as possible, thereby exemplifying a pragmatic, somatic instance of litotes. The prominence of litotes in the film is symptomatic of a (gendered) relation to Otherness embedded in language itself. According to Steve Neale, masculine silence is linked to an attempt to overcome the symbolic castration associated with the entry into language, which profoundly threatens the narcissism of early childhood: "language is a process (or a set of processes) involving absence and lack, and these are what threaten any image of the self as totally enclosed, self-sufficient, omnipotent" (Neale 1993: 12-13). Within Lacanian theory, language signals the subject's dependence upon the "Autre grand A", upon the Symbolic, upon the Name of the Father; more prosaically, language stands in for the object so that the very usage of a word highlights the absence of that which is being spoken of. Masculinity, which typically figures itself as fullness in contrast to feminine lack, has a particular interest in concealing its connections with its Other, in order to paper over its own lacunae. If language displays the manner in which the self is dependent upon and implicated in, indeed, constituted by Otherness, then the laconic structure of the whole film dramatises restraint as a form of recuperation and masking of loss of power. A significant expression of Mick's desire for Sue is his roundabout comparison of himself to the crocodile, which, in her words "was going to eat me alive". Mick's growled comment ("The same thought had crossed by mind once or twice") expresses affection through deadly aggression. Thereupon he puts his hat over his face and goes to sleep, thus terminating face-to-face contact, sealing off language and silencing the symptoms of sexual or emotional hunger. Reserve is thus a means of dealing with implicit powerlessness, configured here under the sign of gender. Reserve is a way of reworking the imbalance of power and the intimate imbrication with the Other who limits the power of the self, as a form of what Lyotard has called "retorsion": the capacity to seize effects wielded by a stronger power, and to reroute those effects in a manner radically opposed to the original imbalance of forces (Lyotard 1977: 66, 127). The reserve and litotic elements of the film thus implicitly reveal in national masculinity a structure which is in no way autonomous, but predicated upon its Other; the film necessarily works to admit this fact, and simultaneously to elide it.

It is in this light that the film's seeming contestation of gender stereotypes needs to be regarded. *Crocodile Dundee* is replete with apparent subversion of images of traditional masculine power. In the inaugural pub scene, Mick kisses Donk on the lips, thus replacing the traditional punch in the stomach which has never yet unbalanced the glass of beer on the muscle-man's head. Mick openly deflates his own elevated tone or punctures images of hyper-masculinity: when shaving in the bush, he smartly replaces his razor with the enormous bush-knife as soon as Sue appears in the corner of the frame, but cannot help laughing at his own patently staged backwoodsman pose. In reply to Sue's admiration of her defender on the New York streets with the epithet "Tarzan", Mick utters not a bellow but something resembling a bleat. The self-deprecating deflation of stereotypical masculinity which repeatedly occurs in *Crocodile Dundee* can be seen, on the one hand, as part of the film's comedy, which constantly takes aim at masculine pretentions to power. On the other, more disturbingly, it can be conceived as an aspect of the litotic strategies of the film, by which hegemonic masculinity is recast in a ironic, negative form in order to pre-empt symptoms of its own deep vulnerability.

Recuperation

The gender characteristics of *Crocodile Dundee* are not merely utilised in the film to figure the place of the Australian nation in relation to the US; as suggested above, they also work to describe the position of the diminutive Australian film industry in relation to its Hollywood counterpart. Significantly, at the end of the film, Mick Dundee walks over the heads of a cheering American crowd in the subway station, in a proleptic mise-en-abyme of the film's resounding success. Tom O'Regan suggests that it is precisely the Australian film industry's engagement on Hollywood's own terrain – a gendered engagement, because the Australian film industry is small and not particularly powerful on the American cinema stage – which reveals to what extent Australian film is closely linked to the other national cinemas in competition with whom it quite consciously defines itself. O'Regan speaks of strategies which work "to transform what is the culturally weak Australian position into a comic vehicle that turns the tables on the culturally strong": "moving from outright mimicry, to ironic imitation, adjustment, negotiation, transformation, resistance and subversion. All these movements entail relations of implication, not violent resistance" (O'Regan 1996: 234). A similar complicity is revealed, ironically, in Mick's confession, when asked about his nickname "Crocodile", that it was suggested by his colleague Wally: "He reckons it makes be more colourful for the tourist business." Thus the very name which has since become an international synonym for stereotypical outback Australianness is quite openly admitted to be a strategy for inviting the world to intrude upon the Red Centre of Australia. Thus the film directly addresses not only the imbrication of self and Other, of masculinity and femininity, but also, more cannily, that of vulnerability and recuperation for an immensely successful marketing ploy.

The penetration of the American woman into the realm of Australian masculinity is figured by Sue's camera, whose brand-name, Canon, signals its close connection with the rifle which very nearly perforates Mick's foot. The journalist's camera in turn is a metonymy of the gaze in its double capacity in this film. The gaze can undermine masculine confidence, as in the episode when Mick, fearing the intrusion of the chambermaid Rosina into the New York hotel bathroom, seizes his bush hat in a movement of panic to cover up his vulnerable private parts. Likewise, his own hypnotic gaze, capable of overwhelming water buffaloes and dogs, fails to subdue the pimp and his sidekick thugs in the concrete jungle. And in sexually liberated New York, Mick's mistrustful gaze functions as an index of his own anxiety about the erasure of gender difference as he finds himself obliged to carry out manual verification of the gender of transsexuals. Yet on the other hand, it is precisely in New York, where Mick's masculinity is most tested by the danger of the loss of differentiation, that the same telephoto-lens which tracks him in the outback subsequently establishes him as a form of photogenic and commodifiable difference. Thus Mick's conquest of New York is captured by Sue's camera as he stands atop the Empire State Building, pointing across the panorama with a deictic gesture which appropriates the mastery endowed by the photographic gaze – a gaze in turn replicated by that of the cinematic camera. Here the film makes a self-reflexive gesture about its own offering of a narcissistic view of an Australian national identity – an identity simultaneously emasculated *and* masculine in its engagement with the powerful forces of Hollywood film industry. For it is this gaze, both at home and abroad, which has guaranteed the establishment of an artificial yet immensely successful version of Australian identity – and one subsequently marketed by other commercial enterprises such as Foster's.

The anxious gaze trying to ascertain sexual difference in danger of erasure ("just making sure", explains Mick after a cautious grope) indicates one potential consequence of the problematic process of chiasmus and interlocking which the film undertakes in order to equalise the patently unequal relationship between Australia the US. Cross-dressing in the colonial context, Diana Brydon has pointed out, is the site of a precarious vulnerability in cultural and nationalist discourses, because it destabilises the borders of identity at crucial moments of cross-cultural exchange (Brydon 1994: 29). As suggested above, the mapping of masculinity and femininity onto Australia and the US and their subsequent spatial exchange comes close to endangering its own project, because chiasmus and interlocking threaten to blur the very boundaries upon which gendered national identity are predicated. Yet if the escalator at JFK airport, as a machine in which Same and Other blend together in a vicious toothed embrace figures the process by which two genders meet, with possibly dire consequences for the individual identity being carried by the process, the same escalator also explains how the film successfully averts the possible melting of gendered identity. For in actual fact, at the point on the escalator where self and Other meet, difference *is* maintained, despite the "catastrophic" moment at which the two structures intersect and blend. Here the film gives a visual image of the way sexual difference is both eroded, *and* perpetuated by being co-opted for a project of commodification of cultural and gender difference. In that image, radical differences meet and indeed interlock in a process of unceasing destabilisation and reconfiguration, without for all that disappearing.

The chiastic reversal of gender hierarchies undertaken by the film carries with in the danger of the eradication of gender difference, something that is thematised in the second part of the film in Mick's encounters with transsexuals. This problem is resolved by converting masculinity as a structure involved in a difference-suppressing chiastic relationship, into masculinity as a commodified difference whose regional origin can be assimilated to a commercial process. Lawrence Grossberg has proposed that: "In its originary – colonial – mode of operation, the discursive machine apparently operated – somewhat like an ideology – by hiding the primacy of difference and producing what appeared to be essential (at least for the colonizer, positive) identities. This is no longer true: the machine not only tolerates but seems to demand the visible production of difference everywhere" (Grossberg 1999: 39). Rather than being suppressed, difference becomes the principle product of global media: "My argument is that media produces the local – (as territories or places – whether as the village, the nation, or the region) – in fact, a heterogeneity of locales. [...] Globalization is producing a reality in which differences proliferate in a highly reterritorialized world (hence, there is a reinvestment in the local and identities as places). [...] This constructed equivalence of place and identity constitutes in my opinion the primary power of the media as a global force" (Grossberg 1999: 41). If Grossberg's suspicions are founded, then the cultural difference of Mick Dundee is a dramatised, staged commodification of a distinct identity linked to a specific place whose broad outlines are sketched out in the first part of the film, and whose marketing abroad is proleptically indicated in a grand mise-en-abyme in the second half of the film. *Crocodile Dundee* is a perfect example of what Grossberg sees as a modern community identity which is "less a matter of relations than of images of lifestyles (themselves defined by the aura of commodities) embodying imaginations of 'becoming American' [read: Australian], i.e. of entering into the auratic space of the commodity located in specific imagined places" (Grossberg 1999: 43).

More importantly, the cultural difference which is so successfully commodified in *Crocodile Dundee* (both within its own fictional world, and in the success enjoyed by the film itself) is based upon a gender difference, one whose threatened erasure is subsequently recuperated as a further form of difference. For the masculinity produced by *Crocodile Dundee* is both quixotically naive and close to the feminine and, at the same time, traditionally sexist and conservative. In a very pertinent warning to cultural studies, Grossberg cautions: "If this is the case, it makes the current faith in difference (and even hybridity) as the form and site of resistance and agency quite problematic" (Grossberg 1999: 39). The same warning could be recast for the exponents of an anti-ideological gender studies in the light of *Crocodile Dundee*'s use of feminine attributes to reinforce traditional masculism.

Finally, as noted above, the gaze which so threatens Mick Dundee is the key to his success on the New York scene, and as a film icon internationally. Regarding the visibility of masculinity, Jonathon Rutherford has written that masculine identity "is an identity that is in continual struggle to assert its centrality in cultural life, yet it attempts to ensure its absence, and to evade becoming the object of discourse" (Rutherford 1988: 23). Following Foucault, it is the invisibility of power which ensures its perfect functioning (Foucault 1976: 113). Yet Frank Mort's work on the recent prominence of highly stylised masculinity in fashion advertising and lifestyle magazines has shown that an intense spotlight cast upon the masculine body as a visual icon in no way necessarily implies a genuine questioning of male social power, but can go hand in hand with the continued exclusion of women from public space and positions of power (Mort 1996: Part 1). The "difference" of a masculinity rendered visible does not necessarily lead to the demystification of its ideological underpinning, to the detachment of its "metaphoric" adherence to a naturalised real for the "metonymic" shifting of hitherto manipulated signifiers. Far more, enhanced mobility injected into the illusory "metaphorical" fullness of the signifier can lead to an eternal metonymic succession of signifiers desired as commodities (or commodities as signifiers); each impulse towards the impossible "metaphorical" act of possession of the commodity only triggers a further metonymical desire for acquisition. In the words of Fredric Jameson, these impulses "are initially awakened within the very texts [or commodities] that seek to still them" (Jameson 1981: 287). Precisely this transformation can be seen at work in the episode of the swish New York party. "Just checking", explains a relieved Mick, having grabbed at the drag queen Ben's nether regions and thus re-established the clear dividing lines of gender difference – whereupon Sue is left to justify Mick's behaviour: "Don't worry, he's Australian". This scene marks exactly the point of suture where the anxious gaze verifying the presence of clearly delineated sexual difference is recycled as commodified national difference. Here, masculinity abroad as a structure undermined by proximity to a constitutive Other which threatens it with the loss of boundary-based difference, is rescued as commodified difference. Exemplary of this troubled border is Mick's statement of derived phallic superiority, ridiculing a New York switch-blade with a flourish of his enormous outback machete – "That's not a knife, *that's* a knife", perhaps the film's most famous one-liner – which pithily summarises the film's gender project, that of shoring up endangered difference in service of profitable (inter)cultural capital. In this second phase, the "lack" displayed by the naive lad from the bush – his sexual innocence, his ignorance of drugs, his inability to adapt to the anonymity of a large metropolis – become part of his "aura", that of unpolluted and nostalgic purity. The commodification of masculinity, and not its demystification through the de-naturalising work of the intensely visual culture of the 80s and 90s, is expressed by Mort's succinct description of the motivations of the artists and designers working in the men's magazine scene: "What were the contours of this consumption-led discourse, and how did the new form of magazine publishing hope to intervene in men's lives? Publishers and journalists confronted these matters not as ethical or political dilemmas, but as business questions demanding practical solutions. Shifting the boundaries of masculinity, defining new identities and styles of life were immediately bound up with the search for markets [...]" (Mort 1996: 44). Clearly, Paul Hogan's Mick Dundee character is a far cry from the slick fashion boys of contemporary men's lifestyle magazines. What this unlikely juxtaposition should illuminate, however, is the links between masculinity, an increasing degree of visual attention to differentiated masculine identity, and consumerism, as evinced in the chiastic relationships between Foster's Lager and *Crocodile Dundee* explored at the beginning of this article.

Anne McClintock provocatively writes: "All nationalisms are gendered, all are invented and all are dangerous" (McClintock 1995: 352). Given the world-wide resonance of *Crocodile Dundee* and conversely its success within Australia – Paul Hogan was voted Australian of the Year in 1988 –, its significance as a moulder of social representations and values, in particular in the field of gender and national identity, cannot be underestimated. Even if the relationship of the Australian public to the Ocker legend exemplified in the film is never one of direct imitative appropriation, as Hodge and Mishra intimate (Hodge/Mishra 1990: 172-177), the impact of such images nevertheless remains powerful and extensive.

To begin with, what the film *elides* should be of some concern. There is no real confrontation with Australia's participation in American overseas policy (including, for instance, the presence of American military bases on Australian territory). There is no mention of and therefore no reflection on Australia as a multicultural, urban society located in Southeast Asia.

Further, the *active* symbolic work of the film is even more concerning. *Crocodile Dundee* can in no way be seen as a politically progressive film. Typical of its apparently innocuous, but in the last analysis deep conservatism is, for instance, Mick's opinion of Aboriginal land-rights. When interrogated by Sue on Aboriginal demands for restitution of their land, he replies that the Aborigines do not own the land but that they belong to it, thus co-opting one partial aspect of Aboriginal lore in order to dismiss their political activism. This ostensibly well informed riposte, which claims to reflect the Aborigines' own cultural standpoint over against a "politicised" stance (invented by White activists?), merely echoes the findings of Justice Blackburn in 1971 which rejected Aboriginal claims in the Milirrpum case on the ground that the Aboriginal people had a sense of obligation to the land rather than a relationship of possession, thus disqualifying them from proprietary interest in tribal lands (Yunupingu 1997: 4). The profoundly disturbing character of the film's contribution to the further history of relations between Black and White Australia becomes evident when one reflects that the current Australian government in power continues to resist the process of transfer of land to indigenous custodians, and reconciliation with indigenous Australians. *Crocodile Dundee*'s active contribution to gender politics is equally reactionary. The identification by men of their selfhood with the nation as described by Hroch (1996: 90-91) means that gendered figures of nationhood can in turn be appropriated by individual men within their everyday lives, with the association of nationhood and masculinity serving as legitimisation for a particular masculine habitus of domination, a phenomenon epitomised in Mick Dundee's "This's a man's country love". The few aspects of an alternative, non-hegemonic masculinity which are offered to the audience in *Crocodile Dundee* are rapidly recuperated for a commodified version of victorious masculinity. In terms of gender politics, *Crocodile Dundee* supports a traditional hegemonic masculinity (uncommunicative, sexist, racist, violent); this masculinity's areas of weakness are revealed by contact with a strong and assertive form of femininity, but those weaknesses are rapidly turned to its own advantage, helping to get the public on its side. *Crocodile Dundee* can be thus seen as belonging to a genre of contemporary films which "[put] masculinity into crisis" without "[offering] a radical critique either of masculinity or of violence"; Mick Dundee can be regarded as exemplifying a generic hero "who redeems himself through loss" (Cook 1982: 39-40). The notion of redemption through failure has particularly strong cultural resonance in Australia, whose popular mythology of masculist national identity reposes upon the ANZAC legend and the military debacle at Gallipoli in 1915, a myth of stoic soldier heroism seriously eroded by Australian participation as an ally of the US in the Vietnam war – and, significantly, a myth which numerous films and plays have attempted to rehabilitate in recent years (Turner 1993: 21; Gilbert 1998: 190-191). These strategies of recuperation of hegemonic versions of masculinity have a broad base in social practices. Like other erstwhile liberal Western societies enthusiastically embracing neo-liberal economic policies and dismantling socially progressive state services for its citizens, Australia has also experienced a vehement reaction against transformations in gender practices in private and public life. Ronald McKie for instance has recently bemoaned the encroachment of feminism upon Australian males' privileges:

> His bewilderment grows as his position and status is undermined. His certainties have degenerated into uncertainties as his place as a man is being more and more assaulted. This [...] is such a profound historical and emotional change that it is impossible to guess how far the [feminist] movement will go and what damage it will do, since it is only just beginning. If the movement slows down in the years ahead, largely through the natural commonsense of women, evolutionary change rather than revolutionary may be more easily absorbed and the influence on the individual and the family may be more easily accepted. But a female revolution which destroys male position and self-confidence, and attempts to make the male virtually obsolete, could produce a community that is a social disaster – and not only for the male. What women do not seem to have yet understood is that they are in grave danger of losing those characteristics which make them such a strong, perceptive, compassionate and superb sex – their essential dignity and their hidden power.
>
> I have only seen one matriarchy, and its male components were miserable and demoralised specimens. (McKie 1989: 245-246)

McKie's simplistic populist stance is symptomatic of a strong trend in Australian society in times of social change coupled with economic recession. Eleanor Hogan, in her contribution to the present volume, explores further instances of increasingly conservative public discourses of gender in Australia. It is at this point that images of national identity, particularly when propagated by a cultural medium as seductive and suggestive as film, need to be scrutinised in their legitimating force within everyday practices of employment, educational opportunities, social services resources and so on. *Crocodile Dundee* projected an image of masculine Australia and of Australian masculinity on the international screen which gestured towards acceptance of such change in gender patterns while in reality offering renewed legitimisation to traditional hegemonic masculinity; furthermore, the film stamp that legitimisation with the seal of success on the international market for identity-commodities and of corresponding global fame.

Works Cited

Anderson, Benedict 1991. *Imagined Communities: Reflections on the Origin and Spread of Nationalism*, 2nd ed. London: Verso.

Anzieu, Didier 1985. *Le Moi-peau*. Paris: Dunod.

Beck, Ulrich 1997. *Was ist Globalisierung?* Frankfurt/Main: Suhrkamp.

Brotton, Jerry 1996. "Mapping the early modern nation: cartography along the English margins." *Paragraph* 19:2 (July 1996), 139-155.

Brydon, Diana 1994. "Empire's Bloomers: Cross-Dressing's Double-Cross." *Essays on Canadian Writing* 54 (1994), 23-45.

Butler, Judith 1995. "Melancholy Gender/Refused Identification" in Berger, Wallis and Watson (eds.) *Constructing Masculinity*. New York: Routledge, 21-36.

Chodorow, Nancy 1978. *The Reproduction of Mothering: Psychoanalysis and the Sociology of Gender.* London: University of California Press.

Cohan, Steven and Ina Rae Hark 1993, "Introduction" in Steven Cohan and Ina Rae Hark (eds.). *Screening the Male: Exploring Masculinities in Hollywood Cinema.* London: Routledge, 1-8.

Cook, Pam 1982. "Masculinity in Crisis? Tragedy and Identification in *Raging Bull.*" *Screen* 23: 3-4 (1982), 39-46.

Crofts, Stephen 1992. "Cross-Cultural Reception: Variant Readings of *Crocodile Dundee.*" *Continuum* 6: 1 (1992), 213-227.

Dinnerstein, Dorothy 1987. *The Rocking of the Cradle and the Ruling of the World.* London: The Women's Press.

Douglas, Mary 1980. *Purity and Danger: An Analysis of the Concepts of Pollution and Taboo.* London: Routledge and Kegan Paul.

Foster's 1999. URL: http://www.fosters.com.au/ftb_advert.asp

Foucault, Michel 1976. *Histoire de la sexualité, 1: La Volonté de savoir.* Paris: Gallimard.

Gilbert, Helen 1998. *Sightlines: Race, Gender and Nation in Contemporary Australian Theatre.* Ann Arbor: University of Michigan Press.

Grossberg, Lawrence 1999. "Globalization and the 'Economisation' of Cultural Studies" in Bundesministerium für Wissenschaft und Verkehr/Internationales Forschungszentrum Kulturwissenschaften (ed.). *The Contemporary Study of Cultures.* Vienna: Turia + Kant, 23-46.

Hodge, Bob, and Vijay Mishra 1990. *Dark Side of the Dream: Australian Literature and the Postcolonial Mind.* Sydney: Allen and Unwin.

Hroch, M. 1996. "From national movement to fully formed nation: the nation-building process in Europe" in G. Balakrishnan (ed.). *Mapping the Nation.* London: Verso, 78-97.

Irigaray, Luce 1984. *Ethique de la différence sexuelle.* Paris: Minuit.

———— 1990. *Je, Tu, Nous: Pour une culture de la différence.* Paris: Grasset.

———— 1992. *J'aime à toi: Esquisse d'une félicité dans l'histoire.* Paris: Grasset.

Jameson, Fredric 1981. *The Political Unconscious: Narrative as a Socially Symbolic Act.* London: Methuen.

Johnston, George 1981 [1964]. *My Brother Jack.* Blackburn, Victoria: Collins Fontana.

Kaplan, E. Ann 1997. *Looking for the Other: Feminism, Film and the Imperial Gaze.* New York: Routledge.

Krutnik, Frank 1991. *In a Lonely Street: Film Noir, Genre, Masculinity.* London: Routledge.

Langer, Beryl 1991. "The Real Thing: Cliff Hardy and Cocacola-Nisation." *SPAN* 31 (1991), 29-44.

Lyotard, Jean-François 1977. *Rudiments païens: genre dissertatif.* Paris: UGE 10/18.

Mayer, Tamar 2000. "Gender Ironies of Nationalism: Setting the Stage" in Tamar Mayer (ed.). *Gender Ironies of Nationalism: Sexing the Nation.* London: Routledge, 1-22.

McCaughey, Patrick 1998. "Likeness and Unlikeness: The American-Australian Experience" in Elizabeth Johns, Andrew Sayers, Elizabeth Mankin Kornhauser and Amy Ellis (eds.). *New Worlds from Old: 19th Century Australian and American Landscapes.* Canberra: National Gallery of Australia/Hartford, Conn.: Wadsworth Atheneum, 15-21.

McClintock, Anne 1995. *Imperial Leather: Race, Gender and Sexuality in the Colonial Contest.* New York: Routledge.

McKie, Ronald 1989. *We Have No Dreaming.* Syndey: Collins.

Mercer, Kobena 1990. "Welcome to the Jungle: Identity and Diversity in Postmodern Politics" in Jonathon Rutherford (ed.). *Identity, Community, Culture, Difference.* London: Lawrence and Wishart, 43-71.

Morris, Meaghan 1988. *The Pirate's Fiancée: Feminism, Reading, Postmodernism.* London: Verso.

Mort, Frank 1996. *Cultures of Consumption: Masculinities and Social Space in late Twentieth-Century Britain.* London: Routledge.

Neal, Steve 1993, "Masculinity as Spectacle: Reflections on men and mainstream cinema" in Steven Cohan and Ina Rae Hark (eds.). *Screening the Male: Exploring Masculinities in Hollywood Cinema.* London: Routledge, 9-20.

Nelson, Dana 1998. *National Manhood: Capitalist Citizenship and the Imagined Fraternity of White Men.* Durham, NC: Duke University Press.

O'Regan, Tom 1996. *Australian National Cinema.* London: Routledge.

Rickard, John 1995. *Australia: A Cultural History.* London: Longman.

Sami-Ali 1982. *L'Espace imaginaire.* Paris: Gallimard/Tel.

Schneede, Uwe M. 1994. *Joseph Beuys: Die Aktionen: Kommentiertes Werkverzeichnis mit fotographischen Dokumentationen.* Stuttgart: Verlag Gerd Hatje. 330-353

Silverman, Kaja 1992. *Male Subjectivity at the Margins.* New York: Routledge.

Thom, René 1983. *Paraboles et catastrophes: Entretiens sur les mathématiques, la science et la philosophie.* Paris: Flammarion.

Tisdall, Caroline 1988. *Joseph Beuys: Coyote.* Trans. Dominique Le Bourg. Paris: Hazan.

Turner, Graeme 1993. *National Fictions: Literature, Film and the Construction of Australian Narrative.* 2nd ed. Sydney: Allen and Unwin.

Turner, Victor 1982. *From Ritual to Theatre: The Human Seriousness of Play.* New York: PAJ Publications.

White, Richard 1981. *Inventing Australia: Images and Identity 1688-1980.* Sydney: George Allen & Unwin.

Willemen, Paul 1981. "Anthony Mann: Looking at the Male." *Framework* 15-17 (1981), 16.

Yunupingu, Galarrwuy 1997. "From the Bark Petition to Native Title" in Galarrwuy Yunupingu (ed.). *Our Land is Our Life: Land Rights: Past, Present, Future.* Brisbane: University of Queensland Press, 1-17.

American Culture X:
Identity, Homosexuality, and the Search for a New American Hero

Stefan Brandt

> The modern hero is no hero; he acts heroes.
> Walter Benjamin 1973: 97

> ESMARELDA: Butch. What does it mean?
> BUTCH: I'm an American. Our names don't mean shit.
> *Pulp Fiction* Screenplay (Tarantino/Avary 1994: 94)

The man in modern-day America is a cultural hermaphrodite. At least he feels like one. Says self-declared he-man Tom Leykis on his nationally syndicated radio talkshow: "I'm the Mother Teresa of broadcasting" (show 2/15, 2000). And a picture on Leykis's internet web page that shows the talkshow host with two showgirls from Las Vegas reads: "His name was Tom, he was a showgirl..." It is very same talkshow that tells "men how to get more tail for less money" and "women how men think" (trailer, mon through fri, 3:00 p.m.); the very same talk show instructs male listeners in cars to flip on their headlights "if they want women in nearby cars to 'flash' their breasts" (Lippman 1998). Just like Howard Stern, his celebrated colleague on the same radio station, Tom is a declared macho, but his web page also contains links to gay sites; and the trailer for his show boasts that it is "not hosted by a right wing wacko." What reveals itself here is a deep ambivalence in the identity of modern males. While continually unfolding die-hard macho opinions (for instance in his ritualistic labelling of "soft-minded" men as "pussies"), the talk show host is not ashamed to act just as hysterically as the "babbling women" whom he despises so much. The continuous affirmation of male identity and the (involuntary) deconstruction of that identity seem to be close brothers. As Wayne Munson has suggested, the radio talk host has since the 1950s been a figure very susceptible to projections of androgyny, due to his position in an arena-like section of the public sphere (Munson 1993: 112-113). But how does the performance of this figure relate to certain developments in the cultural consciousness of the American 1990s and 2000s?

This article wants to show that the sexual ambiguity of the male radio persona is not an isolated case. My thesis is that the construction of male hero figures in contemporary American culture is closely connected to a general search for cultural identity. It is the underlying conflict between opposing concepts of masculinity that not only reverberates in the cultural practice of gender representation, but also informs the way in which overarching concepts like identity and subjectivity are negotiated in public. If Rush Limbaugh was a signifier for a deep political crisis in the early 1990s, Tom Leykis is a signifier for the deep identity crisis that has seized American males around the turn-of-the-millennium. And radio listeners in the United States who have made "The Tom Leykis Show" one of the most popular radio programs nationwide, seem to feel a need for such an identity figure (Lippman 1998). Identity becomes an important issue, as Kobena Mercer puts it, "when something assumed to be fixed, coherent and stable is displaced by the experience of doubt and uncertainty" (Mercer 1994: 259). As the traditional conceptions of what is seen as "masculine" and "feminine" are changing in our society, the ambiguous male has emerged as an important signifier. The openly displayed gender ambiguity of so many male characters in contemporary films and literary texts has thus proved to be both an expression of and an answer to this widely felt ambiguity in the culture.

In the following passages, I will focus on the contradictoriness and contestedness of heroic masculinity in modern-day America. How do these hybrid models of heroic masculinity function in our culture? And what kind of aesthetic background makes them work? I want to explore the role that the sign "homosexuality" plays in the construction of the male self in contemporary culture. In order to analyze these aspects I will make use of various theoretical concepts developed by Mikhail Bakhtin, Jacques Derrida and Kaja Silverman.

In our turn-of-the-millennium culture, the long symbolic battle of constructing and deconstructing masculinity has reached a symbolic climax. The gradual erosion of male stereotypes that has taken place in the 1970s and 1980s is coming into a new phase. Recently, movies like Quentin Tarantino's *Pulp Fiction* (1994) and Luc Besson's *The Fifth Element* (1997) have concentrated on the vulnerability of the male subject and built a whole plot around this motif. In both movies, masculinity constitutes the recognizable – albeit constantly challenged – center around which the narrative revolves. The interplay between center and margin, presence and absence, subjectivity and objectivity, is of great importance here. These movies stand in a long tradition of validating traditional masculinity, but at the same time they partially distance themselves from these roots. The types of male characters that are offered here have came a long way from the tough guy heroes of the fifties à la Mickey Spillane: the insecure guy (Travolta), the raped man (Rhames), the drag queen (Tucker), etc. Travolta in *Pulp Fiction* always gets into trouble when he is on the toilet. Rhames's portrait of the raped gangster boss Marsellus Wallace is not only sad, in its absurdity it is almost comical, as well. And Tucker's performance is so much over the top that it reaches the point of not only being comical but also tragic.

These often serious and often comical subversions of the male role evoke the notion of carnival (which itself, of course, has a strong element of catharsis). Like the institution of carnival, the imaginary world in these films shows both the absurdity and the sadness, the "real" and the "surreal" sides, of human experience. According to Mikhail Bakhtin's definition, carnival stages reality as a "syncretic pageantry of a ritualistic sort" (1984: 22). In both films, *Pulp Fiction* and *The Fifth Element*, masculinity (as a central part of reality) is relived and reconstructed in a very similar way. The playful and often deliberately ambiguous reinvention of maleness in these films turns out to be a kind of cultural self-observation that is at the same time a symbolic valve and a means of reaffirming existing values. While openly addressing and even criticizing certain aspects of masculinity (for instance the hyper-masculinity of the father figure and the endangerment of masculinity in modern life), the films leave untouched other pivotal aspects (for instance the notion of the "true hero" which is again very much in tune with conventional portrayals of maleness). This double effect is due to the fact that every discourse is in a sense "the marriage of a limitation with an opportunity" and therefore bears the potential of being read both ways (Derrida 1979: 6).

Luc Besson's *The Fifth Element* (1996-97) is a good example of this double discourse of masculinity. In the movie, Bruce Willis plays Korben Dallas, a cab driver and American Everyman who, in the year 2214, is asked by the government of the United States to save the world. The Willis character seems to be the paradigm of the American hero. He is masculine, healthy, brave, strong-willed, and almost Herculean in his ability to master the most difficult situations. And compared to the other figures, he is recognizably the only one who can cope with the task of saving the world. The pattern for the hero's rise to glory seems to be a direct quote from the bible of both popular mythologists and Hollywood producers, Joseph Campbell's *The Hero with a Thousand Faces* (1968 [1949]). The five stages of heroism that Campbell lists in his book could be also a summary of the narrative in *The Fifth Element*:

> (1) 'The Call to Adventure,' or the signs of the vocation of the hero; (2) 'Refusal to the Call,' or the folly of the flight from God; (3) 'Supernatural Aid,' the unsuspected assistance that comes to one who has undertaken his proper adventure; (4) 'The Crossing of the First Threshold': and (5) 'The Belly of the Whale,' or the passage into the realm of the night. (1968 [1949]: 36)

The call to save the world that reaches Korben Dallas through the President's aides (who serve as representatives of a higher power) (1) is followed by the hero's initial refusal to fulfill the call ("Korben Dallas didn't mean to be a hero", tagline for *The Fifth Element*) (2) and the arrival of Leeloo, the "perfect being" (3); the difficulties that Korben and Leeloo meet at the airport mark "the crossing of the threshold" (4); their journey to

69

the giant spaceship Phloston Paradise where the hero wages the conclusive battle against his enemies stands for the passage to the realm of the night (5). This affinity to the mythological structures of our cultural knowledge clearly establishes a sense of heroism that is not man-made but of divine origin. It is not human will but spiritual fate that constitutes the final goal of heroism.

All this echoes the idea of an extra-systemic authority which motivates the hero's actions. This authority is undoubtedly masculine and heterosexual; it is unquestionably transcendental, but at the same time it comes across as extremely pragmatic. For the most part of the movie Bruce Willis is shown "doing things" or getting things done. Yet there is a metaphysical quality that pervades his actions. The movie's finale shows a romantic kiss between the hero and the heroine – he on the top, she, half-unconscious, on the bottom. From this heterosexual kiss (which ritualistically stands at the end of virtually *every* Bruce Willis movie up to *The Sixth Sense*), a magical beam emerges that finally defeats the alien invaders. Significantly, masculinity is shown as a driving force throughout the film, while femininity is characterized as being passive and rather reactionary. For instance, it is Korben alone who manages to finally trigger the beam by kissing the heroine. Leeloo's task consists of merely being there and functioning as the receptacle for the generating male sperm. Like in the famous fairytale, Leeloo figures as a "Sleeping Beauty" who is being kissed awake by her prince. Heroic masculinity has, once again, reached its goal: the achievement of the heterosexual act.

In his theory of a "metaphysics of presence", Jacques Derrida argues that in most languages the construction of a symbolic center is needed in order to give meaning (1989: 108-123). This center constitutes itself through the continuous reference to an extra-systemic authority like "God", "man", or "truth." Only by constantly evoking the notion of this "pre-given law", can the center be perceived as "a point of presence, a fixed origin" (Derrida 1978: 278). In *The Fifth Element*, the notion of a fixed origin is underlined by the frequent evocations of natural elements and laws (wind, sand, air, fire, and as the fifth element, love). It is notable that the movie also uses the concept of a male generative force that produces the woman. Leeloo – "the perfect being" as she is repeatedly called – is artificially created by a bunch of exclusively male scientists in a giant laboratory. Her body is literally reconstructed by the scientists *from one body part*. This scene clearly echoes the patriarchal myth of "Adam's rib" from which Eve is formed by the hands of God. "Woman" is thus established as a creation of a higher, privileged authority that is coded as "male". The aesthetic effect is a synecdochical one; the "hand" stands (like the Biblical "rib") for the whole woman; the transformation of the part to the whole is implemented through the power of male authority.

What do these observations tell us about the construction of the "masculine hero" in *The Fifth Element*? Since the movie presents us a very strong, culturally saturated hero figure (in the tradition of other films of the adventure genre), the effect can be both a manifestation of traditional images and a deconstruction of those images. The character played by Bruce Willis is both comical and serious, the perfect hybridized figure that appeals to action fans and intellectuals alike. The movement of play that is induced by the constant allusion to other film characters allows the possibility of a subversive reading that may even destabilize the notion of a strong, monolithic masculinity. To counteract this movement, the movie must evoke a mythological framework that can deactivate the subversive potential. Consequently, the mythological motif of the heroic savior penetrates both the subtext and the meta-structure of the movie. The marketing for the film was almost completely based on Bruce Willis's hero persona. One of the movie posters for *The Fifth Element* depicts him at the center of the picture radiating confidence and charisma. The aesthetic structure of this sharp-contrast photography relies almost exclusively on the centeredness of the hero figure from which the other objects seem to originate. Like the metaphorical sun, Bruce Willis/Korben Dallas is the focal point of this universe. The flying space cars that emerge at the bottom and the top of the picture seem like beams coming from an imaginary center. Also the position of the two other figures, Milla Jovovich and Gary Oldman, at the upper left and the lower right of the picture suggests such a focus. This configuration is echoed in the narrative structure of the movie. The film starts with a nightmare that its main protagonist, Korben Dallas, has, and it ends with the realization of his romantic dreams. The hero is undoubtedly the determining force and center of the narrative.

Interestingly enough, the same radial configuration as in the movie poster is used in the film still that was most often taken up in reviews. Here, the hero stands in the midst of grim-faced aliens whose machine-guns are directed towards him from many different sides. Again, the hero is at the center of the action. But there is a certain tension in this picture that cannot be observed in the movie poster. The hero is obviously a prisoner here. Both his hands are lifted, and the ape-mouthed aliens point their guns at him. But the threatening pose quickly resolves into absurdity when one looks at the inner structure of the still. Although clearly superior in number, the aliens direct five or six big guns at the hero which gives their action a notion of ridiculousness. And even though Willis lifts both of his hands like a prisoner-of-war, his posture seems everything else but helpless or passive. Since we know from other similar movies (with or without Bruce Willis) that a true hero "can be destroyed but never defeated" (to pick up the famous Hemingway line), the only question that remains is *how* he will rescue himself from the unfortunate situation. Nonetheless, the photography plays with the notion of male vulnerability. This notion is clearly hinted at here, but at the same time neutralized through the hero's confident aura – and especially his cocksure smile. This smile tells us that the hero will, once again, master the situation. The film still can be seen as a *mise-en-abyme*, a bottomless, repetitive image for the leitmotif of the wounding/rescue pattern that goes through the whole movie. While the narrative is often completely confusing and even illogical, the concept of the heroic male, embodied by Bruce Willis, with all his recognizable features of masculine strength and solidity, safely guides us through the plot. "Without his familiar face and sanity," one critic wrote, "*The Fifth Element* would be completely unwatchable" (Denby 1997: 63). It is very important for the movie's aesthetic message that it has such a strong symbolic center. As spectators we need such a focal point in order to be able to access the depicted imaginary world. Here, it is precisely the notion of presence that is evoked through the continuous allusions to heroic images (to Willis's own auratic image, but also to other mythological concepts) which leads to a satisfying cinematic experience.

Nowhere else in the movie is this presence of "masculinity" as obvious as in the scene in which Korben is sent in the ballroom on Phloston Paradise to negotiate with the aliens. Korben walks in without further ado and shoots the leader right in the head. His following question "Anybody else wanna negotiate?" is an echo of the hard-boiled adventure movies where the hero (and sometimes the evil guy) shoots one of his enemies and then provokingly asks the others if they also want to defy his rule. But Korben's martial behavior is also an echo of an earlier scene in the movie. When the President's staff debates the correct strategy how to defeat the enemies, the commander-in-chief explains his view that you should "always shoot first and ask questions later." The President's comment, "Shoot first!", is dutifully enacted by Korben in the latter scene. With its implied ideology of an uncompromising pragmatism, the scene reflects the old dualism between heroes and losers. After Korben has successfully "negotiated" with the aliens by killing their leader, a baffled security chief stutters "W-W-W-Where did he learn to negotiate like that?" The comical element comes from the old patriarchal truth that it should not be the brave guy who is the subject of ridicule, but the coward. Heroism, the movie tells us, is deeply injected with codes of masculinity like strength, courage and the will to *do* things. And this code is evaluated here as good and necessary.

While the concept of masculinity is continuously placed at the center of the narrative, femininity is rather something from "outside". Not only does Leeloo literally come from another planet, she is also consistently situated outside the action (for instance when she passively follows Korben's instructions at the airport or unconsciously lies in his arms in one of the film's most decisive moments). The crucial shot of the couple Korben/Leeloo is a scene in Korben's taxi where the young heroine utters the words "Help me. Help me" that she reads from a commercial that advocates orphanages. Korben's decision to help Leeloo does not occur until she repeats her plea for help for the fourth or fifth time. It is only for the duration of 2 minutes and 10 seconds in the second half of the movie that Leeloo finally leaves her passive role behind to beat up the aliens before she is once again rescued by Korben and transported to the pyramid. As the "fifth element", Leeloo stands for nature and metaphysics. While Korben acts, Leeloo just "is". Here the film echoes stereotypical beliefs about gender (male = culture, female = nature) that have been predominant in our culture for a long time (cf. Ortner 1996: 21-42). The other female figure that embodies this image of immanence is the diva, Plava Laguna (*Maïwenn Le Besco*), who is metonymically equated with Leeloo. Her aura of immanence and her potential for motherhood becomes clear when Korben literally fetches the four stones – a symbol for both nature and the divine will – from the inside of her body. The woman's body is seen as a receptacle for reproduction here, since the stones are not only needed to save Leeloo's life but also to guarantee the continued existence of the human race. The other *Gestalt* of motherhood appears in form of the voice of Korben's mother. The image of the annoying mother is the movie's running gag. In one of the final scenes, a repulsed President is shown as his aides erroneously hand him a phone with the mother's nagging voice. This theme not only encapsulates the cultural prejudice about the persistent mother; it also manifests the film's fear of a domineering femininity.

Significantly, the hero's identity in *The Fifth Element* is established through the interplay with the other figures. It is especially through the representation of *other*, non-heroic masculinities that Korben Dallas's own, heroic personality can be constituted. It can be shown that the identity of virtually *every* figure in the movie, male or female, is organized by the question of male authority. While the women in *The Fifth Element* are basically only gimmicks in the path of the male hero (as divine creature, airport stewardess, bearer of divine stones, etc.), the men serve as ridiculous geeks whose only function is to make the hero's masculinity and heroism look God-like in comparison. Every other male figure except Korben Dallas (and perhaps the black president played by Tom "Tiny" Lister, Jr.) is characterized as extremely unmanly. Korben's evil counterpart Zorg (Gary Oldman) is portrayed as an "extravagant villain" (Welsh 1998: 187) who is at once overtly effeminate in gesture and speech (hysterical laugh, etc.) and ridiculously hyper-masculine in his similarity to Adolf Hitler. There is also Ruby Rhod – a "super-freak entertainment queen" (Welsh 1998: 187), something between RuPaul and Dennis Rodman, whose repulsively shrill voice stands in a sharp contrast to Willis's pleasantly soft organ. The other male characters in the movie are equally caricatures of a man: the disturbed priest Cornelius (Ian Holm) who constantly falls over his own feet and utters inaudible nonsense words; the stupid General Munro (Brian James) who is accidentally locked up with his crew in a freezing chamber; the baroque actor Baby Ray (Ian Beckett) who hands Korben a pair of marbles when the latter asks him for a gun; and an unnamed mugger (Mathieu Kassovitz) whose dumbness even keeps him from finding the trigger of his own gun.

All these pitiful characters are thick as two short planks; they are idiotic clowns who are obviously not capable of coping with the demands that a "real" hero has to face. At the same time, these figures are of great importance for the construction of heroic masculinity in the movie. First of all, they legitimize the "phallogocentric" pattern by which "masculinity" is held to be the decisive criterion for the evaluation of any person's identity (cf. Derrida 1975: 31-113). And secondly, their apparent non-masculinity can function as a generative impulse that complements the hero's (supposed) masculine core identity. The signifiers of effeminacy that emerge from these male supporting characters are used, in the Derridean sense, as indicators of a productive non-presence that foreshadows the hero's true masculinity (1982: 11). Since these radical elements are obviously absent in the hero's persona, they allow him to reach a degree of masculinity that could not be attained without such a negation. On the other hand, all of the hero's masculine qualities (his pragmatism, his strong will, etc.) are unquestionably absent in the peripheral characters. The periphery, in this sense, fertilizes the center through negation, and vice versa. Both sides, center *and* periphery, inform the other by creating signifiers (coded as either "masculine" or "feminine") that are seemingly non-present in their opposites.

This interplay between the center and the periphery has the potential of either stabilizing or deconstructing the concept of heroic masculinity. On the one hand, the lead character's tough guy performance comes across as very masculine, but on the other hand, we are continuously confronted, in the form of all the "non-masculine" supporting characters, with the possibility of "otherness", of an alternative, possibly "effeminate" masculinity. No wonder that critic David Denby calls the sad crowd of losers in *The Fifth Element* "a carnival of geeks" (1997: 63). Even the movie's smallest figures – Ruby Rhod's unmistakably queer co-workers or the priest's dorky assistant – are vivid instructions on how a man should *not* be. The mocking inversion of gender hierarchies in the movie, of course, knows its limits, too. In the same manner in which many old-fashioned notions of masculinity are irreverently debunked, the underlying structure is revalidated on a subtextual level. The traditional concept of heroic masculinity is continually reaffirmed through signifiers of a symbolic order which knows basically just two sorts of men: "real" men and mollycoddles – Bruce Willis and the rest of men.

But the Willis character is not totally monolithic. The character successfully integrates some of the deviant elements of masculinity (a certain sense of sensitivity and self-irony) and at the same time encapsulates the necessary residual components of masculine heroism. On the one hand, the figure of Korben Dallas echoes the aura of ruggedness and vigor that was already established in other Bruce Willis movies like, for instance, the *Die Hard* series in which he fights, although smeared with blood, against evil. But his movie persona also encapsulates elements of the wise-guy character from the TV series *Moonlighting* and even child-like components that we remember from baby Mikey whom Willis gave his voice in *Look Who's Talking* (1989). The masculinity that we associate with Bruce Willis in his roles is partly a product of an already existent image and partly the product of an interplay with other concepts of maleness in his movies. In this sense, the Willis character in *The Fifth Element* is a kind of hybrid construction, a palimpsest that presents the material in a new form, but still echoes its old meaning (and also a range of other possible meanings). Out of the oscillating tension between the different meanings and images of masculinity (infantile, effeminate, masculine, etc.) in the movie, Bruce Willis emerges as both an anchor of stability and a decentralizing impulse towards dissent. Following Bakhtin's terminology, the Willis persona can thus be interpreted as an example of heteroglossia, of a range of voices, perspectives and meanings that produce "polyphony". "Heteroglossia", writes Bakhtin, "is *another's speech in another language*, serving to express authorial intentions but in a refracted way" (Bakhtin 1996 [1981]: 324). Male authority in *The Fifth Element* is at the same time manifested and refracted. The hybridization of differing concepts of masculinity in the movie can be interpreted as an expression of the "instability and mutability of identities which are always unfinished, always being made" (Gilroy 1993: xi). It is precisely this realization of the multi-facetedness of human identities (ethnic, sexual, etc.) that is finally being discovered as a central theme in contemporary popular texts.

As men openly struggle with their inner sense of the "correct" gender role, a need for a public forum has emerged in form of countless radio programs, TV shows and films, in order to negotiate this conflict. The battle that so many men are fighting in their private lives has turned out to be a useful paradigm for a general debate on identity and the loss of authority in our culture. Who could deny that the discussion about "gays in the military", for instance, is also rooted in a deep fear that the inner framework of our society might slowly be turning into something else? But this struggle is not only a struggle between different masculinities. The "enemy outside", i.e. woman as a specter generated by male fantasies, is still more useful in the dominant rhetoric than ever. This brings us back to Tom Leykis and his macho radio show. On his program, Leykis ritually tells stories of mean-spirited, deceitful women and their poor male victims. At the same time, the host often speaks in a high-pitched, woman-like voice and even lets his listeners know that a good reason to listen to his program would be that "I turned gay all of a sudden" (using a clip from the Cary Grant movie *Bringing Up Baby*). Despite these comical allusions to all sorts of disturbing cultural phenomena there is no doubt left in his listeners' devoted minds that this talk show host, as he declares over and over again, is a "real man". No doubt at all. Or is there? Critical listeners might also enjoy Leykis's exaggerated masculinity as an act of (involuntary) self-parody. Leykis's declarations that he has "big brass balls" and is, of course, enormously well-endowed ("It's huuuuuuuge....") can both be interpreted as a hilarious spoof and a sign of dumb male arrogance. These exaggerations echo the concept of "grotesque realism" which Mikhail Bakhtin describes in his book on Rabelais. In carnivalesque literature, Bakhtin argues, gargantuan size and huge protuberances are used to celebrate physicality and conquer a symbolic terrain that is still forbidden in society (1997: 227-244). As in folklorist fiction, the emphasis on the grotesque male body in modern-day culture serves the purpose of mocking the medieval religious repudiation of the flesh. The male body is celebrated as the locus of pleasure and empowerment, but at the same time also exposed to the dangers of objectification and ridicule. On "The Tom Leykis Show", this double discourse is constituted through both Leykis's constant accentuation of a man's atheist beliefs and the allusions to his vivid heterosexual love life and his bodily endowment.

From this point of view, the vulgar radio talk shows are at the same time a playground for absurd and often hysterical male behavior and a manifestation that a "real guy" can be as hysterical as he wants if he's white and strictly heterosexual. The verbal escapades into the world of the "Other" are quickly exposed as trips of a mere carnivalesque nature, but they are still strong elements in the formation of the radio persona. The dominant plot that runs like a thread through the "Tom Leykis Show" is the spectacle of fraternal bonding between Leykis and his male listeners that is established over and over again on the show. Women, in this audio world of male fantasies, serve as "babbling chicks" that ought to be "banged" on the first date ("Three strikes and you're out"). The male is clearly the superior being, intellectually speaking ("Women under 50 never talk politics"), but there's also danger lurking out there: Many of these "lazy bitches" and "modern-day hookers" just want your money, warns Leykis, to lead an oh-so-fulfilling life as rich men's wives. "Dump that Bitch!" – gongs a ritual trailer with Leykis's technically darkened voice, when, once again, a frustrated listener is pouring out his heart to the "professor".

What do these macho slurs on commercial radio have in common with our visual culture? Everything, it seems. The Tom Cruise character in P. T. Anderson's *Magnolia* (1999), a foul-mouthed, female-bashing guru who teaches men how to be real machos, is clearly a copy of the modern day he-man talk show host. Masculinity, once again, seems to be deep, ankle-deep, in a crisis. The furious boost of he-man talkshows on radio since the late

MALE BODY.

female bashing — petty.
machos - gurus.
futile counterreaction

1990s is not the only sign that there is an intense longing for a reaffirmation of straight masculinity in American culture. There is also a never-before-seen boom of male fitness studios, men's magazines and (almost completely) male wrestling shows. And tough guy characters, from grim-faced Governor Jesse Ventura to sunny boy film star Bruce Willis, have become omnipresent in the visual world of modern-day America.

These outspoken celebrations of physical masculinity are not thoroughly consistent though. The male body has obviously become more visible today, but is it still a monolithic "male" body after all? Almost all major Hollywood stars, ranging from Arnold Schwarzenegger to Wesley Snipes, from Dustin Hoffman to Patrick Swayze, have played characters in which the traditional male stereotypes are transformed into a charade, a grotesque travesty of their gender. It seems almost a cliché today to claim that the modern hero is a composite figure. The male body has turned out to be a composite, not only socially (*Kramer vs. Kramer* has made the point in 1979 that men can also fill traditional female roles in the household), but also physically. The finale of Ivan Reitman's *Junior* (1994) in which Arnold Schwarzenegger plays a male scientist who becomes artificially pregnant in the course of tests for an anti-miscarriage drug seems symptomatic here. After Schwarzenegger has successfully carried the child he and his wife (Emma Thompson) are having a barbecue at the beach with another married couple (Danny DeVito and Pamela Reed). There they jokingly debate who could be the next male guinea-pig to become pregnant. DeVito at whom the attention is immediately directed coyly backs up. But something tells us that he will soon overcome his initial resistance and be the second in a line of truly changed "new men".

Since the blossoming of the Women's Liberation and Gay Liberation movements in the 1980s the public perception of male and female identity has decisively changed. The drag and transgender scene has since then conquered the stages and screens. Also the increasing visibility of all sorts of deviant masculinities has influenced the public image of the male. In the nineties, once again, this trend has finally reached mainstream Hollywood fiction. The superhero of the eighties, it seems, has stepped back to make way for a more sensitive, realistic and vulnerable figure in the nineties. To put it in a brief formula: Conan the Barbarian has cleared the way for Private Ryan. "While eighties action-adventure films gloried in spectacular scenes of destruction, nineties films are telling audiences that these men were actually being self-destructive" (Jeffords 1993: 200). The display of emotions and vulnerability by a male character is no longer a sensation in contemporary films. The mixture of traditionally "female" and "male" characteristics has proven to be almost a necessity for survival. In an era that has understood the dangers of hyper-masculinization, the realization of a man's communicative potential (that used to be identified as "effeminate" in former fictions) appears to be a *sine qua non*. Without it, also the

established masculine virtues that support the fundaments of our society would seem in danger. In this view, the " 'gentling' of white masculinity" can be read as a "strategy for holding on to power during shifting times" (Bingham 1994: 4).

This dynamic interplay of different masculinities is acted out far more openly in the 1990s and 2000s than for instance in the 1930s. While Clark Gable could only make a coy statement about his hesitation to cry in one scene in *Gone With the Wind* (1939), most leading male Hollywood actors today are quite outspoken in their willingness to act in an unmanly way or play "unmanly" characters on screen. Softness and gentleness have become important characteristics that do not so much destroy the gender credibility of that figure as help to make a male figure appear "whole". They serve as complements to the otherwise quite unquestioned masculinity of the movie persona. As Yvonne Tasker has pointed out, Bruce Willis's soft voice is often deployed in his films to function as a corporeal counterpart to his physical harshness thus constituting him as "more wise-guy than tough-guy" (1995: 239). In mainstream film criticism, this partial correction of former depictions of manhood in the nineties is almost seen as a revolution. "It is refreshing," writes Barbara Creed, "to note the increasing tendency in contemporary texts to play with the notion of manhood" (1987: 65). And Susan Jeffords asserts: "While eighties men may have muscled their way into our hearts killing anyone who got in their way, nineties men are going to seize us with kindness and declarations that they are changed, 'new men' " (1993: 198). However, a close look at the dominant images of maleness in contemporary culture casts doubt upon the idea that an actual paradigm shift has taken place in the nineties. Fair enough, images of a non-traditional masculinity have become more frequent in mainstream cinema, television and other fields of our culture in the 1990s. An actor like Tom Hanks can receive an Oscar for his portrayal of a gay man who is suffering from AIDS, and men dressing as women are populating films like *The Birdcage*, *Flawless*, and *The Crying Game* and also TV programs like the Jerry Springer Show. The Gay Pride March, it seems, has finally emerged as an extremely symbolic spectacle in American culture both embodying and negotiating all these floating ideas, fears and hopes surrounding the (in)stability of sex and gender. All these changes have not occurred over night, as most studies seem to suggest; they are, quite to the contrary, the explication of a broad, long-term transformation in our culture. This process has involved both the normalization of formerly "deviant" forms of masculinity and the "queering" of dominant types of masculinity. It is a process of hybridization that may have blurred old boundaries but has also entailed a virulent rediscovery of conventional masculinity that is ritualistically rejuvenated, reanimated and reinforced in cultural and social practice.

This double spectacle of a playful questioning and a systematic reinvention of traditional male stereotypes I want to call (following Bakhtin) "the carnival of sex" (Bakhtin 1997 [1984]: 195-206). Like the laughter in carnival, the gaze directed toward the male (representing the dominant principles in our society) may both objectify and affirm traditional masculinity. It reduces man to an object of the look and even an object of scorn. But it also acknowledges his previous authority. "The whole world is seen in its droll aspect. [...] This laughter is ambivalent; it is gay, triumphant, and at the same time mocking, deriding. It asserts and denies, it buries and revives" (Bakhtin 1997 [1984]: 200). The wide range of carnivalesque representations mirrors the range of possibilities in the cultural practice to deal with the question of (male) authority. The "carnival of sex" is not a new phenomenon in American culture though. A closer look at the "great" American heroes in film shows that most of the prominent figures consist of multi-faceted, sometimes contradictory aspects. For example, Rudolph Valentino is – in his screen presence – both aggressive male invader and a rather passive object of desire. Even the screen character embodied by Gary Cooper the archetypal model of the super-cool "yup-and-nope-hero" – bears, as James Naremore has competently shown, elements of a domineering masculinity as well as elements of a coquettish, even narcissistic femininity (1990: 131-156). In the American culture of the beginning 21st century this contestedness and ambiguity of the concept of masculinity seems more obvious than ever. But there has also been a strong revival of archaic male figures since the mid 1980s – from Sylvester Stallone's unforgettable impersonation of Vietnam war hero John Rambo to various characters played by Bruce Willis and Jean Claude Van Damme where the hero fights for liberty and world peace with his bare fists and a machine gun. Films like Ted Kotcheff's *First Blood* (1982) and John McTiernan's *Die Hard* (1988) have often been understood to sound the bell for a new round of (re-)masculinization in American culture. The typical character in these films is certainly not free from irony – he seems indeed often more like the "excessive parody of an ideal" (Tasker 1993: 1) – but the narrative built around these figures is in many cases much too serious, too much loaded with the viewer's expectations to be taken only as irony. Of course, both serious and comic elements often blend together in these characters, but at the same time the ideological element is many times privileged in favor of the goal of creating a (more "imagined" than "real") cultural consensus. In an era determined by concepts of role reversal and sexual "indeterminacy" (to pick up a term used by Wolfgang Iser in literary theory), it seems to be important for a culture to draw the line between chaos and order, between sexual anarchy and the imagined well-functioning structure of social practice and "real life". No wonder that this element of "crisis" can be easily detected in many popular depictions of masculinity.

One of the movies that attempt to play with this notion of a "crisis of masculinity" is Quentin Tarantino's much celebrated *Pulp Fiction* (1994). Men are "real men" in this movie (at least they do their best), and women are again these little playthings who are suited best as sex objects or loving housewives. But, yeah, everything is just a spoof, a merely intellectual negotiation of genres and cultural stereotypes. "Tarantino's gangsters", one critic assures us, "are not 'real' " (Denby 1995: 228). Another critic claims that "the general tone of Tarantino's work is a rejection of anything resembling the 'real' world" (Dowell 1995: 4; cf. Indiana 1994: 108). *Pulp Fiction*, in this view, seems to be just an innocent play, "a commentary on old movies" (Denby 1995: 228). Inspired by the popular "black mask" series, the film clearly alludes to the '50s trash culture à la Mickey Spillane and simultaneously plays with "the '70s pop culture mindset" (Connors/Craddock 1999: 731). But does this play with cultural signs and genres automatically reduce *Pulp Fiction* to a mere treatise upon other discourses, a stylistic performance of signifiers rather than a negotiation of "real" ideas and feelings? Absolutely not. If the movie were so deeply entangled in the arrangement of "unreal" concepts, one might ask why it has then gained such an enormous crowd of enthusiastic followers. In his interview with the movie's director, Gavin Smith elaborates on this paradox:

> On the one hand you're making films in which you want the audience emotionally involved, as if it's "real". On the other you're commenting on movies and genre, distancing the viewer from the fiction by breaking the illusion. (Smith 1994: 41)

It is an interesting observation that it is often paradoxically those movies purporting to be formally *distant* from "real life" on the formal level (e.g. genre flicks and genre spoofs) that are so anxious to appeal to our *visceral perception* and thus *close* to "real life" on the sensual level. A look at the ovations from reviewers for action movies like *The Fifth Element* and *Pulp Fiction* shows a clear picture. *The Fifth Element* was called "eye-popping" (Bill Diehl, *ABC Radio Network*), "jaw-dropping, mind-blowing" (Joe Leydon, *NBC-TV*), "a visual knockout" (Peter Tavers, *Rolling Stone*) (Welsh 1997: 186). And *Pulp Fiction* produced reactions among its reviewers like: "Electrifying!" (Howard Feinstein, *New York Post*), "A knockout!" (Mike Caccioppoli, *WABC Radio*), "It will leave audiences laughing, gasping and applauding" (Jack Matthews, *New York Newsday*) (Adams 1994: 470). What makes these appraisals so interesting is not only their abundance of exclamation marks as an indicator for intense engagement, but also the extensive use of terms that allude to visceral sensations like breathing, looking, laughing, thinking, even getting "knocked out". The spectator of these films, it seems, is addressed as a "corporeal-material being", a "human being with skin and hair" (Siegfried Kracauer cited in Hansen 1993: 458). We are introduced into the fictional world of these movies on a decisively corporeal level, a level which lets us participate in the action shown on screen immediately and fully. And it is on that same tangible level that the identification with the protagonists takes place. Since both movies, *Pulp Fiction* and *The Fifth Element*, are deeply concerned with the theme of masculinity, this kind of aesthetic involvement is most meaningful. In her foreword to the screenplay for *Pulp Fiction*, Manohla Dargis draws a parallel between the drastic images of corporeality in the movie and the complexity of the (mainly male) film characters:

> Bone-shattering, skin-splitting, blood-spurting, Tarantino's cinema of viscera is written on the flesh of outlaw men and women, all of whom are far more complicated than their underworld types would suggest. (1994: 1)

The more our body is involved with the action on screen, it seems, the more we feel forced to deal with the overwhelming tactile dimensions of the depicted world. And the bone-shattering, skin-splitting, blood-spurting, as we all know, is a part of the male world rather than the female one. In the movie, it's just the men who do the blood-shedding. And one wonders if the film's stubborn insistence on this symbolic cleavage between the two worlds, male and female, is more a parodic imitation of stereotypes or more a validation of mythological patterns. There is indeed a strong parodic element in the movie's depiction of male cinematic archetypes (the gangster boss, the fighter, the bad-ass brother). "[B]y repicturing cinema's rituals of masculinity in wildly exaggerated forms," claims Gary Indiana, "he [Quentin Tarantino] has achieved a more daring deconstruction than even directors like Martin Scorsese and Francis Ford Coppola" (1994: 65-66). This statement seems to be a grotesque exaggeration of the film's actual deconstructive potential. Sure, there are playful, parodic references to male cinematic stereotypes in the movie; but parody, as John Fried points out,

> is a double-edged sword. It also protects and reinforces the very "norm" it seeks to disclose. And each segment of *Pulp Fiction* reaches a point at which postmodern self-awareness becomes indistinguishable from good ol' fashioned heterosexual paranoia about "appropriate" representations of masculinity. (1995: 6)

While *Pulp Fiction* is formally redundant with allusions to all sorts of conventions and hoary clichés from gangster and kung-fu movies, it is far from looking at these texts in merely referential terms. What is recovered in *Pulp Fiction*, is not so much the semiotic heritage of these texts, but their lived cultural agenda. The camaraderie of males that is shown in the movie clearly has its mirror in phallogocentric Western thought, particularly in the acceptance of certain fundamentals – eidos, archē, telos (Gestalt, origin, goal), etc. – as continuous points of reference (cf. Derrida 1989 [1978]:

110). These fundamentals, especially the notion of the "true hero" or the "true man" are portrayed as still valid in modern times, although they are continuously contested. The various references to mythological heroes from the past in the movie (e.g. the Hemingwayesque boxer who refuses to give up his honor) are not just empty moves, they actually constitute a vivid dialogue between the action on screen and the spectator's visceral feelings toward these figures. The themes that this aesthetic "dialogue" with the audience – to pick up a phrase from Mikhail Bakhtin (1998 [1981]: 301-331) – touches upon are highly loaded with emotionality and sensuousness: Loyalty, temptation and pride are just a few of the male-coded subjects that are negotiated and reaffirmed in this discourse.

On the aesthetic level, these allusions to patterns of heroic masculinity are deployed to evoke a tangible impression of the dangers and fears to which the male protagonists are constantly exposed. The viewer is at the same time confronted with a "collage of American male heroism and sexual bravado" (Fried 1995: 6) and with a political agenda that reveals itself through these allusions.

> In fact, it is precisely the film's play on classic *film noir*, blaxploitation and kung-fu films, among other action genres, that leads one directly to the core of its power politics: masculinity and the anxiety of the male hero. (Fried 1995: 6)

Most importantly, the aesthetic grounds on which masculinity and male heroism are based are not debunked at all. Quite to the contrary, *Pulp Fiction* endeavors aesthetically to provide conventional masculinity with a halo of postmodern hipness while at the same time playing business as usual in the portrayal of deviant masculinities. Kaja Silverman has identified the deviant masculinities that the dominant fiction is so much afraid of, as "those which not only acknowledge but embrace castration, alterity, and specularity" (1992: 3). Tarantino's film recognizes the existence of those masculinities, but he doesn't depict them as sources of empowerment, but rather as hazards to mainstream masculinity. And these secret hazards are apparently lurking everywhere: in the cellar of a pawnshop, in the boxing ring, on the toilet, even in the hero's own personality. By focusing on the dangers from within the hegemony, *Pulp Fiction* reconstructs a masculinity that needs to be constantly *renewed* and *defended*. This kind of masculinity derives its stability not so much from a reliance on the center, but from the vigilant containment of the margins.

Despite this concentration on the margins, the construction of a strong narrative center is a very important element in *Pulp Fiction*. This center is embodied by the two killers Vincent (John Travolta) and Jules (Samuel L. Jackson) who are shown in the very first scene after the intro and also in the final scene (even in the final shots) of the movie. Another representative of this masculine center is the black boss Marsellus Wallace (Ving Rhames) who is described as "a cross between a gangster and a king" (Tarantino/Avary 1994: 34). It is very significant that this masculine, patriarchal center is shown as being constantly under attack. Not surprisingly, this attack often comes from the bathroom – as a symbolic location of a man's nakedness and vulnerability. After the killers have just shot the two boys in the living room, a fourth man (Alexis Arquette) comes bursting out of the bathroom. Although he manages to stupefy the two hit men for a moment, his bullets miraculously miss their goals. This is, of course, a blunt allusion to the typical shooting scene in a gangster movie where the male hero stays alive within a hail of bullets. The metaphysical quality of the hero's survival is underlined by Jules's evocation of God after the incident. "That was ... divine intervention. [...] God came down from heaven and stopped the bullets" (Tarantino/Avary 1994: 139). Here the movie plays with the old concept that the hero is not enthroned by earthly powers, but through a divine will. Despite the mocking allusion to genre conventions in this one point, the basic structure of the scene with the four boys is more or less conventional. This becomes very clear when one looks at the gender components that constitute the protagonists' looks and behavior.

While the killers are characterized as straightforward and "cool" ("Jules has got style", Tarantino/Avary 1994: 29; see interview with Quentin Tarantino in Smith 1994: 42), the preppie guys who they meet and eventually kill are in every respect coded as cowardly and effeminate. The three guys from the first part of the sequence are described as "obviously in over their heads" (Tarantino/Avary 1994: 24): a metaphor for the bodily implosion, or inversion, that characterizes them throughout the scenes. The "Fourth Man" who emerges as the episode is continued later is portrayed just as stupid and hysterical – too dumb to hit a target as big as Mount Everest. He is a cartoon-like character who has "a yellow look of fear on his face" (Tarantino/Avary 1994: 136) and who screams idiotically while trying to shoot his enemies (Tarantino/Avary 1994: 137). His over-exaggerated tough-guy behavior when he jumps out to shoot the killers "ready to blow in half anybody fool enough to stick their head through that door" (Tarantino/Avary 1994: 136) is just another piece in the puzzle of his hysterical, effeminate personality. Like the Gimp, another cartoon-character that is introduced later, these figures' gender is ambiguous. The Gimp, physically a male, is even referred to as "it" in the screenplay (Tarantino/Avary 1994: 128). This creature is a grotesque caricature of a male. But in his behavior he is not so different from the other victim figures who are all at the verge of hysteria in the "moment of truth". "The Gimp flails wildly, trying to get the leash off the hook. He tries to yell, but all that comes out are excited gurgles and grunts" (Tarantino/Avary 1994: 128). While the lack of masculinity in these losers is staged with relish, the masculinity of "true heroes" like Butch (Bruce Willis) is treated in a reverent, almost worshipful way. While the one type of maleness is "deconstructed" as unfit for life, the other is shown as intact as ever. The film offers basically just two male identity choices: "One is either part of the masculine code or outside of it. Although *Pulp Fiction* certainly revels in deconstructing codes of masculinity, a surfeit of macho images and rhetoric still permeate the film, gratifying spectators who long nostalgically for traditional heroes" (Fried 1995: 7). True masculinity, it seems, can only be conquered and kept by a "few good men" like Butch the boxer who is allowed to "peel away" with his girl on a stolen motorcycle after he has just slaughtered two homosexuals. This is the reward of heroism: Butch and his girlfriend have "places to go" – Bora Bora, Tahiti, Mexico? (Tarantino/Avary 1994: 103) – and, in Carolyn Dinshaw's words, "a big bike, courtesy of a dead homosexual, to take them there" (1997: 125).

This negotiation of homosexuality as a stylistic gimmick brings us back to the scene where Vincent and Jules shoot the boys. The most important victim figure in this scene is Brett (Frank Whaley) whose very name already suggests gender ambiguity. Not only is the character closely associated with butt-fucking ("why did you try to fuck 'im like a bitch?!" Tarantino/Avary 1994: 32) and other anal images ("Brett has just shit his pants," Tarantino/Avary 1994: 29), he is also identified as being very timid and insecure about his bodily presence as he lazily hangs around with other sissies in shady rooms. When Jules shoots Brett's sissy friend Roger in cold blood during the interrogation, Brett is "so full of fear, it's as if his body is imploding" (Tarantino/Avary 1994: 29). The notion of "imploding" is very significant here since it points to Brett's "inversion", his (latent) homosexuality. "Imploding" also stands in a sharp contrast to Jules and Vincent's "explosive" and masculine behavior that characterizes them as tough guys. To implode, the movie suggests, is to turn inside, to become an "invert".

As Brett cowers into the chair while being tortured and finally finished off, he is the perfect example of a sissy, an "invert". He feels so intimidated by Jules's raw, masculine behavior that he withdraws into complete passiveness and effeminate fussing. His behavior is marked by ponderous rhetorical excuses, hysterical stuttering and a final "No! No!" when the killers assassinate him. While completely acknowledging Jules's authority – for instance, he immediately sits down after Jules makes a small indicative movement with his hand –, Brett himself has no authority at all (in which he resembles the typical homosexual in Hollywood movies). He comes across as a ridiculous queen who just deserves to be shot in his squirming body. The camera literally revels in his suffering when he is mentally tortured and finally killed. The screenplay repeatedly emphasizes his agony and his "shaking/trembling spasm" (Tarantino/Avary 1994: 32). Brett's physical pain has its counterpart in Jules's explicit sensuousness when the killer is, for instance, shown eating a cheeseburger or drinking a soda with relish ("Uuummmm, that's a tasty burger", Tarantino/Avary

1994: 26; "Uuuuummmm, hits the spot!", Tarantino/Avary 1994: 27). A similar sensuous pleasure like when eating and drinking, we understand, Jules gets from systematically torturing and finally executing his male victim.

Most disturbingly, the victim, Brett, acts just like the stereotypical victim of an anti-gay murder. When it comes to dying, he simply gives in to the aggressive attack, as if in a secret agreement to the legitimacy of the murder. "It's too late. Cause you're a faggot", these last words that the killers in the Billy Jack Gaither murder case barked out at their gay victim ("Assault on Gay America", program on KCET, Feb 15, 2000), would seem fitting in Brett's case, too. There's obviously no escape for the little queer boy when the messengers of male authority strike "with great vengeance and furious anger" (Tarantino/Avary 1994: 32). And who cares what the sissy boy thinks or feels when Jules and Vincent, the executors of the male heterosexual will, finally have to "do what a man's gotta do"?

It is clearly the overtly heterosexual aggressors, not the effeminate and possibly queer victims, whose perspective interests Tarantino's film. While the figures of Jules and Vincent have enough time to unfold themselves and their problems in front of a sympathetic camera eye, the four guys are mainly shown in unfavorable camera angles from behind the two hit men – a structure which establishes the killers as the domineering force of the action. Later, when Vincent accidentally shoots Marvin (Phil Lamarr) in the car, both camera and narrative exclusively focus on the killers and their problems in getting rid of the corpse. The victim's perspective seems entirely removed from the aesthetic conception of the movie. Even when the victims fill the frame solely, the view is everything else but sympathetic since it always comes from a slightly upper position that suggests both inferiority and weakness. This privileging of the straight male aggressor's perspective in *Pulp Fiction* reflects a very real pattern in Western thought: the hierarchization between dominant heterosexual masculinity and its deviant "Other". Or, as a translation for *Pulp Fiction*: the hierarchization between "cool" (as identified with masculine) and "uncool" (as identified with effeminate). What distinguishes the world in *Pulp Fiction* from representations of the same dualism in other movies, is that Tarantino focuses more on the potential conflation of these opposites than on their "natural" separateness. In the (imaginary) world, as Tarantino sees it, the dangerous "Other" has already infiltrated the dominant discourse and is no longer situated "outside". Male heterosexual identity is portrayed as constantly in the state of siege; it is incessantly attacked and endangered. Tough battleground! But, as in other gangster movies, the demarcating of masculinity as the dominant force works both ways. The constant gun shooting that characterizes male behavior in *Pulp Fiction* points simultaneously to the defense of masculinity through the hard-boiled heroes and to the "homoerotic associations of the images of bodily penetration that are so common in the action genre" (Tasker 1993: 127).

Consequently, the metonymic focal point in *Pulp Fiction* is *not* the phallus (as a symbol for an unquestioned authority), but the locus of man's *greatest* vulnerability: the male anus. The film's play with images of anal longing and physical penetration (either with a firearm or with a penis) clearly establishes a pattern of semi-erotic, sado-masochistic interaction that permeates all scenes of violence in the movie. Everything that is violent and penetrative in the movie thus gains a slight notion of suppressed sexuality and desire. The anus, writes William Ian Miller, "[is] more than any other orifice, it is the gate that protects the inviolability, the autonomy, of males" (1997: 100). The danger of a possible penetration of body and self is apparently lurking everywhere for the average male killer or Mafia boss. "Ya tried ta fuck 'im and Marsellus Wallace don't like to be fucked by anybody except Missus Wallace," Jules barks at Brett who is at this point already trembling in pain (Tarantino/Avary 1994: 32). The correct punishment for attempting to "fuck" another man, it seems, is to be put into a state of "trembling" as well, trembling not in lust, this time, but in agony. This draconian revenge for any kind of "incorrect" use of the anus constitutes what Carolyn Dinshaw has called "[the film's] anal surveillance project" (1997: 121). When the two hillbilly queers, Zed and Maynard (Peter Greene and Duane Whitaker) later dare to rape black gangster boss Marsellus Wallace, the reaction is equally a libidinous and sadistic one:

> I'm gonna call a coupla pipe-hitting' niggers, who'll go to work on the homes here with a pair of pliers and a blowtorch. [...] Hear me talkin', hillbilly boy?! I ain't through with you by a damn sight. I'm gonna git Mcdieval on your ass. (Tarantino/Avary 1994: 131)

Not only does this monologue pick up the earlier description of the two rapists in the screenplay ("two hillbillies", Tarantino/Avary 1994: 124), also does the film reflect and secretly reaffirm Marsellus Wallace's bloody consequences in its aesthetic structure. Just as in the scene where Brett the sissy is assassinated (in pretty much the same sadistic way), the two hillbilly rapists are executed for "butt-fucking" another man. Death comes as a punishment for sexual perversion. Surprisingly enough, this punishment comes along in precisely the same clothes as the original offense. Thus Butch "thrusts" (Tarantino/Avary 1994: 129) his sword into one of the queer brothers, and Marsellus, freed from the other brother, "blasts" him in the groin (Tarantino/Avary 1994: 130). The sexual terminology in this scene is obvious. But its logic also has a decisively Biblical undertone (similar to the earlier scene where Jules quotes Ezekiel). "[T]hose who take the sword", the film seems to tell us here, "will perish by the sword" (Matthew 26: 52).

The message that the film sends out here is clear: he who embraces "castration, alterity, and specularity", to use Kaja Silverman's phrase (1992: 3), will be embraced by it. But Zed is not only going to be castrated for butt-fucking another man, he is also about to be tortured in the good ol' medieval way, as the film assures us. But at least that queer boy is good for something: leaving a motorcycle – symbol for the American freedom – to one of his heterosexual murderers. bell hooks points to the political implications of this conception when she writes:

> If this isn't symbolic genocide of gay men, what is? [...] No doubt had John Singleton, or any other homeboy filmmaker, shot a scene as overtly gay-bashing as this one, progressive forces would have rallied en masse to condemn – to protest – to remind moviegoers that homophobia means genocide, that silence equals death. But it's fine to remain silent when the cool straight white boy from the wrong side of the tracks offers a movie that depicts the brutal slaughter and/or bashing of butt-fuckers and their playmates. (hooks 1994: 108)

Marsellus Wallace's threat to "git Medieval on your ass" and "call a coupla pipe-hitting' niggers" (Tarantino/Avary 1994: 131) is a direct quote from the cult gangster film *Charley Varrick* (1973) (Dinshaw 1997: 119). It is also an echo from Butch's earlier choice of the medieval Samurai sword as a means of taking revenge (Tarantino/Avary 1994: 128). The ritualized sexual revenge that Marsellus announces here is just as dark and perverse as the sexual act itself that provoked it. The taboo that it touches upon lies not in another foreign region, but as deep in the heart of America like the country music that is played during the rape (Tarantino/Avary 1994: 129). Fittingly, the location of the taboo is the cellar of a seemingly ordinary pawnshop, precisely a room that is called "Russell's old room" (Tarantino/Avary 1994: 126). "Russell," the screenplay notes, "was some other poor bastard that had the misfortune of stumbling into the Mason-Dixon pawnshop" (Tarantino/Avary 1994: 126). This suggests that it may happen to everyone. The perverse sexuality that is acted out in that room is obviously hidden anywhere in the modern world. Like the "Gimp", the asexual leather slave that Zed and Maynard keep down in a dungeon next to Russell's room, it may come into the open any time. Perverseness constitutes itself as the metonymic pre-modern torture chamber that seems to lie in the heart of every American home. The "getting medieval" functions here as the "absence" that refuses to be ignored anymore in contemporary society. As Carolyn Dinshaw explains, the phrase has since then entered American public culture becoming especially popular among "street-smart teenage boys" (1997: 116).

This broad public echo shows how the spectacle of a violation of the anus in the movie must have rung a bell in the viewers. It is the last element of a series of anecdotes and jokes about the anus and anal intercourse in the movie. The motif is first established in a flashback sequence where the young Butch is given a gold watch (after which the whole episode is named) from Captain Koons, a friend of his late father who died as a prisoner in the Vietnam War. The watch, it turns out, was hidden by Butch's father in his own ass for five long years before he died of dysentery. "Then," the Captain tells the boy, "he gave me the watch. I hid this uncomfortable hunk of metal up my ass for two years. Then, after seven years, I was sent home to my family. And now, little man, I give the watch to you" (Tarantino/Avary 1994: 86). The analogies to male sodomy are almost too graphic: The Captain hides a "hunk" in his ass, the same "hunk" that has been hidden up his buddy's ass for five years. Yet the scene shows how central the anus is in male bonding, and especially in the construction of patriarchy (cf. Dinshaw 1997: 120). The watch is transported from "great-granddaddy" (Tarantino/Avary 1994: 85) to "granddad [who] was a marine" (Tarantino/Avary 1994: 86) to grandson ("little man", Tarantino/Avary 1994: 86) via the detour of the anus. And the watch also motivates Butch's actions as a grown-up since he drives back to his apartment where his girlfriend has left it. Finally, it is the reason why he later ends up with a ball gag in his mouth down in the cellar of the Mason-Dixon pawnshop. But couldn't it be that Tarantino is just showing us the absurdity of male bonding with this bizarre anecdote? Isn't he exposing the hyper-masculinity that lies at the basis of male sexual politics by caricaturing men's patriarchal legacy? With bell hooks who poses the same questions, I contend that *Pulp Fiction* "titillate[s] with subversive possibility [...] but then everything kinda comes right back to normal" (hooks 1994: 66). With the "gold watch" anecdote, the film purports to generate a niche for male self-irony in its otherwise monolithically masculine aesthetic, but by reinventing the very same myths it pretends to be deconstructing, it wastes this possibility in the same breath.

> Yeah, like it's really funny when Butch the hypermasculine phallic white boy – [...] who comes straight out of childhood clinging to the anal-retentive timepiece of patriarchal imperialism – is exposed. Yet exposure does mean nothing to intervene on this evil, it merely graphically highlights it. As the work progresses, little Butch is still doing it for Daddy – a real American hero. (hooks 1994: 65-66)

The gold watch scene is very important in this respect since it not only establishes the grounds, but also the *limits* of male bonding. The "hunk" that the Captain puts up his ass during Vietnam is, as he clarifies, "uncomfortable", i.e. not pleasurable. Anuses, the film assures us, are for one use only: shitting. What happens when one crosses this line and confuses the necessary with the pleasurable, is shown in the case of Vincent. As Carolyn Dinshaw observes, "Vince's time in the toilet has been not only useful but pleasurable – he dallies in a leisurely read of an action novel at Butch's apartment – and thus its distinction from another pleasurable use of the anus becomes blurred" (1997: 121-122). Shitting proves to be both a dangerous and a pleasurable ride in *Pulp Fiction* – a conflict which is already indicated in the film's first insertion, a definition from the *American Heritage Dictionary*: "**PULP** (pulp) n. 1. A soft, moist, shapeless mass of matter. 2. A magazine or book containing lurid subject matter and being characteristically printed on rough, unfinished paper" (Tarantino/Avary 1994: 2). No wonder, it seems, that the film is so obsessed with all kinds of "soft, moist, shapeless masses of matter". When it comes to shitting, even the toughest guys become susceptible to dangers. Butch's father, we learn, has died of it (Tarantino/Avary 1994: 86). And every time when Vincent goes to the toilet, something terrible happens. After he leaves for the bathroom in the coffee shop scene ("I gotta take a shit", Tarantino/Avary 1994: 175), suddenly a robbery is taking place. Even worse, when he later uses the toilet to read an action novel, he is blown to pieces by Butch, the film's archetypal heterosexual hero (cf. Willis 1993-94: 40-73).

In its almost paranoid fear of the anus, *Pulp Fiction* resembles other films from the 1990s that have discovered the theme as a symbol for the contestedness of modern masculinity. In Tony Kaye's *American History X* (1998), the moral awakening of the bad boy hero (Edward Norton) is depicted as a process of being humiliated, physically abused and finally raped. The anal intercourse, in both films, constitutes the ultimate evil that either kills the hero or transforms him forever. It is, as *Time* magazine wrote in an article on *Pulp Fiction*, "a fate worse than death": not only rape, but, crucially, male homosexual rape (Corliss 194: 73). In *American History X*, the hero survives the offense; also, he undergoes a painful process of catharsis after which he is saner, more human, and, most importantly, more heroic than before. This narrative echoes the old formula that "the heroic man is always physically beaten, injured and brought to breaking point" (Smith 1995: 81). A man's ability to deal with the challenges that derive from the anus is seen in these movies as a pivotal mode of survival in everyday life. The possibility of a deconstruction of male identity is clearly implied here, but also the concrete option of homosexuality. The anus has thus become a pivotal symbol for the erosion of the masculine self in the lived social practice. The modern male, it seems, is fascinated with the idea of sexual deviation and repulsed by it at the same time. He flirts with the thought of experiencing a different dimension of identity and also understands that the realization of his dirty little secret might involve a dramatic risk. It is bound to be a dramatic struggle, since it challenges the binary structure of our consciousness which is formed along the dualisms of objectivity and subjectivity, presence and absence, essence and surface. Mark Simpson has summarized this cultural *anomie* in the following words:

> Men's bodies are on display everywhere; but the grounds of men's anxiety is not just that they are being exposed and commodified but that their bodies are placed in such a way as to passively invite a gaze that is *undifferentiated*: it might be female *or* male, hetero *or* homo. (Simpson 1994: 4)

While works like *Pulp Fiction* and *American History X* have chosen to handle this topic by delimitation (a whole passage that dealt with the subject of political gayness was cut from the latter film's original screenplay [McKenna 1996: 43-45]), other recent films have decided to focus more on the *hybridization* between the masculinities. Consequently, in Gregg Araki's *The Doom Generation* (1995), Anthony Minghella's *The Talented Mr. Ripley* (1999) and Sam Mendes's *American Beauty* (1999), it is not the homosexual in general, but, more specifically, the closeted gay man who constitutes a risk for society. Not the *lived* homosexuality is stigmatized here, but the *closeted* one. Not homosexuality itself, but (internalized) homophobia. Moreover, open gayness often figures in these films as the more interesting and more gratifying alternative. TV sitcoms like NBC's "Will & Grace" have adopted openly gay and lesbian lead characters. The former taboo, it seems, has turned into a promise. Araki's film *The Doom Generation* can be interpreted as an example of this paradigm shift. If the "Z" in *Pulp Fiction* and the "X" in *American History X* are seen as symbols for an unappetizing otherness, the "X" in Araki's film is the indicator of an attractive and emancipated "polymorphous perversity". The central figure in this movie is Xavier Red (Johnathon Schaech) who is continuously called "X" by the other characters. He is attracted to both males and females, masturbates outside the door while watching a straight couple make love and even licks his own cum off his hand. This character is quite the opposite of all the restrained, effeminate fags that we've been shown in other Hollywood productions.

The X, it seems, has finally found its place not at the margins of Hollywood fiction, but in its very center, as a character that stands for an empowerment of all kinds of masculinities (gay and other) that have been singled out for too long. Comparing Araki's *Doom Generation* to Tarantino's *Pulp Fiction*, Robin Wood concludes that "Araki's work is, in spirit and nature, authentically subversive" (Wood 1998: 342). No matter which movie is really the "more subversive", the important point is that the various representatives of the dominant fiction have obviously started to wrestle for the most effective, most adequate concept to deal with the realities of modern life.

The "American Culture X" that used to be a dark, alienating world of despicable deviations has, in the course of this development, been transformed into a tempting garden of forbidden fruits. Homosexuality, no longer excluded from the topics in Hollywood fiction, is becoming a symbol for all kinds of deviant identities that have been suppressed too long. Film heroes like the ones embodied by Bruce Willis and Jonathon

Schaech are, in this view, complex answers to a whole gamut of problems and standpoints that are articulated in our cultural practice. Therefore they can be read as aesthetic dictionaries for all sorts of different behavioral, sensory and visual possibilities that are existent in this culture. The apparent contradictoriness of these heroes is no criterion of exclusion, it is rather an integral part of their dynamic structure and proves to be closely connected to the aesthetic effect that the viewer will experience while watching them on screen.

Filmography

American History X. USA, 1998. (R). New Line Cinema. P: Turman-Morissey Company. D: Tony Kaye. S: David McKenna. C: Edward Norton (*Derek Vinyard*), Edward Furlong (*Danny Vinyard*), Avery Brooks (*Bob Sweeney*), Stacy Keach (*Cameron*), Guy Torry (*Lamont*), Ethan Suplee (*Seth*).

The Doom Generation. USA, 1995. (R). Trimark Pictures. P: Andrea Sperling, Gregg Araki. D: Gregg Araki. S: Gregg Araki. C: James Duval (*Jordan*), Rose McGowan (*Amy*), Jonathon Schaech (*Xavier*).

The Fifth Element. USA, 1997. (PG-13). Columbia Pictures. P: Patrice Ledoux. D: Luc Besson. C: Bruce Willis (*Korben Dallas*), Milla Jovovich (*Leeloo*), Gary Oldman (*Zorg*), Chris Tucker (*Ruby Rhod*), Ian Holm (*Cornelius*), Brion James (*General Munro*).

Pulp Fiction. USA, 1994 (R). Miramax Films. P: Lawrence Bender. D: Quentin Tarantino. S: Quentin Tarantino & Roger Roberts Avary. C: John Travolta (*Vincent Vega*), Samuel L. Jackson (*Jules*), Uma Thurman (*Mia Wallace*), Bruce Willis (*Butch*), Ving Rhames (*Marsellus Wallace*).

Works cited

Adams, Michael 1994. "Pulp Fiction." in Frank Northen Magill (ed.). *Magill's Cinema Annual.* Englewood Cliffs, N.J.: Salem Press, 470-472.

McKenna, David 1996. *American History X. Original Screenplay.* School of Cinema and Television at the University of Southern California, 12/17.

"Assault on Gay America." 2000. KCET (PBS), Los Angeles: Feb 15.

Bakhtin, Mikhail 1984. *Problems of Dostoevsky's Poetics.* Trans. & ed. C. Emerson. Bloomington: Indiana Univ. Press.

———— 1997. *Rabelais and His World.* Trans. H. Iwolsky, in Pam Morris (ed.). *The Bakhtin Reader: Selected Writings of Bakhtin, Medvedev, Voloshinov.* London/New York: Arnold.

Benjamin, Walter 1973. *Charles Baudelaire: A Lyric Poet in the Era of High Capitalism.* London: New Left Books.

Bingham, Dennis 1994. *Acting Male. Masculinities in the Films of James Stewart, Jack Nicholson, and Clint Eastwood.* New Brunswick, NJ: Rutgers University Press.

Bronski, Michael 1998. *The Pleasure Principle: Sex, Backlash, and the Struggle for Gay Freedom.* New York: St. Martin's Press.

Campbell, Joseph 1953 [1949]. *The Hero with a Thousand Faces.* New York: Pantheon Books.

Connors, Martin and Jim Craddock (eds.) 1999. *VideoHound's Golden Movie Retriever.* Detroit/San Francisco: Visible Ink.

Corliss, Richard 1994. "Saturday Night Fever." *Time*, 6 (June 1994), 73.

Creed, Barbara 1987. "From Here to Modernity: Feminism and Postmodernism." *Screen*, 28: 2 (1987), 47-67.

Dargis, Manohla 1994. "Foreword" in *Pulp Fiction: A Quentin Tarantino Screenplay*. (Stories by Quentin Tarantino and Roger Avary). New York: Miramax Books, 1-2.

Denby, David 1995. "Pulp Fiction" in Peter Keough (ed.). *Flesh and Blood: The National Society of Film Critics on Sex, Violence, and Censorship*. San Francisco: Mercury House, 227-231.

————— 1997. "Hack Work." *New York*, 30: 19 (19 May 1997), 63.

Derrida, Jacques 1975. "The Purveyor of Truth." *Yale French Studies*, 52 (1975), 32-113.

————— 1978. *Writing and Difference*. Trans. Alan Bass. London: Routledge.

————— 1979. "Me-Psychoanalysis: An Introduction to the Translation of 'The Shell and the Kernel' by Nicolas Abraham." Trans. Richard Klein. *Diacritics*, 9 (1979), 4-12.

————— 1982. *Margins of Philosophy*. Trans. Alan Bass. Chicago, IL: University of Chicago Press.

————— 1989. "Structure, Sign, and Play in the Discourse of the Human Sciences." Trans. Alan Bass, in David Lodge (ed.). *Modern Criticism and Theory: A Reader*. London and New York: Longman, 108-123.

Dinshaw, Carolyn 1997. "Getting Medieval: *Pulp Fiction*, Gawain, Foucault" in Dolores Warwick Frese and Katherine O'Brien O'Keeffe (eds.). *The Book and the Body*. Notre Dame: University of Notre Dame Press.

Dowell, Pat 1995. "Pulp Friction: Two Shots at Quentin Tarantino's *Pulp Fiction*" (with John Fried). *Canasta*, 21: 3 (1995), 4-5.

Fried, John 1995. "Pulp Friction: Two Shots at Quentin Tarantino's *Pulp Fiction*" (with Pat Dowell). *Cineaste*, 21: 3 (1995), 6-7.

Gerzon, Mark 1992. *A Choice of Heroes: The Changing Face of American Manhood*. Boston, New York & London: Houghton Mifflin Company.

Gilroy, Paul 1993. *The Black Atlantic: Modernity and Double Consciousness*. London: Verso.

Hansen, Miriam 1993. "'With Skin and Hair': Kracauer's Theory of Film, Marseille, 1940." *Critical Inquiry*, 19: 3 (1993), 437-469.

hooks, bell 1994. "Cool Tool." *Artforum* discussion "Pulp the Hype on the Q. T." 33: 7 (March 1994), 63-66, 108.

Indiana, Gary 1994. "Geek Chic." *Artforum* discussion "Pulp the Hype on the Q. T." 33: 7 (March 1994), 63-66, 108.

Jeffords, Susan 1993. "The Big Switch: Hollywood Masculinity in the Nineties" in Jim Collins, Hilary Radner and Ava Preacher Collins (eds.). *Film Theory Goes to the Movies*. New York and London: Routledge, 196-208.

————— 1994. *Hard Bodies: Hollywood Masculinity in the Reagan Era*. New Brunswick, NJ: Rutgers University Press.

Lippman, John 1998. "High-Frequency, Low-Brow Chatter Starts To Take Over the FM Airwaves." *The Wall Street Journal*, 29 October 1998.

Mercer, Kobena 1994. *Welcome to the Jungle*. London: Routledge.

Miller, William Ian 1998. *The Anatomy of Disgust*. Cambridge, Mass.: Harvard University Press.

Munson, Wayne 1993. *All Talk: The Talkshow in Media Culture*. Philadelphia: Temple University Press.

Naremore, James 1990. *Acting in the Cinema*. 1988. Berkeley: University of California Press.

Ortner, Sherry B. 1996. *Making Gender: The Politics and Erotics of Culture*. Boston: Beacon Press.

Schulberg, Pete 1999. "It's a Man's World." *The Oregonian*, Saturday, 26 June 1999.

Sedgwick, Eve Kosovsky 1991. *Epistemology of the Closet*. Berkeley and Los Angeles: University of California Press.

Silverman, Kaja 1992. *Male Subjectivity at the Margins*. New York: Routledge.

Simpson, Mark 1994. *Male Impersonators: Men Performing Masculinity*. London: Cassell.

Smith, Gavin 1994. " 'When you know you're in good hands': Quentin Tarantino interviewed by Gavin Smith." *Film Comment*, 30: 4 (1994), 32-39.

Smith, Paul 1995. "Eastwood Bound" in Maurice Berger, Brian Wallis, and Simon Watson (eds.). *Constructing Masculinity*. New York and London: Routledge, 77-97.

Tarantino, Quentin and Roger Avary 1994. *Pulp Fiction: A Quentin Tarantino Screenplay*. New York: Miramax Books.

Tasker, Yvonne 1993. *Spectacular Bodies: Gender, Genre and the Action Cinema*. London and New York: Routledge.

———— 1995. "Dumb Movies for Dumb People. Masculinity, the Body, and the Voice in Contemporary Action Cinema" in Steven Cohan and Ina Rae Hark (eds.). *Screening the Male. Exploring Masculinities in Hollywood Cinema*. London and New York: Routledge, 230-244.

"The Tom Leykis Show." On 97.1 FM radio US-nation wide, 3p.m. – 8 p.m.. http://www.blowmeuptom.com/altshockwave.html

Welsh, James M. 1998. "The Fifth Element" in Frank Northen Magill (ed.). *Magill's Cinema Annual*. Englewood Cliffs, N.J.: Salem Press, 186-188.

Willis, Sharon 1993-94. "The Fathers Watch the Boys' Room." *Camera Obscura*, 32 (1993-94), 40-73.

Wood, Robin 1998. *Sexual Politics and Narrative Film. Hollywood and Beyond*. New York: Columbia University Press.

Disclosure's Disclosure

Neil Badmington

I

> If you want to know, I'm really tired of feminists, sick of them. They've really dug themselves into their own grave. Any man would be a fool who didn't agree with equal rights and pay, but women, now, juggling with career, lover, children, wifehood, have spread themselves too thin and are very unhappy. It's time they looked at *themselves* and stopped attacking men. Guys are going through a terrible crisis right now because of women's unreasonable demands.

Although these words, spoken by the actor Michael Douglas and reproduced in Susan Faludi's *Backlash: The Undeclared War Against Women* (Faludi 1992: 150-151), refer specifically to the controversy surrounding *Fatal Attraction* (dir. Adrian Lyne, 1987), they would not have seemed out of place seven years later, as the release of *Disclosure* (dir. Barry Levinson, 1994) provoked a brief media frenzy. I want in this essay to focus upon Levinson's film, assessing its contribution to a wider backlash against feminism, before suggesting that the text actually reveals how that backlash forever lashes back against itself. While *Disclosure* calls for an unreconstructed masculinity, that is to say, it at once discloses the manner in which patriarchy harasses and subverts itself from within.

The film, of course, claims to be anything but reactionary. In the afterword to the original novel (a passage which has, it sometimes appears, been quoted more often than the book itself), Michael Crichton describes his desire to approach sexual politics from an unusual angle in order to "examine aspects concealed by traditional responses and conventional rhetoric" (Crichton 1994: 405). The movie, like the novel, attempts to do this by telling a role-reversal story which poses a troubling question: can a woman sexually harass a man? The male in question is Tom Sanders (Michael Douglas), a division manager in the Seattle office of Digital Communications, who learns at the very beginning of the film that the promotion he has been expecting has been given to a woman, Meredith Johnson (Demi Moore). Later that day, Meredith attempts to seduce Tom in her office, reminding him of their passionate affair of some ten years earlier. Now a family man (with a wallet full of photographs and a toothpaste-stained tie to prove it), Tom initially resists, concedes a little in allowing her to perform oral sex upon him, and finally calls a halt to proceedings. The following morning, Sanders arrives at work to discover that Meredith is alleging that *he* forced himself upon *her*. Faced with a transfer to another office which would result in the loss of his bonus from an impending corporate merger, Tom enlists the services of prominent lawyer Catherine Alvarez (Roma Maffia) to file a sexual harassment suit against Meredith. "I never even heard of such a thing – a woman harassing a man," cries Phil Blackburn (Dylan Baker), but – reprising the roles he played in *Fatal Attraction* and *Falling Down* (dir. Joel Schumacher, 1993) – Michael Douglas refuses to go quietly.

Blackburn's incredulity aside, it might be argued that the question *Disclosure* claims to be posing is a timely one, for, after years of struggle, small numbers of women have finally begun to take up positions of power within American society. Thanks to feminism, the chance, however remote, that a man will find himself with a female boss is greater than ever before, and if – as *Disclosure*'s publicity posters would have it – "sex is power", female-male sexual harassment becomes at least a possibility. For a text, such as *Disclosure*, which claims to be concerned with contemporary sexual politics, it would not, therefore, be entirely unreasonable to approach the theme, to ask a "what if?" that seemingly speaks to the times. (I must admit, however, that I share Philip Green's anxieties [Green 1998: 95] about the way in which recent Hollywood cinema has been far happier to show men being *wrongly* accused of sexual assault than it has been to depict genuine cases). It seems to me, however, that *Disclosure* quietly and cleverly fails to address what it nonetheless claims to be its *raison d'être*. Unwilling at the end of the day to explore the complex question towards which it gestures, the text turns out to be a backlash against feminism, a champion of traditional masculinity and, moreover, a perfect example of the "conventional rhetoric" so readily brushed aside by Michael Crichton.

The film's disingenuousness springs largely from its calculated construction of Meredith as a liar. Simply because the crucial sexual encounter is shown at length and in detail at the time of its occurrence, the viewer is never in a position to doubt precisely who initiated proceedings and how those proceedings developed. There is, in this respect, little in the way of mystery. Everything – or as much as mainstream cinema will allow – is put on display, disclosed. Consequently, during the deposition – which is intended to restage, or re-present, the event in question – the viewer, like Sanders, knows all along that Meredith is lying. The question of female-male sexual harassment is eclipsed by a lingering fascination with a woman who is quite clearly engaged in a damaging act of deception. The tears and the trembling voice, not to mention the tale recounted, are clearly fake. From this point onwards, the film slips comfortably into an old-fashioned struggle between truth and falsehood, between an innocent man and a lying woman, between good and evil.

To a viewer familiar with the history of Hollywood cinema, Meredith's character and fate should come as no surprise. From the moment at which she first stamps her mark on the narrative – in the metonymical form of a black, spiked heel – Demi Moore repeatedly conjures up images of the *femme fatale*, the dark and dangerously powerful seductress of *film noir*. In keeping with tradition (and this is truly a film that loves all forms of tradition), *Disclosure* builds towards the destruction of its spider woman: Sanders eventually gathers enough evidence to prove his innocence, and Meredith is publicly stripped of her position within the company. The march of the single, sexually aggressive "career girl" who will do anything to break through the glass ceiling has been stopped, and although Tom is not promoted in the aftermath of Meredith's departure, he ends the film a company man, a family man, a (relatively) safe man. While the new team leader is another woman, Stephanie Kaplan (Rosemary Forsyth) is different: she is older, has a family, took Tom's side throughout (she was, quite literally, "A Friend"), and announces in her inaugural speech that she is counting on Sanders to work alongside her on future projects. The *femme fatale* has given way to the more comforting *femme maternelle*.

It is not difficult to see why Carol Watts (Watts 1995) should read *Disclosure* as a particularly cynical example of the backlash, to be counted alongside the movies singled out for attention by Susan Faludi. In Faludi's influential account, feminism's victories during the 1970s have provoked, in recent times, a widespread recuperative panic – a backlash – which declared feminist theory and practice to be dead languages:

> To be a woman at the close of the twentieth century – what good fortune. That's what we keep hearing anyway. The barricades have fallen, politicians assure us. Women have "made it", the style pages cheer. Women's fight for equality has "largely been won", *Time* magazine announces. Enrol at any university, join any law firm, apply for credit at any bank. Women have so many opportunities now, corporate leaders say, that we don't really need equal opportunity policies. Women are so equal now, lawmakers say, that we no longer need equal rights legislation. (Faludi 1992: 1)

Not only has feminism become unnecessary, the argument continues; it has at once engendered a host of new anxieties for women:

> You may be free and equal, [the backlash] says to women, but you have never been more miserable.
>
> This bulletin of despair is posted everywhere – at the newsagent's, on the TV set, at the cinema, in advertisements and doctors' offices and academic journals. Professional women are suffering "burn-out" and succumbing to an "infertility epidemic." Single women are grieving from a "man shortage" [...]
>
> [I]t must be all that equality that's causing all that pain. Women are unhappy precisely *because* they are free. Women are enslaved by their own liberation. They have grabbed at the gold ring of independence, only to miss the one ring that really matters. They have gained control of their fertility, only to destroy it. They have pursued their own professional dreams – and lost out on the greatest female adventure. The women's movement, as we are told time and again, has proved

women's own worst enemy. (Faludi 1992: 1-2)

There is, of course, a simple solution: turn back the clock, turn away from feminism and fall adoringly back into the arms of patriarchy. In tradition, whispers the backlash, lies salvation.

And this is precisely the message of *Disclosure*. Feminism, in the form of the powerful single woman, is the its demon (Sanders, after all, has to call upon an angel to help him defeat Meredith in cyberspace). There may be, as Yvonne Tasker has pointed out (Tasker 1998: 132), the vaguest of gestures towards liberalism in the decision to distinguish between "good" and "bad" women in the workplace, but this is liberalism that has promised to honour and obey the backlash. The "good" women are either loving mothers, generally supportive of Tom (no matter how unreconstructed his everyday conduct within the office may be), or, more simply, paid by Sanders to take his side in the legal proceedings. To be single, dismissive of domesticity ("A family makes you stupid", remarks Meredith at one point), and sexually aggressive is to be the villain, the liar, and ultimately the loser. Far from subverting traditional assumptions about masculinity, the film seems, in other words, to long for the halcyon days of patriarchy, a simpler time when men were unproblematically men. Contemporary North American culture, with its feminism and political correctness, is seen as a threat to male pride and job security. If he fails to defeat Meredith, Tom risks becoming exactly like the pathetic "surplussed" figure whom he regularly meets on the ferry. This is clearly "familiar backlash territory" (Watts 1995: 278).

And yet, this is by no means the end of the story. The familiar, as Freud concluded, can all too easily become unfamiliar, uneasy, uncanny (Freud 1998). As Catherine Belsey has argued in the introduction to her recent book on Shakespeare and family values, much of what currently takes place in the fields of literary and cultural studies is "predominantly thematic" in character and, as such, shies away from readings which would bring out the undecidability of the signifier (Belsey 1999: 14). Close attention to a whole range of signifying practices reveals, in fact, that the family has throughout its history been an unstable institution. "From its first moment," writes Belsey towards the end of her book, "the family, as a place of passion, is also, and correspondingly, the source of our greatest peril" (174). Common sense turns out to have never quite made sense. With this in mind, I want to attempt a reading of *Disclosure* which pays attention to the text's uncertainty, its disclosure and dis-closure. While the film dreams of an unreconstructed masculinity, I want to suggest that there is a sense in which those dreams become nightmares.

II

Freud's great discovery, of course, was that the "interpretation of dreams is the royal road to a knowledge of the unconscious activities of the mind" (Freud 1965: 647). In dreams – as in slips of the tongue, lapses of memory, the experience of *déja vu*, and the other phenomena detailed so memorably in the *Psychopathology of Everyday Life* (Freud 1938) – the unconscious finally has its say. What has been repressed from consciousness momentarily returns under cover of sleep. A dream is the saying of what must normally remain unsaid.

Published sixty-six years after the *Traumdeutung*, Pierre Macherey's *Pour une théorie de la production littéraire* imported a marriage – blessed largely by Althusser – of psychoanalysis and Marxism to the field of literary studies. If the human subject is forever split between its conscious and unconscious thoughts, could it be the case, he asked, that the same principle applied to literature, that – quite contrary to the claims of traditional criticism – "the work never has, except in appearance, the coherence of a unified whole"? (Macherey 1966: 53; my translation). Fictions, Macherey argued, are forever haunted by unmasterable, unconscious elements which disrupt the intended textual project. Criticism should no longer seek to elaborate and celebrate the organic unity of the text, but should instead aim to "make a *difference* explode within the work [*faire éclater en l'œuvre une différence*], to make it seem *other than it is*" (15; emphasis in original):

> The postulate of the unity of the work, which, more or less explicitly, has always haunted the critical enterprise, must therefore be denounced: the work is not *created* by an intention (objective or subjective); it is *produced* out of determinate conditions. (97; emphasis in original)

Macherey's Marxism keeps watch over the final part of this sentence, and this unflinching conviction no doubt accounts in part for the unfashionable status of *Pour une théorie de la production littéraire* in the post-Marxist moment. As critical theory has drifted slowly but steadily away from socialism, Macherey has gone unread and, worse still, out of print. But if the time of Marxism (whether classical or Althusserian) has passed, I want to suggest that the actual way in which Macherey reads literature should be neither forgotten nor repressed.

This approach is perhaps at its most seductive in the section of *Pour une théorie de la production littéraire* devoted to the fiction of Jules Verne. Turning his attention to *L'Ile mystérieuse*, Macherey produces a devastating (and devastatingly documented) account of what "appears between every line of Jules Verne's book" (225). While the fantastic narrative is founded upon a firm belief in the benefits and, moreover, the possibility of colonization, the margins of the text tell a strikingly different story. In ultimately revealing Nemo to be the orchestrator of the strange happenings, the text, Macherey suggests, unconsciously undermines the entire imperialist project. Colonialism is deposed as it is imposed:

> When the colonists' ordeal is over, when Captain Grant's ship arrives to put an end to the suffering of the abandoned man, all that had been based on this illusory nature disappears with it: not a trace remains of the work accomplished; the colonists can hold to nothing of the object of their quest. They are no longer what they believed themselves to be: the agents of a real change. The attempt at colonization has failed [*échoué*]. (247)

L'Ile mystérieuse, that is to say, harbours a troubling secret. It drifts away from itself, pulls itself apart from within, "provides the principle of its own decomposition" (224). The narrative is, to take a phrase from Marx that Macherey might well have known, "pregnant with its contrary" (Marx 1973: 299).

This, of course, sounds remarkably like deconstruction's desire to open "a reading by locating a moment of alterity within a text" (Critchley 1999: 28). Macherey's book, in fact, appeared in the same year that Jacques Derrida presented "Structure, Sign, and Play in the Discourse of the Human Sciences" to the now-legendary Baltimore conference, and one year before the publication of *L'Écriture et la différence*, *De la grammatologie*, and *La voix et le phénomène*. Both theorists share a fascination with the gaps, silences and slippages that trouble a text or system of thought from within. While Macherey writes that the "calling into question of the fiction is carried out [*opérée*] by the fiction itself" (246), for instance, Derrida describes the manner in which every structure "bears within itself the necessity of its own critique" (Derrida 1978: 284). But no kinship is acknowledged: Derrida ignores Macherey, who in turn leaves Derrida out of *Pour une théorie de la production littéraire*. And that common ground has become even more difficult to discern in recent times, for the unstoppable rise of deconstruction has been matched, in the English-speaking world at least, by Macherey's drift into obscurity. With the notable exception of Catherine Belsey's *Critical Practice* (Belsey 1980), few overviews of critical theory, and even fewer anthologies, grant Macherey more than a passing mention in a paragraph which will, without fail, be concerned solely with Marxist literary criticism.

This is, no doubt, an effect of the waning of Marxism. While Derrida and Macherey both insist upon the undecidability of meaning, the former's explanation for that very instability – discarding as it does all talk of ideology and contradiction (in the strictly Marxist sense of the term) – is, to some degree, more at home in the space of post-Marxism. To a contemporary reader (and particularly one born, like me, five years after the publication of *Pour une théorie de la production littéraire*), some of Macherey can only be seen through sepia. He gives at times a glimpse of another era. I want, however, to read Macherey as more than just a Marxist thinker, for it seems to me that his work contains something that deconstruction too readily casts aside. While a text like *De la grammatologie* depends to some extent upon a psychoanalytic understanding of meaning, the actual language of Freud remains unspoken. Derrida listens carefully to what Rousseau "says [...] without wishing to say it" (1976: 200), for instance, but never once describes Rousseau's texts as divided between *conscious* and *unconscious* elements. I want to cling to Macherey's psychoanalytic terminology not merely as a way of staging the return of what deconstruction has repressed, but because I find it useful for a reading of *Disclosure* which does not seek to hide from the fact that the film reveals – in its slippages, its gaps – how the fixity of meaning is nothing but a dream.

The film, of course, has a dream. Quite literally so. It comes approximately thirty-seven minutes into the narrative, shortly after Tom has escaped from the clutches of Meredith. As he sits with Susan in the safety of the marital bed, the camera pans down into the darkness beneath and the film cuts to a daytime scene, presumably the following morning. Arriving for work, Tom steps into the lift with Garvin, who soon takes an interest in Tom's suit. And an unhealthy interest at that, for he suddenly leans in to kiss Tom. But this is only a dream, a nightmare from which Sanders awakes with a start. The following morning (the time lapse is, on this occasion, made clear through the use of an inter-title), Tom – dressed now in casual clothes – arrives for work and makes it to the office without incident.

I am by no means the first to take an interest in the nightmare. Yvonne Tasker, for instance, sees this "short but indicative" scene as lying "at the heart of *Disclosure*", and – through a fascinating account of the text's subtle articulation of dress, power, and feminization – concludes that:

> [a]lthough this sequence doesn't suggest that the film's anxieties aren't really about women, it does reveal that they are not *solely* about women. The image [of Garvin attempting to kiss Sanders] expresses a fear that the hero might be produced as object of (homo)sexual (as well as heterosexual) attentions, situated within the specular. (Tasker 1998: 133)

While I have no desire to challenge this reading, I do want to approach the dream from a slightly different perspective (one which nonetheless stresses the indicative quality identified by Tasker).

The dream sequence is brief, perhaps something of a cheap trick. It depicts an event that never actually takes place; it is merely a figment of the protagonist's over-active imagination. On one level, it is meaningless, of no importance to the final outcome. And yet, as Freud insisted, the material upon which psychoanalysis bases its observations is "usually provided by the inconsiderable events which have been put aside by the other sciences as being too unimportant – the dregs, one might say, of the world of phenomena" (Freud 1973: 52). Dreams are never meaningless, never innocent, never to be ignored. Psychoanalysis, that is to say, is about seeing and reading differently, about paying careful attention to the marginal, the apparently trivial. Writing three years before Freud's death, Walter Benjamin made precisely this point:

> Fifty years ago, a slip of the tongue passed more or less unnoticed. Only exceptionally may such a slip have revealed dimensions of depth in a conversation which had seemed to be taking its course on the surface. Since the *Psychopathology of Everyday Life* things have changed. This book isolated and made analyzable things which had heretofore floated along unnoticed in the broad stream of perception. (Benjamin 1969: 235)

Dreams, like slips of the tongue, always point to, or point out – quite literally *indicate*, to return to Tasker's phrase – something. While Freud glimpsed unconscious desires in his patients' dreams, I want to take *Disclosure*'s nightmare to be the point at which the unconscious of the text returns from repression. Here, to return to Macherey's words, the film begins to seem *"other than it is"*.

While the main body of the text positions Meredith as the villain, Tom's nightmare shifts the focus elsewhere, to Garvin. The difference, of course, is sexual difference: Tom is, in his dream, sexually harassed by another man. While this may be to some extent yet another eruption of Hollywood's rampant homophobia, I think that it at once discloses a slightly different fear, a fear which begins to turn the film's backlash back upon itself and which might be named "power-phobia". In the dream, sexual difference is evacuated from the scene of sexual harassment: the perpetrator and the victim are of the same sex. And yet, the spectre of the form of harassment with which *Disclosure* claims to be concerned (female-male) returns when Garvin, like Meredith, alludes to power ("Now you've got all the power" she remarked, just as Garvin says "Now you have the power – you have something I want"). Power, that is to say, inhabits both scenes. Sex is power.

And the dream, in fact, pursues this truism to a conclusion which, while perfectly logical, nonetheless undermines the more general demonization of the powerful professional woman. If the main body of the film confines sexual harassment to a situation in which a tyrannical female threatens her male subordinate, the unconscious moment of the dream tells another story. Here, in the margins of the text, the space of the perpetrator is occupied by a man. Garvin is able to harass *not* because of his sex, but simply because he has power over his victim (the suggestion, made by both Garvin and Meredith, that Tom has access to power is, of course, untrue). Power, rather than sexual difference, lies at the heart of harassment. Meredith, that is to say, is dangerous *not* because she is a powerful woman but *simply because she is powerful*, and while the main body of the film would efface such a distinction, the dream sequence effuses it. Sex might be power, but power is not necessarily bound to either sex.

Meanwhile, a closer look at *Disclosure* as a whole suggests that the "real power belongs to the anonymous men on the Conley-White team" (Francke 1995: 36), whose growing anxiety makes Meredith's dismissal inevitable. The *femme fatale* is destroyed but the larger power structure remains untouched. Even Garvin – who floats effortlessly between the banal space of the office and the potent world of hotel lobbies – survives the affair, welcoming Meredith's replacement just as he had introduced the spider woman herself at the beginning of the film. Only one figure has fallen. Little has really changed. Tom's troubles, in other words, will not disappear with Meredith (who, it transpires, was never actually that powerful a character). Power remains and, as the nightmare knows, so does the possibility of sexual harassment. The backlash might appeal to natural male power, but the unconscious of the text reveals that there is nothing to stop that power turning upon men themselves. Although Meredith is "a fantasy spiderwoman, product of the patriarchal power system, dreamt up and subsequently destroyed by men because they find her just too scary" (Francke 1995: 36), the film cannot bear to look its real fear in the eye. The full implications of power must be repressed. Meredith is, to some extent, a smoke-screen, a straw target set up to distract patriarchy from its true nightmare. And yet, in true Freudian fashion, the repressed returns. The nightmare comes back quite literally as a nightmare. Traditional masculinity is at once asserted and troubled from within. The text, to borrow a formulation from Philippe Lacoue-Labarthe, desists where it insists (Lacoue-Labarthe 1998). Patriarchy subverts itself, lashes back against itself, harasses itself.

For Freud, dreams frequently "admit impossibilities" (1965: 87). Having shaken off reality and repression, they "accept the most violent contradictions without the least objection [...] they disregard knowledge which carries great weight with us in the daytime" (87). *Disclosure*'s dream admits impossibility in a slightly different sense, for it describes how patriarchy forever deposes itself as it imposes itself. It turns out to have always already been impossible, a construction founded upon its own deconstruction. In rushing to reaffirm traditional masculinity, the film cannot silence a lingering doubt about the power that makes such a discourse possible. This is not for one moment to say that *Disclosure* is not a film of the backlash, but it is to insist that the text forever undermines itself and, by extension, patriarchy. There is a wandering between two positions: on the one hand, there is a clear drive towards traditional masculinity; on the other hand, in the fleeting nightmare, that same hegemony pulls itself apart from within. *Disclosure*'s dream is *Disclosure*'s discerption, its discordance, its discrepancy. The calling into question of patriarchy, to paraphrase Macherey, is carried out by patriarchy itself.

It is perhaps worth recalling the understanding of hegemony found in the work of Ernesto Laclau and Chantal Mouffe. As part of the construction of an anti-essentialist "Post-Marxism without Apologies" (Laclau/Mouffe 1987), the concept of hegemony is refashioned into a process by which contingent and incomplete formations are assembled. In this account – one that "goes far beyond Gramsci" (Laclau/Mouffe 1985: 3) – hegemony comes to name the making of meaningful articulations in the radical absence of guarantees. Taking the concept of "society" as an example, Laclau and Mouffe argue that a claim to the meaning of "society" (patriarchy, for instance) might appear to be totalizing, but a finite totality is forever deferred by the movement of meaning. The "moment of the 'final' suture never arrives." Closure is denied by an eternal dis-closure. Each and every discourse "is subverted by a field of discursivity which overflows it", and which keeps the thinking of difference alive (Laclau/Mouffe 1985: 86, 113).

It does not follow, however, that anything goes, that there is no such thing as meaning, for "a discourse incapable of generating any fixity of meaning is the discourse of the psychotic" (112). The opposition between absolute fixity and absolute non-fixity is, rather, deconstructed:

> The social is not only the infinite play of differences. It is also the attempt to limit that play, to domesticate infinitude, to embrace it within the finitude of an order. But this order – or structure – no longer takes the form of an underlying essence of the social; rather, it is an attempt – by definition unstable and precarious – to act over that "social", to *hegemonize* it [...] [T]he social always exceeds the limits of the attempts to constitute society. At the same time, however, that "totality" does not disappear: if the suture it attempts is ultimately impossible, it is nevertheless possible to proceed to a relative fixation of the social through the institution of nodal points. (Laclau 1990: 91)

Here lies hegemony. Each hegemonic formation is a claim to a certain space which it can nonetheless never hope to master. Because hegemony can only ever be about a *relative fixation* of meaning, because any form of political solidarity (whether reactionary or subversive) is always – to use Diane Elam's phrase (Elam 1994) – a *groundless solidarity*, intervention and rearticulation are always possible. In the absence of essence, in the bright moments of discursive dis-closure, the thinking of change finds its force.

To approach hegemony in this way is to realize that the subversion of traditional masculinity need no longer consist solely in turning away from the backlash. While an outright or outraged dismissal of the reactionary certainly has its place and its seductions, I think that there is a more complicated, more challenging response which a combination of Macherey,

Laclau, and Mouffe permits. Moreover, it seems to me that there is a real sense in which a stubborn refusal to engage with the culture of traditional masculinity implies that patriarchy is actually capable of coherence, capable of constituting itself as a determinate object. In the wake of Macherey, the kind of cultural criticism I am proposing refuses to see either text or discourse as an organic unity. By seeking out the gaps – those moments at which things become *other than they are* – criticism no longer turns the other cheek but turns its face towards the "necessity of lodging oneself within traditional conceptuality in order to destroy it" (Derrida 1978: 111). Change can come precisely because it always already inhabits every meaning and moment in the form of undecidability. If traditional masculinity can be shown to subvert itself, a space for rethinking and reviewing sexual politics is opened up *within* patriarchy itself. The challenge, from this perspective, is one of exploiting the contradictions, disclosing the differences and the ways in which "dubious discourses" (LaCapra 1989: 16) forever doubt themselves. To ignore a text like *Disclosure*, simply because it longs for traditional masculinity, is to ignore the way in which such longing is always left wanting. This is not blind perversion; it is wide-eyed subversion.

I owe thanks to Catherine Belsey and Jean-Jacques Lecercle for talking about Macherey when no one else wanted to, Emma Mason for discussing *Disclosure* when the whole world wanted to, and to Ruth Evans for putting me in touch with the editors of this volume.

Works cited

Belsey, Catherine 1980. *Critical Practice*. London: Methuen.
———— 1999. *Shakespeare and the Loss of Eden: The Construction of Family Values in Early Modern Culture*. London: Macmillan.
Benjamin, Walter 1969. "The Work of Art in the Age of Mechanical Reproduction" in Hannah Arendt (ed.). *Illuminations*. Trans. Harry Zohn. New York: Schocken, 217-251.
Crichton, Michael 1994. *Disclosure*. London: Random House.
Critchley, Simon 1999. *The Ethics of Deconstruction: Derrida and Levinas*. 2nd ed. Edinburgh: Edinburgh University Press.
Derrida, Jacques 1976. *Of Grammatology*. Trans. Gayatri Chakravorty Spivak. Baltimore and London: The Johns Hopkins University Press.
———— 1978. *Writing and Difference*. Trans. Alan Bass. London: Routledge and Kegan Paul.
Elam, Diane 1994. *Feminism and Deconstruction: Ms. en Abyme*. London and New York: Routledge.
Faludi, Susan 1992. *Backlash: The Undeclared War Against Women*. London: Vintage.
Francke, Lizzie 1995. Review of *Disclosure*. *Sight and Sound* (March 1995), 36.
Freud, Sigmund 1938. *Psychopathology of Everyday Life*. Trans. A. A. Brill.

Harmondsworth: Pelican.
———— 1965. *The Interpretation of Dreams*. Ed. and trans. James Strachey. New York: Avon Books.
———— 1973. *Introductory Lectures on Psychoanalysis*. Ed. James Strachey and Angela Richards. Trans. James Strachey. Harmondsworth: Pelican.
———— 1998. "The 'Uncanny' " in *Writings on Art and Literature*. Trans. James Strachey. Stanford: Stanford University Press, 193-233.
Green, Philip 1998. *Cracks in the Pedestal: Ideology and Gender in Hollywood*. Amherst, MA: University of Massachusetts Press.
LaCapra, Dominick 1989. *Soundings in Critical Theory*. Ithaca and London: Cornell University Press.
Laclau, Ernesto 1990. *New Reflections on the Revolution of Our Time*. London and New York: Verso.
———— and Chantal Mouffe 1985. *Hegemony and Socialist Strategy: Towards Radical Democratic Politics*. London and New York: Verso.
Laclau, Ernesto and Chantal Mouffe 1987. "Post-Marxism Without Apologies". *New Left Review* 166 (1987), 79-106.
Lacoue-Labarthe, Philippe 1998. *Typography: Mimesis, Philosophy, Politics*. Ed. Christopher Fynsk. Stanford: Stanford University Press.
Macherey, Pierre 1966. *Pour une théorie de la production littéraire*. Paris: François Maspero.
Marx, Karl 1973. "Speech at the Anniversary of the *People's Paper*" in David Fernbach (ed.). *Surveys from Exile: Political Writings, Volume 2*. Harmondsworth: Pelican, 299-300.
Tasker, Yvonne 1998. *Working Girls: Gender and Sexuality in Popular Cinema*. London and New York: Routledge.
Watts, Carol 1995. "Thinking *Disclosure*: Or, the Structure of Post-feminist Cynicism". *Women: A Cultural Review* 6:3 (1995), 275-286.

Part II:

Literature

From *Trainspotting* to *Filth* – Masculinity and Cultural Politics in Irvine Welsh's Writings

Stefan Herbrechter

> Men still have everything to say about their
> sexuality. You still have everything to say
> about your sexuality: that's a challenge.
> (Alice Jardine and Hélène Cixous in
> Chapman/Rutherford 1988: 21)

This powerful challenge, I am going to argue, is taken up in Irvine Welsh's work. What turns this work itself into a challenge is that it combines the search for sexual identity with aspects of the wider contexts of contemporary cultural politics. It critically reflects the transition from Thatcherite to Blairite Britain. From *Trainspotting* to *Filth*, Welsh's texts have been gravitating from Scottish marginality to mainstream British culture and economic and cultural thirdwayism. This development is reflected and find its (displaced) articulation in the crisis of masculinity which has increasingly become the focus of his writings. Welsh writes about social exclusion and individualism; the local, national and global; neoliberal economy and the commodification of drugs; but maybe, above all, about the dissolution of patriarchy and the de(con)struction of masculinity, about the erosion of gender categories and the family.

Welsh's male working-class and subcultural (anti)heroes have to come to terms with the social changes of their roles and their relationships to their "mates", partners and children. As individual subjects, they are portrayed in their psychotic world of self-destructive masculine sexuality and identity, and, as members of post-industrial society, in their parasitic and anachronistic position within contemporary "postfeminist" and "post-gender" culture.

Cultural Politics

> It's coming back to me. It's all coming back. I
> wish it wasn't but it is. I don't suppose any of
> us stopped being on trial. It was her own fault;
> she fuckin well asked for it. (Welsh 1996b:
> 177)

Irvine Welsh is rapidly developing into a cult writer. It is not so much the undeniable quality of his writings than their "social message" that seems to appeal to his readership which, as he claims, is not merely the average middle-class fiction addict whose "culture" Welsh, in fact, "challenges", but people who identify with the kind of *milieu* he describes. As Welsh believes "half the people who have bought the books have never bought a book before, never even read a book before [...] obviously it's no challenge to them, because it's an affirmation of their culture" (Welsh cited in Berman 1996: 58). The affirmation lies in the doubly marginalised position from which Welsh writes: from a regional, Scottish position against the hegemonic centre of "English" Britishness, in a time of political devolution; and from a variety of oppositional subcultures against hegemonic middle-class values. In the face of this double threat it is no wonder that Welsh's texts are primarily concerned with identities and cultural politics. They dramatise at once "the repressive processes of post-industrial individualism" (Freeman 1996: 251) and the "anger and volatility of post-Thatcherite Britain" (Berman 1996: 56). The legacy of Thatcherism and the rise of New Labour communitarianism and thirdwayism serve as the political backdrop for representing the destruction of working-class identities, the effects of new social exclusion and the forms of subcultural escapism in the absence of any serious possibilities for radical social change. Welsh describes the resulting social dynamic of his characters in the following words:

> There are two kinds of working-class philosophies, a radical or revolutionary one that sees the middle and upper classes as enemies; and another more individualistic desire to escape from the working class and assimilate into the upper classes. That antagonism is always going on in a working class head. It's wanting to be in a different situation. (Welsh, in Berman 1996: 57)

Welsh's characters thus play out the drama of self-destructive identities in an alienating environment. At once against a nostalgic return or the preservation of a mythical and archaic working-class Scottishness and deeply sceptical of New Labour's politics of communitarian inclusion Welsh's texts invoke a radically different scenario to a "third way" which believes that "[n]o one any longer has any alternatives to capitalism" (Giddens 1998: 43). Rather than comply and accommodate, Welsh's anti-bourgeois rebels spitefully announce: "I think I'll stick to drugs to get me through the long, dark night of late capitalism" (Welsh 1995: 240).

Thus, Welsh's texts muster the devastating effects of neoliberalism in relation to questions of identity and difference. With growing disillusion, they are both a reflection of post-Thatcherite society and of New Labour politics. Chronologically, they demonstrate the failure of metropolitan politics to face rampant individualism, as seen from the Scottish margins. From pre-New Labour *Trainspotting* (which developed out of a number of short stories written from 1991 onwards, first edited as a novel in 1993):

> [...] the socialists go on about your comrades, your class, your union, and society. Fuck all that shite. The Tories go on about your employer, your country, your family. Fuck that even mair. It's me, me, fucking ME, Simon David Williamson,

NUMERO FUCKING UNO, versus the world, and it's a one-sided swedge. (Welsh 1994: 30)

and:

> In the kitchen, two guys are arguin aboot the poll tax. One boy's sussed oot, the other's a fuckin spineless Labour/Tory Party servile wankboy. "You're a fuckin arsehole oan two counts. One, if ye think the Labour Party's goat a fuckin chance ay ever getting in again this century, two, if ye think it would make a blind bit ay fuckin difference if they ever did," ah jist butt in and tell the cunt. (Welsh 1994: 237-238)

to *The Acid House* (first published in 1994):

> He launches into a long and bitter attack on the politics and personalities of Scottish Labour Militant. I'm thinking, what can I do, really do for the emancipation of working people in this country, shat on by the rich, tied into political inaction by servile reliance on a reactionary, moribund and yet still unelectable Labour Party? The answer is a resounding fuck all. Getting up early to sell a couple of papers in a shopping centre is not my idea of the best way to chill out after raving... I think I'll stick to drugs to get me through the long, dark night of late capitalism. (Welsh 1995: 240)

and, after New Labour's election, in *Ecstasy* (1996):

> ...responsibility-oriented society. That's why people should be free to choose the sort of health care and education they want.
> – That's just Tory rubbish, my dad says.
> – I think we have to face facts – that old-style socialism, as we used to perceive it, is long dead. It's now about appeasing different interest groups in a more diffused society; about taking what's best from both traditional right and left philosophies.
> – Well, I'm afraid I'll always be a Labour man...
> – I'm Labour as well, always have been, says Hugh.
> – You're New Labour. Tony Blair Labour. Which is the same as Tory, only Major's probably further left than Blair. Blair's just a snidier version of Michael Portillo, which is why he'll do better than Portillo will ever do... Labour and Tory are now both exactly the same, I tell them. (Welsh 1996: 190)

However, if Thatcherism and New Labour are rejected and a return to "old-style" socialism is also impossible, what kind of alternative is "left"?

A Fourth Way?

> You don't have to decide that culture should be only for the middle classes. (Welsh, in Berman 1996: 58)

Welsh's work certainly is political rather than escapist in that it engages with the negotiation between marginalised and hegemonic cultural identities in late capitalism. Strategic "Scottishness", working class and subcultures, masculinity and parenthood, "weak" and strong femininities are some of the main subject positions that are explored in Welsh's fictional discourse.

Alan Freeman, who gives a post-structuralist interpretation of *Trainspotting* and its place in Scottish literature sees the originality of Welsh's texts in their "playful" distortion of realism and their displacement of the ubiquitous struggle between realism and antirealism (Freeman 1996: 251-62). This is also what places Welsh's texts within the wider context of postmodern literature. According to Freeman, the "trainspotters" represented in the novel "exemplify Late Capitalism's replacement of work with leisure, of action with consumption, of meaning with system, of life with lifestyle" (Freeman 1996: 256). They expose the myth of individualism and the privatisation of experience through consumption. The downsides of late capitalist individualism – social exclusion, the destruction of the family and traditional forms of employment and work-based identities, changing of drug cultures (from heroin to ecstasy), sexuality and masculinity, and English colonialism – are dwelt upon in a "non-judgmental way".

> With its allusion to pop culture and junk fads, to chemically altered consciousness and artificial lifestyles, in its form, language and action, *Trainspotting* dramatises the desperate margin between meaning and being, between possession and creation, between the repressed and the expressed in human life. (Freeman 1996: 261-262)

If *Trainspotting* still "grieves for selves that cannot be", Welsh's later work constitutes the representation of the complete breakdown of identity. Sexuality and masculinity become the main focus. Whereas *Trainspotting* can be read as a negotiation of sexual identity and difference that explores the variety of identity positions available within the realm of sexual consumption, in his most recent work, *Filth* (1998), Welsh zooms in on the extreme masculinist position in order to further dissect and advance its psychotic self-dissolution. The sexist psychopath figure (*Trainspotting's* Frank Begbie) is singled out and becomes the analysand of a more psychologised introspective narrative: the "strange" and deranged Roy Strang of *Marabou Stork Nightmares* (first published in 1995) and the (male chauvinist) "pig" Bruce Robertson in *Filth*. It seems as if the later texts are playing mindgames with the obsessive sexual self and its self-hatred, projected onto others. The absence of a moralising social realism is by now a familiar feature in the contemporary representation of violence.

You're Filth!

> My father. It was my brother. It was the coal,
> the dirt, the filth. The darkness. I hate it all.
> (Welsh 1998: 339)

Filth is the story of a police detective (D.I. Bruce Robertson) who is gradually spiralling into insanity while leaving a trail of violence, murder, verbal and drug abuse, and general hatred behind. The novel starts with a "Prologue" that contains Robertson's inner "dialogue" commenting on the reasons why he murdered the black lover of his wife, who has left him:

> The trouble with people like him is that they think that they can brush off people like me. Like I was nothing... You've pushed me away mister. You rejected me. You tricked me and spoiled things between me and my true love. I've seen you before. Long ago, just lying there as you are now. Black, broken, dying. I was glad then and I'm glad now. I reach into my bag and I pull out my claw hammer. Part of me is elsewhere as I'm bringing it down on his head. He can't resist my blows. They'd done him in good, the others. [...] There's no fear or regret but no elation or sense of triumph either. It's just a job that had to be done. (Welsh 1998: 1-2)

Gradually, the reader discovers that the first person narrator has committed a murder he is going to investigate himself, in his function as a detective: the police's and the press's hypothesis that the victim, a black journalist, was subjected to a racist attack, is only half the truth. Although Bruce's act itself was not devoid of racism it was mainly a re-enacting of the key scene in his traumatic childhood.

The story is narrated through Bruce Robertson's eyes with regular short interruptions and comments by his wife, Carole. The third perspective of narration is that of Robertson's tapeworm – visually set off from the main text by the superimposition of speech bubbles represented in the form of bowels. It is the worm – Bruce's "Other" – who reveals the background to his unhappy childhood. But the worm's speech bubbles also contain a parallel story of the parasite's physical and psychological coming into being through the consumption and exploitation of its host (it could be argued that the worm here re-enacts the rise of bourgeois capitalism). The worm is developing a Self which is mainly concerned with its own survival and gradually takes over the place of Bruce's Me (Welsh 1998: 98) – a process which in psychoanalytical terms corresponds to the definition of psychosis, an ego's idea of "being lived by the Other". According to Laplanche and Pontalis, psychosis is a "primary disturbance of the libidinal relation to reality", "leaving the ego under the sway of the id". The ego thus has to reconstruct a "new reality in accordance with the desires of the id". Psychotic delusional behaviour is the result of specific mental mechanisms like "*Verwerfung*"/ foreclosure and projection (Laplanche & Pontalis 1985: 369-372).

The worm begins a psychological exploration of its host (Welsh 1998: 130) while Bruce is sinking ever more deeply into paranoid states of persecution and schizophrenia (170). On its identitarian journey, the tapeworm begins wondering about significant others to confirm its sense of self (191) while starting to develop a critical distance from its "friend", the host – complaining e.g. about his "proletarian habits" (192). The worm's bulimia – "eat... eat for the Self... consume for freedom..." (219) – is coupled with the realisation that its external reality is becoming hostile ("the host is now aware of my presence", 230) and with the knowledge of "not being alone" any longer, of falling in love due to the presence of a "significant other", a second tapeworm:

> I can feel the one that I must now refer to as The Other. I am not alone. My soulmate is here... We engage with one another in that most delicious and intimate of congresses, that exchange of the chemicals through our bodies as our means of the joining of the souls... to merge... to become one with our universal identity... (230-231)

The rejoicing in a humanist idea of unified universal identity in turn spurns the "religious" gratitude for the Host (or God): "We feed each other through our breathing, eating, excreting bodies, intwined infinitesimally through the intestines of our most glorious Mine Host" (231). The worm gains more and more scope despite Bruce's "chemical warfare" against it; it starts "internalising Bruce's ghosts" (242), a process which finally sets off the analytical reading of Bruce's repressed past (242).

The worm-narrator's insistence on exposing Bruce's childhood creates a parallel commentary for Bruce's "current" social behaviour and his anti-union and anti (New) Labour outbursts. The parasite's narration thus serves to link Bruce's personal with his political:

> But there are people in the unions now who don't give a fuck about democracy. Maggie sorted them out, but they're still there, just waiting for that Tony Blair spastic to show signs of weakness and let them back. That was why things got so messed up with the last Labour government. These bastards held sway. Scargill and the likes. That's why we had to sort them out. (245)

When Bruce's anti-worm treatment causes the death of the worm's soulmate, its "significant other", the worm starts with Bruce's (psycho)analysis proper. The first revelation is Bruce's identitarian reliance on – and his love-hate relationship to – his work as a policeman:

> You need to be at work. You need the job; hating, yet at the same time thriving on it, its petty concerns. These concerns are enough to distract you from the Self you must only face up at night between the extinguishing of the television set and the onset of a jittery and fitful descent into a physically bruising sleep. How can I

forgive you Bruce, after the ruthless shedding of my most significant Other? That creature of sublime beauty, that purest of souls who trusted you, our Host, who didn't want to hold on grimly for life, here in those exploding gaseous bowels. That soul who believed that you had the purest of intentions towards the Other, just as the Other did to all the others in this world of ours... How can I forgive you? But forgive you I must. I know your story... (260)

The worm's theodicy mirrors that of the host in his own society. Bruce's loss of his loved one, Carole, his traumatic experience of "being shed" by his adoptive father, Ian Robertson; but also Labour's and the British public's "shedding" of the mineworkers' cause under Thatcherism.

Bruce comes from a mining family but he joined force with the "other" side, the side of the police who enforced the new "anti-union laws on behalf of the state" (261):

You were on the other side. Power was everything. You understood that. It wasn't for an end, to achieve anything, to better one's fellow man, it was there to have and to keep and to enjoy. The important think was to be on the winning side; if you can't beat them join them. Only the winners or those sponsored by them write the history of the times. That history decrees that only the winners have a story worth telling. The worst ever thing to be is on the losing side. You must accept the language of power as your currency, but you must also pay a price. Your desperate sneering and mocking only illustrates how high the price has been and how fully it has been paid. The price is your soul. (261-262)

Socially and historically, thus, Bruce's story is combined with the 1984-85 miners' strike and with Thatcherism's destruction of the last traditional working-class communities in Britain. For Bruce, being rejected by his mining family and the mining village community causes injustice and self-hatred that push him towards revenge. He joins "the other side" in the strike and becomes part of the police force whose main aim it was to divide the strike support within the mining communities.

In political terms these specially trained police forces were the instrument of the Conservative Government to combine the idea of the "rule of the law" with the justification of their liberal economic programme, the inescapable "law of the market" (Fine/Millar 1985: 2-3). Both "laws" served crucial roles in Conservative paternalism and authoritarianism, to perpetuate the "law of the father". Cathie Lloyd gives an account of how this police force threatened many mining villages:

Wherever these substantial police reserves were held, nearby villages felt their oppressive and intimidatory presence. Away from the picket lines key people in the strike were harassed as squads of police pursued them in raids on pubs and clubs, creating tension in villages which sometimes erupted into street fighting. All members of the community felt themselves to be "fair game" to the police when these clashes took place. (Lloyd cited Fine/Millar 1985: 68-69)

The (b)latent police racism – which recently regained public attention in the controversy about the Stephen Lawrence murder case – is an omnipresent feature in Bruce Robertson's discourse and his policing practices. As Paul Gordon remarks, the miners' strike riot policing "had been developed in the 1960s and 1970s largely in response to the presence of black people in Britain" (Fine/Millar 1985: 161).

But the socio-political background is only the field in which Bruce's psychological reality is subjected to the repetition compulsion brought about by a repressed trauma. Bruce's first rebellion against his mining father was acted out by a resistance to eating which in turn provoked his "force-feeding" on the coal his father had dug up – the filth – to earn the family's living (292). "Can you taste the filth, the dirt, the oily blackness of that fossil fuel in your mouth as you choke and gag and spit it out? [...] Now you can consume to your heart's content or your soul's destruction, whichever comes first. So eat" (295). When his little brother Steven – the father's favourite – is born Bruce is made to understand that the reason for being rejected, hated and stigmatised – by his father and the people of his mining village – is that he is not his mother's legitimate child. During the strike Stevie and Bruce steal coal from their father's pit. Bruce pushes Steven after having been provoked by him and Stevie dies buried by coal – "battered, broken, lifeless and... [black]" (354) – the traumatic scene that is being repeated at the beginning of *Filth* (quoted above). In his rage the father spells out the "truth" to Bruce and the community:

> This thing killed [Steven], your father screams, this bastard spawn ay the fuckin devil killed ma laddie! You look straight at him. You want to deny and affirm his assertions all at once. You're no ma son! You've never been ma fuckin son! You're filth! (355)

Bruce's uncanny and threatening Other takes on internal and external representations. Internally, the "enemy within" is the growing parasite that weakens Bruce physically (anorexia – Bruce's refusal to eat) and mentally (by forcing him to face his sexual bulimia and his self-hatred that expresses itself in his violence against others). Of course, the "enemy within" is also the phrase used by Thatcher to describe the cause of the miners – a political ploy to combine the exclusion of political "others" and to legitimate their policing by employing techniques of "moral panic" (Samuel/Bloomfield/ Boanas 1986: 2ff). Ironically, since the miners' strike was in fact inspired by "radical conservatism" – "a defence of the known against the unknown, the familiar against the alien, the local and the human against the anonymous and the gigantesque" (Samuel/Bloomfield/Boanas 1986: 22) – the Conservative Government helped accelerate the destruction of moral values, especially those associated with the traditional family, that subsequent governments have come to deplore.

The paternalistic ideology Bruce paradoxically makes his own as the very reaction against his adoptive and biological fathers, is itself based on the psychotic exclusion and oppression of others (as demanded by the omnipotent threatening Other) – a process which feminist theories have come to perceive as the fundamental mechanisms of hegemonic Western heterosexual masculinity.

The Psychosis of Masculinity

> Scotland is one of the most repressed societies. It completely sustains [...] misogynistic behaviour. The pubs, dark inside... a completely masculine environment. And then there is this militaristic, football thing, and adults in positions of trust. (Welsh, cited in Berman 1996: 60)

While in "real time" Bruce Robertson's social disintegration continues – he is suspended from duty after having been attacked by a gang of thugs while dressing up as Carole; he has to withdraw his application for promotion; he lives in a state of complete apathy in the mess of his flat – the narrator-worm grows increasingly "worried" about his host. As Bruce's story of his past fully unfolds the attention turns to an analysis of his sexual identity. Bruce gradually comes to use the pronoun "we" instead of "I" referring to himself while the speech bubbles begin to merge with the main text (352ff.; 367ff.) and begin to prompt Bruce's main narrative (368). His psychological reality progressively invades his social reality. The remaining boundaries between Bruce's real and psychological world begin to fuse.

The worm recounts Bruce's first love, for a "lassie in a caliper" named Rhona, and how his inferiority complex about his difference turns into the opposite by affirming his masculinity:

> You started to thrive on this difference. You had always felt different but inferior, but now you were coming to feel yourself to be different but superior. This was how you were coming to be seen as well. All you needed to do was to assert that difference and accept the consequences. (370)

The incipient love story and sexual education is brutally interrupted by lightning. Rhona is killed – another accident for which Bruce is responsible:

> She was your first love but you never really knew her as well as you wanted to. She liked music and she looked and smelt nice and she wore a caliper and your heart used to and still does break, if you're honest with yourself, every time you think of her. (376)

Later, when Bruce finds out the identity of his real father – a convicted rapist with a series of pathologies: acute schizophrenia, depression, anxiety attacks (381) – his sexual identity turns sour. As the offspring of a sexual perversion, fathered by "The Beast" – the Other – Bruce goes to see his "real" father in jail looking for some reassuring essential difference:

> You had to tell yourself that you were nothing like him. But the women. You wanted them. You always wanted them. But so did all the young men. It was normal. [...] You left the pits and joined the force. Then got married. You settled down. You had a child. You were normal. Only, there came the anxiety attacks. The depressions. The desires. (381, 386)

The worm's narrative from this point is struck by an anxiety of its own. It becomes more and more desperate in reminding his host of his instinct for survival (385; 388 ff) and it is indeed the insane Bruce who now threatens to invade the worm's world [in the guise of Margaret Thatcher!]:

> You are repulsed and proud. The urge to hurt, demean and control is great in you. To somehow get back at them. You consider politics as a career. How wonderful it would be to start a war. To send thousands of people to their deaths. You idolise Thatcher over the Falklands. (389)

The last stage is the worm's frantic appeal for Bruce to desist his suicidal thoughts, but the story ends in a final closed speech bowel, the worm being shed at the point of death:

> I feel myself slipping out of my Host in a large pile of his excrement and sliding down his leg inside his flannels. Then I'm away from him. There's a piercing scream... somebody's in pain... like the Other was when the Host was disposing of it... the Other I loved... now the Host is gone and I cannot sustain this any longer. I can't sustain life outside of the Host's body... like the Other I am gone, gone with the Host, leaving the screaming others, always the others, to pick up the pieces... (393)

Filth can be read as a negotiation of repressive oedipal masculine identity. Bruce's *raison d'être* is his role as Don Juan, "playing at being man". He undertakes the sexual re-education of his "effeminate" mate Bladesey, who is something like a New Man, deeply insecure of his manhood and the relationship with his wife. The not entirely altruistic plan is to teach his friend/rival a lesson in "strong" masculinity by seducing his wife. Bruce's relationship with his mate(s) – just like the relationship among the group of mates in *Trainspotting* – is based on masculinity as "homosocial competition" (Kimmel cited in Brod/Kaufman 1994: 121). Constant sexual activity and the permanent renewal of conquests serve as reassurance of Bruce's compulsive identity. After having achieved the conquest of his friend's wife he expresses his fundamental misogyny:

What I usually do with a new bird is hole up with them for a weekend and spoil them with loads of foreplay, champagne, takeaways and undivided attention to all the preposterous shite they drivel. That usually does the trick for getting into them on a casual basis for months. The best thing to do is to give a new bird the very best possible time, and then she knows you have the capacity to do that again and she's always looking inwards blaming herself for not being able to reactivate that passion in you. The best lovers ken that you only need tae be a good lover once with one bird. Get it right the first time and then ye can basically dae what ye like. Eventually they tipple that you're just a selfish cunt, usually eftir a few years ay fruitless self-analysis, but by that time you've generally had your fill and are firing into somebody else. (299-300)

Seen in perspective, Welsh's male psychos come at a time when masculinity has been forced out of its hegemonic silence. Feminism, the gay, lesbian and transsexual movements and postcolonial and postmodern theories have been attacking the hegemonic model of the white heterosexual patriarch as masculinity's natural "norm". Essentialism has given way to social constructivism and insistent questioning of male identity construction. The effect has led to a perpetuation of crisis, a "demythologisation" and a destabilisation of patriarchal authority in general – provoking a series of male introversions and backlashes, the New Man and the New Lad (Chapman/Rutherford 1988: 17).

In academic but also increasingly in popular discourses identity is being represented as a social and historical construct rather than as static and essential given. While this affects all forms of identity the hegemonic identification process within white heterosexual patriarchy has been scrutinised for its violent exclusions of "others" and its projections of anxieties and desires outside of itself. Difference and otherness play a key role in these processes of self-identification. Significant others serve as touchstones and anchoring points of self-assured, internalised identity, while difference remains necessarily ambivalent. Otherness as a structural and ontological "void", is usually projected as a passive space that constitutes an inversion of the self – the other side of the mirror, so to speak. However, by definition, this otherness remains other or mystical like death. The taming and manipulating of otherness which is at once threatening and desirable is assured by the epistemological process of differentiation, a process which is subject to pre-existing value systems and hierarchies. Power struggles are fought out on the terrain of difference while necessarily ignoring or repressing the always preceding (structural) otherness that cannot and must not be articulated.

A Bit of the Other?

> Even his anti-sexism was therefore overlayed with sexist self-interest. Men are pathetic cunts, [Renton] thought to himself. (Welsh 1994: 141)

Bruce's scornful male chauvinism is in a sense "sanctioned" by its inverted other: traditional femininity. Carole's interspersed comments in which she claims to "really know [her] man" and his "sexual aura" (42) represent woman conspiring in her own oppression, thus illustrating Simone de Beauvoir's idea of woman as *man's* other. "I feel a need and an aching for him, I'll have to get back to him soon" she says (43). It has to be said that Welsh's text leaves open the possibility of Carole's interventions actually being projections or discursive appropriations by Bruce's imaginary.

Bruce's imagined impact on women is greatly exaggerated: at work for example he is being outdone by a new female colleague, a specialist in "equal opportunities". It is indeed Amanda Drummond who comes closest to Bruce's true identity:

> Bruce, you're an ugly and silly old man. You're very possibly an alcoholic and God knows what else. You're the type of sad case who preys on vulnerable, weak and stupid women in order to boost his own shattered ego. You're a mess. You've gone wrong somewhere pal, she taps her head dismissively. (338)

Carole, on the other hand, in her intervening chapters sticks to "her man" despite everything, waiting for "true love" beyond sexuality:

> Bruce knows that our wee games and flirtations only serve to strengthen a true love, by making it confront the depths and heights of itself. He did it for me, and it worked. I'm a different person now. A better person. (122)

In her own state of delusion, Carole embraces patriarchal oppression, including Bruce's political views which she sets within the context of the break-up of the traditional family:

> [W]hen I first met Bruce's parents... They were good people, from a mining village in Midlothian. This was before they were corrupted by that Scargill, who split up families and turned everyone against each other. Bruce doesn't bear any grudges though, even though they were cruel to him and rejected him, their own son. That's what these people want though: to split up the family. It's not important to them but the way I see it, if you haven't got family then you haven't got anything. (165)

Carole represses the profound dysfunctionality of her traditional family and Bruce's abuse of their daughter Stacey: "It's so unfortunate that Stacey's said those horrible things, but we don't blame our little girl, all children go through a phase when they tell silly wee lies" (166):

> I'm looking forward to seeing Bruce again, so we'll be back together as a family; me, Bruce and our little girl Stacey. She has got to accept the wrong she's done and the hurt she's caused everyone with her silly little lies. I often feel guilty, I feel that I should have taught her better, taught her the difference between right and wrong. She's a good girl really though and it's important for her to know Bruce and I forgive her. All families go through these kind of traumas and it's important not to make more of these things than is necessary. It's a complicated world enough to grow up in these days. (211)

Carole's last intervention in the story, "More Carole?" (following the chapters "Carole", "Carole Again", "More Carole", "Carole Remembers Australia"), however, is in fact Bruce's narrative displaying his delusion of going out "with"/as Carole, him being dressed as her. The pronoun used for narration is again the schizophrenic "we" descending further into mental delusion:

> We're remembering how this all started: that when Carole first left with the bairn we used to set the table for two and then we started wearing her clothes and it was like she was still with us but no really... Carole... Carole, why did you dae it, with that fucking nigger, those whores they meant nothing tae me... you're fucking big-moothed hoor ay a sister... fanny like tha fuckin Mersey tunnel... and the bairn... oh God... God... God... we want to live... all we're asking for is some law and order... it's the job... (343)

Bruce manages to escape the cruel death the gang of thugs had prepared for him but his self seems beyond repair. Carole and Stacey return too late and find Bruce after he has just hanged himself:

> ...I want more than anything for Stacey not to be there and see this and I'm trying to shout No go away and I hear her screaming Daddy and I want to live and make it up to her and Carole, I can hear her now too, screaming BRUCE because I care and I've won and beaten the bastards but what price victory
> STACEY PLEASE GOD BE SOMETHING ELSE SOMEONE ELSE... (393)

The inescapable and incurable psychotic masculinity with its constant use of violence against others and itself, with which *Filth* engages seems to be driven by a fear of the absolute power of the malevolent Other. It is thus impossible for Bruce to form intersubjective relations with others that are not based on anxiety and (self)hatred. *Filth* is to be read as an illustration of the self-destruction of masculinity. The protagonist is eaten up from inside by an unspeakable Other, symbolised by the tapeworm who speaks Bruce and fills him with voices: "If only I could sleep, but I get the voices in my heid at night and then I start thinking of that thing inside me, eating my guts out" (274). "We hear voices... Aw the time. Do you hear them? All our life we've heard them. The worms. [...] We say this, they say that... I, we, I

hear myself singing in a low, tuneless voice, – Why not take all of me..."
(333). "I'm hearing the voices and I'm pressing the buttons on the handset
to change the channels but it's the voice in my head. That same, insistent
soft voice, eating me up from inside..." (381).

Bruce's story represents the psychotic's loss of control over his reality.
This control is the product of an identity strongly related to his work and
the power with which it invests him. Sexuality, violence and the way they
are "encouraged" by and exploited through his policework set the
framework of Bruce's world, and this framework is being undermined by
Bruce's "worm": namely his past, his sexual bulimia, his nervous skin
disease – on a psychological level – and his unsuccessful application for
promotion and his losing out against a the new female generation – on a
social level. The process is also mirrored in the transformation of Bruce's
sexuality from his homophobic machismo on which his compulsive
heterosexuality relies to his transsexual "incorporation" of Carole.

Bruce has transposed the absurdity of the double law of the father – his
abusive adoptive father who rejected him and his unavowable real father,
the rapist and "Beast" – onto his work or vocation. As a policeman he used
to be able to live out his "dreams of revenge against those who transgress
the laws of the state [or the father]" (384). "My own father. The one who
never abused me, never forced me to eat coal, never called me the spawn of
the devil. But he was still the one I hated most" (387). The Beast or
"Thing" constitutes the Other who governs the Lacanian order of Bruce's
real, the repressed that conditions his imaginary and symbolic reality and
forces his compulsive, repetitive, psychotic violence against others. In a
final monologue, shortly before his suicide, Bruce seems to speak as the
archetypal traditional patriarch on his exit from history. Trying to imagine
how Carole would find him hanged and feeling the ultimate enjoyment and
justification for his tortured self-hatred, his misogynistic masculinity,
Bruce explains:

> We wait and think and doubt and hate. How does it make you feel? The
> overwhelming feeling is rage. We hate ourself for being unable to be other than
> what we are. Unable to be better. We feel rage. The feelings must be followed. It
> doesn't matter whether you're an ideologue or a sensualist, you follow the stimuli
> thinking that they're your signposts to the promised land. But they are nothing of
> the kind. What they are is rocks to navigate past, each one you brush against,
> ripping you a little more open and there are always more on the horizon. But you
> can't face up to that, so you force yourself to believe the bullshit of those that you
> instinctively know to be liars and you repeat those lies to yourself and to others,
> hoping that by repeating them often enough and fervently enough you'll attain the
> godlike status we accord to those who tell the lies most fervently and most
> passionately. But you never do, and even if you could, you wouldn't value it,
> you'd realise that nobody believes in heroes any more. We know that they only
> want to sell us something we don't really want and keep us from what we really
> do need. Maybe that's a good thing. Maybe we're getting in touch with our

condition at last. It's horrible how we always die alone, but no worse than living alone... (392-393)

This description of the self-destructive process of masculinity echoes the death of the male psycho embraced at the end of *Marabou Stork Nightmares*. The comatose Roy Strang, who is trying to escape from his violent masculinity by retreating ever deeper into his imagination, is castrated by his former rape victim. He conspires in his own mutilation with a kind of (masochistic) relief as he experiences "woman's" revenge:

> She's looking into my eyes, my lidless eyes and we see each other now. She's beautiful. Thank God. Thank God she's got it back. What we took. I'm trying to smile. I've got this severed cock in my mouth and I'm trying to smile. I can't breathe and she's showing no mercy. I understand her... We both understand everything. (Welsh 1996: 263-264)

This parody of a romance displays the deep ambiguity and desire that still lurks even behind the self-destruction of masculinity as represented in Welsh's work. Desperate sympathy and cynicism seem to be inextricably linked. Already Renton in *Trainspotting* confessed that he "didnae know much aboot women" (Welsh 1994: 13). Asked why he is sometimes thought not to be able to effectively write female characters, Welsh replies:

> [...] it's not so much that I can't write women characters, it's a question of being very wary of doing it. It's about acknowledging that you're not a woman, and acknowledging the other-ness... of how women characters think, feel, react and all that. I don't think women and men do think, feel, react differently. But again, it's this whole imperialist thing. You've got to be aware of the issues and acknowledge the possibility of other-ness. So, it's been a tentative process, for me, writing about women characters. (Welsh, cited in Berman 1996: 59)

Whether and how to "acknowledge the possibility of female otherness" constitutes the entire dilemma of "men in feminism" with their irrepressible desire of "Getting a Bit of the Other" (Suzanne Moore in Chapman/Rutherford 1988: 165-192) and the ambiguity of sexual difference.

Current (post)feminist thought has moved away from direct confrontation towards precisely this problem of difference. Some would say that this lack of political activism is deplorable and guilty of complicity with the "enemy". Others would see this development as a more effective and more "subversively" cunning way to explain to men and women alike what a rough deal they get out of a patriarchy that relies on heterosexual masculinity as its norm that persists by constantly reconfiguring itself (see for example Faludi 1999). This development constitutes the cultural background against which Welsh's stories about masculinity have to be seen.

What becomes precarious in the postfeminist scenario is not so much (sexual) identity as such – there is rather an increase in possible identity positions and their commodification – but the otherness preceding (sexual) difference. In a post-gender society, i.e. a society in which gender difference is no longer the fundamental structuring device, the utopian ideal of androgyny can turn oppressive. (What would the "other" of androgyny be?) It can serve as a conservative device for masculinsism's repeated "forgetting of woman" – an otherness that manifests itself in difference – and thus a renewed denial of woman (Chapman/Rutherford 1988: 169). Sexual difference cannot be forgotten as long as the process of working through masculine repression and oppression remains incomplete. In other words, as long as sexual politics is to have an emancipatory goal, an evaluation of differences must be possible.

Filth symbolically plays out this drama of utopian androgyny in Bruce's "becoming woman", his incorporation of Carole by impersonating and dressing up as her. Internally this androgyny is mirrored by the parasite's sexlessness. Bruce's "male autism" (Horrocks 1994: 107-124) is the price he pays for rejecting and incorporating the oedipal law of the father. His misogyny and homophobia express themselves in his violence and self-hatred, which are the two sides of the same problem. *Filth* reflects the cultural evolution of masculinity of the present. However, the text ultimately seems to opt against androgyny and for a redefinition of difference, and thus for a new way of constructing masculinity. It is quite revealing that Renton's memorable statement about the future "indifference" of sexual identity occurs in John Hodge's script only and not in Welsh's novel *Trainspotting*:

> Diane was right. The world is changing. Music is changing. Drugs are changing. Even men and women are changing. One thousand years from now there will be no guys and no girls, just wankers. Sounds great to me. It's just a pity no one told Begbie... You see if you ask me, we are heterosexual by default not by decision. It's just a question of who you fancy. It's all about aesthetics and it's fuck all to do with morality. But you try telling Begbie that. (Hodge 1996: 82)

Conclusion: Literature and Cultural Politics

> [...] the disarray of the Left in face of the miners' strike is, in one aspect, part of a larger discomfort both about the alternative to Thatcherism, and of the very possibility of a socialism which is in any sense representative of popular desire and will.
> (Samuel/Bloomfield/Boanas 1986: xiv-xv)

Literature is certainly no straightforward or even less a "true" reflection of society. But it is that aspect of social discourse that most obviously tries to mediate between individual imaginary and social symbolic. The interest it is able to raise and which thus continues to make it an important discursive formation to inform cultural analysis is its proximity to the "real", which is never an entirely personal or social fact but always relates to the intersection of individual psychological reality and social history. Bruce's identity for example is the product of such an intersection. The only place where all levels of Bruce's reality cross – childhood, father figures and worms; sexuality and identity; politics and society – also constitutes the turning point in Bruce's story of decline:

> ... no signs of the alien monster. I know it's up there though, like an Arthur Scargill in the healthy body politic of eighties Britain, the enemy within. (171)

Arthur Scargill, the miners' leader and president of the NUM, became the main scapegoat of the majority of Britain during and after the failure of the strike – the "enemy within" personified. He was the target of an "unprecedented campaign of vilification by the government and the national press" and the "symbolic object of national execration" (Samuel/Bloomfield/Boanas 1986: 26). The miners' strike has to be understood as the turning point in late-twentieth-century British history. As far as foreign policy is concerned, the Thatcherite "enemy within" strategy of moral panic was the reflective legitimation for fighting the "enemy without", morally justifying and politically exploiting the Falkland War against Argentina. On a party political level it led to the continuation of Thatcherite neo-liberal economic restructuring beyond return. For Labour the miners' strike "by its intransigence [...] threatened to expose the hidden doubts which gnaw at the Socialist project, and the absence of any clear left-wing or even Keynesian alternative to the economic policies of the [Thatcher] government" (Samuel/Bloomfield/Boanas 1988: xiv). It is thus the beginning of New Labour and its post-Thatcherist legacy (Driver/Martell 1998).

Welsh's texts attempt to reconcile sexual identity with this legacy and its culminating point, the traumatic event of the 1984-85 miners' strike, in a way that situates them in juxtaposition to New Labour and thirdwayism. Welsh's texts contain a (sexual and cultural) politics of their own. Against patriarchal exclusion and traditional (psychotic) masculinity, but also against neo-liberal commodification of identity politics; opposed to the individualism that lurks behind the "transformation of intimacy" thesis (Giddens 1992 and 1998) and communitarian models of equality as inclusion, they seem to invoke the impossible: dialogic romance beyond patriarchy and the destruction of oppressive oedipal masculinity. Is this incredulity towards patriarchy, as the greatest "metanarrative" of all, a harbinger of the beginning or of the end of change and thus also of difference? Are justice and equality beyond "apocalyptic" masculinity thinkable? This seems to be the way in which Welsh's work returns feminism's challenge to Cixous and Jardine (with interest).

Works cited

Beck, Ulrich 1998. *Democracy Without Enemies*. Trans. Mark Ritter. Cambridge: Polity Press.

Berger, Maurice, Brian Wallis, and Simon Watson (eds.) 1995. *Constructing Masculinity*. London: Routledge.

Berman, Jennifer 1996. "Irvine Welsh." *Bomb* 56 (1996), 56-61.

Braidotti, Rosi 1993a. "Discontinuous Becomings. Deleuze on the Becoming-Woman of Philosophy." *Journal of the British Society for Phenomenology* 24:1 (January 1993), 44-55.

——— 1993b. "Embodiment, Sexual Difference, and the Nomadic Subject." *Hypatia* 8:1 (Winter 1993), 1-13.

Brod, Harry and Michael Kaufman (eds.) 1994. *Theorizing Masculinities*. London: Sage.

Chapman, Rowena and Jonathan Rutherford (eds.) 1988. *Male Order: Unwrapping Masculinity*. London: Lawrence & Wishart.

Connell, R. W. 1995. *Masculinities*. Cambridge: Polity Press.

Driver, Stephen and Luke Martell 1998. *New Labour: Politics After Thatcherism*. Cambridge: Polity Press.

Eisenstein, Hester and Alice Jardine (eds.) 1994. *The Future of Difference*. 2nd ed. New Brunswick, NJ: Rutgers University Press.

Faludi, Susan 1999. *Stiffed: The Betrayal of the American Man*. London: Chatto & Windus.

Fine, Bob and Robert Millar (eds.) 1985. *Policing the Miners' Strike*. London: Lawrence & Wishart.

Freeman, Alan 1996. "Ghosts in Sunny Leith: Irvine Welsh's *Trainspotting*" in Susanne Hagemann (ed.) 1996. *Studies in Scottish Fiction: 1945 to the Present*. Frankfurt am Main: Peter Lang, 251-262.

Giddens, Anthony 1992. *The Transformation of Intimacy: Sexuality, Love and Eroticism in Modern Societies*. Cambridge: Polity Press.

——— 1998. *The Third Way: The Renewal of Social Democracy*. Cambridge: Polity Press.

Hodge, John 1996. *'Trainspotting' and 'Shallow Grave.'* London: Faber & Faber.

Horrocks, Roger 1994. *Masculinity in Crisis: Myths, Fantasies, Realities*. Houndmills: Macmillan.

Jamieson, Lynn 1999. "Intimacy Transformed? A Critical Look at the 'Pure Relationship'." *Sociology* 33:3 (August 1999), 477-494.

Kimmel, Michael S. (ed.) 1987. *Changing Men: New Directions in Research on Men and Masculinity*. London: Sage.

Laplanche, Jean and J.-B. Pontalis 1985. *The Language of Psycho-Analysis*. Trans. D. Nicholson-Smith. London: The Hogarth Press.

MacCannell, Juliet Flower 1991. *The Regime of the Brother: After the Patriarchy*. London: Routledge.

Samuel, Raphael, Barbara Bloomfield, and Guy Boanas 1986. *The Enemy Within: Pit Villages and the Miners' Strike of 1984-5*. London: Routledge & Kegan Paul.

Thomas, David 1993. *Not Guilty: In Defence of the Modern Man*. London: Weidenfeld & Nicolson.

Weed, Elizabeth (ed.) 1989. *Coming to Terms: Feminism, Theory, Politics*. London: Routledge.

Welsh, Irvine 1994. *Trainspotting*. 1st ed. 1993. London: Minerva.

——— 1995. *The Acid House*. 1st ed. 1994. London: Vintage.

——— 1996a. *Ecstasy*. London: Jonathan Cape.

——— 1996b. *Marabou Stork Nightmares*. 1st ed. 1995. London: Vintage.

——— 1998. *Filth*. London: Jonathan Cape.

The Moor's Last Sigh (Salman Rushdie): Marginal Alternatives, the Reconstruction of Identity through the Carnival of Indetermination

Madelena Gonzalez

> "Indeterminacies pervade our actions, ideas, interpretations; they constitute our world."
> (Ihab Hassan, "Pluralism in Postmodern Perspective")

Subversion as creative creed

Since the publication of *The Satanic Verses* in 1988, the status of a subversive has been thrust upon Salman Rushdie, of somebody who dares to formulate the unthinkable and thus threaten with ruin the well-established systems of thought with which we gird ourselves as a protection against contingency. Effectively, the thematics of Rushdie's work has been a ceaseless interrogation of our certitudes, a political, historical and metaphysical questioning of reality which situates him not only within the debated space of postcolonialism, but also on the *terra infirma* of postmodernism. However, the interest of Rushdie's work lies not simply in the provocative subject-matter he dares to choose (the processes of colonization and decolonization, political and religious oppression), but more largely in the importunate manner in which he engages with it. The Rushdian *œuvre* constitutes an immense monument to subversion, balanced upon the shaky cornerstones of the contesting of norms, the reversal of roles, the questioning of certainties and the beleaguering of dominants, and inscribing itself within a larger disharmonious project of deconstruction, undertaken via a gigantic jamboree of fertile confusion. Rushdie's house of fiction is purposely built upon sand, a compromised construction whose undoing is written into its being from the outset. In his later work, from the first pages of *The Satanic Verses* (1988) to the last of *The Ground Beneath Her Feet* (1999), it seems that, by increasingly destructuring his own discourse, he desires to expose it to the drives and inconsistencies of a species of feminine "writing-effect" as it strives against itself, attempting to break free from the prison of gender and genre in order to embrace the rebellious impulses of a non-institutional art.

The Moor's Last Sigh, which takes in a large swathe of recent Indian history, seeks to overthrow the dominant systems of conventional thought and power by putting them on stage to participate in their own destruction, clearing a discursive space in which other voices constituting marginal alternatives can come to the fore. Thus the norm is foregrounded to be mocked and laid low in a perverse celebration of its compromised status so that what is other or different can move to center-stage to suggest a concept of identity which is discursive, digressive and hybrid, from a position which Catherine Cundy defines as "mongrelised and relativist" (Cundy 1996: 113).

The novel unfurls within the confines of a vision of male prepotency based on hierarchical colonialist power structures. Indian society with its highly organised and rigid caste system and its inherent discrimination against women makes the frame of the book a distinctly masculine one, set within the male dominant of colonialism. However as Rushdie sets up all the familiar hegemonies, organised around centralised patriarchal power, he also sows the seeds of their downfall. Slowly, but surely, by undermining traditional gender models he reconstructs an a-gendered fictional world, making it the province of autonomous indetermination and a parallel of the new independent state's problematic struggle for self-direction. By giving room to other visions and other voices in a carnival of plurivocity, he creates a new late-twentieth century fictional space built on a concept of open power-sharing. Multiple possibilities become the new democratic dominant instead of univocal impositions as his universe splinters outwards into a myriad of marginal alternatives, in relation to which the former predominancies must struggle for identification. Thus the balance of power is shifted from masculine to feminine and the ultimate bastion of male domination, the authorial voice, is feminized and democratized, liberating subject, discourse and reader.

"Framing" the Dominant

The historical setting of the story, the colonial past of India and its postcolonial present, seems to place it firmly within the framework of dominant discourses, as does its mental and physical geography, "this country of parental absolutism [...] never-darken-my-doorstep scenes [...] fierce hierarchies and ancient moral certitudes" (Rushdie 1995: 278), conferring on it the elephantine proportions of the monolith, a fact to which the size of the volume itself draws attention. Yet from the outset, the majority is identified as threatening, "Majority, that mighty elephant, and her sidekick, Major-Minority, will not crush my tale beneath her feet" (Rushdie 1995: 87) and the perspective chosen is a minority one, that of the Indo-Portuguese, Catholic spice merchants of the south. It is also a perspective fragmented by repeated shifts of time and place, setting up a disconcerting relativism in the stead of unquestionable absolutism. The narrative will constantly slew away from the centre, not only due to the disturbed narrative voice itself but also thanks to the vehicles it chooses for its story, "the hooks on which it hangs its tales" (Rushdie 1995: 145, *sic*), electing, as it does, to stand on the same shaky ground as postmodernism which aims to " 'decentre' unitary and normative conceptions of sexual, ethnic, racial or cultural identity" (Brooker/Selden/Widdowson 1997: 213).

Very early on, the authority of the family or the clan around which the narrative turns, a frequent metaphor in Rushdie's fiction for political oppression, as readers of *Shame* will remember, is challenged by the irruption into its prison of tradition of characters who seem, at first sight, apparently minor or parallel to the main story; the young Aurora, for example, a child and a woman, who significantly rids the family home on Cabral Island of its precious elephant statues, liberating herself and her surroundings from the weight of myth, as gods are thrown to the winds; or the younger son of the house who, on his wedding night, travesties the institution of marriage by dressing up in his new bride's dress and going to meet his homosexual lover. As elsewhere in Rushdie's fiction, one senses not merely the desire to give space to other voices but more than that, a deliberate problematizing of the dominant as it is confronted with subversive forces. From being "a gap or absence that troubles and destabilizes the master narratives" (Brooker/Selden/Widdowson 1997: 215), women and other minority groups move to centre stage to openly challenge the official organization of thought. The child defying parental, familial and even religious authority serves to throw into relief the panic reaction of a beleaguered order, for the more it seeks to validate itself by oppression, the more its efforts prove counter-productive and foment rebellion. Being locked up as a punishment will prove a spur to Aurora who will take creative control of her destiny by decorating the walls of her "prison" with her drawings, using art as a radical force with which to combat imposed myth through the creation of her own, alternative, provisional, and openly subjective story:

> Aurora had composed her giant work in such a way that the images of her own family had to fight their way through this hyperabundance of imagery, she was suggesting that the privacy of Cabral Island was an illusion and this mountain, this hive, this endlessly metamorphic line of humanity was the truth; and wherever Camoens [her father and heir to the Da Gama family spice kingdom] looked he saw the rage of the women, the tormented weakness and compromise in the faces of the men, the sexual ambivalence of the children, the passive uncomplaining faces of the dead. (Rushdie 1995: 60)

The girl-child's revolt is an early intimation of the guilt to be laid at the dominant's door as alternative truths surface and the subversive force of the female as other challenges the established male order. Behind the myth of enlightened British rule, hides the brutal suppression of indigenous revolt, behind the security of identity and clan, savage rivalry and injustice, behind the desire of the majority, fascist fundamentalism, behind the "glittering monetarist vision" (Rushdie 1995: 334) of a new capitalist India, corruption. It is a world where in an inversion of the "normal" order of things, symbols which should or *could* be reassuring, the father, the family, organized religion, and finally a democratically elected government (Rushdie's fictional version of the *Shiv Sena* or Hindu nationalist party which is increasingly popular now in India), lose all sense of benignity to tower oppressively over the weak, thriving on their destruction. Indeed the father of the narrator becomes a risible parody of the ultimate in wicked father-figures, "Big Daddy [...] ruling boss or *dada* [...] *capo di tutti capi* [...] the biggest dada of them all" (Rushdie 1995: 331), "God in Paradise [...] shadow-Jehovah, anti-Almighty" (Rushdie 1995: 336-337), for he is suspected of having his wife and daughter killed for political reasons and of sleeping with his son's girlfriend. In an ambience reminiscent of the Gothic novel, authority is foregrounded as abuse, hysterically overreaching itself, and combated by the traditionally powerless (women, children, minorities, effete young men such as Moor), while the convolutions of the text resemble nothing so much as the tortured ichnography of a Gothic castle where the narrator is imaginatively and indeed effectively held hostage, for, having fled to Spain to avoid the riots in Bombay and his own imagined part in the chaos, as well as to track down some of his mother's stolen paintings, he is trapped in a castle in Spain by a former lover of his mother, Vasco Miranda, and, like Scheherazade, must tell his story to put off the moment of his death.

The overbearing and suffocating "Law of the Father" which looms large over the text provides then its ostensible framework. Colonialism, patriarchy, religion and even matriarchy (which reveals itself to be a parallel version of male oppression in the person of the hero's great-grandmother, Epifania, reminding us of *Shame* where the women condone by imitation the existing hegemony), jostle for supremacy in a battle of the gods, all providing blueprints for the persecution of the enfeebled. However, while rejoicing in its sovereign status and imposing strictures and structures on those less powerful, the dominant not only manifests itself as oppressive, but overplays its hand, until the edifice begins to crumble and the disorder latent and inevitable underneath the rule of order, indeed necessary for creating that order, comes to the fore, in a parallel of what befalls the narrator, as he repeatedly struggles to impose form on what seems formless. Caught within the paradoxical postmodern praxis of "unrepresentability" (Hassan cited in Jencks 1992: 197), he recognizes the inevitability of the indeterminate as the only viable structure for experience,

> and it is around here that my words run out, so you will not learn from me the bloody details of what happened when she, and then he, and then they, and after that she, and at which he, and in response to that she, and with that, and in addition, and for a while, and then for a long time, and quietly, and noisily, and at the end of their endurance, and at last, and after that, until... phew! Boy! (Rushdie 1995: 89)

By the same token, the well-oiled and highly successful commercial empire built up by the narrator's father has its foundations in corruption, "the power of corruption being equal to that of the gods" (Rushdie 1995: 185), but also in the anarchy of capitalism, and will be destroyed by the very chaos which nurtures it, as it becomes a prisoner within the frame of its own definition, trapped within the destructive dynamics of domination,

> For the barbarians were not only at our gates but within our skins. We were our own wooden horses, each one of us full of our doom [...] the explosions burst out of our very own bodies. We were both the bombers and the bombs. The explosions were our own evil [...]. We have chopped away our own legs, we engineered our own fall. And now we can only weep, at the last, for what we were too enfeebled, too corrupt, too little, too contemptible to defend. (Rushdie 1995: 372-373)

The enterprise of self-validation which attaches itself to power, whether it be narrative or other, is already a sign of in-built decadence, of a falling away or a *rapprochement* with death as the narrator's losing battle with his story proves,

> but on that occasion she, my mother, – instead of, – when I fully expected, – she turned on me, and, just when I needed her most, she, – against her own flesh and blood ... you see that I am not able, as yet, to tell this story either. Once again, the words have let me down. (Rushdie 1995: 90)

Indeed the scene into which the reader is thrust on opening the novel is one of chaos and confusion, structured by uncertainty and defined by the disorganization of narrative and language which will find a disturbing echo in the final pages, when the hero's weepy monologue or epilogue brings his story to a self-conscious clichéd end which is also the final sleep or death of the narrator. Hence the story which started with a bang of the unexpected in a fracas of broken and hysterical word-play, demanding of its reader instant implication, fizzles out in the damp squib of the inevitable, inscribing in its very form a cynical comment on the fate of all fiction. That all experience, however rich, is limited by a frame, of time, and/or, places, drawing attention to its fundamentally flawed and artificial status, seems to be the message conveyed. The narrative voice, traditionally and, one might add, necessarily, strong and even overweening, colludes in a postmodern parodying of its omniscience as it lays itself open to criticism and revels in setting itself up as an unreliable source of truth. The very premise of the novel from the outset is clearly to create a space for contradiction as an obsessive desire for control will have the dominant manoeuvre itself into a position where compromise of its status becomes inevitable and indeed desirable. Thus the dominant is given space only to be questioned, not solely by a militant counterforce but, above all, by its own realization of its probable bankruptcy, positioned as it is in a problematic relation to what is other. Nowhere is this more evident than in the stance adopted by Rushdie's narrator, Scheherazade in drag, condemned to fight for his life through his story and gasping for breath as he nears the inevitable and "final surrender": THE END, "When you're running out of steam, when the puff that blows you onward is almost gone, it's time to make confession. Call it testament or (what you) will; life's Last Gasp Saloon" (Rushdie 1995: 4). Structuring is therefore merely a necessary prelude to dismantling and valid above all on this level, for the narrator works from a position of fundamental compromise having shot himself in the foot, so to speak, a metaphor which is consciously mirrored by his deformed, hammer-like right hand, as he claims truth from a position of unashamed subjectivity. Situating his narrative within an aporia, constructed around different and conflicting voices, he "undecides" and "relativises" (Hassan in Jencks 1992: 196) his discourse, undermining his own story to the extent of handing over at least part of the responsibility of its future fate to the reader, witness and participator in its dialogism:

> The above is my understanding of what lay behind the stories I was told; but there is also a confession I must make. In what follows you will find stranger tales by far than the one I have just attempted to debunk; and let me assure you, let me say to-whom-it-may-concern, that of the truth of these further stories there can be no doubt whatsoever. So finally it is not for me to judge, but for you.
> And as for the yarn of the Moor: if I were forced to choose between logic and childhood memory, between head and heart, then sure; in spite of all the foregoing, I'd go along with the tale. (Rushdie 1995: 85-86)

If the narrative is crooked and sabotaged like its narrator from the beginning, it tilts ever more off balance as its world of discourse is increasingly subjected to doubt, oscillating between the authority of the real and subversive fantasy, existing in a shadow land between the two which implies a radical interrogation of the certainties of literature and the situation of the reader and which finds a disturbing reflection in the ceaseless destabilizing of traditional gender models. Through travesty, pastiche and parody all official discourse is mocked, whether it be religious, literary, political or historical; stripped of its mythical attributes by the critical scrutiny of the narrator. Hence, for example, a sarcastic recycling of Homi Bhabha's essay dealing with *The Satanic Verses* (Bhabha, "DissemiNation: time, narrative, and the margins of the modern nation" in Bhabha 1990: 291-322) which is applied to the work of the artist heroine, Aurora Zogoiby, to tease out the modish contradictions of postcolonial critical theory, while at the same time formulating the contested standpoint of the narrator and artists in general, *"Imperso-Nation and Dis/Semi/Nation: Dialogics of Eclecticism and Interrogations of Authenticity in A.Z."* (Rushdie 1995: 329). Such plagiarism, or should one say "playgiarism" (Hassan in Jencks 1992: 197), fulfils the double function of dragging the dominant from its pedestal and simultaneously reworking it democratically in a process of de-definition and de-formation. Likewise, a piece of daring and disrespectful intertextuality inspired by Shakespeare's *The Merchant of Venice* proposes a less normative reading or *re*-presentation of a classic text,

> when I say that our tale's Aurora was no Portia, I do not mean it wholly as a criticism. She was rich (like Portia in this), but chose her own husband (unlike in this); she was certainly intelligent (like), and, at seventeen, near the height of her very Indian beauty (most unlike). (Rushdie 1995: 114-115)

More interesting than direct and aggressive problematizing of the dominant, whether that dominant be radical chic or traditional lore, is the way the narrator also manoeuvres the story he is telling into a laughable impasse where it must partake of myth while drawing attention to its bankruptcy, "As Yul Brynner, in Pharaonic mode (that is, a rather fetching short skirt), was so fond of saying in *The Ten Commandments*: 'So let it be written. So let it be done'" (Rushdie 1995: 322). The iconic "Law of the Father" is here trivialized into a parody of the typical objectification of the feminine as seen through the male perspective which thus acts against itself to undermine its own discourse. Mixing Shakespeare and other texts from the Canon, fairytale and the Bible into a frenzied vaudeville, stirring in a generous dose of word-play and muddling high and low registers, Rushdie concocts a subversive feast for the reader where writtenness is foregrounded and the self-mythologizing inevitable in any text, including the one in front of our eyes, is deconstructed by way of alternative proposals of what could be the case.

At the same time as the reader is presented with a cliché of male domination (the domineering father, state, colonial master, religion, authorial voice, text), his certainties are undermined from the word go by the narrator's indeterminism. Coming significantly after his three sisters, he is "a hollow beat, a silent space where a fourth word should be" (Rushdie 1995: 140). Taking his name, "Moor", from a distant ancestor and historical figure, Boabdil, last Moorish king of Granada, renowned for his lack of courage and womanish failure to defend his kingdom, his narrative will represent a whole project of deconstruction of male ways of seeing. The cruel barb addressed to Boabdil by his vicious mother, "*Well may you weep like a woman for what you could not defend like a man*" (Rushdie 1995: 80) becomes Moor's defining slogan and if, as Patricia Duncker insists in her essay, "Post-Gender: Jurassic Feminism Meets Queer Politics", "The feminine role is associated with vulnerability, submission, lavish clinging desire" (Duncker in McQuillan/MacDonald/Purves/ Thomson 1999: 55), the hero is certainly "effeminate". In fact masculinity itself is shown to be fatally compromised. Thus Moor's father, the impressive Abraham, "a veritable czar, a mughal of human frailty" (Rushdie 1995: 182) is also "a complaisant husband" (Rushdie 1995: 176), despised by his wife as an example of the weakness of all men, " 'Here's a tautology [...] *Weak man*' " (Rushdie 1995: 169), while the heteropatriarchal discourse of society is questioned by the bothersome and discordant interference of homosexuality and bisexuality which propose alternative performances of self.

However, it is the relation between effeminacy and parody which is most significant and the larger sense in which this effects and affects the gendering of Moor and his story, raising as it does, the question of identity. If gendered behaviour is not the consequence of a prior identity as Judith Butler affirms (Butler 1992), if identity is *signifying practice* and gender is something we "do", dependent like all signifying practices on *repetition* – the repetition of words and acts which make the subject culturally intelligible, the result is that not only are categories of identity such as femininity recognized as varied and contested (rather than fixed), but a subversion of identity also becomes possible. This means that Butler's privileged model of subversion in action is the practice of parody in which gender is produced as a "failed copy", as fundamentally flawed and split (Butler 1992). With his mangled right hand, premature ageing-disease and doubtful origins, ancient and modern, Moor is such a failed copy, a subversive reference to the original, and thus intrinsically a challenge to the norm in a more radical sense. Postmodern parody and colonial mimicry unite in the text as Anglophile Indians are depicted as "mimic men" who, "obliged to internalize the laws of the colonizing nations, do so only imperfectly so that they are almost the same, but not quite, and this imperfect repetition or imitation highlights the flaws and fissures of the colonial project" (Brooker/Selden/Widdowson 1997: 216). Equally, the narrative mimics the languages of the dominant but draws attention to a breach in their coherence through mockery and humour or pinpointing the little detail which is not quite right. Behind the amusing clichés riddling the text and in some cases foregrounded by them, lurk challenging questions as the abnormal raises its head,

> "To be the offspring of our daemonic Aurora," I was told when young by Goan painter V; (for Vasco Miranda), "is to be, truly, a modern Lucifer. You know: son of the blooming morning." [...] I remember it as a prophecy, because the day came when I was indeed hurled from that fabulous garden, and plunged towards Pandemonium. (Banished from the natural, what choice did I have but to embrace its opposite? Which is to say, *unnaturalism*, the only real ism of these back-to-front and jabberwocky days. (Rushdie 1995: 5; original italics)

The controlling and defining force of the novel, Moor, "that appalling monster in whom a child's mind peered out through the portals of a young man's beautiful body" (Rushdie 1995: 189), is ailing, "queer", peculiar and querying, nothing but "manhood's simulacrum" (Rushdie 1995: 192), engaged in speaking differently or otherwise about what we take to be the norm. Such a narrative voice sets the reader free from identification, involving him instead in a revolutionary process of disidentification which throws into question dominant discourse and leads to alternative conceptions of the subject.

Debating and debated spaces

The Moor's Last Sigh is an obvious meeting point for the debated spaces of postmodernism and postcolonialism as such issues as the questioning of the subject and the disintegration and confusion of identity would seem to prove. Although the postcolonial agenda is obviously relevant to Rushdie's work, it is within the discourses of postmodernism that his writing seems most at ease, or at least at the points where postcolonialism and postmodernism intersect, as for example in Homi Bhabha's "invocation and transformation of the Bakhtinian notion of 'hybridity'" (Brooker/ Selden/Widdowson 1997: 229), seen as a " 'problematic of colonial representation' which 'reverses the effects of the colonialist disavowal of difference, so that other "denied" knowledges enter upon the dominant discourse and estrange the basis of its authority'" (Brooker/Selden/Widdowson 1997: 229). The concepts used by theorists of the postmodern seem to provide a model for Rushdie's writing, making his books a *mise en abyme* of such problematics. Placing postmodernism under the sign of Heisenberg's principle of uncertainty, Ihab Hassan identifies indeterminacy as a key feature in the writerly text which gives rise to "all manner of ambiguities, ruptures, and displacements affecting knowledge and society" (Hassan cited in Jencks 1992: 196). According to Hassan,

> Indeterminacy often follows from fragmentation. The postmodernist only disconnects; fragments are all he pretends to trust. His ultimate opprobrium is "totalisation" – any synthesis whatever, social, epistemic, even poetic. Hence his preference for montage, collage, the found or cut-up literary object [...] The age demands differences, shifting signifiers. (Hassan in Jencks 1992: 196)

This is one of the demands met by Rushdie's text where a poetics and a thematics of fragmentation are united in the work of the artist heroine, Aurora Zogoiby. In the words of D. C. R. A. Goonetilleke,

> In her earlier Moor pictures, Aurora had created "a romantic myth of the plural, hybrid nation" (Rushdie 1995: 227) [...]. Now, for the first time in Aurora's series of paintings, the reader is informed of the breaking-up of this concept of nationhood. In the "Moor in exile" sequence, the most important work of Aurora's later years, she abandoned [...] the notion of "pure" painting itself [...] elements of collage became the most dominant features [...]. The unifying

narrator/narrated figure of the Moor was usually still present, but was increasingly characterised as jetsam, and located in an environment of broken and discarded objects [...].
"When the Moor did reappear it was in a highly fabulated milieu, a kind of human rag-and-bone yard." (Goonetilleke 1998: 180)

As Marc Porée and Alexis Massery point out, Rushdie's style is part interrogation, part provocation, part play, part seriousness, but above all it situates the text in a no-man's-land where all points of reference are compromised (Massery/Porée 1996: 203) and where, in the words of the narrator, "There are no guiding stars" (Rushdie 1995: 62).

Criss-crossing with the idea of fragmentation, is the familiar palimpsest motif, also one of the defining preoccupations of postcolonial culture. The tension between fragment and palimpsest creates an indeterminate space where the complexity of layers of meaning, composed of the subparticular, reinforces the climate of uncertainty, "Call it Mooristan [...]. Water-gardens and hanging gardens, watchtowers and towers of silence too. Place where worlds collide, flow in and out of one another, and washofy away [...]. Call it Palimpstine" (Rushdie 1995: 226). If we examine more closely the defining features of Aurora's "palimpsest art" and its "intermingling of land and water" (Rushdie 1995: 226), we can see how it is reminiscent of some kind of semiotic flux for it is fluid and open, as yet unformed, "a vision of weaving, or more accurately interweaving" (Rushdie 1995: 227), a "land-sea-scape in which the land could be fluid and the sea stone-dry" (Rushdie 1995: 227). If woman is defined as "the silence or incoherence of the prediscursive" (Brooker/Selden/Widdowson 1997: 142), as representing "the 'Other', which stands outside and threatens to disrupt the conscious (rational) order of speech" (Brooker/Selden/Widdowson 1997: 142), relying on intuition rather than reason and argument, we can see how it is possible to analyse both the narrator's "art" and the paintings done by his mother which can be considered as a *mise en abyme* of his narration, in the light of a kind of feminine "writing-effect" such as that described by Hélène Cixous (Cixous 1975) and Luce Irigaray (Irigaray 1974) and not far from Julia Kristeva's theory of the semiotic and the symbolic where the former is associated with the "Body-of-the-Mother" and the latter, "The-Name-of-the-Father" (Kristeva 1974).

This feminine "writing-effect" appears at the intersection not only of the postmodern and postcolonial, but also at a meeting point with feminism and "queer theory" where "speaking 'otherwise', rethinking the relationship between subjectivity, sexuality and representation, decentring foundationalist narratives based on sex or reason" (Brooker/Selden/Widdowson 1997: 254) are high on the agenda. A sort of feminine ethos enters the text *qua* text as theory and practice overlap and the "creatively open dynamic" of feminism, its "viviparous" and "self-problematizing nature" (Brooker/Selden/Widdowson 1997: 145) become some of its defining features. Aggressive interpellation of the norm, what Hassan calls "Decanonization", a "massive 'delegitimation' of the mastercodes in society, a desuetude of the metanarratives, favouring instead *les petites histoires* which preserve the heterogeneity of language games" (Hassan in Jencks 1992: 197), will result in the laying low of the dominant and the emergence of subversive forces. In the words of Hassan, "from 'the death of god' to the 'death of the author' and 'death of the father', from the derision of authority to revision of the curriculum, we decanonise culture, demystify knowledge, deconstruct the languages of power, desire, deceit" (Hassan in Jencks 1992: 197). As he sees it, "Derision and revision are versions of subversion" and, " 'subversion' may take benevolent forms such as minority movements or the feminisation of culture..." (Hassan in Jencks 1992: 197). Aurora's paintings represent this feminization, for they will increasingly become the locus of a debate between a feminine fantasy and a masculine reality which her husband tries to impose on her. As in *Shame* and *Midnight's Children*, Rushdie shows how private is public and public private or, in the familiar terms of a feminist slogan, "the personal is political" (Brooker/Selden/Widdowson 1997: 235), as the heroine's art becomes increasingly representative of the embattled zone of India's identity, and history just one of many "*petits récits*" told from an openly subjective and minority point of view instead of constituting an imposed epic or "grand narrative" to which the reader is subjected.

In *The Moor's Last Sigh* the subversive presence of a Kristevean "Body-of-the-Mother", challenging the "Name-of-the-Father", constantly disrupts the "logic" of the narrative, questioning established verities and opposing closed to open systems of representation,

> an invisible reality moved phantomwise beneath a visible fiction, subverting all its meanings, [...]. How could any of us have escaped that deadly layering? How, trapped as we were in the hundred per cent fakery of the real, in the fancy-dress, weeping-Arab kitsch of the superficial, could we have penetrated to the full, sensual truth of the lost mother below? How could we have lived authentic lives? How could we have failed to be grotesque? (Rushdie 1995: 184-185)

(There are in fact two palimpsest canvases in the book. The first, by Vasco Miranda, is painted over a picture of Aurora and shows the defeated Boabdil weeping over his loss at Granada, while the second, Aurora's "The Moor's Last Sigh" depicts a reconciliation between mother and son and is painted over the picture of her murderer). The fantastic and the abnormal become the defining features of the text as it embraces otherness through dissent. By disorganizing syntax, for example, it can be considered as subverting the Law-of-the-Father and identifying with the mother through the recovery of the maternal semiotic flux. The very first pages of the book define the reader's troubled interaction with the narrative voice as a tension arises between the semiotic and the symbolic and s/he struggles to impose a familiar structure of reference on what seems irrational and free-floating. As the semiotic and the symbolic meet, the former is released in the latter and the result is linguistic "play", where phonology prevails over semanticism and the metonymical process of combination outdoes metaphorical selection,

> A last sigh for a lost world, a tear for its passing. Also, however, a last hurrah, a final scandalous skein of shaggy-dog yarns (words must suffice, video facility being unavailable) and a set of rowdy tunes for the wake. A Moor's tale, complete with sound and fury. You want? Well, even if you don't. And to begin with, pass the pepper.
> – *What's that you say?* –
> The trees themselves are surprised into speech. (And have you never, in solitude and despair, talked to the wall, to your idiot pooch, to empty air?) (Rushdie 1995: 4; original italics)

A Kristevean rapture stemming from the overwhelming sensuousness and anarchical abundance of a text which refuses to choose between alternative voices, results in a doubtful "pleasure" or "rupture" as the reader is left suspended, obliged to crack a confusing combination if s/he hopes to ward off disjuncture.

As the leitmotif of incest suggests, Moor's double rôle as son and narrator literally enacts this dialectic between the maternal body and paternal law as primary processes or drives attempt to invade the rational ordering of language and threaten to disrupt the unified subjectivity of the "speaker" and the reader. Moor is not so much the source of meaning as the site of meaning, undergoing a radical dispersal of identity and loss of coherence, caught up as he is in the irrationality of sexual textual congress for, as Brooker, Selden and Widdowson remind us, "Writing in the feminine or *écriture féminine* [...] deconstructs the opposition body/text" (Brooker/Selden/Widdowson 1997: 253):

> It is hard for me to speak of our lovemaking. [...] I remember its ease and tenderness, its quality of revelation; as if a door were opened in the flesh and through it poured an unsuspected fifth-dimension universe [...]. Its whirling galaxies. Its bursting suns. But beyond expression, beyond language was the plain *bodyness* of it, the movement of hands, the tensing of buttocks, the arching of backs, the rise and fall of it, the thing with no meaning but itself, that meant everything [...]. (Rushdie 1995: 252; original italics)

Rejected by his parents, Moor goes into hiding, making himself invisible to the male gaze of the dominant and assuming a sort of "phantasmal existence in hysteria and mysticism" (Irigaray 1974; Brooker/Selden/Widdowson 1997: 145). Like the mystic, by losing all sense of personal subjective being as he exposed to the rigours of a

Bombay jail, he is able to "slip through the patriarchal net to the maternal body below" (Irigaray: 1974; Brooker/Selden/Widdowson 1997),

> And one day I awoke from such a sea-dream in which, while attempting to escape from unknown pursuers, I came upon a lightless subterranean flow, and was instructed by a shrouded woman to *swim beyond the limit of my breath*, for only then would I discover the one and only shore upon which I might be safe for ever, *the shore of Fancy itself*; and I obeyed her with a will, I swam with all my might towards my lungs' collapse; and as they gave way at last, [...] the ocean rushed into me [...]. (Rushdie 1995: 290; original italics)

The scopophilia which Luce Irigaray associates with the male vision is opposed here to the tactile and physical quality of Moor's narration. Defined by fluidity and touch, what Irigaray calls "her style" is a way of writing which "resists and explodes all firmly established forms, figures, ideas, concepts" (Irigaray 1974; Brooker/Selden/Widdowson 1997: 145). Both Aurora's canvases and Moor's narration promote the radical "otherness" of women's eroticism and its disruptive enactment in language, but more than that, they help to create a radical space for art where identity is the result of constant revision and multiple voices, "a miraculous composite of all the colours of the world" (Rushdie 1995: 227).

Marginal alternatives: art as a-gender and a-genre

According to Irigaray, it is only "the celebration of women's difference," her "fluidity and multiplicity" which can "rupture conventional Western representations of them" (Irigaray 1974 ; Brooker/Selden/Widdowson 1997: 145). It is in the term of "multiplicity" that we get close to the truth of Rushdie's text and its "writing-effect", for the place where postmodernism, postcolonialism, feminism and "queer theory" most interestingly meet each other in *The Moor's Last Sigh* is in its use of polyphony, the multiple voices of Bakhtin's carnival, what Hassan calls "the 'gay relativity' of things, perspectivism and performance, participation in the wild disorder of life, the immanence of laughter" (Hassan in Jencks 1992: 198). Having openly deconstructed the masculine and embraced the feminine, it is above all as performance that the text creates its true identity, thus setting itself finally outside the prison of gender and of genre. It is its cultural impurity, the speaking in different tongues, the plurality of its sexuality, which sets it beyond the pale of what is identifiable as fitting into the pre-ordained categories of hierarchy. Locked in the riotous embrace of carnival, where the gender of the protagonists is confused, the text itself is in perpetual mutability and mobility, interpellating fixed notions and constantly raising questions as to its own species, comically crowning and uncrowning different deities as the unstable "I" provides a pretext for different voices to be king or queen for the space a line,

On the run, I have turned the world into my pirate map, complete with clues, leading X-marks-the-spottily to the treasure of myself. When my pursuers have followed the trail they'll find me waiting, uncomplaining, out of breath, ready. *Here I stand. Couldn't have done it differently.*
(Here I sit, is more like it. In this dark wood – that is, upon this mount of olives, within this clump of trees, observed by the quizzically titling stone crosses of a small, overgrown graveyard, and a little down the track from the Ultimo Suspiro gas station – without benefit or need of Virgils, in what ought to be the middle pathway of my life, but has become, for complicated reasons, the end of the road, I bloody well collapse with exhaustion.)
And yes, ladies, much is being nailed down. Colours, for example, to the mast. Bit after a not-so-long (though gaudily colourful) life I am fresh out of theses. Life itself being crucifixion enough. (Rushdie 1995: 3-4; original italics)

When subjected to close scrutiny, it appears that the text's resistance to interpretation comes from its heteroglossic nature, at the centre of which the unreliable narrator mischievously places the audience, witnesses to, but also participators in, a fickle floor-show where they may be unwittingly thrust on stage at any moment to improvise their part in the "play". By refusing to let itself be "nailed down" and thus assume the certainty of scripture, humorously deconstructing itself, the text invites us to read subversively, doubting always its authority, as sacred and profane, familiar and non-familiar, high and low, are mixed in a carnival of indeterminacy, transforming it into a monument of non-identity.

Patricia Duncker affirms that, "gender is performance", making the body "ambiguous", so that "power and knowledge cannot be so easily allocated to the masculine". By "fucking with gender" (Duncker 1999: 57), putting on different performances, the text not only demolishes established authority, but reconstructs itself through a new abnormal norm so that finally, "it is the idea of the norm which is bizarre" (Rushdie 1995: 206). Not only does it collude in its own dismantling and degendering, but creates a "transgressively transgendered" (Duncker 1999: 58) space where a "dream of a multiplicity of genders, of each one of us giving radically different performances, in any register, whenever we like" (Duncker 1999: 60), can come into being. Thus it is precisely the "ludic and subversive elements" of carnival and its "antisystem" (Hassan in Jencks 1992: 198) which promise renewal. The doubt which characterizes the narrative voice/s, its "fucked-up dissident mindset" (Rushdie 1995: 206) which is so disconcerting to the reader (Mark Wormald says that: "[...] both [Winterson and Rushdie] have inserted metafictional commentary and commentators into their narratives; the effect can be disconcerting, invigorating, or even sufficient to raise doubts as to their own faith as writers in the power of story" [Wormald in Mengham 1999: 199]) is expressly vocalized in order to lay bare the constructedness of all discourse, leaving an empty husk of meaning represented by the stuffed dog nicknamed Nehru which accompanies Moor on his travels. However, this doubt also fosters a liberating "selflessness" as, through loving interaction with others, skin peels off, categories disappear and hegemony is renounced, "To love is to lose omnipotence and omniscience ... without that leap nobody comes to life" (Rushdie 1995: 289). By tearing away layers of certainty, the hidden potentialities of the uncertain come to light, leaving the path open to the "second life" of carnival, the "feast of becoming, change and renewal" (Hassan in Jencks 1992: 198), which appears both universal and provisional at the same time: Wormald says that: "mingled images, confused but familiar metaphors of creativity, are capable of renewing perspectives on the future and the past not just of any one novel or novelist's world but of fiction itself" (Wormald in Mengham 1999: 200). Through its figuration of the alternative, Rushdie's novel attempts to remain always above or below recuperation, putting itself beyond the reach of hierarchy as the narrator seeks constantly to free his fictional space of determinism. The antidote to the *diktats* of the dominant and its dangerous imposition of meaning requires the renunciation of self as power. It is the narrator's vision of openness to the other of the "feminine", to the free-flowing liberation of indeterminism as self meets another, not in conflict, but in the shared harmony of the democratic ideal of love, which remains its only defining space, *"the most profound of our needs, [...] our need for flowing together, for putting an end to frontiers, for the dropping of the boundaries of self"* (Rushdie 1995: 433; original italics). A "last sigh", a "breath" (Rushdie 1995: 4), the text is "ex-haled", dragged out of the confines of itself as fixed identity, projected beyond the objectifying stare of the masculine and its reductive categories so that, like Moor, it becomes, *"weightless, floating free of burdens"* (Rushdie 1995: 432). Breathing itself "out" as a radical but fragile "body" of creation undergoing constant metamorphosis, defined only by its resistance to discernibility, its final refuge is inevitably in the nothingness of sleep/death, the "blank page" at the end of the story which alone can guarantee its eternal openness and, thus, immunity from the domination of recuperation.

Works cited

Bhabha, Homi K. (ed.) 1990. *Nation and Narration*. London: Routledge.
———— 1994. *The Location of Culture*. London: Routledge.
Brooker, Peter, Raman Selden and Peter Widdowson 1997. *A Reader's Guide to Contemporary Literary Theory*. Hemel Hempstead: Prentice Hall, Harvester Wheatsheaf.
Butler, Judith 1992. *Gender Trouble: Feminism and the Subversion of Identity*. London: Routledge.
———— 1993. *Bodies That Matter: On the Discursive Limits of 'Sex'*. London: Routledge.
Cixous, Hélène 1975. "Le rire de la Méduse." *L'Arc* 61 (1975), 3-54.
Cundy, Catherine 1996. *Salman Rushdie*. Manchester: Manchester University Press.

Goonetilleke, D. C. R. A. 1998. *Salman Rushdie*. London: Macmillan.

Hennard Dutheil de la Rochère, Martine 1999. *Origin and Originality in Rushdie's Fiction*. Bern: Peter Lang.

Irigaray, Luce 1974. *Le spéculum de l'autre femme*. Paris: Editions de Minuit.

Jencks, Charles (ed.) 1992. *The Post-Modern Reader*. London: Academy Editions.

Kristeva, Julia 1974. *La révolution du langage poétique*. Paris: Editions du Seuil.

——— 1975. *La traversée des signes*. Paris: Editions du Seuil.

Massery, Alexis and Marc Porée 1996. *Salman Rushdie*. Paris: Editions du Seuil.

Marret, Sophie (ed.) 1999. *Féminin/Masculin: Littératures et cultures anglo-saxonnes*. Rennes: Presses Universitaires de Rennes.

McQuillan, Martin, Graeme MacDonald, Robin Purves, and Stephen Thomson 1999. *Post-Theory: New Directions in Criticism*. Edinburgh: Edinburgh University Press.

Mengham, Rod (ed.) 1999. *An Introduction to Contemporary Fiction*. Cambridge: Polity Press.

Rushdie, Salman 1982. *Midnight's Children*. London: Picador.

——— 1984. *Shame*. London : Picador.

——— 1988. *The Satanic Verses*. London: Viking Penguin.

——— 1995. *The Moor's Last Sigh*. London: Jonathan Cape.

——— 1999. *The Ground Beneath Her Feet*. London: Jonathan Cape.

From Hard-Boiled Detective to Kaspar Hauser?: Masculinity and Writing in Paul Auster's *The New York Trilogy*

Monika Müller

Paul Auster's *The New York Trilogy* (1985) is a book that has created quite a bit of genre trouble. Because of its generic affinities with detective fiction, critics have uneasily identified the trilogy as "postmodern detective fiction" or even "anti-detective fiction" (Lewis 1994: 59; Rowen 1991: 224; Russell 1990: 71-72). In the following, I want to argue that Auster conceptualized *The New York Trilogy* as a fictional experiment which takes the generic mode of detective fiction as a point of departure for an exploration of how professional authorship affects his protagonists' masculine identity. In the trilogy Auster explores concrete notions of masculinity in relation to professional writing through his engagement with the works of his nineteenth-century literary predecessors Emerson, Hawthorne, Melville, Poe and Thoreau – the "ghosts" of the eponymous section. Nineteenth-century notions of solitude in particular serve as sounding boards for Auster's exploration of the exigencies of authorship as "manly" profession. Frank Lentricchia quite compellingly describes the difficulties a male author experiences "in a society that masculinized the economic while feminizing the literary" in *Ariel and the Police* (1988: 168). Furthermore, in *Unmasking the Masculine: Men and Identity in a Sceptical Age*, Alan Petersen points out that being the main provider is still expected of males in contemporary society: "The idea of 'success' for males in the modern West is bound up with paid labours and with being the breadwinner and head of the household. The idea that men sacrifice themselves or 'do it all for their families' is strongly rooted [...]" (1998: 49). In keeping with this notion, in *The New York Trilogy* Auster focuses on the problems and pressures that males who are more or less professional writers experience when they also try to function as providers. Yet by insisting that males fulfill their roles as "breadwinner" – or "head of the household" – in spite of all the difficulties they might encounter, he ultimately furthers hegemonical views of masculinity, even though he undercuts the usual machoism of detective fiction through his ironic presentation of the conventions of the hard-boiled detective novel.

To point out the conflict between "manly" and "unmanly" ways of gaining one's livelihood, he juxtaposes the supposedly dangerous masculine profession of the private investigator with the economically rather unproductive – and hence feminized – vocation of the professional writer. In all three sections of the book, Auster presents more or less besotted male protagonists, who only partially realize that they are in the midst of what seems to be an insoluble dilemma to them, namely how to reconcile the demands of domesticity with those of professional authorship. Thus, the individual sections of the trilogy provide a rather ironic comment on the fact that the notorious poverty associated with the literary profession makes it hard for a writer to fulfill the traditional masculine role of provider and thus "head of the household" that Auster, or at least the narrator of *The New York Trilogy*, still seems to cling to. The writer's need for solitude, furthermore, severely limits the emotional rewards to be gained from a harmonious family life and inspires fantasies of flight from domesticity.

All three sections tell very similar stories of a man who gives up his previous life in order to embark upon a solitary quest that first boosts his imagination, then leads to the discovery of "alternative selves", and finally to some sort of (self-)annihilation. Quinn, the protagonist of the first section, *City of Glass*, barely understands that it is his solitude, which is at first self-imposed, but then forced on him by his detective case, that ruins his life, whereas Blue, the protagonist of the middle section, *Ghosts*, has a firmer grasp of his situation as an involuntarily recruited writer who has to give up his former life in order to learn how to write. The protagonist of the final section, *The Locked Room*, however, seems to find a way of dealing with the conflicting demands made by his professional life and his family life by first splitting his "selves" into that of a writer, Fanshawe, and that and of a "family man", the narrator, and then being able to integrate both selves again.

Auster employs the detective/writer binary throughout the trilogy. Quinn is a writer of detective stories; Blue is a private detective; and Fanshawe is a writer. In *City of Glass*, the narrator deconstructs the opposition between the "manly" and "unmanly" profession by explaining that being a detective or being a writer is ultimately the same thing:

> The detective is one who looks, who listens, who moves through this morass of objects and events in search of the thought, the idea that will pull all these things together and make sense of them. In effect, the writer and the detective are interchangeable. (9)

As the narrator of *City of Glass* explains rather optimistically, the detective – and, by implication, the writer – is searching for nothing less than "the truth":

> [Quinn] had always imagined that the key to good detective work was a close observation of details. [...] The implication was that human behavior could be understood, that beneath the infinite facade of gestures, ties, and silences, there was finally a coherence, an order, a source of motivation. (80)

Quinn's assignment in *City of Glass* is to find out what Peter Stillman senior, a man who abused his son Peter Stillman jr. by denying him access to language in a bizarre experiment designed to find "God's language" and who allegedly still wants to kill his son, will do after his release from prison. Quinn, whose wife and son are dead, apparently seeks to relive his fatherhood – and thus to assert his masculinity – by protecting Stillman jr., who seems severely retarded due to his father's experiment, from his murderous father: "He knew he could not bring his own son back to life, but at least he could prevent another from dying" (41). Ironically, Quinn cannot realize at this point that it is precisely this assignment as protector of an innocent which ultimately prevents him from ever finding himself in the role of protector and provider again. And, perhaps even more importantly, he also does not understand that by taking up the breadless activity of being a writer/detective he might express a subconscious wish to escape the traditional masculine role.

By means of affirmative passages about Quinn's abilities as a detective – like the one quoted above – the narrator of *City of Glass* initially convinces his readers that Quinn is up to his detective's mission. But from the very beginning, he also gives out hints suggesting that Quinn finds himself in a very unstable situation, which he has partially brought on himself by becoming a writer and a recluse after his family's death. Indulging in the quasi-luxury of being able to live his life as a fantasy life, Quinn has developed "a triad of selves" (6). This triad is made up of Quinn, the "actual writer" of detective fiction, William Wilson, the pseudonym he has adopted for his story, and Max Work, the detective-protagonist of his fiction. The unnamed narrator and protagonist of *Ghosts* also splits his "personality" into a "writer self" and a "provider self" in order to deal with the pressures of his everyday life, thus suggesting that the conflicting demands made by masculine roles can lead to an almost schizophrenic "split personality". Critics usually call attention to the fact that in *The New York Trilogy* the narrators' and characters' identities are often self-invented and destroyed in the process of writing. Alison Russell argues that "[i]n *The Locked Room*, Auster suggests that language can destroy identity as well as create it" (Russell 1990: 80). By stressing the fabricated rather than innate nature of the self, Auster seems to align himself with poststructuralist theorists who view identity as culturally constructed by and in discourse (Grossberg 1996: 89-90; Hall 1996: 2-6). Yet considering that in the first two sections of the trilogy, along with the construction of "multiple male selves" in language Auster presents their complete annihilation (as a result of a life botched partly due to misunderstood notions of masculinity), it remains debatable just how blithely he accepts a truly postmodern view of the self.

In *City of Glass*, Quinn's three selves serve to distance him from his work – and himself –, as the narrator explains in a passage which sounds like an elaboration of a poststructural denial of the truth-seeking claims of "agency" inherent in the "author-function" (Barthes 1990: 167-172; Foucault 1986: 142-145):

> Because he did not consider himself to be the author of what he wrote, he did not feel responsible for it and therefore was not compelled to defend it in his heart. William Wilson, after all, was an invention, and even though he had been born within Quinn himself, he now led an independent life. Quinn treated him with deference, at times even admiration, but he never went so far as to believe that he and William Wilson were the same man. (5)

The William Wilson self (an homage to E. A. Poe as the "father" of the American detective story) foreshadows the at least partial self-annihilation of the protagonists of the *New York Trilogy* who, like Poe's William Wilson's "good" and "evil" selves, "cancel each other out" and provides yet another hint at the *doppelgänger*-motif which is so prevalent throughout the trilogy. The narrator furthermore indicates that Quinn actively creates the discourses that make up his multiple writer/detective selves:

> Private eye. The term held a triple meaning for Quinn. Not only was the letter "i," standing for "investigator," it was "I" in the upper case, the tiny life-bud buried in the body of the breathing self. At the same time it was also the physical eye of the writer, the eye of the man who looks out from himself into the world and demands that the world reveal itself to him. For five years now, Quinn had been living in the grip of this pun. He had, of course, long ago stopped thinking of himself as real. (10)

In this passage, Auster's narrator raises the question whether or not somebody who is "not real" can actually solve a "real" detective case and protect a "real" person. The tricky question of how Quinn as a "triad of selves" (or any of the "split" protagonists of the trilogy) is to take up "agency" and function in his masculine role as protector and provider is further exacerbated by the fact that Quinn receives yet another self from Stillman jr. who hires him as "Paul Auster of the Auster Detective Agency". Auster involves his own life in his book by dropping many clues that hint at his own biography, such as his stay in France and his divorce from his first wife. While it might therefore be tempting to read the trilogy's "domestic plot" in terms of his biography, I would still refrain from such an interpretation for the obvious reasons that Auster stated when he was asked whether *City of Glass* was a disguised autobiography:

> I think [the autobiographical quality] stemmed from a desire to implicate myself in the machinery of the book. I don't mean my autobiographical self, I mean my author self, that mysterious other who lives inside me and puts my name on the covers of books. [...] The self that exists in the world – the self whose name

appears on the covers of books – is finally not the same self who writes the book. (Auster 1993: 301)

Quinn, nevertheless, seems quite hesitant about taking over his creator's identity and only very reluctantly becomes the "hard-boiled dick" Paul Auster. In describing his reaction to the first phone call by which he is interpellated as a detective, the narrator almost seems to be making fun of the term "hard-boiled dick", and of the ultra-masculine conventions of hard-boiled detective fiction, by making Quinn react in the following way: " 'Then I suggest you dial again. This is not a detective agency.' Quinn hung up the phone. He stood there on the cold floor, looking down at his feet, his knees, his limp penis" (8). However, after the phone conversation, Quinn dreams about finding "himself alone in a room, firing a pistol into the bare wall" (10). He finally accepts the challenge on the third call on the night of May 19th – a day that he celebrates as his "birthday" because he was told that this was the day of his conception. Due to the significance of this date, Quinn is finally able to "conceive" of himself as a "real detective".

Norma Rowen and Alison Russell, who write about *The New York Trilogy* as somewhat off-kilter detective fiction, point out that "Quinn's case seems at first to take him into the world of Chandler or Macdonald" (Rowen 1991: 227), but that "by denying closure, and by sprinkling his trilogy with references to other end-dominated texts, Auster continually disseminates the meaning of this detective story" (Russell 1990: 72). In addition to this, he also undermines the "hc-man" type of masculinity presented in detective fiction. Auster himself concedes that with *The New York Trilogy* he deconstructs the genre of detective fiction:

> Not that I have anything against detective fiction [...] I refer to it in the three novels of the *Trilogy*, of course, but only as a means to an end, as a way to get somewhere else entirely. If a true follower of detective fiction ever tried to read one of those books, I am sure he would be bitterly disappointed. Mystery novels always give answers; my work is about asking questions. (Auster 1993: 277)

While the detective-part of *The New York Trilogy* nevertheless exhibits some characteristics typical of the hard-boiled detective novel, such as the "hero's marginality" (Hamilton 1987: 29), his becoming (almost) involved with an attractive femme fatale (Virginia Stillman, in Quinn's case) and the view of the city as "a conglomeration of individuals without a sense of community, where people become lost or lose themselves among the faceless" (Hamilton 1987: 26), there is no real hard-boiled action to be found in the trilogy. In keeping with Auster's understanding of the detective as kin to the writer, his protagonists do not get involved in any shoot-outs or any other life-threatening situations, but instead, in all three sections, sparked by the "domestic nature" of their cases, more or less consciously investigate the writer's possibility of functioning as traditional provider in a society that does not value his profession. The investigator becomes a mere observer.

In the first of these domestic cases, Quinn is paid by Virginia Stillman to spend most of his detective assignment observing Stillman senior on his walks around Manhattan. But he cannot find any evidence for the fact that Stillman indeed wants to kill his son. Instead, he finds out that the old man, who has made it his life's purpose to discover an almost Emersonian "analogue [of spiritual matters] in the material world" in order to invent a new language which "will at last say what we have to say" (92) "walks" the words TOWER OF BABEL into the streets of New York in order to reverse the "fall of language". Quinn cannot elicit any violent or in any other way significant response from Stillman senior when he tells him that he is Peter Stillman junior. He fails to realize that his attempts to make sense of Stillman's behavior are completely futile and that through his insistence to detect meaning where meaning simply cannot be detected, he is becoming more and more like Stillman senior and his son whom the narrator compares to Kaspar Hauser because of his linguistic handicap (see Kendall 1995: 209). Deprived of access to language as a child, Peter Stillman junior usually speaks a moronic gibberish, but, nevertheless, like his abusive father who tells Quinn, "I invent new words that will correspond to the things" (94), he claims that due to his father's bizarre but ultimately successful experiment, he knows how to speak "God's language" in the dark where "no one can hear me" (25). Because Quinn cannot accept what he already knows, namely that "Stillman was a crazy old man who had forgotten his son" (78), he continues to observe the Stillmans' apartment even after he has to assume that they have moved.

Waiting for Stillman senior at Grand Central Station before first starting to observe him, he subconsciously does what Black, one of the characters from *Ghosts*, does consciously: he turns to a nineteenth-century American writer in order to a gain a better understanding of his life as a male writer in an alien society. Thus, he suddenly recalls

> Melville and the opening pages of *Moby Dick*. From there his mind drifted off to the accounts he had read of Melville's last years – the taciturn old man working in the New York customs house, with no readers, forgotten by everyone. Then, suddenly with great clarity and precision, he saw Bartleby's window and the blank brick wall before him. (63)

Unfortunately, he is not able to heed the lesson implicit in the story of Bartleby, the human Xerox machine, who, because of having taken up the pointless and "breadless" activity of "writing", of copying what others have authored, becomes melancholic to the point of committing suicide by continually reducing his activities. And, of course, he also does not understand that with "Bartleby" Melville, having experienced literary failure, commented on the hopeless situation of the writer in a hostile environment. Like Bartleby, Quinn lives his life in solitude. He does not have a family to provide for (and to lean on) and just like Bartleby, he observes a brick wall – after he has moved into an alley opposite to the Stillman's building. Also like Bartleby, he receives shelter after becoming a bum (Quinn finally moves into the Stillman's empty apartment after Paul Auster has told him that Peter Stillman senior has long since committed suicide) and does not eat the meals that miraculously turn up in front of him. Unlike Bartleby, Quinn does not die – he has merely vanished when Paul Auster and the narrator of *The City of Glass* turn up at the apartment in order to check on him.

But before vanishing and leaving behind his red notebook, Quinn seems to have found the meaning of his life in his writing:

> [T]he case was far behind him now, and he no longer bothered to think about it. It had been a bridge to another place in his life, and now that he had crossed it, its meaning had been lost. Quinn no longer had any interest in himself. He wrote about the stars, the earth, his hopes for mankind. He felt that his words had been severed from him, that now they were a part of the world at large, as real and specific as a stone, or a lake, or a flower. He remembered the moment of his birth and how he had pulled gently from his mother's womb. He remembered the infinite kindnesses of the world and all the people that he had ever loved. Nothing mattered now but the beauty of all this. (156)

The beautiful language of this passage, which almost seems to echo Emerson's linguistic theory, masterfully conceals the dark irony that at the end of the *City of Glass* section, Quinn seems to have discovered "God's language", which makes words as specific as the things they describe. By reducing himself to language, Quinn emulates both Peter Stillman senior and junior whose nasty family affair he has become involved in. Thus, instead of restoring Quinn's "manhood" through saving an innocent victim and enabling him to become a family man once again, detective work for the Stillman case has furthered his pathology of wanting to be a recluse to the point of wanting to disappear entirely.

Perhaps not surprisingly, in *Ghosts*, Auster tells another variant of the story of the conflicted masculinity of the detective/writer whose work keeps him from being a family man. The middle section of *The New York Trilogy* repeats the most important thematic components from the first section. Again, a man – this time he is named Blue and is a proper private investigator – is sent on an investigation that chiefly requires observation. Like Quinn, the detective-protagonist of *City of Glass*, Blue encounters alternative selves while on his mission, becomes intrigued by the signifying power of language through writing (detective's reports in his case) and, strangely enough, also fantasizes about avenging harm done to an innocent boy. Ironically, Blue remains just as unaware as Quinn that it is his more or less enforced vocation of "detective turned writer" that keeps him from being able to become a provider for a family of his own whom he could "protect from any harm". Stuck in a professional endeavor that enforces a solitude which keeps him from communicating with his fiancée, Blue continues to be unable to reconcile the conflicting demands made on his masculinity.

At the beginning of *Ghosts* it seems as if this time Auster's narrator really leads his readers into the world of the hard-boiled detective-novel. The section's opening lines feature what Hamilton deems the "objective technique" of the hard-boiled novel. This stylistic technique focuses on a portrayal of facts rather than emotion and is characterized by "the use of simple, stripped down sentences, the portrayal of actions as series of component movements, the use of understatement [...]. These devices emphasise brutality by objectifying those involved; people are treated as mechanisms, equated with things" (Hamilton 1987: 140). Auster indeed seems to employ this technique in the middle section of the trilogy:

> First of all there is Blue. Later there is White, and then there is Black, and before the beginning there is Brown. Brown broke him in, Brown taught him the ropes, and when Brown grew old, Blue took over. That is how it begins. The place is New York, the time is the present, and neither one will ever change. Blue goes to his office every day and sits at his desk, waiting for something to happen. For a long time nothing does, and then a man named White walks through the door, and that it is how it begins. (161)

Furthermore, Blue, who is a more hard-boiled character than Quinn, seems to want to act out the tough guy, as his attitude towards "the future Mrs. Blue" reveals:

> [H]e thinks about calling her up on the phone for a chat, hesitates, and then decides against it. He doesn't want to seem weak. If she knew how much he needed her, he would begin to lose his advantage, and that wouldn't be good. The man must always be the stronger one. (165)

Yet, as readers of *City of Glass* might suspect, *Ghosts* is as different from a real hard-boiled detective story as the previous section of the trilogy. Auster immediately checks the hard-boiled quality of the opening passage by ridiculing its "objectivity" through his use of colors for names (which, of course, also points out the exchangeability of the characters and their identities). By indicating that Blue spends a good part of his time sitting around the office waiting for something to happen, he furthermore – but this becomes evident only much later – hints at the absolutely boring nature of Blue's detective assignment and, by implication, detective work as such.

In *Ghosts*, Blue, an aspiring young private eye, is hired by a man named White to observe somebody named Black. At first he thinks that he has been hired by a jealous husband who suspects Black to be his wife's lover, but then he realizes that "the case has nothing to do with marriage" (162). He finds out that Black, whom he observes from an apartment across the street, seems to be doing exactly the same thing that he is doing – reading and writing: "For in spying out at Black across the street, it is as though Blue were looking into a mirror, and instead of merely watching another, he finds that he is also watching himself" (172). Like Quinn, Blue is sent on an assignment that is senseless and destructive to his personality and like Quinn, he discovers a William Wilson-like alternative self, a *doppelgänger*, in Black.

As with the detective plot of *City of Glass* – which, ultimately, is about domestic life – the detective story of *Ghosts* becomes mixed up with domestic concerns in spite of Blue's earlier protestation that the "the case has nothing to do with marriage." Quite to the contrary, the narrator incorporates hints suggesting that the case has everything to do with domesticity, marriage, and male fantasies of evading domestic responsibility by absconding. Blue, who necessarily realizes that his assignment (like Quinn's) has trapped him "into doing nothing, into being so inactive as to reduce his life to almost no life at all" (201) cannot keep his mind from drifting off to previous cases having to do with the demands of domestic life as, for example, the case of Gray, a missing husband who, suffering from amnesia, walked out on his wife. After Blue has accidentally "stumbled on Gray in a bar" (167), he takes the stray husband, who had changed his name to Green, back to his wife and a happy ending: "[A]lthough he didn't remember her and continued to call himself Green, he found her to his liking and some days later proposed marriage" (167). The next case he remembers is one that he has read about in a magazine called *True Detective* and that "he finds difficult not to keep thinking about" (169) because it is about a little boy who was murdered in the woods of Philadelphia and never identified:

> [The coroner] whose name was Gold, became obsessed with the murder. Before the child was buried, he made a death mask of his face [...]. Blue is deeply moved by this. If it were possible, he would like nothing better than to drop what he's doing and try to help Gold. There aren't enough men like that, he thinks. If the boy were Gold's son, then it would make sense: revenge, pure and simple, and anyone can understand that. But the boy was a complete stranger to him, and so there's nothing personal about it, no hint of a secret motive. It is this thought that so affects Blue. (169)

Unlike Quinn, who, in some strange way wants to protect his own dead son by protecting Peter Stillman junior, Blue has no apparent reason to think about a child. But, there is the vague possibility of his becoming a father because, as already mentioned, he has a fiancée whom he left behind when he started working on his assignment. Strangely enough, he does not realize that, in a way, he has fled impending domesticity and abandoned her (and, by implication, his not yet conceived child) in a fashion similar to that in which the amnesiac Gray has left his wife. When by pure chance he encounters her on the street holding on to another man's arm, she only manages to say "You! . . .You!" (195). Blue immediately understands that she "will never be his wife" (195) and henceforth only refers to her as the "ex-future Mrs. Blue".

Yet while he does not seem to understand the implications that the Gray case has for his own life, he – unlike Quinn – gains a deeper understanding about the nature of (his) writing. In the beginning Blue, confident about writing his detective's reports, has the same kind of optimism about writing that Quinn acquires towards the end of his section: "Words are transparent to him, great windows that stand between him and the world, and until now they have never even impeded his view, have never even seemed to be there" (174). But later on, after he has watched Black's monotonous activity of reading *Walden* and writing something for weeks and weeks, he is appalled at the paucity of his report and becomes less confident about the ability of language to make sense: "For the first time in his experience of writing reports, he discovers that words do not necessarily work, that it is possible for them to obscure the things they are trying to say" (176).

Unlike Quinn, Blue, in spite of having learned to identify with Black because of the shared experience as his alter ego, finally becomes fed up with his assignment: "There is no story, no plot no action – nothing but a man sitting alone in a room and writing a book. That is all there is, Blue realizes, and he no longer wants any part of it" (202). He also comes to understand that this situation is detrimental to his well-being: "Months go by and at last he says to himself out loud: I can't breathe anymore. This is the end. I'm dying" (203). When he finally confronts Black, who also claims to be a detective who is having to work on a boring case – namely watching somebody write –, he actually receives a partial explanation for what is going on: "He needs my eyes looking at him. He needs to prove that he's alive" (216). Blue suddenly understands that Black does not really exist, that White and Black are the same person, and that White has created both Black and Blue as alternate selves. He decides to seek out Black in his apartment to confront him, but Black is not there. After Blue goes through the papers on Black's desk and finds that they are his own reports, he loses all his bearings. That same night, he remembers significant events and people from his previous life as in a near-death experience; he thinks about the people whom he feels he has let down: the ex-future Mrs. Blue and the little boy whose murder case he, too, could not solve. Black's existence becomes unbearable to him because he feels that he cannot separate himself from him anymore: "To enter Black, then, was the equivalent of entering himself, and once inside himself, he can no longer conceive of being anywhere else. But this is precisely where Black is, even though Blue does not know it" (226). A few days later he goes back to Black's apartment, in friendship as he says, but finds Black sitting on his bed with a gun in his hand, ready to kill him because Black has decided that Blue's assignment is over:

> "No Blue, I've needed you from the beginning. If it hadn't been for you, I couldn't have done it.
> "Needed me for what?"
> "To remind me of what I was supposed to be doing." (230)

After this exchange, Blue becomes enraged and possibly kills Black. Before he leaves the apartment, in order to go out West, or to China – as the narrator informs us – Blue reads Black's manuscript, which he finds on his desk.

While the outcome of this detective story is equally unsatisfying as the ending of *City of Glass*, the story's possible "meaning" might be a little more accessible because there are more clues planted in this section. Whereas Quinn seems to be quite unaware of what is happening to him, Blue, while not fully understanding what is going on, has some sort of inkling about his situation, as, for example, when he realizes that he and Black are *doppelgängers* and that his self has become unstable because it has been reduced to language (the texts that he and Black produce) or when he comprehends that by rejecting domesticity and walking out on the ex-future Mrs. Blue: "He has lost whatever chance he might have had for happiness, and if that is the case, then it would not be wrong to say that this is truly the beginning of the end" (196).

Yet there is still a subtext to the story which Blue (as Quinn in regard to the Bartleby-hint) does not seem to be aware of and which reveals an important thematic component dealing with the conflict between the exigencies of being a professional author and those of domesticity. Throughout *Ghosts*, Blue's alter ego Black gives examples from the lives and stories of the nineteenth-century writers whose writing informs *The New York Trilogy* and which, in way, "demystify" the *Ghosts*-section, even though Blue does not seem to understand the lessons inherent in them. As Black puts it: "I like to know how writers live, especially American writers. It helps me to understand things" (208). He thus tells Blue about Hawthorne's "literary apprenticeship", which lasted twelve years during which the writer supposedly shut himself up in a bedroom in his mother's house, and he also retells the story of Hawthorne's protagonist Wakefield (from the short story "Wakefield") who, like Gray, the amnesiac, walks out on his wife, watches her from a house opposite his own, decides to return years and years later and is then happily welcomed back into the home. Hawthorne, by the way, is not the only American male to tell such a story of a male's flight from a domestic situation: in "The Wanderer" (on the U2 album "Zooropa") Johnny Cash sings about a man who "in search of experience" leaves his wife without previous warning ("I went out for the papers / told her I'd be back by noon"); one of the characters of Dashiell Hammett's *The Maltese Falcon* tells his girlfriend – as a word of warning – the story of a husband who one day just walked away from the responsibilities of family life. Moreover, Leslie Fiedler has notoriously argued in *Love and Death in the American Novel* that in American literature males flee from domesticity and "civilization into each others arms" (Fiedler 1982: 12).

By telling the "Wakefield"-story, Black alerts Blue and the readers of *Ghosts* to the demands and dangers inherent in the profession of authorship. Readers familiar with Hawthorne's biography will know what Blue perhaps does not know; namely, that Hawthorne's long literary apprenticeship made him put off marriage by several years and that even after he did get married, his poverty forced him and his family to move in with his Salem relatives (see Miller 1991: 175-298). Moreover, as "Wakefield", which – after all – tells about a husband's flight from home and hearth, suggests, Hawthorne might not have been all that happy with his domestic situation because having to provide for a wife and children certainly took away time from his writing, time that he perhaps would much rather have spent engaging in the "useless activity" of first observing life around him and then writing about it.

The story of Blue's detective assignment rewrites the domestic defection of Wakefield, but beyond that it also tells a success story about the birth of a writer. By acquainting Blue with Thoreau's *Walden*, which focuses on solitude as one of the main requirements for introspective writing, Black makes the point that in order to be productive the writer has to become dead to the world. In an interview about *The New York Trilogy*, Auster pointed to the difficulties inherent in such a lifestyle by calling it "a passionate excess": "[i]n *Ghosts*, the spirit of Thoreau is dominant – another kind of passionate excess. The idea of living a solitary life, of living with a kind of monastic intensity – and all the dangers that entails" (Auster 1993: 271).

In *Ghosts*, Black (or White) seems to have created Blue because – perhaps in order to overcome writer's block – he needed to spend time being watched while writing in solitude. Forced into the seemingly non-productive life of a recluse, and having lost the initial optimism about his words making perfect sense, Blue actually develops his imagination, even though he feels as if "his life is reduced to almost nothing":

> Then, suddenly aware of what his mind is doing, he wonders why he has turned so sentimental, why all these thoughts keep coming to him, when for so many years they have never even occurred to him. It's all part of it, he thinks, embarrassed at himself for being like this. That's what happens when you have no one to talk to. (180)

The final product of Blue's forced literary apprenticeship is – presumably – the text of the *Ghosts* section. Ultimately, it does not matter at all, whether White, Black, or Blue wrote the text because they all are facets of a self created in and by language. Yet, as in *City of Glass*, the selves created in the text are solitary, unhappy selves that are so unstable that they can disappear at any time without further notice.

Thus, *Ghosts* does not solve the conflict between creativity and responsibility, solitude and domesticity, which is already latently dramatized in *City of Glass*. As the example of Blue shows, a man who finds himself in the situation of wanting to be both a writer and a traditional provider is facing an insoluble dilemma: domesticity keeps a man from writing, whereas solitude will drive him crazy. Towards the ending of *City of Glass* even Quinn, who had more than his share of solitude, seems to have understood this:

> Quinn had always thought of himself as a man who liked to be alone. For the past five years, in fact, he had actively sought it. But it was only now, as his life continued in the alley, that he began to understand the true nature of solitude. He had nothing to fall back on anymore but himself. And of all of the things he discovered during the days he was there, this was the one he did not doubt: that he was falling. (139)

It perhaps does not come as a surprise at this point that *The Locked Room*, the final section of *The New York Trilogy*, tells a story that again is very similar to the two previous ones. Unlike Quinn and Blue, the unnamed narrator-protagonist finds an – albeit rather bizarre – way of reconciling the conflicting demands made on his masculinity by his vocations as a writer and a "breadwinner". In his section, the narrator of *The Locked Room*, initially splits his "composite self" into that of a writer, Fanshawe, and that of a husband and father, the narrator. Towards the end of his narrative, however, he manages to integrate Fanshawe's personality within his own self, and thus becomes the only protagonist of the trilogy to come to terms with his roles of professional writer and provider. This time, the story begins after the hard-boiled detective, a man (also rather unsurprisingly) named Quinn, has somehow vanished from the disappearance case that he was supposed to solve. Instead, the protagonist of *The Locked Room*, a writer, is asked by the pregnant wife of the disappeared man – a close childhood friend of his – to help her publish his friend's book manuscript. Though the narrator has not seen his friend in a long time, it is clear from the beginning that Fanshawe has always been his alter ego:

> Early on, his influence was already quite pronounced. This extended even to very small things. If Fanshawe wore his belt buckle on the side of his pants, then I would move my belt into the same position. If Fanshawe came to the playground wearing black sneakers, then I would ask for black sneakers the next time my mother took me to the shoe store. If Fanshawe bought a copy of *Robinson Crusoe*

with him to school, then I would begin reading Robinson Crusoe the same evening at home. (247)

Almost exactly the same age as the narrator, Fanshawe, his childhood bloodbrother, has always been everything the narrator ever wanted to be because no matter what he attempted, he always was a little bit better than everybody else. Apart from his many talents "there was more innate goodness in him than in others" (247). Pointing out the truly unusual closeness between the two boys, the narrator recalls that "when we were six, we asked [my mother] if it was possible for men to get married" (252). The irony already hidden in this childish question does not become evident until later when Fanshawe's dark side is revealed, after the narrator has "taken over" his wife and son and thus has managed to participate in a marriage with Fanshawe without actually marrying him. He eventually receives a letter from his friend explaining that this was exactly what he had set up to happen:

> At the risk of causing you heart failure, I wanted to send you one last word – to thank you for what you have done. I knew that you were the person to ask, but things have turned out even better than I thought they would. You have gone beyond the possible, and I am in your debt. Sophie and the child will be taken care of, and because of that I can live with a clear conscience [...]. Above all, say nothing to Sophie. Make her divorce me, and then marry her as soon as you can. I trust you to do that – and I give you my blessings. The child needs a father, and you're the only one I can count on. (281)

Fanshawe thus becomes another character from *The New York Trilogy* to act out the "Wakefield"-story: "The man wanted to leave and he left. He simply got up one day and walked out on his pregnant wife, and because she trusted him, because it was inconceivable to her that he would do such a thing, she had no choice but to think he was dead" (282-283). Readers familiar with Hawthorne will also have noticed other references pointing in his direction. *Fanshawe* (1828) is the title of Hawthorne's earliest work, which features a pair of college friends who are in love with the same woman. Fanshawe, the protagonist, who is the more handsome and studious one of the two friends, "wills" himself to death and the narrator eventually marries the woman. Sophie was Hawthorne's pet name for his wife, Sophia. Considering that Auster named his character's deserted wife after Sophie Hawthorne, one might perhaps conclude that he attributed to Hawthorne a wish to walk out on his wife.

The way in which the "Wakefield"-story is incorporated in *The Locked Room* illustrates Auster's author's comment that each section of the trilogy represents a different stage of awareness of what the story is about. At one point in *The Locked Room*, the trilogy's author, who invented the narrator of the section, steps in and explains why he has told the same story over and over again:

> The entire story comes down to what happened at the end and without the end inside me now, I could not have started this book. The same holds true for the two books that come before it, *City of Glass* and *Ghosts*. These three stories are finally the same story, but each one represents a different stage in my awareness of what it is about. I don't claim to have solved any problems [...]. If words followed, it was only because I had no choice but to accept them, to take them upon myself and go where they wanted me to go. But that does not necessarily make the words important. I have been struggling to say goodbye to something for a long time now, and this struggle is all that really matters. The story is not in the words; it's in the struggle. (346)

Interestingly enough, this awareness also seems to result in a less traumatic ending to the section. While *Ghosts* still rather obliquely suggests that a male author might experience a conflict between his vocation and the demands of the traditional masculine role of providing for a wife and a child, this topic is treated quite openly in *The Locked Room*. In an interview printed in the aptly entitled *The Art of Hunger*, Auster practically admitted an autobiographical component by describing his own situation as a young writer:

> The year before my father died was a particularly bad period. I had a small child, a crumbling marriage, and a minuscule income that amounted to no more than a fraction of what we needed. I became desperate, and for more than a year I wrote almost nothing. I couldn't think of anything but money. (Auster 1993: 290)

This situation is paralleled by the domestic plot of *The Locked Room*. Thus, Sophie informs the narrator that throughout their relationship "Fanshawe had never any regular work, nothing that could be called a real job" (241). The narrator corroborates this by his seemingly off-hand remark about the Fanshawes' apartment "If nothing else, it proved that Fanshawe had not spent his time making money" (238). But, in spite of Fanshawe's initial poverty, after the narrator (a minor writer of journalistic pieces) has successfully placed Fanshawe's manuscript with a publisher, he is able to provide for himself and Fanshawe's family rather nicely by means of the royalties coming in from his friend's literary works. But he soon realizes that there are some drawbacks, too. Thus, he has to admit to himself that he is jealous of Fanshawe's literary accomplishments and he also notices that even though he has no financial problems anymore, he is not writing:

> I no longer had to write articles. I could move on to other things, begin to do the work I had always wanted to do. This was my chance to save myself, and I decided I'd be a fool not to take it.
> More weeks passed. I went into my room every morning, but nothing happened. Theoretically I felt inspired, and whenever I was not working, my head

was filled with ideas. But each time I sat down to put something on paper, my thoughts seemed to vanish. Words died the moment I lifted up my pen. [...] I looked for excuses to explain why I couldn't get going. That was no problem and before long I had come up with a whole litany: the adjustment to married life, the responsibilities of father, my new workroom (which seemed too cramped), the old habit of writing for a deadline, Sophie's body, the sudden windfall – everything. (288)

His unhappiness about his writing not in spite but because of his seemingly perfect domestic situation causes the narrator to engage in self-destructive behavior. Under the guise of working on Fanshawe's biography, he sets out to find Fanshawe. In keeping with the earlier observation that the writer and the detective are the same, he states: "I was a detective, after all, and my job was to look for clues" (332). His search for his alter ego first leads him to Fanshawe's mother. Apparently motivated by an outburst of anger directed at Fanshawe because he has put him in a situation that has become unbearable, the narrator has violent sex with Fanshawe's mother:

> I was fucking out of hatred, and I turned it into an act of violence, grinding away at this woman as though I wanted to pulverize her. [...] I was using her to attack Fanshawe himself. As I came into her the second time – the two of us covered with sweat, groaning like creatures in a nightmare – I finally understood this. I wanted to kill Fanshawe. I wanted Fanshawe to be dead, and I was going to do it. I was going to track him down and kill him. (315)

This strange sex scene, which suggests something akin to murderous homosexual incest (since, in a way, the narrator as Fanshawe's alter ego is both having sex *as* Fanshawe and *with* Fanshawe), drives home the point that the narrator is Fanshawe, but that Fanshawe, who has instrumentalized the narrator to serve as his domestic self, which will provide for wife and child, is losing control over his creation.

After this traumatizing event, the narrator decides to look for Fanshawe in France, to run away from Sophie, and thus to reenact Fanshawe's earlier defection. This time around, Sophie seems to understand what is about to happen and says: "We're coming to the end, my darling, and you don't even know it. You're going to vanish, and I'll never see you again" (337). And at first it really looks as if this is what the narrator is going to do (he acts just like Blue who always meant to call the "ex-future Mrs. Blue"): "I wanted to call Sophie. One day, I even went so far as to walk to the post office and wait in line for the operator, but I didn't go through with it" (341). In France, the narrator relives Fanshawe's life; he talks to his friends and his literary connections and even sleeps with his ex-girlfriend, but he finally understands that he does not need to track down Fanshawe in France because

> Fanshawe was exactly were I was, and he had been there since the beginning. From the moment his letter arrived, I had been struggling to imagine him, to see him as he might have been – but my mind had always conjured a blank. At best, there was one impoverished image: the door of a locked room. Fanshawe alone in that room, condemned to a mythical solitude – living perhaps, breathing perhaps, dreaming God knows what. This room, I now discovered, was located inside my skull. (344-345)

In order to exorcise Fanshawe from his head, the narrator stays drunk for days, has sex with prostitutes and meets a man he keeps calling Fanshawe even after he tells him that his name is Peter Stillman. The narrator, still suffering from writer's block, suddenly fantasizes that Peter Stillman (whom we remember as a character from *City of Glass* who cannot use words very well) has to do with his death, attacks him, and barely survives being beaten up by him. But after all of this, he nevertheless simply returns to Sophie, as he had promised on a postcard he had finally written to her.

Sophie takes him back – but only after living apart from him for almost a year –, they have another baby boy, named Paul, and even though the final showdown with Fanshawe has not come yet, the story seems to proceed to a rather benign ending. This might be due to the fact that the narrator has accepted that a story can be told, even if words fail instead of making perfect sense as they once did to Peter Stillman senior and Blue:

> For when anything can happen – that is the precise moment when words begin to fail. To the degree that Fanshawe became inevitable, that was the degree to which he was no longer there. I learned to accept this. I learned to live with him in the same way I lived with the thought of my own death. Fanshawe himself was not death – but he was like death, and he functioned as a trope of death inside me. (355)

The narrator thus decides to live with the possibility of not being able to say everything precisely in the way he wants to say it and the fact that this compromise is an accomplishment might be one of the central messages of the trilogy.

The Locked Room finally comes to an end when Fanshawe summons the narrator to a last meeting during which he will disclose everything. On April 1 in Boston, Fanshawe finally reveals what the readers already know for the most part – that he was upset that his work was published because "the book was garbage" (363), that he only wanted Sophie to show it to the narrator since he wanted "to find a new husband for her" (364) and that he camped outside the narrator's apartment building for almost a month watching "you and Sophie and the baby" (365) in Wakefieldian manner. He furthermore admits that he – just like the narrator in regard to Fanshawe – was "filled with murderous thoughts" (367) on the subject of the narrator, that he then decided to kill himself instead and "took poison hours ago" (368), but left a red notebook (just like Quinn's) which will explain everything. The narrator reads the notebook – just as Blue read Black's manuscript after finding it – and describes what is on the notebook pages as follows:

> All the words were familiar to me, and yet they seemed to have been put together strangely, as though their final purpose was to cancel each other out [...]. Each sentence erased the sentence before it, each paragraph made the next paragraph impossible. It is odd, then, that the feeling that survives from this notebook is one of great lucidity [...]. These were not the words of a man who regretted anything. He had answered the question by asking another question, and therefore everything remained open, unfinished to be started again. (370)

While this paragraph also seems to describe the experience of reading *The New York Trilogy*, one might still be tempted to conclude that the book's final section provides ways of dealing with some of the problems raised in the two previous sections. Thus, the writer-protagonist of *The Locked Room* has made a tenuous peace with the fact that words fail to convey precise meaning, that there is no language like Stillman senior's "God's language", in which signifier and signified correspond perfectly. Perhaps even more importantly, although the Fanshawe-self disappears at the end of the section, it seems that the narrator of *The Locked Room*, in a way, has finally been able to integrate the "bad, disruptive William Wilson-part" of his split personality. Thus, by returning to Sophie and the boys, he becomes the only *New York Trilogy*-protagonist who is able to return to his former life and live his role as provider and protector. Yet by reverting to a very traditional model of gender relations which still views the male as main provider for the household even though he might feel a strong urge to abscond from this function, Auster ultimately supports masculine hegemony while at the same time subverting the ultra-masculine conventions of the macho-masculinity presented in hard-boiled detective novels.

Even though *The New York Trilogy* does not give its readers ordinary solutions to ordinary detective cases, the "domestic case", the conflict between authorship and domesticity has nevertheless been "solved" – even though the outcome is characterized by an uneasy compromise and a very traditional solution to the demands of masculinity. Auster himself – basically reiterating what the "author" of the trilogy says in *The Locked Room* – reveals in an interview that he has provided more than a fair amount of closure to his perhaps after all not that postmodern trilogy:

> In the end [the narrator] manages to resolve the question for himself. [...] He finally comes to accept his own life, to understand that no matter how bewitched or haunted he is, he has to accept reality as it is, to tolerate the presence of ambiguities within himself. That's what happens to him in relation with Fanshawe. He hasn't slain the dragon, he's let the dragon move into the house

with him. That's why he destroys the notebook in the last scene. (Auster 1993: 272)

Works Cited

Auster, Paul 1990. *The New York Trilogy.* New York: Penguin.

Auster, Paul 1993. *The Art of Hunger.* New York: Penguin.

Barthes, Roland 1990. "The Death of the Author" in David Lodge (ed.). *Modern Criticism and Theory: A Reader.* London: Longman, 166-172.

Foucault, Michel 1986. "What Is an Author?" in Hazard Adams and Leroy Searle (eds.). *Critical Theory Since 1965.* Tallahassee: Florida State University Press, 138-48.

Fiedler, Leslie A. 1982 [1960]. *Love and Death in the American Novel.* New York: Stein and Day.

Grossberg, Lawrence 1996. "Identity and Cultural Studies: Is That All There Is?" in Stuart Hall and Paul Du Gay (eds.). *Questions of Cultural Identity.* London: Sage Publications, 87-107.

Hamilton, Cynthia S. 1987. *Western and Hard-Boiled Detective Fiction in America: From Noon to Midnight.* Basingstoke: Macmillan.

Hall, Stuart 1996. "Introduction: Who Needs 'Identity'?" in Stuart Hall and Paul Du Gay (eds.). *Questions of Cultural Identity.* London: Sage Publications, 1-17.

Kendall, Joshua 1995. "Psychische Zersplitterung in der postmodernen Polis: Kaspar Hauser in Paul Auster's New York Trilogy" in Ulrich Struve (ed.). *Der imaginierte Findling: Studien zur Kaspar-Hauser-Rezeption.* Heidelberg: Winter, 207-223.

Lentricchia, Frank 1988. *Ariel and the Police: Michel Foucault, William James, Wallace Stevens.* Madison: University of Wisconsin Press.

Lewis, Barry 1994. "The Strange Case of Paul Auster." *The Review of Contemporary Fiction* 14 (1994), 53-61.

Miller, Edwin Haviland 1991. *Salem is My Dwelling Place: A Life of Nathaniel Hawthorne.* Iowa City: University of Iowa Press.

Petersen, Alan 1998. *Unmasking the Masculine: "Men" and "Identity" in a Sceptical Age.* London: Sage.

Rowen, Norma 1991. "The Detective in Search of the Lost Tongue." *Critique* 32 (1991), 225-234.

Russell, Alison 1990. "Deconstructing the New York Trilogy: Paul Auster's Anti-Detective Fiction." *Critique* 31 (1990), 71-84.

Patriarchal Poetry: Fathers and Sons in Contemporary Poetry

Peter Middleton

When the American poet Neal Bowers discovered that some of what he considered his best poems had been repeatedly plagiarised and published in leading poetry magazines by a shadowy individual who sometimes answered to the name of David Sumner, he felt that not only his work but his very memories and identity had been robbed (Bowers 1997). He was so traumatised by the experience that he took the unusual step of writing a memoir about the theft of his memories and his search for the plagiarist in the hope that the cathartic narrative might restore his confidence and alert others to the danger from this predator on the poetry scene. The memoir itself is interesting enough as an honest confession of the ambitions, fears and beliefs of a representative contemporary poet, but along the edges of the central narrative a revealing picture also emerges of the wider affective investments and internal workings of the contemporary poetic economy as a whole. Uniting these personal concerns and the field of poetic production is a preoccupation with fathers, for the core of Bowers' anguish was produced by the textual *Entstellung* (a distortion or displacement which Freud said sometimes "resembles a murder" partly because "the difficulty is not in perpetrating the deed, but in getting rid of its traces" [cited in Dickson 1985: 283, 356]) of an autobiographical poem about a father. Freud was talking about his theory that the "mighty prototype of a father", Moses, was murdered by his followers; the poem whose textual murder caused most pain was a poem about Bowers' own father. Bowers' account of this strange affair will serve to introduce the significance of fathers as both bodily progenitors and symbolic prototypes of the engendering of certain key relations between writers, readers and contemporary poetry; this enquiry continues my earlier work on masculinities (Middleton 1992, 1998, 2001).

Bowers was the author of two volumes of poetry, autobiographical free verse lyrics that employ memory as the basis of brief narrative episodes and emotional cruxes, usually end on a rising note of insight even if the concluding affect is downbeat (an effect which can reinforce the impression of sincerity). Like many dedicated poets, he was earning his living by teaching creative writing, although in his case at a university (Iowa) which pioneered the now ubiquitous poetry workshop, when in January 1992 a friend told him that another author appeared to be republishing slightly altered versions of his poems in magazines, under a different name. A poem in memory of his father and published in the September 1990 issue of *Poetry*, "Tenth-year Elegy", had been given a cosmetic makeover and then reprinted under the title "Someone Forgotten" and under the name of David Sumner. Here are the opening lines of the two poems:

SOMEONE FORGOTTEN
He is too heavy and careless, my father
always leaving me at rest-stops, coffee shops,
some wide spot in the road. I come out,
rubbing my hands on my pants or levitating
two foam cups of coffee, and I can't find him
anywhere, that beat-up Ford gone.
                                        David Sumner
TENTH-YEAR ELEGY
Careless man, my father,
always leaving me at rest-stops,
coffee shops, some wide spot in the road.
I come out, rubbing my hands on my pants
or levitating two foam cups of coffee,
and can't find him anywhere,
those banged-up fenders gone.
                    (Bowers 1997: 27-28)

"The name on it was David Sumner, and it had been published in the December 1991 *Mankato Poetry Review*, but it was my poem" (Bowers 1997: 26). Initially he intended to dismiss the whole incident as unimportant, a course of action urged on him by many friends, advisors, and poets, even when later he discovered a whole series of plagiarisms by the same man – wasn't this a postmodern thing, perhaps even improving the poem a little – but "the poem itself wouldn't let me do that" (Bowers 1997: 30). It is soon clear to the reader that Bowers, far from thinking the incident unimportant, was profoundly upset by it, and not consoled even when Mark Strand, a much more famous poet, also plagiarised by Sumner, insisted that the whole business was trivial (as did his editor at Knopf). Why wouldn't the poem let him shrug it off?

Bowers explains that he was severely disoriented by seeing his work appropriated by someone else, and this was what helped drive his search for the culprit and to write an account of the affair. Once when he unexpectedly encountered one of the plagiarised texts he felt himself rendered uncanny by what felt like a doubling of identity. "I was stupefied to turn the page while reading for enjoyment and see my own face, slightly distorted, looking back," he reports, adding that it was an experience which reminded him of waking at night and seeing his own face unexpectedly in a mirror, a face that was his "but changed [...] empty of personality" (Bowers 1997: 52). Freud's essay on "The Uncanny" obviously provided a useful heuristic for interpreting the associations produced by these experiences, giving voice to the fear of murder by textual distortion, but the deeper source of this reaction remains unclear. Anger, outrage, and disgust seem more likely responses than evacuation of identity, so what was it that made the poet feel so victimised? A clue appears when Bowers insists that the worst damage to his identity was done by plagiarism of "Tenth Year Elegy", the poem in memory of his own father: "The poem was a bittersweet bloom I planted on my father's grave. The thief dug it up, pruned it to his liking, and damaged the roots in the process. Worse, he replanted it in the soil mounded over my father and pretended the loss was his" (Bowers 1997: 30). Bowers refers to the "ground" from which the poem arose as the reason for his intense reaction to the affair, and therefore one likely contemporary interpretation of this would be that the memories on which the poem is built are the foundations of the author's identity. Damage them and the whole construction of self might crumble. According to the sociologist Anthony Giddens, the answer to a masculinised version of Freud's infamous "What do men want?" is that although many men think they want recognition from other men in the form of material reward, what they really need, and ought therefore to want, is to have their identities validated. This is not a passive process. Men themselves have to engage in a "reflexive project of self" which "involves an emotional reconstruction of the past in order to project a coherent narrative towards the future" (Giddens 1992: 60). What men ought to want is memories capable of sustaining their identity in the face of others. Bowers was trying to do this, and yet instead of recognition along came a thief who deconstructed his past by stealing his poetic memory, and left him unable to project "a coherent narrative into the future". His poem had after all mapped out a future after his father's death in which he had "settled", "built a house" and planted trees in whose branches he could sometimes hear in the rustling wind the sound of a highway like that place where he used to meet his father. He had, in psychoanalytic terms which echo distantly in the poem, successfully introjected his father. The plagiarist's appropriation of the phrases "settled", "built a house" and the final line about the wind, appear to Bowers to deconstruct this formation of identity.

The key to his pathological emotional reaction to the plagiarism lies in the effects on his identity of the plagiarism, which is particularly evident in the use of the metaphoric discourse of flowers, graves, exhumations and reburials to project an imaginary shadow re-enactment of the funeral rites for Bowers' father from the point of view of the usurping son, Sumner. This fantasy should give us pause, given that publication of a poem has certain dissimilarities from the privacy of a family funeral. The poem/anthos is unlike the flowers on a grave, or private prayers for the dead, because it is intended to be dug up from the site of authorship, published in anthologies (of the poet's work or as in a magazine, of the work of a number of poets) and then displaced into the minds and emotions of strangers. The poem I shall discuss later, Seamus Heaney's "Digging", also a poem about a father, even proposes a homology between acts of digging, writing, and publication. Isn't there always a risk, indeed even an expectation, that readers will pick the flower of the poem, and place it on the graves of their own dead fathers, especially those metaphoric fathers whose loss might be felt in many areas of a life, through an ordinary process of empathetic identification as they read? The plagiarist had of course done more than this, he had pretended to be the son to Bowers' father, because the reference to a father in "Tenth Year Elegy", as in so much other contemporary poetry, is intended to be read as a true statement of paternity. The onetime living existence and continuing memory of an actual man who helped engender the poet son guarantees the statements about him made by his son. When the plagiarist affixes his own name to a slightly altered version he is murdering Bowers the poet by erasing the kinship on which Neal Bowers depends for his own identity as man and poet, leaving him an uncanny figure, a ghost of himself.

Even so, we might ask why this should elicit such an intense reaction. Bowers had other father poems which were not plagiarised – there are several in *Night Vision* (Bowers 1992) in some of which his mother is also mentioned. Couldn't these suffice as an anchor to withstand the plagiarising force dislodging his identity? One of them, "Dead Weight," suggests why not. It begins: "My father lifted all his life – / limbs, stumps, loads of dirt [...] I finished the job he started [...] I brought what I could carry/ these words piled here" (Bowers 1992: 19). Without the father as a guarantor of this tropology of poetic transmission on which the legitimacy of the public voice of the poet rests, there would, according to this poet, be no words "piled here". The Bowers Affair highlights the significance of paternal transmission for contemporary poetry, suggesting that a male poet's identity can be secured by a narrative of filiation that grounds the authority of the author to speak as a poet. The founding gesture in the Bowers case takes the form of what has been called a familial elegy to a father, and absolutely relies on a reader's confidence in its authenticity.

In the remainder of this paper I shall investigate the issues raised by Bowers' account of the horrors of plagiarism. What I shall show is that fathers are not just one more autobiographical subject to add to the wealth of possible topics; they play a central role in the legitimation of the personal lyric, and they do this within a highly contested field. Father poems need to be read also as contributors to a larger genre of parent poems and therefore as participants in a gender politics defined by both patriarchy and to a lesser extent by its challenges from feminism and occasionally, the men's movement. More tentatively I shall suggest that the treatment of fathers in contemporary poetry can be read back into contemporary culture as a diagnosis of contemporary ideologies of paternity. Throughout the discussion I shall emphasise that this poetry needs to be treated as part of a complex economy of reception, whose interpretative investments are cognitive, affective, and interdependent on many different institutions including the academy, publishing, the family and the market. This is why, tempting as it is to psychoanalyse the poems – father figures, Oedipally murderous textualities, and questions of origin all beckon to Freud – it cannot be the sole reason why psychoanalysis is both central and inappropriate as a key interpretative method. These poets, like Bowers when he analyses his experience through unacknowledged reference to Freud, know their Oedipal complexes, castration anxiety and names of the father, extremely well, and will use psychoanalytic allusion as part of their cultural poetics. What is needed (but lies beyond the scope of this paper) is a psychoanalytic reading of the appropriation of psychoanalysis in contemporary poetry's economy. Here I shall focus on the autobiographical turn in contemporary poetry and its elicitation of tropes of parenthood, before offering a comparison of a nineteenth-century father poem with a conventional late twentieth century example, and then contrasting the significance of fathers in the work of poets who have questioned expressivism and voice in contemporary poetry.

The market penetration of the father poem is evoked by the first stanza of a poem by Mark Vinz, "Passages":

> The first poem in the book
> I just happen to open
> is about a dead father–
> how many like it I've read
> before I knew what they meant.
> And now, every book I pick up
> has one of those poems in it–
> every book in every room.
> (originally from *Mixed Blessings* [Spoon River Poetry Press, 1989], cited in Moramarco/Zolynas 1992: 49).

Recall that "stanza" is etymologically connected with words for "room" and "dwelling", and note that the second, final stanza recalls his father's anxious need as an old man to have his son in the room with him, a situation in which his father hated his son for the dependency he felt, and the haunting's emotional roots become obvious. Yet the exaggeration still finds considerable confirmation across the range of contemporary poetry, as if patriarchy were internal to the structures of poetic textuality. It can indeed seem as if almost every book of poems has a poem about the poet's father, or, although Vinz doesn't say so, the poet's mother. Many of the best known poems of the past three decades are poems about mothers and fathers. Sylvia Plath's "Daddy", Allen Ginsberg's "Kaddish", Robert Lowell's *Life Studies*, Seamus Heaney's "Digging", Tony Harrison's *The School of Eloquence*, and poems by Sharon Olds, Charles Olson, Denise Levertov, Robert Duncan and Susan Howe, have helped define the contours of post-war poetry, its divisions and its developments, and their common interest in parents and filiation is all the more striking because these poets have little in common otherwise – they belong to different schools, classes, genders, sexualities, nationalities and generations.

Mark Vinz's poem appears in *Men of Our Time: An Anthology of Male Poetry in Contemporary America* (Moramarco/Zolynas 1992), and is thematically located with thirty six other poems about "Sons Seeing Fathers", a context that almost ironises its attempt at seriousness. The majority of the poems about fathers are elegiac variations on Simon Ortiz's bare emotional statement, "I miss my father tonight" ("My father's song", originally from *A Good Journey* [University of Arizona Press, 1985], cited in Moramarco/Zolynas 1992: 7). Even the living fathers, like Robert Creeley's in his memory of watching an ambulance take away his father to die when he was a small boy, are near death, or laid out like Joe David Bellamy's on the operating table with a heart that is only just "still undulating" ready for the surgeon's knife ("Memory, 1930", originally from *Mirrors* [New York: New Directions, 1985] and "Opening Up", from *The Frozen Sea* [Orchises, 1988], cited in Moramarco/Zolynas 1992: 35, 68). The preponderance of well-known names in this section supports the explicit claim in the introduction that "the contemporary male poet who hasn't written a poem about his father is rare."

Charles Olson, a poet whose preoccupation with his own father led the critic Andrew Ross to conclude that "a family romance is writ very large in Olson's work," and that he therefore oscillates between "the desire to owe everything or nothing to the father," and suppress the feminine, certainly explains his own filial poetics as an ethical act of self-fashioning through a familial historicism, and claims this imperative as an important affinity with other poets (Ross 1986: 130-131). To be a poet today, he implies, you have to write about parents:

> What strikes me [...] is, the depth to which the parents who live in us (they are not the same) are our definers. And that the true work of each of us is to find out the true lineaments of ourselves by facing up to the primal features of these founders who lie buried in us – that this is us, the Double-Backed Beast. (Olson 1974: 39)

Sex ("the Double-Backed Beast"), death, and origins, commingle in these metaphorical discourses of the face and habitation that sustain the paradox of parents who are both living and dead, because they have come to be a dominant tropology for the representation of the past. Michele Roberts uses an umbilical metaphor that neatly combines these issues in a poem which argues that the parent within must be persuaded to move out:

> this women's work is thrifty and grim:
> learning to save myself, learning to live
> alone through the long winter nights
> means so much unknotting, unknitting

unravelling, untying the mother-cord
– so much undoing.
("Poem on St Valentine's Day", Roberts 1986: 85)

Roberts and Olson write as if the parent poem has become the necessary precondition for the construction of an autonomous and self-conscious individuality capable of creating poetry. Their convergence on this belief despite the radical difference between their British feminist and Black Mountain poetics exemplifies the way this preoccupation with the composition of detailed poems about one's parents crosses many boundaries. Despite sometimes antagonistic poetics, most authors of parent poems share David Dabydeen's conviction that "the ancestors curl and dry to scrolls of parchment./ They lie like texts/ Waiting to be written by the children" ("Coolie Odyssey", Dabydeen 1994: 73). Individual popular successes like those by Plath, Ginsberg, Lowell, Heaney, Harrison and Olds, are only a handful of the enormous number of post-Freudian parent poems now in circulation which exceed critical and canonical recognition. The warning implicit in Dabydeen's ambiguous phrase, "they lie like texts", that these parental figures, however circumstantially authentic, may also be rhetorical figures in a textual mortuary ritual whose cultural purposes extend beyond mere sharing of personal memories, has gone largely unexplored, and even it is noticed in a single writer, it is usually treated as Ross does, as an occasion for psychoanalytic biography. Judging by the critical indifference to the topos, its fundamental preoccupation must now seem so self-evidently reasonable that its explosive emergence in the nineteen-fifties, and continual reappearance in almost every new book of poetry, needs no explanation.

The filiative topos is now so familiar to readers of contemporary poetry that its novelty is easy to forget: very few poems about parents were ever written before the Second World War. Literary critics who have noticed this new phenomenon have either taken it for granted as a confirmation of psychoanalytic theory, or explained it in terms of political and social changes in the significance of filiation. Alicia Ostriker, for example, treats the daughter's poem about a mother as an inevitable consequence of the politics of feminism, since the mother-daughter bond is a "primary erotic relationship" in which the mother's influence over the daughter poet still "seems infinite" and therefore constitutes the core of femininity with which feminism must reckon (Ostriker 1987: 179). A woman cannot fully access her powers as a poet until she has successfully negotiated a viable co-existence with the mother's power because the mother-child relationship inaugurates individual history, an "emotion-laden intimacy antedating all others" (Ostriker 1987: 179). This redemptive model of poetic transmission makes the writing of such self-transforming poems seem inevitable: "Rather than Oedipus and Laius at the crossroads, the model among women writers, critics as well as poets, is Demeter and Kore; except that it is the daughter who descends to Hades, step by step, to retrieve and revive a mother who has been raped, or perhaps seduced, by a powerful male god. For as the mother returns to earth, the daughter expects to blossom" (Ostriker 1987: 16). In this archetypical scenario, to write about a mother is to challenge a father's influence, and equally, by implication, a man's poem about his father may well be read as an affirmation of patriarchal sovereignty.

Feminism might help explain women poet's interests, but it would be much harder to claim that a similar radical sexual politics was motivating men poets, whose poems on fathers are at least as common, if not more so, than the poems by women poets about their mothers. The men critics who have noticed the new genre of father poems, have like Ostriker, nonetheless tried to explain the popularity of the father poem written by a man as a function of the self-evident importance of parents in our dominant cultural narratives of identity. Robert Peters believes that although "the wealth of poems on fathers is amazing" at first glance, it is an inevitable consequence of the hegemony of the "ego-poem or first-person poem" in contemporary poetry (Peters 1989: 134). His analysis of the causal relation is disappointing however, because it relies on his fundamental claim that the hegemony of the first person anecdotal narrative exemplifying a common truth or ethical insight within contemporary verse (which accounts for most of the poems in Neal Bowers' collection *Night Vision*, for example) means that these poems categorise themselves not by their form, ontology or rhetorical address, but quite simply by their theme or topos. There are "wise child poems", "nuclear poems", "prison poems", "celebrity poems" as well as the mother and father poems. Contemporary poets writing in the autobiographical mode inevitably choose pressure points in the narratives of their lives, and not suprisingly many of these are familial: in the anthology where Vinz's poem appeared it is the moment when the son and his mother take money out of the newly dead father's wallet to pay for the transport of his body back to the funeral, or the moment of discovery of a briefcase or shoebox of treasures that belonged to the newly deceased father (Raymond Carver, "My Dad's Wallet", originally from *Where Water Comes Together With Other Water* [New York: Random House, 1985]; Ronald Wallace, "Off the Record", originally from *The Makings of Happiness* [Pittsburgh: University of Pittsburgh Press, 1991]; Mark Rudman, "The Shoebox", originally from *The Nowhere Steps* [Sheep Meadow Press, 1990], cited in Moramarco/Zolynas 1992: 83, 54, 85). The problem with this explanation is that it overlooks the role of authenticity as a sign of sincerity (the issue which so exercised Bowers) and by focussing on classification it misses the degree to which themes determine not just poetic forms but poetic economies too.

Peters' theory has a counterpart in Blake Morrison's flattering theory that these are explicitly poems of "filiation", a theory which also assumes that fathers are now an obvious theme for poetry, but at least offers a tentative explanation for this (Morrison 1987: 216). He observes that: "no other poetic generation one can think of has *collectively* been so obsessed with parents as the current one", a comment that is particularly revealing because of its suggestion that social fantasy may play a part in its ubiquity. His chosen sample of writers of love poems to fathers is unconvincingly small: Tony Harrison, Seamus Heaney, Hugo Williams, Craig Raine, James Fenton, Paul Muldoon, Andrew Motion and Michael Hoffman, form a conservative tendency in contemporary British poetry with which Morrison is closely identified. The idea that this is a generation which respects the contribution to lasting peace made by fathers who fought in the second world war is also unpersuasive. Piety and respect are not always present in the poems by the authors he mentions, and if we look further afield, even to an earnest collection like *Men of Our Time*, which chooses poems that explicitly strive for understanding and reconciliation with fathers, anger and disgust frequently overwhelm the good intentions. Peter Spiro's father who "up-chucked the boiling black scummy stuff/ from his belly all over me because he/ wanted to show me/ what a young man's life was really worth", represents a fairly frequent trace of the negativity of the father-son relation (Peter Spiro, "He Wanted to Show Me", not previously published). Even Robert Bly who has been making a career out of encouraging men to rediscover an effaced manhood, struggles throughout his poem with condemnation for the way his father used to humiliate him, before he can reach at the end of the poem a point of reconciliation based on identification, and this is still somewhat double-edged: "He never phrased/ what he desired/ and I am/ his son" (Robert Bly, "My Father at 85", originally from *The Best American Poetry 1989* [New York: Macmillan, 1989], cited in Moramarco/Zolynas 1992: 44, 67). Bly's very act of phrasing, the poem itself, is therefore both a failed phrasing because it does not acknowledge desire (to adore/murder the father perhaps), and successful insofar as a poem results and buries his father's reticence within itself, and thereby overcomes the father. Morrison's own admission that some of these poets express Oedipal rage partially undermines his own thesis (and demonstrates the risks of using psychoanalysis, since filial piety and Oedipal rivalry belong to dissonant discourses), and ignores the degree to which these are prototypes of paternity. As bell hooks observes in a discussion of the treatment of black characters in Hollywood movies, our "white supremacist capitalist patriarchy" is frequently represented in popular culture as a white daddy who must be pleased, and poetry is no exception (hooks 1995: 99). Fathers in poetry represent a cultural authority derived from discourses of religion, law, nation and morality. In a poem published in the same year as the volume that did most to inaugurate the parent poem, Robert Lowell's *Life Studies* (1959), the poet John Logan goes to meet the ageing William Carlos Williams, and twice names him a "poet father" in a gesture which underlines the degree to which we need to look beyond family history to understand the significance even of biological fathers in contemporary poetry: "And when we visited a poet father/ we rode to Jersey on a motor scooter... That old father was so mellow and generous – /easy to pain,/ white, open and at peace, and of good taste,/ like his Rutherford house" (John Logan, "A trip to four or five towns", cited in Strand 1969: 212). It is the intersection between cultural authority and the demands of poetic authenticity and legitimation in the father poem, which requires investigation. The father poem is overdetermined, the outcome of at least four prevalent cultural investments which all converge to create the ideal conditions for its continued popularity. The most evident is the belief that, in the words of the theatre director Richard Eyre: "our parents cast long shadows over our lives [...] we carry them within us all our lives." It has become a truism that, in the words of Carolyn Steedman, the nineteenth-century discovery that "the core of an individual's psychic identity was his or her lost past, or childhood," has now become a commonplace, and allied to the belief that this past is determined by parental cathexes (Steedman 1995: 4). Freud played a central role in the consolidation of this nineteenth-century idea which has become an element of many varieties of psychotherapy and even more importantly, childcare advice, to the point where it is sometimes hard to recognise the possibility that other situations, phenomenologies and lived temporalities (for example: childhood peer pressure, adult social and sexual relations, or social structures of feeling and empathy) might also determine psychic identities, and that interiority itself may be more dependent on the textuality of memory than we admit. The second factor in the establishment of the parent poem is its role as elegy. A scarcity of public opportunities for collective mourning (which can become a social pathology when a figure like Kennedy or Diana is killed), and in particular the demise of the formal poetic elegy, has led to the popularity of quasi-elegiac poems which can be sites of empathic mourning, as well as acts of burial of genitive powers, appropriated by readers for their own rituals of grief directed at people whose faces can mask those provided by the poet. A third factor is the problem of finding cultural authority for the public speech of the expressive lyric. The autobiographical turn in a poetry already abandoning the cultural authority of metrical form left it badly in need of means to justify its relevance as more than the personal expression of a mere singular prejudice which also renders largely useless the formerly important, if often invisible, cultural authority of recognisable modalities of literary writing (the socialised intimacy of the sonnet, the civic couplet, the symbolist invocation, or the modernist appeal to historical parallels with the present). The familial narrative of psychic origins and development fills the gap; it is metonymic of the emergence of authorised speech itself by rehearsing the story of how the poetic self came to poetry. The voice of the poem, represents the body of the poet, which in turn was engendered by the parent, whose invocation amounts to a reminder of the way these words of the poem came into being. Repetition of the topos helps affirm commonality in the midst of difference signified by the autobiographical detail of identity (think of the blue dots on Robert Lowell's father's curtains, or the hot water bottle that Tony Harrison's father goes on placing on his dead wife's side of the bed) ("Father's Bedroom" in Lowell 1959: 89; "Long Distance" in Harrison 1984: 134). Finally, these poems represent a renewal of bonds with the past, bonds between individual and cultural memory severely disrupted by the Second World War and the Holocaust, adding to the discontinuities created by slavery, genocide of indigenous peoples, industrialisation, social mobility, and rapid transformations of the institutions and technologies of intimacy. The poem's autobiographical subject's self-display of articulate record signifies individual subjectivity, while the parent signifies history, and the poem is a sewing machine that will demonstrate the suture of subject and temporality in the cloth of history.

This familial trope for history has been most studied by feminist writers. Ostriker cites three lines of a poem by June Jordan, in which, according to Ostriker, the poet's acknowledgement of her mother's influence enables to her to take the difficult step of speaking for other African American women: "help me/ turn the face of history/ *to your face*" ("Getting Down to Get Over", *Things That I Do in the Dark* [New York: Random House, 1977], cited in Ostriker 1987: 190). The poem is not just about her mother, however, it is very much a family romance which includes father too, and these concluding lines are part of an extended elegiac plea to her mother: "turn/ my mother/ turn/ the face of history/ to your own/ and please be smilin/ if you can/ be smilin/ at the family/ and be/ like you/ teach me to survive my/ momma/ teach me how to hold a new life/ momma/ help me/ turn the face of history/ to your face." The Latin etymology of "verse" is "turn", and thus the short lines saying "turn" are so self-reflexive they are completely self-absorptive, as the verse names its defining activity over and over, and asks the introjected mother to facilitate the action of verse. Within this extreme emphasis on its poeticality's engenderment by the mother, another ambiguity begins to play itself out, as the poem first appears to ask her mother to face up to history, to dialogue with it, as if persuading Walter Benjamin's angel to look forwards for once, and then, as the poem repeats the formulation, seems to say that history could be made to appear in the guise of her mother – instead of living outside the history of the hegemonic white world, this newly inclusive history could wear her mother's physiognomy. Like the representation of interiority by childhood, this personification of history has a longer history. The immediate source for the influence of this feminist trope was Virginia Woolf's much quoted assertion about women writers, "we think back through our mothers." Influential theories of phenomenology and hermeneutics had also given history a face. Maurice Merleau-Ponty's discussion of time in *Phenomenology of Perception* (1945) for example, presents what he claims is the commonplace perception of time in similar terms: "Everyone talks about Time, not as the zoologist talks about the dog or the horse, using these as collective nouns, but using it as a proper noun. Sometimes it is even personified. Everyone thinks that here is a single, concrete being, wholly present in each of its manifestations, as is a man in each of his spoken words" (Merleau-Ponty 1989: 421). Instead of dismissing the doxa, Merleau-Ponty finds an acceptable simplification of the actuality in its treatment of time as a kind of person, because he borrows Heidegger's conception of time as a dimension of subjectivity itself, rather than a condition of the world external to subjects: "We must understand time as the subject and the subject as time" (Merleau-Ponty 1989: 422). What we witness in the father poems is a performative engendering of history as masculine subjectivity.

The trope that history ought be like mother has, according to Jane Gallop, been widely used by feminists, precisely in order to wipe the grin off the patriarchal face that usually stares back from the past. She cites a resonant aphorism by Joyce Kegan Gardiner – "history is like mother: if we don't understand her, we are doomed to repeat her" – that cleverly reformulates George Santayana's epigram – "those who do not remember the past are condemned to repeat it" – as a challenge to existing patriarchal canons and authorities made by reversing the gender of patriarchal tropes like those mentioned by bell hooks, used to describe social and historical process. Such a reversal worries Gallop, however, because "history is also not like mother" (Gallop 1992: 239). Institutions like higher education are not structured like families, and the maternal trope too readily invokes the stereotype of self-effacing care on which traditional motherhood rested. In fact, Gardiner herself is acutely aware of the power of these "paradigms" and argues that their power to influence lives unthinkingly would be diminished if the relationship between gender and history was made explicit. This suggests a question for the father poem: to what extent do specific poems that use this paternal tropology resist the recidivism of the stereotype or simply work to promulgate the ideologies against which Jordan, Gallop, Gardiner and other feminists continue to fight? Is the contemporary father poem the attempt by threatened masculinities to retain control over the engendering of the present by history?

As I said earlier, the answers to questions about fathers, memory and history in contemporary poetry might all seem to lie in psychoanalytic theory, but I believe that to interpret the poems directly according to Freudian, Kleinian, or Lacanian models would miss the mediating roles of literary institutions, reception networks, and above all, the dominant knowledge economy. Today's reader puts the poem on the couch, and finds primal scenes, Oedipal romances, subjectivity in process, libidinal economies, castration anxiety, and phallic signifiers at work in it, and therefore the poem prepares confessions, resistances, lures of jargon and hints of symptom in anticipation of this analytic encounter with the knowing (but not too knowing) reader.

Harold Bloom constructed an entire theory of literary history along such lines out of such poetic signs. John Logan's endearing poem "A trip to four or five towns", for example, typifies the willingness of many contemporary poems to employ parental tropes for the origins of poetic vocation. Bloom's algorithm of poetic intertextuality envisages poetic identity-formation through just such actual and idealised parental relations:

> Just as we can never embrace (sexually or otherwise) a single person, but embrace the whole of her or his family romance, so we can never read a poet without reading the whole of his or her family romance as poet. [...] True poetic history is the story of how poets as poets have suffered other poets, just as any true biography is the story of how anyone suffered his own family – or his own displacement of family into lovers and friends. (Bloom 1973: 23)

This confidence about the origins of identity reiterates the dominant ideology of individuality, and so we might speculate that what Bloom has done is to retroject the postmodern ideology into the history of poetry because he is writing within the same hermeneutic circle as the contemporary poet and reader. It is not Milton, Keats and Yeats who perceive history as a struggle with fathers; it is contemporary poets working within an ideological sedimentation of psychoanalysis who do so, and who then backproject a history which Bloom reads as an almost universal literary history. To employ psychoanalytic theory to read the contemporary poem without attending to the poem's own relation to the discourses of theory is to revolve frictionlessly within it; to find an anxiety of Oedipal influence in the prior history of poetry is to elide historicity. In the first case the poem simply drops out of the analysis as the mere medium for the transmission of contemporary psychological ideology and in the second the absence of this ideology in earlier poetry is read as the anxiety which the theory attempts to explain. Bloom's theory is not his alone by any means. Many recent anthologies present the history of poetry as if it culminated in the parental poem (the most striking and influential being *The Norton Anthology of Poetry: Fourth Edition*, where two of the three final poems are constructed around memories of a father and a mother). Although the final poem is not about parents, its last word, and therefore the last word in the anthology, is "home" (Li-Young Lee, "Persimmons", and Cynthia Zarin, "The Ant Hill", cited in Ferguson/Salter/Stallworthy 1996: 1878-1882). Psychoanalytic ideas are background knowledge; to use psychoanalytic methods to study contemporary poetry one would need to psychoanalyse the use of psychoanalysis reflexively, and consider both composition and reception.

A contrast between a poem written when father poems were rare, and the present, and a contemporary poem which helped give further impetus to the new genre (and underwrites Bowers' poem "Dead Weight") will give us a measure of what is actually at work in the new genre, and how we might begin to conceptualise the practices of gender within it. Matthew Arnold's poem "Rugby Chapel" (1857) writes about his father, Thomas Arnold, the founder of Rugby School, as if it were difficult to distinguish his father from the prototypical heavenly father, and memorially assigns traits to his father which are traditionally attributed to the Christian God via paternal metaphors (Arnold 1965: 444). This father was a source of light, like the sun, even in dark Novembers: "seasons impaired not the ray/ Of thy buoyant cheerfulness clear." He was also able to protect others from the sun, like "a mighty oak", and give them shelter, and most telling, he was "a faithful shepherd", echoing the Twenty-Third Psalm's well-known words: "the Lord is my shepherd". Recalling Thomas Arnold's love of hill-walking, life's journey is represented as a particularly difficult climb in the Lake District, and his father as combining the qualities of guide and mountain rescue. This imagery goes through three stages: firstly Matthew Arnold's own sense of the demands of a lived life as similar to the difficulties of following an indistinct trail; then memories of his father on mountain walks caring for all the walkers equally; and finally a general image of humanity's history: "See! In the rocks of the world/ Marches the host of mankind" (imagery that also borrows from *Exodus*). The cumulative judgement is that his father was a hero in the Moses mould, and this is important to Arnold, because through knowing his father's heroism he can believe that the historical accounts of other great heroic figures are also to be believed. By possessing these exceptional qualities, his father was not only deserving of this filial poetic tribute, he also made it possible to maintain links with the past. More riskily, and a little uneasily, and covering his awareness of the danger of blasphemy with overstatement, he says that the ordinary phrase, "servant of God", doesn't fit his father, who was, like other heroic figures, more a son of God ("because/ Not as servants ye knew/ Your Father's innermost mind"), and the effect is to further strengthen the idea that fatherhood is the link to the divine, and the mode whereby consciousness (at its best) is transmitted. Arnold senior knew his father, God's, mind, and Matthew knows his father's mind, and all this is possible, it is implied, because of the power of fatherhood exemplified by God the Father.

Fatherhood therefore, is not imagined as an origin in the sense that it functions for the late twentieth century writer who, as we shall see, will claim poetic authority just so much as he is able to portray himself as the heir to an actual father whose historicity will be attested to by special authentic details. This fatherhood is a quality that has to be achieved (by heroic struggle), or as it were, reached in order to be manifested within a mortal man, and remains transhistorical, a condition that makes life and poetry possible. The cumulative effect of this merging of individuality in the illumination of the patriarchal sublime of the Christian God not only consoles the writer that his father's fatherhood has been reabsorbed into the master pattern, it enables Arnold to give the afterlife more substance than if, like a late twentieth century poet, he had memorialised those distinctively unique signatures of personality which death would erase (like Bowers' father's constant lifting of things). Arnold's father's soul may even retain the power of self-consciousness in "some far-shining sphere,/ Conscious or not of the past" – the very suggestion that he might be still conscious emphasises just how much a continuity of moral, and even psychic, identity is imagined – or may live in a more ineffably metaphysical style, "in the sounding labour-house vast/ Of being." By rhyming "past" with "vast", Arnold places his father in the depths, the soundings of history. The "sounding labour-house", a noisy, sonorous laboratory of being, the place where being is studied, created, analysed, is in one sense of this deeply ambiguous line, sound itself, and the poetry which relies on sound. Here in this poem, what is best in his father is a medium in which he can potentially participate because fatherhood tied his father to God and hence to immanence in sound and meaning – a clever elegiac assertion of continuity in the face of death.

Comparison with a widely celebrated poem by Seamus Heaney, in which the contemporary also acknowledges the significance of his father for his own career, will show that fathers have come to have a quite different valence for men poets today. Now they represent origins as a source of legitimation, manliness, the past and its overcoming.

In the opening of his lecture to the Royal Society of Literature in 1974, "Feeling into Words", Heaney almost but not quite says that it was by writing a poem about his father that he finally became a fully fledged poet. He begins by citing Wordsworth's lines from *The Prelude* where Wordsworth refers to the "hiding places of [his] power", those sites of memory which are only sporadically open to his adult self, and explains that his purpose in writing is to ensure the effective memorialisation of such occasions in the social memory: to "enshrine the spirit of the past/ for future restoration" (Heaney 1980: 41). This, says Heaney, is his own aim also, and is what makes his successful poems work. He aims to write a poetry which is divinatory, capable of both individual and collective self-reflection, and above all capable of digging up the past and memorialising it. A poem is like a small piece of material culture discovered on an archaeological dig, except that its significance is not solely dependent on the glory of the "buried city" from which it came because unlike an inanimate artefact it is capable of growth, like a plant. In this unburying of the past represented by the new growth, we can recognise the familiar trope of the elegist, who finds substitutions for the dead in the renewing growth of flowers and trees; and the archaeological metonym allows him to invoke a popular idea of archaeology as the simple act of bringing to the surface the objects of the past, which effectively treats it as if it were merely data ready for interpretation. Poetry is like archaeology because it too maintains an open route to the past in its "attempt to define and interpret the present by bringing it into significant relationship with the past" (Heaney 1980: 60). Then Heaney offers a history of his development as a poet which takes this archaeological metaphor further. Although he had been writing poetry for a couple of years, it was only when he wrote the poem "Digging", that he had finally managed to produce an authentic poem: "where I thought my *feel* had got into words." In the poem, Heaney sets a scene in which he is indoors with a pen in his hand, and hears the sound of a spade going into the ground, looks out and sees his father's "straining rump" as he digs in a flowerbed. This prompts a Proustian, involuntary memory of his father twenty years before, when the poet was a boy, digging potatoes, and then another image of his grandfather digging peat. From these recharged engrams the poem infers a dilemma of paternal transmission – how can the poet inherit the fathers' power to sustain the world by providing heat, light and food, if he does not know how to use the implement necessary to dig with? Does he lack their phallic mastery, having become feminised? David Kennedy's recent article on Tony Harrison and Douglas Dunn, argues that a negotiation with the construction of conventional masculinities has been as necessary a part of their development, as the widely noticed issue of class relations for writers whose profession takes them away from their working class history: "the masculinity personified and literally embodied by Harrison's father and other working-class men is found to be a problematic patrimony" (Kennedy 2000: 119). To become a poet it may be necessary to acknowledge the femininity of writing which (as in Heaney's poem) belongs to the indoor domestic space. In "Digging" the poet takes milk, a powerful symbol of feminine nurture (think of how important it is to the opening of James Joyce's *Ulysses* that it is an old woman who brings the milk to the tower for Stephen and his friends), to his grandfather, in what is a hint at how his poetry is needed to nurture these men like his grandfather. But the most striking feature of the poem is a certain implicit crudity in the image, already cited, of his father bending over and exposing his bottom to the gaze of his son who is holding up a phallic pen. It is a poet's gesture of male dominance, and in being so, a reaffirmation of what Kennedy reminds us is a largely unchallenged binary opposition of conventional masculinity and femininity that still dominates our literary histories of postwar poetry: "Dunn and Harrison, like their immediate contemporary Seamus Heaney, accept conventional masculinity and femininity as rigid but entirely natural categories with measurable accountabilities and performativities and their work naturalises the homophobia attendant upon this binary" (Kennedy 2000: 133). The engendering of the poet's voice entails an endorsement of stereotypical masculine traits.

Although famous as a poem about the relation between working class fathers and sons who move into the middle class as writer intellectuals, Heaney side-steps this class-based family romance in his lecture, as if this theme were now too well-known to bear repetition, and perhaps also because he assumes that its mechanisms are best not discussed, and instead reflects on the degree to which the poem is an act of cultural transmission of local wisdom. Memory, individual and social, is the site of a successful transmission of patrimony and cultural knowledge. He says that the idea of contrasting pen and spade derives from a proverb used to encourage him and other schoolchildren to gain an education that would take them out of the sphere of manual work: "the pen's lighter than the spade". Another source was a ditty with a double meaning attributed to digging – the good digger is the phallic male, and therefore the good writer is also phallic. By locating the poem's thematics in Irish oral tradition he also competitively trumps the ready psychoanalytic interpretation of this access of the power to write in Oedipal terms. Just as Thomas Arnold's heroic leadership gave his son a sense of the truth of history's accounts of other great men, and therefore a better sense of the continuity of human life, Heaney's father's digging also presents him with an image of history – the oral tradition made flesh – that he then has to transform or introject in order to be a writer capable of limning the face of history. An interjection – "By God, the old man could handle a spade" – even hints at a divine connection of the kind that Arnold explicitly affirmed.

The most obvious visible difference between Heaney and Arnold is that Arnold has no need of specific authenticating memories presented as actual scenes in a specific space-time, to establish his father's significance as a father. Heaney's poem works hard to convince us that this father is not just a generic role but the specific creator of the poet, the man who fathered him. The poem is the narrative of an event, the Proustian moment of sitting indoors and hearing the spade outside, then seeing the father and experiencing a flashback to an earlier occasion, and this reporting of an authentic moment is crucial to the affirmation of a transmission of power. Only because such technical care goes into the manufacture of authenticity can the almost overexaggerated proliferation of deliberately Freudian symbols, like the pen "snug as a gun", for the phallus, be made convincing. In this context the phallic symbols positively invite the knowing reader to interpret them, and in doing so, to endorse the legitimacy while perhaps feeling knowingly superior to the youth who inadvertently reveals his masculine pride. The connection between the inscription of fathers in poems by men poets, and the attribution of engenderment to the phallus, is a connection everywhere present in the father poems, although rarely made as explicit as it is in a poem by Charles Bukowski which recalls his father interpreting the word "love" to mean merely sex for payment, and then undergoes a revulsion from the thought of his own physical origins:

> the most horrible thing
> I could think of
> was part of me being
> what ejaculated out of the
> end of his
> stupid penis.
> I will never forgive him
> for that.
> (Charles Bukowski, "Three Oranges", cited in Gluck 1993: 37-38).

Parents are origins of the poet's organic life in the most material possible sense, in the face of which any claim to self-birth, or to be a part of the progenitive poetic lineage seems mere denial of the facts. Bukowski's cry of self-loathing at the end of his poem – "I say kill the Father/ before he makes more/ such as/ I" – may be merely an extreme self-loathing but it refers to ways of imagining origins that are widespread. The poem of personal voice both imagines itself as a paternal ejaculation and disavows this in the gesture of poetic substitution. Even Heaney's poem, as we have seen, toys with the idea of destroying his father's phallic power, with its image of the superior poet with pen looking down on his bent progenitor.

Heaney's much-lauded ability to use concrete, sensuous language is put into the service of rendering his father unique – "the coarse boot nestled on the lug" – and the main element of his memory of his father when the poet was a boy, is of seeing his father pull out new potatoes from the ground, an image of his father's ability to engender new life as he had done with little Seamus. Memory does play a part in Arnold's poem, but only in the sense that it can be allegorised as a capacity to be a Moses or Christ leading people towards God, and displaying heroic fortitude. No actual memories are needed to make this point, because they would have undermined Arnold's basic point, since it was the degree to which his father incarnated the invisible power of fatherhood radiating from God that mattered, and individual, local memories would have obscured that radiation with their material contingency. The heroic image of Arnold's father removed from everyday event is what makes it possible for the son and poet to maintain imaginative continuity with the past, but in Heaney's case, it will have to be solid authentic memories of actual deeds by his father that will maintain history for him. The spade becomes almost tangibly Masonic, and his father, the skilled digger, gives metaphorical birth to the author of the poem. The poet of the potato passed on a poetics to his son which makes possible the digging or history that can be presented in poetry, and is actually demonstrated by the very act of this poem itself which inaugurated his career. Poetic power derives from the relation to the past made possible by his relation to his own father.

Arnold's poem was written in response to detractors who had mocked his father's seriousness and mission, but it is secure in its own authority as a poem; it can rely on two interconnecting forms of legitimation, the use of the traditional elegy, and the Christian discourse of election and divine paternity. The contemporary poet who writes in the first person, who relies on an implicit bond between reader and writer that the materials in the poem are an accurate representation of what the author has witnessed, and who uses language that is part of the communicative resources of a speech community, has a problem of authority. Who is he to speak? In the absence of a religious authority, and the demise of public poetic forms like the elegy, how is the poet to announce a vocation and authenticate what is said? Heaney's poem demonstrates particularly clearly how this might be done. Confirmation of his poetic power is made dependent now on a replaying of psychoanalytic narrative, but in order to be convincing, it must appear natural and not simply imposed by the educated poet from a book onto the raw material of memory. Therefore memory has to be seen to be spontaneous. Since psychoanalysis, and its many popular variants, insist that identity depends on the ability to tell one's story, and to maintain a continuity of identity, then the poem must show a coherent chain of memories that define who the poet is. Heaney's poem does this most effectively. Indeed, we might wonder whether the psychoanalytic subtext of flag-waving Freudian symbols is deliberately embedded in the poem in order to add legitimacy to this account of his own accession to symbolic power. The poem itself, almost subliminally, evokes earlier certainties like those in Arnold's poem, when it allows itself an oath: "By God, the old man could handle a spade." A God who represents the power of fatherhood as a digging, still lurks in the cultural background.

The poem is able to perform Heaney's "feel" because it explains who he is and how he can speak poetry. His father is his bodily origin; and by extension, this is where the poet's language originates. And yet, we want to respond, what about his mother? This is not a question that is raised at all by reading Arnold's poem, not because it was written in part for his mother as his letters reveal, but because fatherhood is not imagined in the terms of the genetic transmission and creation of singular individuals as occurs in our contemporary culture. The problem with Heaney's positioning of his father as an origin of the poet's speech is that the claim could equally well be made for his mother. This is a myth of origin that will not stay still, it will need to be constantly revised, and the significance of fatherhood will remain uncertain. What are fathers for? What fathers are for, according to Heaney, is digging – a metaphor for carrying out the work of anamnesia, of memorialising the past and therefore maintaining historical continuity, as well as the lewd, oral meaning of fucking and therefore engendering new poets. Poems about father will have to exaggerate the value of paternal power and yet always risk the poet in doing so, since the poet's own right to speak will depend on a successful transfer of power from father to son. In Arnold's world, God has enough fathering for everyone, so there is no economy of scarcity. Here in Heaney's poetic world, the son has to have what the father once possessed. They cannot both have it at once, and they must deny the role of mothers too.

Contemporary poetry is much more of a struggle over gender authority than we sometimes realize, even when gender politics is kept out of sight. One effect of poems like Bowers' and Heaney's is to provoke dissident poets to rethink the entire nexus of form, voice, subject, language, gender and sexuality. Much of the most interesting avant-garde poetry of the past half-century has been motivated by the instabilities and inequalities of the ideology of the expressive lyric's treatment of gender, even by poets, like Charles Olson, whose public behaviour, and even some of their poetry, can remain misogynist. (Susan Howe has given an excellent and moving account of the difficulties this side of Olson's work has caused her and other women poets, in "Since a Dialogue we Are" [Howe 1989: 166-173]). I shall conclude with just two brief examples of the degree to which the dominant mode of the personal lyric is associated by writers with engenderment. The American poet Charles Bernstein, an important theorist of poetics as well as a leading figure in the avant-garde, sometimes creates brilliant comedy by imitating the earnest tones of the dominant modes of poetry. In *Controlling Interests* he wrote a disjunctive poem mischievously entitled "Sentences My Father Used", which is composed of sentences and phrases that mostly disconnect from one another, a poem which intercuts many of the types of phrase and motif characteristic of the father poem ("Surprising details that/ hide more than announce"; "I don't remember much"; "Misled by the scent, you/ spend the whole day trying to recover/ what was in your pocket, the watch your/ parent gave you if you would only mind/ the hour"). There is no indication in Bernstein's poem of any such sentences as the title refers to, but the smart reader will realize that language-users will use parts or all of most sentences, and this need not mean that they are in direct communication or share subjectivity, and the poem effectively questions the entire model of transmission that so dominates the poetry scene. Bernstein also questions its nostalgic phallicism as well in one of his most barbed poetic parodies, "Memories", a poem in four parts, each devoted to a familial relationship – grandfather, mother, father and sisters – in which the speaker is a manly, firm voice offering the kind of masculine judgements that are associated with unreflective manliness. Part three is called "Tough Love" and begins like this:

My Dad and I were very close
I like to say, int'mately gruff:
We hunted bear, skinned slithy toes ·
You know, played ball and all that stuff.
Daddy had his pride and maybe was aloof
But when he hit me that was proof--
Proof that he cared
More than he could ever share.
How I hated those men who took him away!
(Bernstein 1989: 14).

The use of the first person as a marker of sincerity, the capitals at the start of each line, the rhymes, are all conventional signs that this should be read as poetry, and the missed rhymes (stuff/aloof, cared/share) as well as the irregular lines suggest that the speaker is a naïve poet. Conventional masculinity is represented by the stereotypes of hunting (we might recall William Faulkner's story) as a demonstration of male power, casual references to sports, and the monochrome affect. Bernstein signals a critique to the reader not only by the dissonance between the speaker's feelings about his father's violence and possible insanity (or criminality), but also by the allusion to the "slithey toves" of Lewis Carroll's poem which hints at a dissolution of meaning indicative of the writer's own questionable rationality. Despite the deconstruction of patriarchal engenderment, a fear lingers at the edge of both of the Bernstein poems, that is captured neatly in a poem by a younger avant-garde poet, Douglas Rothschild, who begins his parody of the confessional lyric, "Early Poem", with the stanza: "My dad would always come home/ from his job at the *IG Farben* (Reichold/ Chemicals really) & ask, 'How's/ every thing in Sunny Vale.'" Rothschild's poem ends with the thought that eventually one will become the same: "You get older & there's nothing/ left of you but the empty shell of a joke" (Rothschild 1999: no pagination) and this we realize is an anxiety behind the parody in Bernstein's poem too. Although it is the loathsome hypermasculine speaker who looks forward to treating his son the same way he was treated, with "tough love", it is not hard to draw the inference that such a fate may overtake every male poet too, even if in a less survivalist mode.

Bernstein writes of his own practice: "I have tried to understand who and what I am without assuming the authenticity of my feelings or sexuality," and adds that much of the most innovative modern poetry has been devoted to the "questioning of essentialist ideologies of gender" (Bernstein 1989: 192). The avant-garde parodies work because of the prevalence of parent poems, but they are not aimed so directly at the contemporary family romance as at its employment as an usher to the realist narratives of personal autobiography in the contemporary lyric. What incites them is as much opposition to the authentic voice of personal expression and memory on which the economy of the hegemonic lyric appears to depend, as a radical sexual politics. These poems suggest the possibility that the extraordinary upsurge in parent poems results from an interaction between dominant poetic genres and social change, rather than simply reflecting historical changes in the family and in cultural models of individuation.

The poetry of fathers needs to be examined as a reception economy, in which it is precisely the interest in the lives of strangers presented in personal lyrics which suture a narrative of personal origins to the dramatisation of a speaking self. This is a reception economy in which gender, and in the material examined by this essay, specifically masculinities, is in production. It is precisely that there are so many of these poems, that they repeat with remarkable tolerance of repetition, certain basic performances of memory, recognition and repudiation of masculinity as history, that is most in need of investigation. Poetry's specificity as an institution is also an important part of the story of the parent poem, which is the locus of a wider struggle over the gendering of origins as an intersection between familial and public history, in which masculine anxiety about femininity and motherhood is encoded as a negotiation with the ever-present possibility of rewriting origin stories as narratives of motherlove. This poetic economy is much more than a medium for the relation of an expressive act of the poet and an individual act of readerly interpretation; it is also a process of cultural circulation in which certain collective needs for a renewal of historical continuities and a reflection upon discontinuities, are made self-aware.

Works cited

Arnold, Matthew 1965. *The Poems of Matthew Arnold*. London: Longman.

Bernstein, Charles 1989. "Memories." *American Poetry Review* (September-October 1989), 14.

Bernstein, Charles 1989. "Poetry and (Male) Sex." *Sulfur* 24 (1989), 189-193.

Bloom, Harold 1973. *The Anxiety of Influence*. Oxford: Oxford University Press.

Bowers, Neal 1992. *Night Vision*. Kansas City: University of Missouri Press.

—— 1997. *Words for the Taking: The Hunt for a Plagiarist*. New York: W. W. Norton.

Dickson, Albert (ed.) 1985. *The Origins of Religion*. Trans. James Strachey. Harmondsworth: Penguin.

Ferguson, Margaret, Mary Jo Salter, and Jon Stallworthy (eds.) 1996. *The Norton Anthology of Poetry: Fourth Edition*. New York: W. W. Norton.

Gallop Jane 1992. "History is Like Mother", *Around 1981: Academic Feminist Literary Theory*. London: Routledge, 206-239.

Gluck, Louise (ed.) 1993. *The Best American Poetry 1993*. New York: Macmillan.

Harrison, Tony 1984. *Selected Poems*. Harmondsworth: Penguin.

Heaney, Seamus 1980. "Feeling into Words", *Preoccupations: Selected Prose 1968-1978*. London: Faber & Faber, 41-60.

hooks, bell 1995. "Doing it for Daddy", in Maurice Berger, Brian Wallis and Simon Watson (eds.), *Constructing Masculinity*. London and New York: Routledge, 98-106.

Howe, Susan 1989. *Acts 10: In Relation*, 166-173.

Kennedy, David 2000. " 'What Does the Fairy DO?' The Antithetical Staging of Masculine Styles in the Poetry of Tony Harrison and Douglas Dunn." *Textual Practice* 14: 1 (2000), 115-136.

Lowell, Robert 1959. *Life Studies*. London: Faber & Faber.

Merleau-Ponty, Maurice 1989. *Phenomenology of Perception*. Trans. Colin Smith. London: Routledge.

Middleton, Peter 1992. *The Inward Gaze: Masculinity and Subjectivity in Modern Culture*. London: Routledge.

———— 1998. "The Recognition of British Public-School Masculinities in Modernist Fiction." *Forum for Modern Language Studies* XXXIV: 3 (1998), 237-249.

———— 2001. "The Masculinity Behind the Ghosts of Modernism in Eliot's *Four Quartets*" in Cassandra Laity and Nancy Gish (eds.), *Gender, Sexuality, and Desire in T. S. Eliot*. Cambridge: Cambridge University Press.

Moramarco, Fred and Al Zolynas (eds.) 1992. *Men of Our Time: An Anthology of Male Poetry in America*. Athens, GA: University of Georgia Press.

Morrison, Blake 1987. "The Filial Art: A Reading of Contemporary British Poetry." *Yearbook of English Studies* 17 (1987), 179-217.

Olson, Charles 1974. *Additional Prose: A Bibliography on America, Proprioception, & Other Essays*. George Butterick (ed.). Bolinas: Four Seasons Foundation.

Ostriker, Alicia Suskin 1987. *Stealing the Language: The Emergence of Women's Poetry in America*. London: The Women's Press.

Peters, Robert 1989. *Hunting the Snark: A Compendium of New Poetic Terminology*. New York: Paragon House.

Ross, Andrew 1986. *The Failure of Modernism: Symptoms of American Poetry*. New York: Columbia University Press.

Rothschild, Douglas 1999. *Matchbook*. New York: Situation.

Steedman, Carolyn 1995. *Strange Dislocations: Childhood and the Idea of Human Interiority, 1780-1930*. London: Virago.

Strand, Mark (ed.) 1969. *The Contemporary American Poets: American poetry since 1940*. New York: New American Library.

Part III:

Diverse Cultural Forms

"Manhood," "Boyhood" and Reading the Melbourne Weekend Papers: the My(th)op(oet)ic Consumption of Family Life

Eleanor Hogan

Over the past few years there have been intimations in Australian contemporary life that men are in crisis, that feminism has "gone too far", and that masculinity as a nexus of "special" issues and interests is on the ascendant. The recent emergence of a grass-roots men's movement, popularly presented as matching and superseding second-wave feminism, is mooted as holding the answers to contemporary gender anxieties. The personal is no longer merely political; it is also masculine. Claims for what purportedly represent gains for men in terms of personal empowerment are, however, often performed in highly public sites, not least of all in the print media. As Bary Dowling, a *Sunday Age* reviewer, puts it: "Men are in. [...] Journalistic chaff is already filling newspapers and mags as the pendulum of fashion swings away from women" (Dowling 1997: 9).

This article seeks to examine what interests drive this focus on the crisis in masculinity with particular reference to the Melbourne weekend newspapers. It discusses the public performance of "manhood" as it featured during the period of June to November 1997 in the Saturday and the Sunday *Age* and *The Weekend Australian*. Print media coverage of this crisis often professes to present specialist knowledge mediated by "experts." Indeed, one of the reasons for the high-profile of "manhood" as an issue during the latter half of 1997 was the publication of several local books on men's issues written for public consumption, three of which were reviewed in the weekend papers. These books were: Steve Biddulph's *Raising Boys: Why Boys are Different and What We Can Do to Help Them Develop Into Wonderful Men*, Don Edgar's *Men, Mateship and Marriage: Exploring Macho Myths and the Way Forward*, and David J. Tacey's *Remaking Men: Jung, Spiritual Values and Social Change* (Biddulph 1997; Edgar 1997; Tacey 1997a). Reviews and other related material pitched these books as the timely work of experts (Biddulph is a practising psychologist, Edgar is a sociologist with the Australian Institute of Family Studies, and Tacey is an academic and Jungian expert) written to meet a groundswell of populist and grass-roots male agitation about gender inequities. (Similar pro-male grass-roots activism has occurred on a much larger scale in the United States through the growth of movements such as the Promise Keepers organisation, described by Michael Messner as a means of taming men with patriarchal bargains, and the Million Man March, the MMM [Messner 1997: 24-36, 64-6]).

The "expertise" of these commentators on masculinity can be aligned with what David Buchbinder has identified as a "softer-core" element that predominates in the Australian men's movement. Unlike the "harder-core" material on masculinity, which is more analytic and theoretical in nature, and methodological in approach (Buchbinder 1992: 136), and usually identified with feminist and queer-informed destabilisations of masculinity, the "softer-core" element tends to coalesce with New Age philosophies directed at self-development (of which Robert Bly's *Iron John* [1992] is a prime example) and is aimed at a populist, general readership. In his discussion of "softer-core" men's studies, Buchbinder notes that:

> [i]ndeed, a publishing industry has arisen [...] aimed at a general readership, and producing books and journals which typically call on men to consider the principles of a (generalised) feminism, and to reform their lives towards a more liberal acceptance of difference, whether of sex or of sexuality. (1992: 135)

The recent coverage of men's issues in the print media assists in the promotion of this publishing niche, particularly through reviewing books by "softer-core" experts. In contrast to the high-profile media hype accompanying "softer-core" interrogations of masculinity, "harder-core" investigations of masculinity, such as the work of scholars like David Buchbinder (1994), R.W. Connell (1995), Michael Flood (1992), Michael Gilding (1992) and Lynne Segal (1994), have been largely contained within an academic sphere in Australia. Buchbinder observes that "we have seen recently in Australia the emergence of a men's movement whose objective is to restore male supremacy at home and in society" (1992: 137). This mainstream men's movement operates chiefly from "softer-core" pretexts, often in contradistinction to gay and feminist challenges to models of masculinity which serve to perpetuate a patriarchal socio-economic system, and also to the inroads made on this system by the worldwide recession (Buchbinder 1992: 137).

In this article I offer a symptomatic reading of the issues surrounding manhood as represented in the Melbourne weekend newspapers in relation to other sites of public anxiety and interest such as the future of the nuclear family as a unit of social reproduction, changes to the structuring of the workplace, mounting unemployment and youth delinquency. My concern here is with the narrowness of the familial pretexts on which "manhood" is being established as a public issue in contemporary Australian life. In keeping with the "softer-core" trajectory of commentary on masculinity, recent print media coverage of masculinity relocates gender issues in the private arenas of the psyche and the family, and in terms of gains in self-awareness and self-empowerment for a subject that is, I shall argue, Anglo-Celtic, middle-class and probably middle-aged. Contemporary feminism, on the other hand, is chastised for its pursuit of an equity-based agenda that seeks to redress matters of social injustice concerning equal opportunity, sexual harassment, reproductive rights, and so forth, in the public sphere. Such a shift in popular discussions of gender is in keeping with a political climate that wishes to move issues of social and economic welfare away from the responsibility of the State and onto the individual and the family. Much of the recent print media coverage of the "crisis" in masculinity focuses on the need to limit and contain delinquency, chiefly through deploying effective disciplinary practices for boys within the context of the traditional nuclear family. This article argues that this project for recuperating masculinity within the family domain is a very private, narcissistic and homosocial one, a kind of window-dressing for the male psyche, rather than, as it sometimes claims, an attempt to deal with serious social and economic issues impacting on the community.

I also read the performance of masculinity in the weekend papers as part of a desire to attain to the "good life". While this may sound unduly cynical, much of the earnest stuff about raising sons and discovering one's anima is embedded within a broader schema of lifestyle commodification. The *Sunday Age Life!* supplement, for example, presents self-development and alternative therapies more or less as fetishised commodities, part and parcel of the "good life" that is to be pursued through such activities as cooking gourmet recipes, eating at the right restaurants, following the correct fashions, finding quality childcare, and so forth. The high incidence of articles on "manhood" in the weekend papers indeed suggests the middle-class-ness of recent attempts to privilege masculinity as a site. Alison Caddick has commented on the "yuppification" of *The Age* as part of a marketing strategy to "promot[e] itself as a new kind of commodity" (1998: 15). Both *The Age* and *The Weekend Australian* now supply lift-out magazines with lengthy feature articles similar to those found in magazines aimed at young professionals and the *Sunday Age* also upgraded its *Life!* Supplement to magazine format during 1997. Contemporaneous with the rise of interest in masculinity in the print media has been the advent of new male magazines such as *Ralph, MAX* and *Men's Health*, developments chronicled in A. Close (1997: 5), and C. Webb (1997: 3), which suggests the re-commodification of "masculinity" for magazine consumption through a newer, softer, ostensibly feminised angle on the pre-existing *Playboy/Penthouse* market.

While the "new lad" and the "new man" occasionally featured in the weekend papers as more upmarket successors to the hapless "SNAG" (for example, Tacey 1997: C3; Webb 1997: 3), overall the family predominated as the favoured site for public discussions of masculinity. The advent of the nurturing, more domestically invested father as a parallel but more worthy gain for modern family life than that of the careerist mother received particular attention. The suggestion that the father take individual and specific responsibility for the happy and autonomous functioning of his family, however, owes much to the development of discourses and institutions of social regulation in reference to both the child and the family within the modern State. A broad spectrum of social commentators, from more right-wing and libertarian elements through to the radical left, have examined various aspects of these trends (for example, Elshtain 1981; M. Freeman 1983; Garmarnikow et. al. 1983; Lasch 1997/1978; Oakley 1972; Stacey and Price 1981; Wilson 1977; Zaretsky 1976); here I will be drawing specifically from Nikolas Rose's book, *Governing the Soul: The Shaping of the Private Self* (1990), which presents a Foucauldian perspective on these developments.

The modern family has been widely depicted as a private and autonomous domain, "a haven in a heartless world" in Christopher Lasch's memorable words, that provides its members with both solace and space for the exercise of their own personal and individual desires. As Rose observes, this site has been constructed "through the intense subjectivization, emotionalization, and eroticization of domestic affairs" (1990: 201). Contrary to this perception, however, Rose argues that the family has in fact become heavily implicated in the functioning of the State over the past two centuries. The child and the family have become subject to intense public scrutiny, with the family answerable to the State as an instrument for implementing "normalcy" in the reproduction of the child as governable citizen. Requirements that certain standards of "health, hygiene and normality" (Rose 1990: 129) were met, and that certain social and legislative obligations were fulfilled such as the "adequate education" of children "up into their teens" (Rose 1990: 121), became fundamental to family life. The operations of the family were further enmeshed with that of the State through financial regulation in the form of family benefits and allowances, with some types of families rewarded and others penalised at various moments in recent bureaucratic history. Both the processes of mothering and education provided significant points of intersection for the interaction of State and family. The site of motherhood became the particular focus of disciplinary practices through the obligation from birth to apply certain modes of surveillance in order to meet basic medical, legal, social and later, educational, requirements. Appeals were also made to the mothers desire to produce a "healthy", "normal" and even "exceptional" child, appeals that may in themselves shape that desire. Recent appeals to men to repent from their workaholic and underfatherly ways suggest the co-option of contemporary fatherhood as an extension, or complementary site, of surveillance and disciplinary practices usually aligned with motherhood.

Following the work of Jacques Donzelot (1979) on the policing of families, Rose further stresses the role of the "regulation of images" in mediating between the "family mechanism and the goals of government."

Representations "of motherhood, fatherhood, family life, and parental conduct" (Rose 1990: 129) produced by State agencies and institutions have been influential in appealing to family self-interest and encouraging conformity to certain norms without "the threat of coercion and without direct intervention by political authorities into the household" (Rose 1990: 130). The regulation of these images manipulates the family's hopes and fears about their capacity to meet and even exceed the norms set in place by the family ethic through the inevitable gaps that emerge between actualities and the family ideal. I would extend Rose's argument to suggest that representations of family life produced by the popular media also encourage family members to participate in various modes of self-surveillance and disciplinary practice not only by appealing to fears of inadequacy but also to consumer interests through the fetishisation of family life and the concomitant implication that its ideals are commodities within or maybe just only slightly out of reach.

Within the context of commodifiable family life in contemporary Melbourne, I think that print media representations of the delinquent male youth operate both as an incitement and a supplement to the implementation of certain disciplinary modes of social reproduction. In his discussion of the prison and panopticism as a paradigm for the growth of disciplinary institutions and modes of power, Michel Foucault draws attention to the development of the figure of the delinquent as a supplement to the penitentiary system as well as its desired object of knowledge. He claims that it is not so much the delinquent's "act as his life that is relevant in characterizing him" (Foucault 1986: 219). Corrective technologies are grounded in projections of the delinquent's biography:

> [I]t falls to this punitive technique [the observation of the delinquent], therefore, to reconstitute all the sordid details of a life in the form of knowledge, to fill in the gaps of that knowledge, and to act upon it by a practice of compulsion. It is a biographical knowledge and a technique for correcting individual lives. (Foucault 1986: 219)

The delinquent is thus "not only the author of his acts [...] but is linked to his offence by a whole bundle of complex threads (instincts, drives, tendencies, character)" (Foucault 1986: 220). Troubleshooting the biographical possibilities of the delinquent provides the basis for the exercise of juridical power as well as the often scientised rationale behind the development of penitentiary techniques.

The boy-friendly material appearing recently in the papers presents an apparatus of corrective techniques, especially through the proposed implementation of tribal ritual and initiation rites within the home as a form of protection against the full biographical flourishing of the delinquent youth. In hazarding biographies of the development of the boy and the adolescent male, this material seeks not only to curb the "dangers" of "natural" male drives and tendencies (in which "testosterone" plays a major and demoniacal role) but also the pitfalls of certain kinds of social and educational strategies and influences as exercised by fathers, mothers, teachers and others. All boys are in a sense potential offenders and case studies in the pathology of boyhood, reflections of the spectral figure of the delinquent who often haunts but is never fully present within these accounts, although he is raised more directly in other instances of reportage and reviewing as an object for scrutiny and even romanticisation. In addition, the delinquent youth represents a fall from certain norms and privileges desired by the modern Australian family not merely because he is ungovernable and out-of-control, but because he is tainted with associations from less privileged groups such as the unemployed, blue-collar workers, and occasionally certain racial groups. Rose points to the class agenda linked to the socialisation and education of the child over the past two centuries in his analysis of interactions between the State and the family. Strategies directed at the "child of the well-to-do" have

> [...] sought, by and large, to maximize the potential of the adult that the child will become, seeking to convince parents that a particular way of thinking about and acting upon the child in its infancy will help them promote their own lineage and secure the best future for the offspring. [Those directed at the working-class child have] sought, in different ways, to minimize the threat to social well-being that the future adult might represent, by supplementing the work of the mother in various ways, and by training her in the correct ways of conducting her tasks. (Foucault 1986: 178-179)

In the contemporary Melbourne context of reading pro-male, boy-friendly material in the papers, the protection of the interests of the well-to-do, and perhaps also the aspiration to these interests, may well fuel the desire to avoid the fall into depravity and delinquency traditionally associated with the lot of the underparented, underfathered child of lower socio-economic status.

One of the first newspaper features that drew my attention to the outburst of pro-male material was an issue of the *Australian* magazine on 2-3 August 1997 titled "Boy Trouble: The new gender debate". The lead article outlines the platform for boys' special needs, the problems surrounding their rearing and education, and it draws substantially from an interview with "manhood" guru, Steve Biddulph, in the wake of the publication of his book, *Raising Boys*. Biddulph states that while "[i]t was painfully obvious 30 years ago that women and girls weren't getting much of a go [....] the most recent outbreak of commonsense is to realise that we've dishonoured masculinity, misunderstood it if you like and even tried to say it doesn't exist" (Safe 1997: 15). Biddulph's assertion is typical of claims made for men's specific needs, which are often grounded in a polarised, essentialist and even androgyny-based view of gender difference.

Contemporary feminism tends to be portrayed by pro-male commentators as having gone awry, and as being particularly bereft of human values as a result of women's infiltration into the workplace. Biddulph claims that while feminism has "stopped becoming a liberation movement and [become] 'we want our slice of the cake as well' '', the men's movement is the one offering "a reassertion of human values and community and connecting with each other, caring for the people around you" (Safe 1997: 15). In an article titled "The sagging sex warriors who just can't get used to peace" in the "Opinion" section of *The Sunday Age* Neil Mitchell writes, apparently in response to Germaine Greer's address to the 1997 Melbourne Writers' Festival, "Once, they were right. This was a just war against prejudice and unfairness. But it is won" and "Sexism has come to mean anti-female, not a prejudice based on gender" (Mitchell 1997: 9). (In reviewing Tacey's *Remaking Men*, Roy Masters reports the book's argument as being that "men have copped the bad bounce of the ball in the gender confusion game" [Masters 1997: 8]).

Proponents of this point of view often seek support from quasi-scientistic or Jungian psychoanalytic forms of authority, presenting their understanding of gender difference as natural, intuitive and "only commonsense". The spectre of quasi-scientism looms large in Biddulph's vision of gender inequity. For "those in universities today who would argue that gender is just made up", Biddulph asserts that "it's clear they haven't gone across to the science faculty and talked to the people who study that kind of thing" (Safe 1997: 15). It's equally clear, however, that Biddulph himself hasn't visited the Humanities faculty to talk to the people who study history or history of philosophy of science and those kinds of things. Moreover, as his simplistic construction of a straw liberal feminism indicates, he is ignorant of the history of feminist thought and practice, and of the men's movements dependence on, and even mirroring of, certain positions in the recent history of both feminist and queer theory. As in much pro-male material, Biddulph deploys terms such as "manhood", "men" and "boys" in similar ways to the use of "woman" and "women" by early second wave feminists: that is, as homogenising, universalising and unifying categories. Buchbinder makes a similar observation: "Such publications [softer core men's studies] bear a strong resemblance to some of the early work of feminism and the women's movements, in that these, too, sought a comonalty [sic] in women's experience and responses through a sharing of life-stories. Here, as in other aspects, this more popular form of the nascent men's studies replicates the development of women's studies" (1992: 136). He also overlooks the emphasis of radical, cultural and eco-feminisms on re-introducing "connection" and community, and the feminist sources of many initiatives that critique the structure of the workplace and the heavily "masculinised" valuing of work.

A similar vein of gender determinism emerges through the conception of a post-patriarchal "New Man" promoted by the publication of David J. Tacey's *Remaking Men*. Reviewer Roy Masters informs us that Tacey, a Jungian expert, follows Freud and Jung in their belief that "the human psyche was bisexual", and in doing so, elaborates on the view that man inherits certain traits genetically by positing that masculinity can be led "onward to new, post-patriarchal definitions" through re-conditioning towards a new androgynous ideal (Masters 1997: 8). However, there is certainly nothing new or unproblematic about androgyny, a concept discarded by early second wave feminists. Tacey's psychic paradigm appears to forward yet another polarised view of gender relations. As in Biddulph's commentary on contemporary society, male adolescent delinquency registers as a major sign of gender imbalance, although for Tacey it is also evidence of an underlying psychic disorder. In this instance, the unchannelled male psyche (rather than testosterone) is demonised as the primary source of pathology. Masters recounts the following priestly insight: "Dr Tacey refers to teenage drug overdoses, pub crawls, train surfing and reckless driving as examples of an Australian youth feeling justified '[...] in carrying out life-threatening practices, since he is acting from the authority of the soul' " (Masters 1997: 8). In what sounds like an echo of Lasch, Tacey claims that "[o]ur society has been overtaken by adolescence," and posits the re-introduction of initiation rites, doubling maybe both as therapy and as disciplinary measure, since "adolescence in tribal societies lasted as long as the ceremony" (Masters 1997: 8). With an observation more appropriate perhaps to the milieu of *My Brother Jack* (1964), Tacey suggests that national service previously played the role of initiation rites in Australian society, curbing an excessively prolonged male adolescence.

Tribal societies are a stalwart feature of much "male-friendly" material, and more specifically of mythopoetic men's movement material (Pfeil 1995: 167-232), which depict them as remarkably static and unchanging, unlike contemporary social structures. The pathologisation of the male adolescent psyche, and its need for homosocial monitoring and re-direction through the practice of initiation rites, features in the coverage of Biddulph's work as well as Tacey's. Bettina Arndt comments in her review of *Raising Boys* that: "These dark aspects of the male psyche have become the object of intense interest now [...]. The pitch in *Raising Boys* is to both mums and dads, encouraging them to tackle the problems now plaguing young males" (1997: 8). The onus is on families to nip male aggression in the bud before it blooms; like Tacey, Biddulph endorses the appropriation of initiation rites from tribal contexts as a means of social control, in this instance to be deployed within the family unit. Biddulph advocates that:

A ceremony should be held to honour a boys start of adolescence a rite of passage
for this milestone in his life. The highlight could be a special meal at a venue he
chooses a real grown-up restaurant, not the usual fast food place. (Safe 1997: 14)

This rite is to coincide with and positively validate the 800% jump in
testosterone levels experienced around age 14. Biddulph supports this idea
with references to the practice of initiation rites marking the passage from
boyhood to adulthood in Aboriginal, African and Arabic cultures and, like
Tacey, he believes that this kind of activity will counteract the excesses of
"an adolescence that can go from 11 to 35" which is characterised by
juvenile behaviour – binge drinking, irresponsible sex, risk-taking with that
person's and others' safety" (Safe 1997: 15). Here the responsibility for
warding off delinquency is placed squarely within the domain of the
autonomous family. In addition, Biddulph diagnoses " 'father hunger', the
lack of an adult males guidance in a boy's life" which is also "relatively
new in Western culture" (Safe 1997: 15), as a major source of this
overwhelming social adolescence. While the theory of the fatherless society
has its origins in the Frankfurt School, it has perhaps been best popularised
through the writings of Christopher Lasch. He attributes many social
disorders to the breakdown of the family, and in particular, the absence of
paternal authority, which is replaced by a series of narcissistic
identifications on offer to the individual through commodity culture. Once
again, things were happier for men in far-off times, in this instance prior to
the Industrial Revolution, when boys received "direct fathering" – in the
privacy of their own homes, perhaps in the family workshop or out in the
fields together. The benevolence of this "master-slave"-dialectic-style
enterprise is never doubted, and its economic underpinnings are never
examined. In addition, appeals for renewed direct fathering from
commentators such as Biddulph to the effect that "[i]f you work a 55- or
60-hour week, you won't cut it as a dad" (Arndt 1997: 8) obscure an
implicit consumerist tension: a father must mediate between attaining to the
conventional role of breadwinner to ensure the economic and social
standing of his family unit, and finding and financing the quality time
necessary to attain to fatherhood as a lifestyle choice and form of self-
fashioning.

   That children, and more particularly boys, have become the victims of
underfathering through the ways that public and private spheres structure
men's lives is a recurrent theme in recent print media material. After a
lead-in story about a new ritual, the fathers-only night ("[s]ecret men's
business, or so the publicity intimated", Michael Grose devotes one of his
regular parenting columns in the *Age Life!* supplement, titled "Often, dad's
the word", to mapping a brief social history for the phenomenon of
underfathering (Arndt 1997: 8). Grose argues that while children may have
lost fathers in previous centuries due to natural causes from a higher

mortality rate, they are now faced with the loss of "direct fathering" through divorce and voluntary separation. Grose gestures towards the collusion of psychoanalysis and the legal system in centring family structures round the mother:

> For much of the 20th century we have seen the gradual erosion of real fathering. Thanks in part to the work of Freud and friends, the mother-child bond has been the most celebrated family relationship with fathers playing some kind of support role. The message coming through many sections of society, including the family law courts is that mothers are irreplaceable while dads are an optional extra. (Grose 1997b: 5)

What seems to be on offer as an alternative to this legally- and psychoanalytically-overdetermined family structure is the suggestion that men can and should be able to reconstruct their family lives along the lines of "naturally" occurring homosocial structures – never mind that this type of construction is being endorsed through the imaginative expertise of self-help and New Age counsellors, psychologists and family therapists instead. The opinions of Grose and Biddulph on "direct fathering" at times come close to advocating what sounds like a return to the days of the Victorian papa – a more interactive Victorian papa, perhaps, but one who nevertheless re-stakes his claim to direct the lines of power within the family domain. Elsewhere Don Edgar wonders whether women will want to give up one of their last traditional bastions of power, that of the home (Edgar 1997a: 3), and given that women are still largely responsible for bearing and rearing children, it's a question that should be seriously asked. But, conversely, if men substitute innocence of familial duties for large-scale responsibilities, perhaps they will find themselves shouldering the full burden of blame for the social problems attributed to underfathering. Mike Safe makes the following point: "most of the blame [for young males' problems] is laid at the feet of fathers or, more exactly, absent or inadequate dads who cannot deal with their own emotional flaws, let alone their sons' " (1997: 13). This is a prospect sometimes implied by the confessional mode used to describe men's conversion to "direct fathering". Grose recounts that when he asked the men at the "fathers-only night" "to reflect on their own experience of being fathered, it was as if someone opened the floodgates. Many issues poured out" (1997b: 5). As confessional subjects, the fathers are able to experience liberation by confessing the terrible and often emotionally-charged "truths" surrounding fatherhood, as practised by themselves as well as by their own fathers; by implication the "guilt" for mismanaging fatherhood is also theirs.

The desire to reproduce homosocial sameness and exclude other differences through reinstating a paternalistic family structure is evident even in the more moderate, women-friendly and social-constructivist agenda of Don Edgar's sociological survey, *Men, Mateship and Family*. In the reportage accompanying the publication of this survey, Edgar stresses the good will of many men in building families and striving for equal partnerships with wives. His revelation for family studies is that Australia has not been built on the back of male mateship which is "a straw man set up by our intellectuals that has obscured the real nature of nation-building and identity – the essential gender co-operation that underpins society itself" (Edgar 1997: 3b). As the colonialist ambience of this statement suggests, Edgar's conception of the Australian family as the ideal site for negotiating gender differences omits scrutiny of those other differences it might work to police and exclude. An extract from his book reproduced in *The Weekend Australian* opens with the following reverie on suburbia: "Every time I fly into Sydney or Melbourne, the suburban red roofs and green backyards loom larger and I think: 'Something good must be going on down there' " (Edgar 1997: 3b). The implication is that the "family" ideal Edgar wishes to endorse as he looks out fondly over the nation's suburban roofs is the conventional het, (Edgar's focus on the family occludes gayness, as Dowling notes in quoting from *Men, Mateship and Marriage*: "He insists that 'the family is in essence a male-female couple usually with offspring [...] a homosexual couple is not a family in this sense' " [Dowling 1997: 9]) white, middle-class suburban one, the colonialist authority and functioning of which has been clearly underscored in the recent controversy over native title, for example, through the Australian Government's appeals to misplaced fears about the loss of freehold land. Racial difference, however, emerges elsewhere in a discussion of the place of family ritual. Unlike other commentators, Edgar does not project a large role for ritualised homosociality in rebuilding the modern Australian family, but he does query the loss of ritual as a kind of family glue. He aligns this query with the non-Anglo-Celts in his survey sample, who criticised the "lack of duty of 'Australian' parents", "ask[ing] questions about the place of ritual, responsibility and tradition in modern family life and the sense of family as a binding unity" (Edgar 1997b: 3). As in the Biddulph material, racial difference is fetishised as a metonymy for forgotten, "natural" familial structures – on which the modern white colonialist family has not only been built but can continue to plunder in its own nation-building enterprise.

A tendency to efface race and class differences has also been noted as a criticism of Biddulph's project, particularly in reference to his complaints about the privileging of girls' special education needs at the expense of boys'. Peter West, one of *Raising Boys*' reviewers, suggests that Biddulph oversimplifies the material on boys, equity and education, underlining the "strong ethnic dimension to school achievement. Asian boys and girls often do well in exams and Aboriginal and South Sea Islander boys generally perform badly" (1997: 27). This observation is supported by an article on gender equity and education, "Boys to men: the tough road", from the *Age* on 23 August 1997 in which Gay Alcorn points out that "[t]here has never been a time since World War II [...] when boys were not more disruptive in class than girls or got suspended more often than girls. What has changed is that we are starting to worry about it" (Alcorn 1997: A27). She argues that socio-economic factors have been obscured in discussions of gender and education, and that "a child from a wealthy background will do well regardless of sex" (Alcorn 1997: A27). The most disadvantaged students are boys from poorer backgrounds: "Working class boys who could get apprenticeships in the 1950s, and who left school for secure and often life-long jobs, are the big losers in the huge social and economic changes of the past few decades" (Alcorn 1997: A27). Following Rose's model for the education of the well-to-do child, the focus on boys' special educational needs in isolation from other factors might well present a narcissistic exercise in protecting one's "own lineage and secur[ing] the best future for [one's] offspring" (1990: 179) in economically-troubled times and in minimising the possibility of one's child joining the ranks of delinquency, along with other children of less privileged backgrounds. The deployment of "boys" as a universal and potentially pathological category in much of the coverage of men's issues would appear to support a self-interested middle-class agenda: as long as one is implementing the correct practices and procedures to ensure that one's own son is educable and governable, there is no need to address other equity issues in the community which impact on areas such as unemployment.

The spectre of male delinquency emerges more fully in relation to matters of employment and training. In a *Good Weekend* article titled – very appropriately for the purposes of this article – "When rites go wrong", Sue Neales discusses the rising number of reported cases of workplace violence, especially in relation to young male apprentices. In this article Neales discusses the rising number of reported cases of workplace violence, particularly from young male apprentices employed in "[f]amily-owned, blue-collar small businesses" (Neales 1997: 32). She relates these incidents to the acceptance of terrible working conditions by young people at great cost in the face of mounting unemployment. Neales also quotes the observation of Chris Trafford, "a senior partner with counselling and corporate advisory company Davidson-Trehaire", that these conditions "may be creating a new brutality" (Neales 1997: 33). Significantly, Trafford uses of notions of tribalism and initiation to frame the subject of violence in the often masculinist culture of some workplaces. He comments as follows:

> Systematic violence towards one victim seems to involve overly macho behaviour, often bordering on a form of tribalism, complete with initiation rites and a strong element of power mixed in [...]. There is a fine line between a joke and serious violence – and these bosses have been pretty immune from any form of retribution, so the cycle of violence is perpetuated. (Neales 1997: 33)

Paul McCarthy, a lecturer in the school of organisational behaviour at Griffith University, likewise observes that "[o]n other occasions, apprentices will recognise the primitive bonding involved in these initiation rites and understand that the next time around they will no longer be the victim but the aggressor" (Neales 1997: 37).

The violence of these homosocial workplace rituals and relations undermines the implicitly universalist claims made for the purity and benevolence of "tribalism" and its associated rites in their appropriation by the men's movement as a form of family hygiene for policing boys. Some men's movement material even makes a direct link between employment and initiation rites, with suggestions that the family bolster young men's self-esteem with a celebration of the first male pay packet – or indeed that this ritual once existed but has been lost to the detriment of the young man and his family. The "boy-friendly" family's invocation of this ritual, however, might enact a desire to ward off anxieties stemming from the possibilities of hardship and even violence in relation to education, employment and training issues. Another spectre they may seek to deter is the socio-economic disadvantage associated with blue-collar workers and also certain ethnic groups. "When rites go wrong" is littered with a litany of references to less-privileged locations – examples are given of incidents in a butcher shop in Footscray, a North Melbourne car repair shop, City Edge Panels, MIM Mt Isa, Neil Lennox Automotive, Richmond, Sydney, Clarice Body Group, Box Hill, and two stories of cabinet-makers in Williamstown also feature (Neales 1997: 33, 34-37). A number of the young, victimised apprentices mentioned have non-Anglo-Celtic names: for example, Gabriele Lovisotto, Raffael Galardi and Simon Haug. It is likewise intriguing that violence should be embedded within the practices of family businesses, as presumably these would constitute ideal sites for the exercise of "direct fathering" through the merging of public and private sphere interests. Delinquency is more usually associated in the popular imagination with public spaces, although two recent articles in the weekend papers have suggested that such anxieties about delinquency are purely phantasmic. One article found that the youth crime rate has maintained stable over the past fifteen years (Harari 1997), and the other that, despite beliefs to the contrary, there has been little rise in delinquency in shopping malls (Guilliatt 1997). In contrast, the association of violence with the sacred sites of family and small business in "When rites go wrong" is all the more damning, indicating that homosocial practices implemented within a private sphere will not necessarily protect the interests of the young male and, in some instances, may themselves constitute brutal acts of delinquency.

In summing up this discussion of recent representations of men's issues in the print media, I would like to emphasise the problematic nature of the focus on the individual and the family as the primary site for dealing the so-called special issues surrounding boys. The publication of books in this area, and the accompanying reviews, interviews and spin-off articles in the weekend papers, appear to be directed chiefly towards protecting the specific interests of a middle-class group of consumers with little interrogation of how these interests factor in relation to those of other groups in the community. In keeping with Mark Davis's *Gangland* (1997) thesis, it may also reflect the media dominance of a certain age group's interests: those of a well-established middle class in their 40s and 50s whose preoccupations include personal growth and family matters. The emphasis on the protection of the family as a form of "private enterprise" is in keeping with a political climate that seeks to move responsibility for issues of social and economic welfare out of the public domain, reducing them to the level of personal and private considerations. Don Edgar has railed against the appropriation of the family as a vehicle for policies from the Right, and the Left's preference for issues concerning "women and minority groups", in the following terms:

> If this reassertion of family values sounds uncannily like a Liberal Party election manifesto [...] that is simply because the Right of Australian politics long ago captured the family as an electoral issue.
>
> It was helped by the fact that the Left gave away the issue, in favour of women and minority groups: "They see family policy as soft. Think of the last two decades – the ALP has refused to look at anything other than hard economic policy." (1997b: 3)

Yet I suspect that the family's vulnerability to becoming the mascot for Right Wing policy has much to do with public understandings of equity issues in terms of liberal rather than leftist politics, and of contemporary feminism as a movement focused chiefly on personal liberation. Neil Mitchell's opinion piece on sagging feminist warriors and the end of the gender wars is a good example of where the terrain for gender debate is often located in the print media: that of personal and private gains such as health and sexuality issues, with men in this instance to "catch up" with women through better knowledge of their bodies and hormones. According to Mitchell, the lack of media coverage of "the testosterone surge of puberty, where male hormones can jump 800 per cent overnight" and the "hormonal confusion of the elderly male" (1997: 9) present examples of contemporary gender inequities, (although he cannot be reading "Achilles Heel", Jill Margo's regular column in *The Weekend Australian Review* on male health issues).

This skewed emphasis on personal empowerment at the expense of collective social responsibility has been encouraged not only by the re-emergence of the New Right in Australian politics, but by the receptiveness of certain local intellectual positions, particularly libertarian ones, to colonisation by this climate. As Mark Davis notes in *Gangland: Cultural Elites and the New Generationalism*, "[m]any local campaigners against PC have complex links to earlier intellectual movements" (1997: 65). The libertarian, Andersonian-inspired Sydney Push of the 1940s, '50s and '60s, for example, laid some of the groundwork for local articulations of civil dissidence and protest movements during the 1960s and 70s through its emphases on free thought, sexual expression, individualism and anti-authoritarianism. Public figures such as Germaine Greer and Richard Neville associated with sexual liberation and the counter-culture were more properly the bedfellows of libertarianism than the women's liberation movement (which their activism pre-dates historically: Lynne Segal discusses Greer's participation on the editorial board of *Suck* from 1969 to 1972, and her contribution to *Oz*'s special issue of "Pussy Power" and "Cunt Power" as "a type of feminism *Oz* could handle [...]. It seemed to only encourage the complacent sexism infusing Richard Neville's 'happy, hippie, playful sex' without commitment in Play Power" (Segal 1994: 27). In mapping sexual emancipation in local and international counter-cultural contexts during the late 1960s, Lynne Segal observes that "saying yes to sex" became emblematic of resistance against the dominant social order. She stresses, however, the underlying misogyny of much of the counter-culture (pre-dated by that of the Push in Australia), to which contemporary feminism provided a counter-response as women "moved from seeing sex as liberation to seeking liberated sex" (Segal 1994: 30). While the anti-authoritarianism of libertarianism as a long-standing Australian cultural formation provided some of the pretexts – both positive and negative – for protest movements such as women's liberation, its "anti-collectivist, anti-welfarist, anti-egalitarian idealist" (Davis 1997: 59) underpinnings also lay it open to collusion with Right-wing agendas.

A recent article on John Marsden, the forty-seven-year-old writer of young adult fiction, hints at these kind of antecedents for "boy-friendly" material. Like Tacey, Marsden believes that national service has been replaced by train-surfing, although he is not critical of this latest deployment of testosterone. Instead, Marsden romanticises the male delinquent as a site of civil disobedience and by implication, as the true genealogical successor to libertarian and countercultural resistance, claiming that "there is a government plan against excess, when we speak of things such as drink-free, drug-free, government-organised parties and swear-free rock and roll" (Dickins 1997: 7). The ignorance of some male-positive commentators of their critique's basis in feminist social theory on the public/private sphere likewise points to its libertarian genealogy. Popular articulations of the Australian men's movement tend to import American material accompanied by trappings of an ethic grounded in individualism, family and private enterprise. The "underfathering" thesis, for example, has counterparts in Blankenhorn's *Fatherless America:*

Confronting Our Most Urgent Social Problem (1995) and Burgess's *Fatherhood Reclaimed* (1996), and beyond these, Christopher Lasch's analysis of the fatherless society with its claims that State bureaucracies have undermined the competence of the individual and the family, and that the narcissistic excesses of contemporary society can be remedied by reinstating the ambit of domestic patriarchy (Lasch's positioning is difficult to pin down. A civil libertarian and a member of the New Left, his proposed solutions to contemporary social problems tend to lend support to some rather conservative platforms). The desire to shield family life from the exercise of State power bears similarities to the activities of civil libertarian groups in the late 1970s and '80s mobilised around platforms protecting "family rights" and "children's rights" from intervention and intrusion by State bureaucracies and welfare agencies (Rose 1990: 203-206). The highly personalised understanding of liberation and equity principles that pervades recent pro-male material in the Australian print media sets up the individual adult male to achieve (a my[th]op[oet]ic) self-realisation through a family life grounded in narcissistic homosocial bonds. It is a focus that also opens the door to the privileging of agendas based on competition and the protection of self-interest rather than the representation and negotiation of different interest groups across the community. At the populist level of the Australian men's movement, the promotion of these agendas is evident in the divorce of notions of equity and empowerment from the broader interplay of socio-economic and political determinants. "Being a man" in this context becomes a highly individualistic pursuit of social privilege and status.

Works Cited

Alcorn, Gay 1997. "Boys to men: the tough road." *The Age*, 23 August 1997, A27.

Arndt, Bettina 1997. "Turning boys into men." Review of Steve Biddulph, *Raising Boys*, *The Age Saturday Extra*, 23 August 1997, 8.

Biddulph, Steve 1997. *Raising Boys: Why Boys are Different and What We Can Do to Help Them Develop Into Wonderful Men*. Sydney: Finch Publishing.

Blankenhorn, David 1995. *Fatherless America: Confronting Our Most Urgent Social Problem*. New York: Basic Books.

Bly, Robert 1991. *Iron John: A Book About Men*. Shaftesbury, Dorset, and Rockport, Mass.: Element Books.

Buchbinder, David 1992. "Editorial." *Southern Review*, 25: 2 (1992), 135-140.

——— 1994. *Masculinities and Identities*. Melbourne: Melbourne University Press.

——— and Charles Waddell 1992. "Myth-Conceptions About Bisexual Men." *Southern Review*, 25: 2 (1992), 168-184.

Burgess, Adrienne 1996. *Fatherhood Reclaimed*. London: Vermilion.

Caddick, Alison 1998. "News Comment: A new cool Age." *arena magazine* 34 (April-May 1998), 15.

Close, Alan 1997. "Bloke on top." *The Weekend Australian Review*, 19-20, July 1997, 5.

Condon, Sean 1997. "Cocktails, jujitsu, women and me." *The Good Weekend*, 30 August 1997, 39-42.

Connell, R.W. 1995. *Masculinities*. St. Leonards, N.S.W.: Allen and Unwin.

Darville, Helen 1997. "It's all relative." *The Australian Magazine*, 67, August 1997, 2630.

Davis, Mark 1997. *Gangland: Cultural Elites and the New Generationalism*. St. Leonards, N.S.W: Allen and Unwin.

Dickins, Barry 1997. "Forever young." *The Age Saturday Extra*, 6 September 1997, 7.

Donzelot, Jacques 1979. *The Policing of Families*. London: Hutchinson.

Dowling, Bary 1997. "Why men are the marrying kind." Review of Don Edgar, *Men, Mateship and Marriage. The Sunday Age Agenda*, 5 October 1997, 9.

Edgar, Don 1997a. "The father of all myths." *The Sunday Age Life!*, 7 September 1997, 1,3.

Edgar, Don 1997b. "Man-sized myths." Extract from *Men, Mateship and Marriage, The Weekend Australian Features*, 23-24 August 1997, 3.

Edgar, Don 1997c. *Men, Mateship and Marriage: Exploring Macho Myths and the Way Forward*. Pymble, NSW: HarperCollins.

Elshtain, Jean B. 1981. *Public Man and Private Woman*. Brighton: Harvester.

Flood, Michael 1992. "The Men's Movement: State of the Movement." *XY: Men, Sex, Politics*, 2: 1 (1992), 10-12.

Foucault, Michel 1986. *The Foucault Reader*. Ed. Paul Rabinow. Ringwood, Vic.: Peregrine Books.

Freeman, M. 1983. *The Rights and Wrongs of Children*. London: Pinter.

Garmarnikow et. al. (eds.) 1983. *The Public and the Private*. London: Heinemann.

Garrett, Peter and Elizabeth Jolley 1997. "My dad and I." *The Age Saturday Extra*, 6 September 1997, 1,4.

Gilding, Michael 1992. "AIDS Narratives, Gay Sex and the Hygienics of Innocence." *Southern Review*, 25: 2 (1992), 141-167.

Gordon, Michael 1997. "Lighting the Wik." *The Weekend Australian*, 22-23 November 1997, 23.s

Grose, Michael 1997a. "Do what you do well, Dad." *The Sunday Age Life!*, 7 September 1997, 3.

————— 1997b. "Often, dad's the word." *The Sunday Age Life!*, 17 August 1997, 5.

Guilliatt, Richard 1997. "Hey you ... Boy!" *The Good Weekend*, 22 November 1997, 16-20.

Harari, Fiona 1997. "The usual suspects." *The Australian Magazine*, 29-30 November 1997, 1623.

Harford, Sonia 1997. "Fatherland." *The Age Saturday Extra*, 6 September 1997, 5.

Hope, Deborah 1997. "The age of the hyper parent." *The Weekend Australian Review*, 19-20 July 1997, 1,4.

Johnston, George 1964. *My Brother Jack*. London: William Collins and Sons.

Lasch, Christopher 1977. *Haven in a Heartless World: the Family Besieged*. New York: Basic Books.

————— 1978. *The Culture of Narcissism: American Life in an Age of Diminishing Expectations*. New York: Norton.

McDonald, Roger 1997. "The best of friends." *The Good Weekend*, 30 August 1997, 16-19.

McKenna, Elizabeth Perle 1997. "And what do you do?" *The Good Weekend*, 30 August 1997, 22-29.

Masters, Roy 1997. "Germaine? Er, no." Review of David J. Tacey, *Remaking Men: Jung, Spiritual Values and Social Change*. *The Age Saturday Extra*, 6 September 1997, 8.

Messner, Michael 1997. *Politics of Masculinities: Men in Movements*. Thousand Oaks, CA., London and New Delhi: Sage.

Mitchell, Neil 1997. "The sagging sex warriors who just can't get used to peace." *The Sunday Age*, 28 October 1997, 9.

Nancarrow, Kate 1997. "R toys us?" *The Sunday Age Life!*, 20 July 1997.

Neales, Sue 1997. "When rites go wrong." *The Good Weekend*, 6 September 1997, 32-37.

Oakley, Anne 1972. *Sex, Gender and Society*. London: Temple Smith.

O'Sullivan, Jack 1997. "10 ways to be a better man." *The Age Saturday Extra*, 7 June 1997, 6.

Pfeil, Fred 1995. "Guerillas in the Mist", *White Guys: Studies in Postmodern Domination and Difference*. London and New York: Verso, 167-232.

Rose, Nikolas 1990. *Governing the Soul: The Shaping of the Private Self*. London and New York: Routledge.

Safe, Mike 1997. "Boys to men." *The Australian Magazine*, 23 August 1997, 12-17.

Segal, Lynne 1990. *Slow Motion: Changing Masculinities, Changing Men*. London: Virago.

———— 1994. *Straight Sex: The Politics of Experience*. London: Virago.

Slattery, Luke 1997. "Failing our kids." *The Weekend Australian*, 23-24 August 1997.

Stacey, M. and M. Price 1981. *Women, Power and Politics*. London: Tavistock.

Stewart, Cameron 1997. "Honey, I drugged the kids." *The Weekend Australian*, 23-24 August 1997, 25.

Stone, Deborah 1997. "Boys talk? They don't." *The Sunday Age Life!*, 29 June 1997, 1,5.

Tabakoff, Jenny 1997. "What beats quality time? Free time and play time." *The Sunday Age Agenda* 1997, 4.

Tacey, David J. 1997a. *Remaking Men: Jung, Spiritual Values and Social Change*. Ringwood, Vic.: Penguin.

———— 1997b. "Step aside SNAG, enter New Man." *The Age*, 19 November 1997, C3.

Webb, Carolyn 1997. "Men's magazines take the gloss off the New Age guy." *The Sunday Age*, 22 June 1997, 3.

West, Peter 1996. *Fathers, Sons and Lovers: Men Talk About Their Lives From the 1930s to Today*. Sydney: Finch Publishing.

———— 1997. "Dads have been displaced." Review of Steve Biddulph, *Raising Boys*. *The Weekend Australian Review*, 67 August 1997, 27.

Wherrett, Peter and Richard Wherrett 1997. "No place like home." *The Good Weekend*, 4 October 1997, 16, 21.

Wilson, Elizabeth 1977. *Women and the Welfare State*. London: Tavistock.

Zaretsky, E. 1976. *Capitalism, The Family and Personal Life*. London: Pluto Press.

Queering the Straights: Straightening Queers: Commodified Sexualities and Hegemonic Masculinity

Rainer Emig

> Only straights like footballers dress "straight" now, and the rest of you have looked more gay with every year of the Nineties. Tight V-neck jumpers, hip-hugging Farahs, three-quarter length trousers, tank tops and Levi's, slick city blousons, skinny-rib Ts, smart white casuals and Gucci-oochi anything. You live for the weekend and you let no man put asunder. You can scan *Arena Homme Plus* for tips on arranging your Helmut, you check *wallpaper** for the latest in blonde easy-lays and you buy import disco twelves like Studio 54 never went off-the-boil (believe me darling, it did). You kid yourself that your minimal, precise designer aspirations are some kind of neo-mod Brit lineage, but the plain and simple truth is that you're consuming like a poof.
> Richard X, "Oh You Pretty Things: Lads, Dads, Fags – The British Male Comes out of the Closet", *Arena Homme Plus*, 12 (Autumn/Winter 1999), 199

In what could be a clever piece of self-reflexivity or even self-congratulation, the leading men's fashion magazine in Britain thus addressed it readers recently. The theme of straight men emulating gay attitudes ran through the entire issue, as can be seen in the subsequent essay "Tag Hags R Us" by Murray Healey that not only cleverly puns on both "fag hags" (women who love the company of gay men) and Toys'R'Us as a symbol of unrestrained consumerism, but includes the following memorable description of the contemporary British male: "He's a peacock. He is a preener and he is a big old poof. And I love him to death" (202).

On the one hand, one might argue that there is nothing surprising about a presumed crossing of the line from "straight" into "poof" territory in a fashion magazine for men that, as a media genre, balances precariously on the line of "straight" acceptability. Such magazines only came to prominence in the 1980s and 1990s, and have since wooed a readership that at first seemed to consist predominantly of homosexuals, as could be glimpsed from the abundance of homoerotic imagery employed in editorials and advertisements. Yet this open or covert catering for a gay market was, from the beginning, tempered by an equally pronounced nod in the direction of the straight reader who was supplied with traditional "manly" features on racing, Bond girls, etc.

What is fascinating about the stage that this apparent balancing act or schizophrenia has reached today is that it seems to have worked both ways: homosexuals appear to have swallowed the traditional accessories of "straight" culture and have in fact become integrated in it to the degree of invisibility. A presumedly "gay" lifestyle magazine called *attitude*, founded in the 1990s, indeed printed the following letter of complaint in its December 1997 issue:

> Can someone at *attitude* please tell me what the fuck is gay about the magazine today? After a three month abstention, I plucked it off the shelf and for a moment thought I had picked up a straight magazine. On closer inspection I realised it was straight: in editorial, style and ideas. Please answer the few gay readers who still buy it and don't fob us off with a terse one-liner about "assimilation" and "crossing boundaries" crap [...]. (12)

Interestingly enough, the editors only managed to retaliate in terms that are generally associated with homophobic abuse, i.e. an enforced hostile definition from without that, in the context of the debate just outlined, appears anachronistic: "Gay, gay, gay! Cock, cock, cock! Faggot, faggot, faggot! That gay enough for you? Now bog off" (ibid.).

Perhaps more surprisingly, "straight" men have adopted "gay" consumerist ideals to the extent that one can even address them jokingly as "poofs" without fear of losing their custom. Here Consumer culture seems to be deeply involved in eroding twentieth-century concepts of masculinity – at whose heart lay the seemingly insurmountable opposition between "straight" and "bent". The following essay will attempt to situate this development both historically, economically, and ultimately in the terms of Critical and Cultural Theory. Questions will be asked about the relation of identity, lifestyle, and ideologies of masculinity and sexuality. Ultimately, the relation of gender and sexuality might appear in a rather different light than in the many recent theoretical studies that tend to situate them side by side, as if they were complementary structures, yet generally fail to address their logical entanglement. Thus, a pronouncement like the following by one of the most outspoken theorists of homosexuality, Kenneth Plummer, will be shown to require some modification:

> Gender identity is clearly distinct from sexual identity; a sense of being a boy or a girl is not directly linked to a sense of being heterosexual, homosexual, sado-masochistic or paedophiliac, which usually comes later. Nevertheless, given the centrality of gender identity as an organizing feature of social life it is very likely to shape sexual identity. (Plummer 1990: 214)

Even a sociological study like Alex Thio's *Deviant Behaviour* comes up with results that show masculinity and sexuality as intimately entangled to the degree that causes considerable confusion, for the self-identifying person as well as for academics trying to explain this relation:

> Why are heterosexual men more homophobic than women? According to one explanation, men are more likely to feel pressured by traditional gender roles to be "masculine" and to avoid being "feminine". Since gay men are stereotyped as "feminine", straight men are more likely to display antigay prejudice as a way of assuring themselves that they are "masculine". According to another explanation,

straight men, accustomed to playing the stereotypically masculine role, do not want other men to look at them the way they themselves look at women. They are afraid of becoming what women in a sexist society often are: an object of unwanted sexual attention, or a victim of sexual assault, harassment, lusting, or just plain ogling. (Thio 1998: 222-223)

The present essay will complicate matters further by introducing the notion that perhaps men, some men at least and in some situations, choose or feel pressurised to make themselves the objects of desire. What would be the effects on the traditional gender divide described above?

Despite the humorous and affectionate banter of *Arena Homme Plus*, or the seemingly strict, if complicated definitions outlined by Thio, masculinity in the late twentieth century is generally believed to be in crisis. Traditional role models appear to have become anachronistic, while men's economic and educational dominance over women threatens to become a thing of the past. If men can't be top of the heap, they seem to be ready for the dust heap of history altogether. What one tends to forget in these contemporary debates is that crises of masculinity are as old as the concept itself. For the early Victorian era (another period of economic hardship in which women increasingly entered "male" spheres of wage earning and left that of the dependence on husbands and family) John Tosh points out the following concerning the education of boys: "[i]n an unstable social and economic climate in which self-reliance was at a premium, this was a matter of acute anxiety to many fathers" (Tosh 1998: 83).

One could go back even further and detect anxieties concerning masculinity in the many seventeenth-century tractates on the fop as a caricature of manliness, a debate that continues through the eighteenth- and nineteenth-centuries with the (frequently, but not always effeminate) figure of the dandy, until it culminates in the late nineteenth century in the paradigm of decadence (Adams 1995). Since this late nineteenth-century debate also participated in developing the modern concept of the homosexual (Meyer 1994: 75-109), it is of special interest for the argument of this essay. Yet a look at an even earlier epoch, the one often called "Early Modern", since it is supposed to bring about the concepts of self, reality, but also society that are still current today, also reminds us that anxiety concerning established roles of gender and sexuality and the perception, and sometimes even tolerance of transgression inevitably takes place within their dominant hegemonic framework. Thus, Elizabeth A. Foyster states in her fascinating study *Manhood in Early Modern England*:

Literary texts which praised [male] friendship competed with those which promoted the Puritan notion of the heterosexual relationship within marriage. Marriage provided the setting in which male friendships could be construed as "unnatural" and even branded as "sodomical". (Foyster 1999: 127)

Much closer to our era, the *fin de siècle* dandy provides an early, if generally more dramatic counterpart of the hedonist male of the late twentieth century. Unmanly, possibly deviant (immoral, criminal, pathological), and consumerist in his interest in exquisite objects and dress, he – like late twentieth century man – is characterised as living in front of mirrors, either real ones or the metaphorical ones of competition with his peers. Oscar Wilde's Dorian Gray and Bret Easton Ellis' Patrick Bateman in *American Psycho* share the same lineage here. But more than aesthetic features that determine the similarities of their lifestyles, the underlying economic structures of this "life as style" should interest us here. Both the *fin de siècle* dandy and the late twentieth-century male consumer are products of a time in which production (of goods, children as part of a nuclear family, or culture in the shape of great art) becomes increasingly eclipsed by consumption. The successful man is no longer engaged in increasing the amount of good(s) or his flock, but involved in the fluctuations of consumption, an activity that depends on surface and transience (as in advertising and fashion). In Rachel Bowlby's words: "The fantasy of lawlessness thus operates as a powerful, if not sensational, source of pleasure, one which unites the interests of aesthete and consumer alike" (Bowlby 1993: 23-24).

It replaces traditional essences (that are held to be theologically or biologically determined or both) with roles that have to be adopted and shed, according to the demands of the market. Yet such an economic and consumerist (and ultimately Marxist) model has to compete with the continuing relevance of an equally important structure, that of binary oppositions. In the same way as traditional gender roles are binary and hierarchical (man and woman as essentially different, with man at the top in most respects), even the altered environment brings with it ordering discourses that function in binaries. Terry Eagleton describes this schizophrenic state of the contemporary subject in the following terms:

> The subject of late capitalism, in other words, is neither the self-regulating synthetic agent posited by classical humanist ideology, nor merely a decentred network of desire, but a contradictory amalgam of the two. The constitution of such a subject at the ethical, juridical and political levels is not wholly continuous with its constitution as a consuming or "mass cultural" unit. (Eagleton 1988: 396)

The evolving type of the "homosexual" is a product of this schizophrenia, defined, on the one hand, as "not natural", "not manly", "not moral", in opposition to the centric ideals of the nineteenth century. Michael Foucault describes this new "species" in the following terms that reiterate the idea of surface:

> The nineteenth-century homosexual became a personage, a past, a case history, and a childhood, in addition to being a type of life, a life form, and a morphology,

with an indiscreet anatomy and possibly a mysterious physiology. Nothing that went into his total composition was unaffected by his sexuality. It was everywhere present in him: at the root of all his actions because it was their insidious and indefinitely active principle; *written immodestly on his face and body because it was a secret that always gave itself away*. [...] Homosexuality appeared as one of the forms of sexuality when it was transposed from the practice of sodomy onto a kind of interior androgyny, a hermaphrodism of the soul. The sodomite had been a temporary aberration; the homosexual was now a species. (Foucault 1981: 43; my emphasis)

At the same time, though, the new type of the homosexual still participates in existing hegemonic constructions of masculinity. Though "not manly" and frequently "effeminate", he is equally obviously not female, and indeed often radically misogynist. Out of this conflict, I would argue, derives the preference of many "straight"-identifying men for transvestites. Their impersonation of women helps their straight admirers cushion the possible transgression of sexual norms with the reassurance of the pretended familiar binary of the opposite gender. "Masculine" homosexuals, on the other hand, by emphasising an apparently shared gender role, often deeply trouble straight-identifying men. David Forrest attempts to outline these confusions between masculine and homosexual identification in his essay "We're here, we're queer, and we're not going shopping." In it he describes the ambivalences concerning gender characteristics attributed to gay men:

In a move variously documented as "the butch-shift" or as the "masculinization of the gay man", the last three decades have seen the emergence of such "macho" figures as the moustached "clone", the tatooed "leatherman" or "biker", and more recently the all-American "jock". [...]
However, when we take a closer look at these representations, things appear much less straightforward. Personal ads in the gay press appeal for "similar straight-acting" partners – sexual or otherwise. Gay men still behave in "unmanly" ways. [...] We still hear many gay men referring to others as "she", and hear talk of "drama queens" (emotionally charged men), "size queens" (men who like big cocks) or "muscle queens" (body-builders). The last seems to make nonsense of the traditional association between muscles and physical (masculine) toughness, since "queens", enthroned or otherwise, are hardly synonymous with muscles. (Forrest 1994: 97-98)

While Forrest also arrives at the insight "that gay masculinity must be seen simultaneously as both subversive (in that it challenges orthodox masculinity) and reactionary (in that it reinforces gender stereotypes – a crucial factor in the oppression of gay sexuality)" (Forrest 1984: 105), he is still content to view the issue primarily from the point of view of homosexuality and to regard heterosexual masculinity as hegemonic and ultimately stable. What is important in our context, however, are not merely the facets and complications of homosexuality, but indeed how that which creates this new type of deviance, hegemonic heterosexual masculinity, undoubtedly in order to stabilise its own concept of itself, relates to its abject. More critically, what happens when the abject becomes assimilated to the centric ideology from which it is seen to deviate, or when the deviant outside or margin takes over the centre, as in the teasing description of "the British male" as "a big old poof"? The consequences both for the presumed ideological centre, the hegemonic force and norm, and its excluded Other might be drastic and perhaps either potentially liberating or, on the contrary, worrying. Toby Manning outlines and challenges some of the positive visions associated with a possible participation in hegemonic ideals via consumerism:

> The latest gay positive image – part of the ongoing "gay gentrification of sexual identity" – is that of the pink pound/dollar-rich consumer. This is relentlessly pushed by the new breed of gay lifestyle magazines aimed at mainstream advertisers – *Attitude* in Britain, following on the heels of *Out*, *Genre* and *10 Percent* in the US and finding its extreme in *Victory* – and by the marketing departments of gay consultancies like Ellie Jay Group ("Loyal, discerning, trend-setting ... affluent" goes the blurb in its 1995 brochure). The claim is often made that this display of economic advantage (however limited its application) will bring about recognition from business and therefore *rights* from a business-worshipping political class – a curiously naive and misconceived notion. (Manning 1999: 101)

But rather than tackling the complex from its presumed structural, economic, and theoretical centre, it might be instructive to approach it, as do many theories of gender and sexuality in the late twentieth century, from the surface.

Twentieth-century fashion seemed to exist for women only until the end of the Second World War, perhaps well into the 1950s and probably 1960s. This can be confirmed by a quick comparison of women's fashion (which changed every season) with the standard uniformity prescribed for men: trousers, shirt, tie, hat, jacket or suit, with a severely restricted colour range of black, grey, dark blue, and brown (Schickedanz 1980: 15). When this model was ruptured, to a certain extent by the emerging youth cultures of the 1950s and 1960s, homosexuals tended to act as trendsetters. A recurring pattern emerged in which the fashions (and often subtle identifications) of a presumed subculture were with worrying regularity and increasing swiftness adopted by the presumably "straight" majority. Examples are the pale blue sweaters and silk neckerchiefs of the 60s and 70s, the dyed hair and earrings, but also the "Buffalo Boy" look of jeans, tight t-shirt, bomber jacket, and desert boots of the eighties, all the way to the tattoos and piercings of the 1990s. In the same way as "straight" men seemed busy running after the latest gay fad, gay men found it increasingly difficult to signal their difference in the contexts that they chose.

Why would "straight" identifying men participate in "gay" identified fashion? The answer lies partly in the restrictions that traditional masculinity imposed, as has been mentioned above in connection with clothes. Yet the escape from these restrictions should perhaps not be regarded naively as an expression of the indomitable self-determination of the human individual. This humanist tenet runs into the difficulty of explaining why (traditionally dominant) men had to reclaim a privilege that women have held throughout history. In fact, the liberation of clothes styles should be seen in the context of an increasing consumerism that depended, in the post-war era, on a ceaseless turnover of new lines and styles. When men regularly need a new type of trousers or even an entirely new wardrobe in the style and colour range of the current season, fashion has succeeded in conquering the remaining half of the population as well. The same applies to cosmetics (or skin care products, as they are still embarrassedly labelled when targeting men) and increasingly also to the market for cosmetic surgery.

Secondly, and equally importantly, this participation in formerly "gay" styles by no means implies a willingness to be (even erroneously) identified as gay. While bisexuality has regularly been declared *fashionable* (especially in the 70s and 80s), its acceptance as a self-imposed label has in fact mainly been restricted to the world of pop stardom. The entertainment industry as a sphere of the carnivalesque, where transgression is to a certain extent expected and unlikely to shock, has traditionally been the realm where sexuality mattered least (Forrest 1994: 98).

Yet even there few individuals dared to cross the line permanently and unequivocally, and of those many were in fact forced into "outing" themselves by media pressure (see the recent cases of George Michael and the Boyzone member Stephen Gately). The in-out model implied in "outing" as well as the complementary concept of "staying in the closet" are reminders of the binary nature of sexual roles, with covert homosexuality labelled restricted and inferior compared with the apparently wide open spaces of the acceptable norm. More typical and more instructive for the argument of this essay is the now infamous statement by the lead singer of the British pop group Suede, Brett Anderson, who declared himself to be a bisexual man without homosexual experiences. This attitude of sitting on the fence is sometimes described by homosexuals as "tourism", a term that will be of relevance in the discussion of the recent British television series *Queer as Folk* below. Alan Sinfield characterises the ambivalence of these seeming border-crossings (not without a problematic recourse to a "we" that he himself then unwittingly undermines in his artificial construction "les/bi/gay") as follows:

> Hybridity may or may not disconcert the system. My case is that being always-already tangled up with it, institutionally as well as conceptually, makes it hard for les/bi/gay people to clear a space where we may talk amongst ourselves. We used to say that we were silenced, invisible, secret. Now, though our subcultures are still censored, there is intense mainstream investment in everything that we

Cultural Climate (handwritten marginal note)

do, or imagined as doing. We are spoken of, written of and filmed everywhere, though rarely in terms that we can entirely welcome. (Sinfield 1998: 39-40)

That a complete crossing of the line dividing the binaries "straight" and gay tends to be avoided by "straight" men can be seen in the grotesque debates about the placing of earrings (left ear signalling straight, right ear gay), another distinction that became obsolete when the (once again originally gay) fashion for multiple rings and piercings made it anachronistic. A humorous elaboration of this dilemma is a column by the comedian Richard Herring in the *Guardian* of 21 August 1999 entitled "Glad to be a bit gay" (the pun is on the hymn of the 1970s Gay Rights Movement, Tom Robinson's "Glad to be gay"). It outlines how Herring finds himself increasingly identified as a gay comedian, wrongly as he is at pains to argue:

> It is true that I do a lot of material that is broadly anti-homophobic (as well as a lot that treats homosexuality in a pathetic and puerile manner). It's also true that the character I play on TV is something of a sexual opportunist, and that he is possibly enamoured of his double-act partner (yes, I refer to myself in the third person, but that doesn't mean I'm confused), but he's always struck me as resolutely heterosexual.
>
> He idolises women; he's just too scared of them ever to get anywhere and so prefers to idolise unobtainable media figures such as Princess Diana and Andrea Corr. What gay man would idolise unobtainable women in the media? Um – oh dear. (Herring 1999)

Sexual opportunism, an unrealistic view of women, and a simultaneous preference for homosocial bonding are themes that we will re-encounter below. But Herring goes even further in providing aspects that shift 1990s "straight" masculinity dangerously close to "gay" territory:

> Why is everyone making these assumptions? Maybe it's because I'm single, in my 30s and work in showbusiness. Maybe it's because I'm naturally flirtatious with both men and women. Maybe it's because of that time at my gran's funeral when I was caught by all my friends and family rimming the vicar in the vestry. I'm joking – we were just kissing. No, we weren't. None of that happened. Really. Sorry. I know it's pathetic trying to joke my way out of this, but however liberal a man thinks he is, there is still part of him that is afraid of the feelings he tries to suppress. It's interesting that people who are opposed to homosexuals aren't called homosexualist, but homophobic. It's not about hatred, it's about fear. Not of them. Of yourself. (Herring 1999)

The presumed failure to have formed a stable heterosexual attachment at an age when marriage would have been the prescribed life-form, but also a now itself hegemonic pressure to "liberate" certain feelings, turn "straight" 1990s man into the joke as which he prefers to present himself. Yet these hegemonic pressures that are old and new at the same time also have their mirror images in so-called "gay" culture.

The consumerist-motivated adoption of gay styles by the hegemonic straight majority has an interesting gay equivalent in the tendencies embodied in some 1990s arguments concerning homosexuality. The early gay rights movements of the 1970s had emphasised difference and the right to be tolerated by the majority. This move went hand in hand with the establishment of an aggressively visible subculture and gay fun ghettos, such as San Francisco's Castro area (Sinfield 1998: 23) – in contrast to the well known, but generally discreet subcultures of earlier periods, such as the one in Berlin in the 1920s, for which contemporary sources mention between 90 and 100 gay bars around 1922, while towards the late 1920s gay parties and dances had taken over even the largest venues in the city (Theis/Sternweiler 1984: 63). The 1980s and 1990s displayed a shift of this segregational attitude towards a very different emphasis, no longer on difference and toleration, but on similarity and integration.

The new stance found its potent media expression in the Hollywood film *Philadelphia* (1993), in which the actor Tom Hanks, who throughout his film career has been identified both with Americanness and straightness (see *Forrest Gump* of 1994) plays a gay lawyer unfairly dismissed by his firm for having contracted HIV and dying from AIDS. The film shows how his eventually successful crusade against his firm's bigotry rests on the support of both his gay "family" of friends and that of his real middle-class all-American family. "We are just like you and we want to be part of the hegemonic centre," could sum up such attitudes, and it would also describe the argument of the theoretical proponent of such views, Andrew Sullivan, in his book *Virtually Normal*. The recent debates about gay men yearning for traditional marriages or for children, either adopted or fathered via artificial insemination, are further indications for a centripetal drifting into a presumed centre of normality. (In fairness, not the entire debate about equal partnership rights follows that pattern, although one could be led to think so from the more prominent demonstrations, i.e. the ones that the hegemonic mass media love to pick up as representative, such as same-sex couples in wedding attire in front of registry offices.) Alan Sinfield characterises this discourse of assimilation as that of "the 'good homosexual' – the kind who, unlike the 'dangerous queer', makes him- or herself indistinguishable from heterosexuals" (Sinfield 1998: 168).

Virtual normality, however, just like its equivalent virtual reality, rests on a paradox, since what is to be created relies on the existence, stability and meaningfulness of that whose virtual equivalent it sets out to create. While this essay cannot interrogate the usefulness of assuming the fixity of the American way of life, and can only touch on questions of the family, it has within its agenda a questioning of the stability and meaningfulness of masculinity in its hegemonic and non-hegemonic forms. If straight "tourists" participating in facets of a gay lifestyle as well as gay men yearning to become part of hegemonic normality seem to believe in a centre to which they can either safely return or into which they might eventually be permitted if they ask nicely enough, what does such a centre look like in the late twentieth-century? That which is considered normal and central in hegemonic systems is generally invisible. Yet does it exist at all? Jeffrey Weeks describes this difficulty as enabling for those who appear to be excluded from normality:

> The very idea of sexual identity is an ambiguous one. For many in the modern world – especially the sexually marginal – it is an absolutely fundamental concept, offering a sense of personal unity, social location, and even at times political commitment. Not many, perhaps, say "I am heterosexual" because it is the taken-for-granted norm, the great unsaid of our sexual culture. But to say "I am gay", "I am a lesbian", or even "I am a paedophile ... or sado-masochist" is to make a statement about belonging and about a specific stance in relationship to the dominant sexual codes. It is also to privilege *sexual* identity over other identities, to say in effect that how we see ourselves sexually is more important than class, or racial, or professional loyalties. (Weeks 1987: 31)

The difficulties increase when the "great unsaid" statement "I am heterosexual", whose definition is implied in the term itself, is replaced by "I am a man". Other than its implicit biological opposition to "I am a woman", the statement lacks internal motivation or essence. It is clear that it can only ever be meaningfully filled by cultural norms and regulations, all of which are ideological and thus subject to historical transformations. John MacInnes, in his study *The End of Masculinity*, argues this point in conjunction with his general Marxist and historicist thesis:

> The previous chapter argued that masculinity was an ideology produced by men as a result of the threat posed to the survival of the patriarchal sexual division of labour by the rise of modernity. Their monopoly of power, resources and status which they had previously been able to claim directly by virtue of their sex, they now had to assert was due to their socially constructed gender identity which expressed some undefined natural difference. Since this invention of masculinity was essentially a holding operation, however, it has been in crisis ever since, for three reasons. First, by definition, the essence of masculinity can never be grasped or defined. If it comprises essentially social characteristics or capacities, we have to explain on what grounds women have been incapable of, or prevented from, acquiring them. Masculinity is something for the girls as much as the boys, and over time, it must surely come to have a special connection to either biological sex. (MacInnes 1998: 45)

MacInnes goes on to argue that the second complication is due to the possibility of reversing the hierarchy of the binaries masculine-feminine, while, thirdly, the very modernising tendencies that bring modernity, and with it masculinity as a "holding operation", into being, also force it to transform itself all the time, and thus undermine its stability and produce cracks and gaps. Masculinity, as this essay has set out to demonstrate, is also something for "gays" and "straights", and among the most effective transformations are that of producer into consumer, which finds its expression in hegemonic views of sexuality as a lifestyle and some concepts of sexualities (i.e. bisexuality) as fashionable at times.

As we have seen, self-identifications such as "I am a straight man" or "I am a gay man" help to fill the vacuum of the concept of masculinity, but only at the cost of importing into gender the equally problematic concept of sexual identity. The suspicion has indeed arisen in the above section on the emergence of the homosexual type in the late nineteenth century that, at least since then, gender has been defined predominantly through sexuality. We will pursue this idea further with reference to one of the surprise successes on British television (arguably the most potently hegemonic medium of the post-war era), the eight-part Channel 4 series *Queer as Folk*, written by Russell T. Davies, first broadcast in the early months of 1999.

Queer as Folk depicts the lives of two gay characters, Vince and Stuart, who have been intimate friends since their school-days. Although their careers are very different (Stuart seems to earn plenty of money in some sort of marketing company, lives in a decadently furnished penthouse, and drives a Landrover, while Vince is a junior manager in a local supermarket and spends a lot of time at his mother's), their lifestyles reunite them almost every night. Their evenings are spent in a number of gay bars and clubs, with an array of entertaining and sometime annoying friends and/or potential lovers seemingly at constant disposal. The only difference is that Stuart consumes these apparent options of a gay lifestyle (promiscuity, alcohol, pornography, drugs, and other forms of legal or illegal fun) with abandon, while Vince predominantly watches the goings-on in an apparently amused and detached fashion.

What distinguished *Queer as Folk* from earlier depictions of gay life in the media, and especially in television, was that it did not concentrate on homosexuality as a conflict, as a source of tension and suffering. It also refused to include in its narrative Aids as a threat or source of anguish, although it was mentioned in passing. In total contrast to the traditional narratives of gay men as heroically suffering or offering resistance in an oppressive world, the series showed homosexuality as subversive, yet also remarkably well-integrated fun, an integration also visible in its title, a variant of the proverb "There's nowt as queer as folk", which signals an acceptance of diversity. The remaining degree of its subversion could be seen in the very first episode, though, which showed Stuart engaging in anal sex with a fifteen year old boy, Nathan, who played a further part in the series as the youngster initiated into a gay lifestyle. The action depicted in this scene, tastefully, if quite explicitly filmed, not only violated the British laws of the time (and of today), but was screened while the House of Lords was for the second time engaged in blocking legislation that would bring the Age of Consent for men down from eighteen to sixteen.

Still, the expected and predicted fury of the public was conspicuous by its almost total absence. In fact, Channel 4 had already used the controversy it hoped to create with this outrageous start to a new series as a marketing ploy. What could (and perhaps should) have been transgression designed to create outrage was from the start also a marketing strategy in the arena of media commodification (in the advertising sequence before the episodes, Beck's, the German brewery sponsoring the series, echoed the red of its beer labels in objects such as chilli peppers, symbolising "hot", i.e. exciting). Rather than being outraged, the general public (or at least that constituted by Channel 4 viewers, which has a reputation of being young, hedonistic, but also often aggressively male and heterosexist) loved the series. Surprised media polls discovered that not only did gay men watched the series, but also, besides young women, many straight-identifying young men. What could they have found appealing in a series that had no qualms to depict "straight" reality as dull and mindless?

In episode 2, for example, Vince is persuaded by his supermarket colleagues to have a traditional after-work pint in a local straight pub (their motive is wanting to act as match-makers for Vince and a young female shelf-stacker; Vince's homosexuality having been kept a secret from them). Vince, understandably nervous, uses his mobile phone (perhaps the consumer gadget of the 1990s par excellence and very prominent in *Queer as Folk*) to describe to Stuart the strange world that he is about to enter. The following lines of dialogue are not only typical of the series; they and the scene in which they occur were also frequently repeated on television, either as part of the advertising for the series by Channel 4 itself, but also in reviews of the programme by other stations:

> Vince (over his mobile phone while entering the pub): "It's all true. Everything we've ever been told. Oh my God! Everything but the flocked wallpaper. Ah, and the people! There are people talking in sentences that have no punchline, and they don't even care! Can you believe it? They've got toilets in which no one's ever had sex!"

Here is a gay point of view describing the normally hegemonic straight world not only as an alien territory, but as a world whose inhabitants deserve pity. And Britain as a television consuming nation (and by no means only its gay component) accepted the verdict with glee. This is a step further than the mere acceptance of the depiction of homosexuality as part of reality on TV, a trend that *Gay Times* reported in its issue of 3 February 1998 (albeit with a telling confusion between "sexual activity" and "relationships" that once more points towards the complex link between transgression and hegemonic framework):

The Broadcasting Standards Commission's 1998 survey of attitudes towards the portrayal of sexual activity found that 58 per cent of respondents thought it acceptable to depict gay relationships. In 1992, the figure was only 46 per cent.

Two further scenes from *Queer as Folk* emphasise the series' subversive move of subjecting hegemonic heterosexual norms to an evaluation by that which it traditionally considers deviant. During a board meeting in episode 1, Stuart establishes eye contact with a young executive from another firm. Determined to make a pass at him, he enlists his (female) assistant in finding out details about him. During the lunch break, they arrive via the inevitable mobile phone: "He's married with kids". Stuart's response is simple: "Aren't they all?" As if he was out to simultaneously prove and subvert the concept outlined above by Elizabeth A. Foyster, that marriage proves a defining framework for homosexual deviance, he follows the guy into the men's toilets, makes sure that he gets a good look at what Stuart has to offer, and then makes a pass at him over the wash basin. While pushing him into a cubicle and frantically undressing him, the young executive utters breathlessly "I don't kiss", only to have Stuart's tongue in his throat the same moment.

Several aspects are interesting here. The notion that married life is boredom and inevitably leads to a desire for sexual escapades is the most obvious one. It is a cliché about heterosexuality apparently shared by heterosexual and homosexual men alike (it is also the other side of the coin of the trend that Richard Herring described in passing in his humorous column: men in their 30s increasingly fail to or refuse to form permanent relationships). In the context of contemporary British society, in which people still marry at a relatively young age, the view of marriage as boredom might gain additional plausibility. Yet what remains interesting is that, contrary to traditional advice, marriage by no means protects from the temptations of homosexuality. The guy's plea "I don't kiss" shifts the scene into the area of prostitution (prostitutes often claim not to kiss their customers) and therefore into an accepted form of heterosexual transgression. Yet it by no means manages to integrate it again into a laddish canon of things you do for fun, since by implication the straight guy engaging in homosexual activity labels himself the prostitute, i.e. the object in the commodity exchange of sex.

A further interesting element of this scene, and many others in *Queer as Folk*, is that gay lifestyle and its transgressions are regularly assisted by, and even seem to rest in part on the collaboration of women. Vince's mother offers not only a home to her son, but also to young Nathan, who refuses to live with his homophobic father after his coming-out. Nathan's mother indeed supports this arrangement. Nathan is further aided by his female school friend Donna, whose strongest line occurs in episode 5, when she accuses Nathan of whingeing about his homosexuality:

> Nathan: "You don't know anything. Cause you're straight, right! You're part of the system, right! You're part of the fascist heterosexual orthodoxy!"
> Donna: "I'm black and I'm a girl. Try that for a week!"

Once again: homosexuality as suffering is not acceptable in the series, but there is also an interesting solidarity (though perhaps not equality) across the traditional gender divide. This is taken as far as making Stuart the biological father of the baby of a lesbian couple, a multiple transgression of traditional norms that forms a further subplot.

The second example of measuring heterosexuality through the normative system of homosexuality happens in episode 5 when Stuart humours one of his business associates, a presumedly straight man in his fifties ("Dull as ditchwater. Wife and three kids. One at Oxford"), by showing him the gay life of Manchester, the city in which *Queer as Folk* is set. "Jesus Christ. Is there no straight left in this world?" is Stuart's telling comment on the request. Manchester, and particularly the area around Canal Street, have achieved a reputation as a gay fun quarter throughout Britain, a "gay village" (an interesting term, combining the deviant with an emblem of traditional Englishness). This has in turn led to complaints that are relevant in connection with the argument of the present essay: too many heterosexual punters apparently wish to participate in its gay abandon and thus spoil the atmosphere. When Martin, the business associate, offers Stuart a business deal in exchange for sex Stuart declines and instead sets him up with a man in a gay bar. Martin reports back the following morning that he wishes to extend his stay and continue frequenting the city's gay (sub)culture ("Must be marvellous, doing that all the time"). At this point Stuart becomes surprisingly confrontational. He accuses the man of merely being a "tourist" who wants to have it both ways: a stable and acceptable heterosexual marriage at home, and access to the joys of a homosexual lifestyle elsewhere: "Forget your wife, forget your kids. Just don't be a tourist."

While the notion of the heterosexual with a double life is once again an established one (it could also be applied to the earlier example of the young executive), what is interesting here is that the series makes gay subculture strike back. It refuses to be exploited like a tourist location and demands a kind of serious subscription. This is all the more astonishing since, despite the fact that the main protagonists of the series, Stuart, Vince, and Nathan, are forever participating in this (sub)culture, none of them is a fully subscribed "member". Nathan is out to his parents, but not at school. This, however does not prevent him from engaging in furtive masturbatory sex with the most homophobic boy in his form in episode 4 – and later outing him as a bully when the same boy proudly shows his new girlfriend a gay bar, another example of sexual tourism, here even by a heterosexual couple.

Vince keeps his sexuality secret in his workplace; and even the otherwise outrageous Stuart has not told his parents.

Thus, *Queer as Folk* by no means presents a simple case of inverted reality or perspective. The relationship between heterosexuality and homosexuality is complex. The lines between them are crossed with alarming frequency, and any attempt to outline norms, be they heterosexual (as in the case of Nathan's father who graphically expresses his horror at the thought of anal intercourse being mentioned in front of his young daughter) or homosexual (as in the case of Stuart upholding a strict "membership policy" for gay lifestyle) are doomed to be frustrated by a reality that proves more complicated. Yet the question remains: why could such a series become the uncontroversial success it ended up being? What is attractive about having one's sexual norms challenged and ridiculed especially to a young male heterosexual audience that forms the core of Channel 4's viewers?

The certainly not gay *I Love TV* reviews pages on the internet brought this attitude to a point when they compared *Queer as Folk* to another presumedly "gay" series that was broadcast simultaneously on ITV, *Wonderful You*. *Wonderful You* showed a squeamish camp gay main character sharing a flat with a sluttish female. *I Love TV* wrote: "Compare *Queer as Folk* to ITV's *Wonderful You*, airing in the same slot, on the same night. One had vitality, energy, warmth, humanity and wit. The other was tired, cynical, two-dimensional and dull. I don't think I need tell you which was which." Even the hegemonic straight majority seems to have become tired of traditional clichés of homosexuality. More than that, it is willing to grant "humanity" to a television series, something that is rare enough in a straight series, but almost self-subverting in a "gay" one. Tellingly, and more worryingly, the review concluded with the following praise of *Queer as Folk*: "It's not gay, it's not homosexual – it's great TV" (http://www.escapetv.freeserve.co.uk/ Page2b.htm).

The reasons for such an apparent change of attitudes, of hegemonic values being softened or indeed reversed, have to be sought in the similarities and parallels between so-called "straight" and "gay" lifestyles in the late twentieth-century. My examples from *Queer as Folk* above already indicated that in terms of workplace and ostensible consumerism there is little that differentiates the two. Business suits and mobile phones, Landrovers as fashion accessories in an urban environment, designer flats to impress friends with and seduce lovers in, these are desirable status symbols for gay and straight men alike. That it is men is significant here, because what *Queer as Folk* demonstrates even more explicitly than the sexuality of its protagonists is that they participate in an environment of intense and permanent homosocial bonding, a universe that functions on the basis of relationships between men and in which women merely play a supporting part (although the "supporting" must be taken very seriously).

What might therefore appeal to straight young men in *Queer as Folk* could be the depiction of a lifestyle that also represents their own, or more than that, an idealised version of their own. Promiscuity, living for the weekend, for drink, drugs and clubbing, nice clothes, cars, and designer gadgets, also sums up the "straight" consumerist ideology of the 1990s.

If the gay lifestyle depicted by *Queer as Folk* has the edge over its straight equivalent it is because its fun is not threatened by the inevitable destination of marriage with its added encumberments of children, mortgage, etc. The consumerist images of 1990s masculinity converge in the characters of the series, all of whom are attractive (even the often clumsy and shy Vince is played by an actor with model looks), and all of whom participate in a never-ending series of visits to pub, bars, and clubs. That there might be limits to the gay abandon that fascinates straights and gays alike is only ever insinuated slyly, for instance when a friend of Stuart and Vince's, Phil, claims not to find lovers any more, because he is 35 (in fact, he is just as good-looking as the rest of the cast), and when Vince reports to Stuart over the ubiquitous mobile phone concerning his date in episode 5: "He says he's 36, the liar. I'm sitting here with an old man." Phil eventually dies of an accidental drug overdose that he takes while preparing for sex with a casual pick-up. But even there gay norms (that privilege youth and looks) and heterosexual ideals are not miles apart. In fact, straight males very often think in terms of a life before thirty that is dedicated to hedonistic pleasure along the lines of that in *Queer as Folk* and a responsible (and boring) existence afterwards. For those who have no access to either straight or gay abandon (probably because their realities do not match those depicted by television), *Queer as Folk* still offers a carnivalesque escapism into not so much a better utopian world as one that forever seems to exist at the fringes of acceptable normality.

Yet, as has been argued throughout the analysis of *Queer as Folk*, the price to be paid for what could easily be viewed as superficially subversive, but ultimately harmless fun, is the dissolving of norms of gender and sexuality. This could be regarded as a progressive effect to be welcomed by all those who conceptualise gender and sexuality as social constructs that, while providing orientation and security, also always entail a constitutive degree of oppression. Yet the dissolution that is signalled by contemporary cultural phenomena such as men's fashion magazines and series like *Queer as Folk* is one that also leads into the repetitive sameness masquerading as fashion, into an often mindless consumerism. Not all of this is done in a naive and unreflected way: the discussion of the importance of labels in magazines like *Arena Homme Plus* is designed to simultaneously reflect, criticise, and still promote exactly the phenomenon it addresses. In episode 4 of *Queer as Folk*, Stuart is shown dictating the words of Phil's grief-stricken mother to his secretary over his mobile phone as an new advertising slogan. The assistant's response, when she figures out what is going on, is to shout "You bastard" at him before slamming down the phone. Yet Stuart also disposes of Vince's mobile phone by throwing it into a canal when it becomes an accessory to Vince's indecision and evasion of relationships. More drastically, Vince abandons the car bought for him by his Australian lawyer lover when he realises that it is used to control rather than liberate him. In a similar way, *Queer as Folk* shows an awareness of the power of the media as both the linchpin of hegemony and its escapist safety valve. A dominant part of Vince's evasion of life's realities (albeit the ones prescribed mainly by Stuart as promiscuous sex and endless fun) is his addiction to *Doctor Who* videos, a science fiction series first broadcast on British TV in the 1960s and now a similar cult to *Star Trek*. Life on TV is not life, that is precisely the message of TV, while it at the same time insinuates the opposite.

If the intriguing solidarity between "straight" and "gay" men brought about by commodity culture signals a new hegemony, then it must produce its own exclusions and fringes. What are they? First and foremost it is women who are placed at the margins of this hedonistic homosocial world. They are not actively excluded by it, in the same way that homosexuality is not strictly excluded from traditional heterosexual normality, but used as a benchmark with which to measure normality and its limits. The term "supporting role" has already been employed for the functions that women are assigned in this new ideology. They are the mothers that enable 30 year old men to stay single without, however, having to accept responsibility for all aspects of their lives (such as cooking, cleaning, washing, etc.). They are the assistants, secretaries, and best friends that provide the social lubricant for a hedonistic male lifestyle (in fairness, male homosexuals as best friends have traditionally fulfilled similar functions for women). They are also, at least in the fictions of this new male lifestyle, the adoring and often envious bystanders that glorify this ideology further.

Age, poverty, and ugliness do not feature prominently in the new homosocial visions that undo the sexual binary of straight and gay in order to strengthen the gender binary male versus female to the degree in which even gender hostility dissolves into an ultimate refusal to engage in gender difference at all. This does not mean that the "new men" (straight and gay, hard and soft, traditional and modern) see gender difference as a thing of the past. On the contrary: they leave it untouched, and only deal with it when it can be made to contribute to their hedonistic universe. It is telling that relationships are the exception in *Queer as Folk*, and almost inevitably end in disaster. Vince, apparently suffering for years because of his failure to find a boyfriend, discovers that he experiences a relationship as suffocating once he has secured a partner. Stuart is asked by the girlfriend of the lesbian mother of his child to sabotage an emerging heterosexual liaison of the latter (the act of sabotage is then actually performed by young

Nathan, but only because he, tellingly, thinks that he is "helping", i.e. conforming to his new environment).

The new hegemonic vision of a successful all-male fun culture retains its normalities and norms: this time it is, perhaps not for the first time, but new in its blatantness, the norm of success, a success that is market-driven. As an object in the commodified world of attractiveness, the individual success, and it does not matter whether it is a straight- or a gay-identified individual, as long as it is male. The apparent victory of homosocial bonding over the traditional heterosexual partnership leaves women, whose existences are still to a large degree ideologically structured with reference to such partnerships, or men in general (as mothers, girlfriends, lovers, wives, and widows), in a no-win situation. Even when they are perceived as autonomous of men (as in the case of the lesbian couple, or Vince's single mother), they are still functionalised by them.

For straight and gay men alike this shift brings about a certain relaxation of the seemingly endless struggle to be different (or not to appear different, according to environment), but at the price of an even less precise idea of their identities. Here, Terry Eagleton's otherwise rather too general attack on the questionable ideology of postmodern culture might be accurate. He writes:

> By raising alienation to the second power, alienating us even from our own alienation, it persuades us to recognize that utopia not as some remote *telos* but, amazingly, as nothing less than the present itself, replete as it is in its own brutal positivity and scarred through with not the slightest trace of lack. (Eagleton 1988: 386)

As the abject adjunct to a heterosexual hegemony, homosexual existence might indeed only offer an alienated position, doubly alienated when it meets an equally ideologically structured notion of masculinity (the problems for women and lesbians are different, although they derive from the same structures). Yet a liberation from this alienation that rests on binaries of in and out, acceptable and unacceptable, need not lead to a miraculous state of wholeness and authenticity. It could just as well lead to greater alienation, the alienation raised to the second power to which Eagleton refers. Jo Eadie formulates the problem from a gay perspective:

> Indigestion is at the core of the gay body politic. Its constant invitation to queers to come and join the party (in either sense of the word) results in a discomforting mass of foreign bodies lodged inside, stuck in the throat, or undigested in its stomach. The cure would be to recognize that the signs which have been collected around the figure of the homosexual – camp, music, leather, butch-femme – even the most blatant, secure signs – we fuck men – in fact secure nothing. They are only the available terms through which different identities are enabled to speak. They do not – and this is crucial because it is the very opposite of how those signs are usually read – *tell us anything*. (Eadie 1999: 83)

The vacuums created by the absence of unalienated meaning, by the missing or impossible authenticities concerning sexuality and gender, might be filled superficially by the distractions of a commodity and media culture, yet only in a self-congratulatory and often blatantly cynical way. "It's not gay, it's not straight – it's only TV, but we are already living it (and we are certainly paying for it)," could sum up this end of hetero- and homosexuality as defining marks of masculinity. It would then be an end that brings with it a new hegemony that might be more difficult to tackle than the old one expressed in the charades of role play and the drawing and re-drawing of borderlines and exclusion zones. It might also ultimately create a very lonely reality of hyperindividualised consumers whose seeming bonding is temporary and prescribed primarily by the dictates of consumption. Phil's mother, trying to rationalise the death of her son in episode 4 of *Queer as Folk*, asks Vince: "He'd find himself at the age of 35 taking heroin with a casual fuck if he was straight?" Vince's answer is strategic, but also possibly true: "He might." Yet Vince lacks a response to her blunt reminder of the other side of the coin of endless hedonistic pleasure, namely the isolation that is the price for glorious male singledom: "Four days he lay there."

While Phil's mother only envisages traditional heterosexual partnership as an alternative and Eagleton ultimately looks back from alienation to its seemingly safe origin, namely its original definition in the division of labour, Eadie adds to the debate a further layer. He raises alienation to the third power, so to speak, by insinuating that identities might consist of the very foreign bodies that trouble it. He translates into Queer Theory a concept that Julia Kristeva introduces into Critical Theory in her book *Strangers to Ourselves* (Kristeva 1994). Yet out of this diagnosis evolve no therapies, since there is no state of health that can be reclaimed. What the concept helps to achieve, and this is where its implications for a practice and politics lie that go beyond Kristeva's philosophical assertions, is the unmasking of the notions of healthy and unhealthy, authentic and inauthentic, be they gay or straight, as the expressions of a hegemonic will to power. These determine masculinity as much as they determine hetero- and homosexuality, and, according to my above argument, the former through the latter. It remains up to us to decide how we subscribe to them and how much we are willing to pay for membership or opposition.

Works cited

Adams, James Eli 1995. *Dandies and Desert Saints: Styles of Victorian Masculinity.* Ithaca and London: Cornell University Press.

Bowlby, Rachel 1993. "Promoting Dorian Gray." *Shopping with Freud.* London and New York: Routledge, 7-24.

Eadie, Jo 1999. "Indigestion: Diagnosing the Gay Maladie" in Mark Simpson (ed.). *Anti-Gay*. London and New York: Cassell, 66-83.

Eagleton, Terry 1988. "Capitalism, Modernism and Postmodernism" in David Lodge (ed.). *Modern Criticism and Theory: A Reader*. London and New York: Longman, 385-398.

Forrest, Fred 1984. " 'We're here, we're queer, and we're not going shopping': Changing Gay Male Identities in Contemporary Britain" in Andrea Cornwall and Nancy Lindisfarne (eds.). *Dislocating Masculinity: Contemporary Ethnographies*. London and New York: Routledge, 97-110.

Foucault, Michel 1981. *The History of Sexuality: An Introduction*. Trans. Robert Hurley. Harmondsworth: Penguin.

Foyster, Elizabeth A. 1999. *Manhood in Early Modern England: Honour, Sex and Marriage*. London and New York: Longman.

Healey, Murray 1999. "Tag Hags R Us." *Arena Homme Plus* 12 (1999), 202.

Kristeva, Julia 1994. *Strangers to Ourselves*. Trans. Leon Roudiez. New York and London: Columbia University Press.

MacInnes, John 1998. *The End of Masculinity: The Confusion of Sexual Genesis and Sexual Difference in Modern Society*. Buckingham and Philadelphia: Open University Press.

Manning, Tony 1999. "Gay Culture: Who Needs It?" in Mark Simpson (ed.). *Anti-Gay*. London and New York: Cassell, 98-117.

Meyer, Moe 1994. "Under the Sign of Wilde: An Archaeology of Posing" in Moe Meyer (ed.). *The Politics and Poetics of Camp*. London and New York: Routledge, 75-109.

Plummer, Kenneth 1990. "Understanding Childhood Sexualities." *Journal of Homosexuality*. 20: 1/2 (1990), 231-249.

Schickedanz, Hans-Joachim (ed.) 1980. *Der Dandy: Texte und Bilder aus dem 19. Jahrhundert*. Dortmund: Harenberg.

Sinfield, Alan 1998. *Gay and After*. London: Serpent's Tail.

Sullivan, Andrew 1996. *Virtually Normal: An Argument about Homosexuality*. London: Picador.

Theis, Wolfgang and Andreas Sternweiler 1984. "Alltag im Kaiserreich und in der Weimarer Republik" in Michael Bollé (ed.). *Eldorado: Homosexuelle Frauen und Männer in Berlin 1850-1950 – Geschichte und Kultur*. Berlin: Frölich & Kaufmann.

Thio, Alex 1998. *Deviant Behaviour*. 5th edition. New York et al.: Longman.

Tosh, John 1998. "New Men? The Bourgeois Cult of Home" in Gordon Marsden (ed.). *Victorian Values: Personalities and Perspectives in Nineteenth-Century Society*. 2nd ed. London und New York: Longman, 77-87.

Weeks, Jeffrey 1987. "Questions of Identity" in Pat Caplan (ed.). *The Cultural Construction of Sexuality*. London and New York: Tavistock, 31-51.

X, Richard 1999. "Oh You Pretty Things: Lads, Dads, Fags – The British Male Comes out of the Closet." *Arena Homme Plus*. 12 (1999), 199.

"Sometimes We Wonder Who the Real Men Are" – Masculinity and Contemporary Popular Music

Frank Lay

In the Eighties of the 20th century, the British singer-songwriter Joe Jackson put into the above words the anguish and confusion which he experienced in relation to different and conflicting models of male behaviour. By doing this, he hit on a vital and fiercely debated point of contemporary life in the Western world, and many men continue to share his concerns.

As is the case with all fields of cultural activity, popular music is and has always been a mirror of the social values of the society in which it was created and is embedded. Given this premise, it comes as no surprise that masculinity plays an integral part in the (self)definition of several music styles, especially those that arose directly out of a predominantly male youth subculture, such as Rock'n'Roll, Heavy Metal, and Punk Rock. The perhaps most striking evidence for this can be seen in the fact that the overwhelming majority of the practising musicians, especially the instrumentalists, in these styles are men, as is – according to market research – the largest part of the audience.

It is the aim of this article to trace the different concepts of masculinity in selected popular music styles in Western societies. I will argue that the crisis of what has been designated "hegemonic masculinity" is reflected in the structures of popular music culture with all the appropriate details and the problems entailed. A gender-based analysis of these music styles can be very useful in gaining an insight into the strategies and ideological functions of different, and indeed often contradictory, definitions of masculinity – and femininity for that matter. The spectrum of the different realisations ranges from the aggressive assertion of hegemonic and traditional images of masculinity inherent in Heavy Metal lingo and appearance, to the ambivalent transitoriness of an androgynic Disco tradition, or the bilateral appropriation of gay codes on the one hand and "traditional" Rock style on the other.

Furthermore, it will be necessary to reflect on the capacity of self-analysis that is evinced in the works of musicians like Joe Jackson or Randy Newman.

At first glance, it is striking that there has been so little research on the reception of masculinity in contemporary music. After all, the recent reorganization of women's studies into gender studies has brought men and concepts of masculinity into focus (cf. Petersen 1998: 1 ff). However, it would be misleading to conclude that masculinity is not an issue in the context of the contemporary music scene. On the contrary, a closer look at some phenomena reveals the importance of contending interpretations of masculinity for both the musical and the visual aspects of the music business.

The complexity and potential polysemy of the visual and aural codes in this cultural field inevitably lead to a proliferation of discursive manifestations that have to be incorporated in any analysis along the lines of the categories of sex, gender, and representation. The interaction of these codes is highly complex in itself, since feminist critics, making use of the reflections of Michel Foucault, have pointed out that not only gender, but also sex are produced by and within regulatory discursive formations. Thus, the inherently problematic character of the categories of gender and sex is generated and perpetuated by the fact that its subjects are "[...] produced and restrained through the very structures of power through which emancipation is sought" (Butler 1990: 2). Judith Butler concludes that any attempt at resistance or subversion must take this complexity into account and thus be an act of self-reflexivity. Therefore, since subversion is only possible within the power that restrains it, it can only consist of subversive bodily acts that are capable of disrupting the performative pattern which reproduces oppression. Can music offer a possibility in this sense? In how far does the multimediality of music yield the chance for effective – even if local – resistance? Eliot Fiske and others have shown that it is possible for critically aware audiences to read media messages "against the grain", to identify them as belonging to a hegemonic set of discursive rules, and even to decode them into their opposite (cf. Fiske 1987, Hall 1988). At first glance, the music industry seems to be totally co-opted by a cultural hegemony including set and very traditional images of gender roles. Yet there are instances of ostentatious display of the crossing of gender boundaries, as in Madonna's or Michael Jackson's self-fashioning appearance. Additionally, the artificiality of many Rock and Pop images and videos seems to clearly unmask the presented gender identities as constructs, at least for an audience that knows how to interpret them. In fact, one may say that the demands of feminism as well as the successes of the gay liberation movement have led to a heightened awareness that traditional concepts of masculinity no longer hold good. Instead, many men share the desire for a new "standard" that would have to be defined. Although the realisation that gender, even sex and the conceptualization of the body, is based on discursive formations and strategies renders such an undertaking impossible and misleading in the first place, there lingers an essentialist undercurrent within the debate about a new masculine standard. It appears that the old hegemonic concept of masculinity is still very much alive and alluring to men of all social backgrounds, not only in men's nostalgia for a time when there is thought to have been less anxiety about how a man should behave and look, but also in paradoxical images conjured up by lifestyle journalists and trend scouts who analyse the desires of women and men respectively, trying to distill a new valid model for masculinity. As R. W. Connell says, "[...] there is an active defence of hegemonic masculinity [and] it has formidable resources" (1995: 216). One reason for the longevity of traditional masculinity is undoubtedly to be found in the strategies of co-optation and adaption of potentially subversive discourses that are characteristic for the existing hegemonic power relations, an observation which has been prominently pointed out by Foucault (as in *La volonté de savoir*) and further elaborated with explicit reference to gender in recent feminist theory. The presupposition that the substantiality of the body is regulated and stylized through discourse, that the body is not only "gendered", but also "sexed" in this way, resulting in a Nietzschean notion of a "metaphysics of substance" (Butler 1990: 20) invariably brings up the question whether any resistance is possible within a framework of all-encompassing power. Theorists like Butler consequently tend to limit the possibility of subversion to the exposure of at least parts of the mechanisms that effect this reiterative definition of "substance". Such an analysis is closely related to a strategy of subversive decoding of media messages as proposed by Fiske and others, and accordingly it must try to resist the temptation of labelling any small deviation from the norm as effective subversion. One should always keep in mind the adaptive power of hegemony, capable of turning an instance of original subversion into a commodified corroboration of hegemonic discourse. Given this premise, it must be clear that a mass of divergent phenomena like the contemporary music scene has to be looked at in great detail to be able to determine the degree of subversive potential for specific examples – provided there is any at all. The following is not intented to give detailed analyses in this sense but rather to provide a broad overview of some of the phenomena that might qualify for such an analysis and to pose some questions with respect to the issue of dominant and alternative discourses of masculinity.

A closer examination of the relevant phenomena in the popular music business shows that there is a twofold manifestation of the (predominantly male) concerns in the face of the ongoing debate about a new standard for men – which is, obviously, largely the same as the debate about hegemonic and subversive discourses of masculinity. One is the conscious or unconscious articulation of confusion about one's presumed gender identity, while the other is the equally important aspect of a commodification of these concerns in several forms. Men's increasing anxiety about proving their manhood has thus been discovered as a marketing device. It will be the aim of this article to trace both manifestations with the help of selected examples. It is not surprising, although certainly worth debating, that most of the explicit or implicit problematizing of masculine discourses in the music business is done by men and thus reflects their anxieties and concerns (this is in itself a point of interest because it forms a clear contrast to other areas of theoretical discourse about masculinities which have been heavily influenced by feminist theory). For this reason, the discussion will be limited to male artists and their interpretations and active representations of masculinity. However, one should not overlook in this context that women are very important, both as recipients or fans of representations of masculinity and as participants in the discourse. An increasing number of female artists is beginning to comment on the matter, and their input will be very valuable (see Reynolds/Press 2000).

The Rise of Electronic Pop and the Heavy-Rock Backlash in the 1980s

If one tries to paint a rough picture of the development of popular music since the 1980s, it is necessary to establish a few crucial stylistic distinctions. First of all, even though it has become a cliché, an important transition is marked by the expanded usage of technology, especially in the form of beat boxes, synthesizers, and later on sampling devices. This tendency had developed through the Seventies, with all the experimentation with the new sound possibilities explored by the "arty" Rock bands in the tradition of Cream, King Crimson, and others, and it reached a first climax in the Eighties with the rise of Disco and Dancefloor (a mixture that incorporated a lot of elements from R'n'B and 70s Soul music) in the wake of the experiments with synthesized sound by progressive bands like Kraftwerk. In any case, this new style formed a sharp contrast to the handcrafted art rock of the later 70s and also to the explicitly "low-tech" approach of the Punk Rock movement. Interestingly enough, even Hard Rock – though it continued to exist in a rough and rebellious form as exemplified by bands like AC/DC – appropriated the "new sound" of the decade, and this ultimately led to the creation of a glamorous and highly stylized Hard Rock with an explicitly carnivalesque element to it (compare the stage appearance of bands like Kiss), the inclusion of synthesizers, and again a concentration on the technical skills of the players, perhaps even more than in the 70s. Soundwise, the use of digital effects became a widespread practice, with the result that the personality of the different bands, especially in the Rock genre, was not as readily recognizable as it used to be in the 70s.

Similarly, the evolution of Dancefloor music created an extremely dancable mixture of usually simple melodic lines and bombastic beats in regular 4/4 patterns, and with characteristic drum computer sound, practically void of any dynamics.

In retrospect, the 1980s have come to represent the radical change that was initiated by the quantum leap in electronic music generation. This is not to say, of course, that handcrafted music was dead. One must not forget, when talking about the 1980s, that it was also the decade of Bruce Springsteen's million-selling album *Born in the U.S.A.* And this is just one example of many. But this consideration does not alter the general observation that the music scene and the music industry in the 80s became more technology-based than ever before. Furthermore, synthesized music began to dominate the charts and, perhaps above all, the dancing venues. This, however, had grave consequences for the reception of popular music in Western culture. Especially with regard to gender identity, the shift from mainly handcrafted to generally synthesizer-based music is interesting and reveals much about the hidden mechanisms of gender identity construction. Most importantly, electronic music was always experienced as somehow more remote and unemotional than the "real thing", i.e. handmade music. On the other hand, this meant that it was also experienced as more modern. Perhaps it was precisely this combination of characteristics which appealed to the practitioners as well as to the audience. In a nutshell, the Disco and Dancefloor styles became a prime vehicle for gay culture and lifestyle (see Attig 1991: 185). It remains a point to be argued whether the general and widespread acceptance of this music at the time actually helped gay liberation or not, but the impact on the self-perception of men cannot be overlooked. Of course the overt gay presence in, and even domination of dancefloor (e.g. bands like Erasure, Bronski Beat, Depeche Mode, or the deliberately androgynous appearance of Boy George's Culture Club) provoked an adverse reaction from the Rock scene – traditionally the realm of hegemonic masculinity. Paradoxically, this reaction in itself, even if intended as a backlash, can hardly be regarded as such. For if one takes the trouble to examine the 80s Rock scene a bit more closely, many parallels with the despised Dancefloor-pop are to be found. Behind the scenes of the radical assertion of maleness, the martial symbolism, and the obvious subjection of women in their depiction as sex-dolls inherent in 80s Heavy Metal, there lurks a fascination for the drag poses of 70s Glam Rock and an appropriation of the technological experiments of electronic music, as in the frequent inclusion of keyboards or the use of guitar effects that serve to annihilate sound differences between different instruments or players in favour of a sound that has subsequently been called "overproduced". Precisely in the Heavy Metal macho poses, as in the often employed fantasy elements or ancient macho cults, lies a desire for escapism, the need to flee a world where masculinity is threatened by androgynity or the demands of feminists and gay activists. Stan Denski and David Sholle have rightly pointed out that in the course of the 1980s Heavy Metal "underwent intra-generic transformations" (Denski/Sholle 1992: 43) into Glam Metal on the one hand and Speed/Thrash Metal on the other. Also, they refer to the obvious connection between Heavy Metal and Science Fiction: "[w]ithin heavy metal it is the the heroic and masculine features of science fiction that are emphasized, and, along with this worship of the warrior/hero, technology again in the form of machines of great power and destruction" (Denski/Sholle 1992: 48). Paradoxically, however, the alternative world which is thus conjured up bears several attributes of precisely that which the participants want to shun. The more or less "feminine" appearance of some bands somehow subverts the machismo of the lyrics and the obvious aggression in the music is tamed by a mainstream bombast sound that tends to smooth the edges of the once rough-hewn Rock style. Given the parodic element in Glam Metal, it is tempting to ask about its potential for resistance. Denski and Sholle are not very optimistic about this, since they try to interpret the appropriation of femininity as a subversive bodily practice in the sense of Judith Butler's theory of performativity, and they come to the conclusion that while Heavy Metal may mirror adolescent boys' fears of women, it does not really go far enough in its drag poses as to seriously question the "asymmetrical binary of masculine and feminine" (Butler 1990: 31). Accordingly, they conclude that

> [f]or all its elaborate posturing and outrageous theatrics, heavy metal's appropriation of feminine gender signs fails to offer a meaningful challenge to the socially constructed core identity of binary sex, offering instead a thinly disguised reproduction of traditional masculine roles of power and domination presented in the context of an aggressive heterosexuality. (Denski/Sholle 1992: 59)

This verdict, however, rests on the assumption that performativity is to be understood as performing and acting gender stereotypes, which is at most only partly true. In fact, performativity goes much further than that. It means that gender/sex is a category that is shaped by discursive formations and at the same time generates and reproduces them; the fact that it is located in a system of ever-adapting bio-power leads to the paradoxical state that it creates its own oppressive structures where resistance always and inevitably carries the risk of being assimilated and turned against itself by the power structures. It is not the subject who decides on gender, but the other way round, as Judith Butler put in the preface to *Bodies that Matter*: "[...] gender is not an artifice to be taken on or taken off at will and, hence, not an effect of choice [...]" (Butler 1993: x). Therefore, the relevance of performativity is more than just performing gender in the way that Heavy Metal does. Nevertheless, Denski and Sholle are undoubtably right in arguing that an appropriation of feminine codes does not automatically function as subversion. As for the Heavy Metal audiences, they typically consist of young males, so that an adolescent fear of women may really be an important motivation for their admiration of the staged heroes.

This kind of interpretation is corroborated by the adverse reaction inside the Rock scene in the early 1990s that featured a neo-Punk movement seeking to get rid of the overproduction and the commercialization of 80s Heavy Metal. The heralds of the new sound – called Grunge – were angry young men who favoured dry guitar sounds with heavy distortion, no keyboards or samples, and simple rhythms. Additionally, they totally refuted the typical Metal look by presenting themselves in torn jeans and t-shirts, gritty and deliberately dirty. Their songs were an outcry against the co-opting of rock through the mass music and culture industry. They resisted the urge to render songs melodious and dancable, and, above all, they felt contempt for that epitome of all they hated in 80s Rock, the elaborated guitar solo.

The history of the rock guitar solo merits a short digression at this point. Ever since Jimi Hendrix popularized the use of a distorted, singing lead sound in the 1960s, the electric guitar had been the chief device for rock music soloing. The guitar heroes of the 70s, like Eric Clapton (one only needs to remember the well-known contemporary slogan "Clapton is God!", painted on a wall by a ravished fan in the late 1960s), Led Zeppelin's Jimmy Page, or Deep Purple's Ritchie Blackmore usually were the most important musicians in their respective bands except for the lead singers. The origin of the guitar solo was, as it was for the whole style, the simple but intriguing structure of blues. But before long accomplished musicians like King Crimson's Robert Fripp or Duane Allman of the Southern Rock band The Allman Brothers started experimenting with more complex scales and techniques. This was countered – already in the 70s – by the Punk rockers' famous assertion that three chords had to be enough for a song, but regardless of that the 80s rock bands continued to work on their playing technique. This tendency was met and further strengthened by the establishing of the Musician's Institute, and, more specifically, the Guitar Institute of Technology in Hollywood, California, a school for professionial players that continued to produce fretboard sprinters until well into the 1990s. In sharp contrast to the Punk rockers these guitarists were highly trained both in music theory and in practice, and they wanted to put everything they had acquired into use. Famous musicians who graduated from or taught at this school were, among others, Racer X's Paul Gilbert, as well as Steve Vai, and Joe Satriani – all of them celebrated guitar heroes of the 1980s and 90s. The culmination of this development may – arguably – be seen in mid-80s players like Tony MacAlpine and Yngwie Malmsteen, who tried to compose neo-classical guitar orchestrations in almost symphonic style (cf. Marty Friedman and Jason Becker's aptly titled 1987 record *Speed Metal Symphony* on Shrapnel Records). If one listens to these recordings nowadays, one cannot help wondering how non-guitarists could bear to listen to the whole length of them (which they probably didn't anyway). Overall, the cult of the guitar hero can be seen as symptomatic for the way in which Rock expresses aggression and sexual prowess,

> [...] where technical mastery of the instrument in conjunction with intense volume create a close link between the performer and the (male) audience. The technological power used and represented in heavy metal is one of the primary ways in which the male audience identifies with the masculine pose of the band. The improvisatory pretensions of the heavy metal musician are read as distinct signs of mastery and aggressive "attack". (Denski/Sholle 1992: 48)

In summary, the Grunge rockers of the early 90s recalled an aversion against such excesses of theatricalism, similar to that of the early Punk rockers. Rather, like the latter, the Grunge rockers either eliminated guitar solos completely or just used screaming feedback effects instead of complicated scales and two-hand tapping techniques. This refutation has grave consequences for the received image of the music with respect to gender representations. If the Grunge rockers scorn the use of complicated techniques, they also modify the implications of a link between the guitar hero and the male audience. Thus, it is no longer possible for would-be heroes in the audience to identify with the band in terms of masculinity. As Jason Middleton has observed,

> [t]he breakthrough of Nirvana can be understood in terms of a number of currents related to the aesthetic of heroin chic. [...] Nirvana was regarded as the antithesis of the hyperbolic, sexist, and masculinist spectacles of the 'Hair metal' bands popular through the late 80s. Cobain's boyish, even childlike appearance, with oversized sweaters and a sloppily cut blond mane; his affirmation of gay sex, and televised screen kiss with bassist Chris Novoselic [...] all negated the values of aggressive masculinist heterosexuality prevalent in much rock music in the period preceding Nirvana's emergence. (Middleton 1999)

Therefore, the Grunge movement can be seen as a double refutation of 80s Heavy Rock that was perceived as "effeminate" and highly commercial. By then, one could surmise, the inherent equivocal machismo-drag-parody opposition had become untenable, above all in a cultural environment that was characterised by the constant deconstruction of gender identity and an increasing anxiety of men who felt uneasy about their own behaviour and about what women (and other men) could possibly expect them to be (these expectations of course mirroring the hegemonic constructions of gender identities). The result was a pretty traditional (and stoical) return of a "boys-will-be-boys" style, a gritty and dirty reaffirmation of Punk values, but without the specifically "punk" outward appearance. In a nutshell, Grunge is a late 20th century version of Punk, lacking the ideological impetus or rather the simplicity of a "no future" slogan. Greg Wahl (1995) points out that the 90s version of Punk rock is characterised by a specifically male adolescent narcissism, the drama of male coming of age and finding a way to define one's masculinity, that is somehow less radical – and certainly less political – than the anarchic and highly neurotic misogyny of the Sex Pistols. Even if Grunge rockers like Nirvana's Kurt Cobain were not explicitly presented as a new kind of male rock persona, they have nonetheless come to impersonate the new type of man, torn angrily between hegemonic masculinity and the "new men" of the 1970s, and, most of all, the unreachable ideal man of the "post-feminist" era, incorporating all extremes, the macho and the softie, everything to the presumed "right" degree. Simon Reynolds and Joy Press in *The Sex Revolts* (2000) argue that the problematizing of gender differences peculiar to Grunge is grounded on a double tradition of "phallic" hard rock beats and riffs on the one hand and a worshipping of the feminine inherent in Pschychedelic music. This opposition can be traced back as far as Jimi Hendrix, who "for every hard rocking number like 'Crosstown Traffic' (in which he's running from a clinging lover so frantically he runs her over, leaving tire tracks on her back) [has] a song like 'Belly Button Window' in which he imagines himself an unborn child nestled in his mum's comfy womb". It is from this conflicting but coexisting aesthetics of refuting and embracing the feminine that Grunge's disturbing quality arises, the "[...] castration blues [,] the flailing sound of failed masculinity that made Nirvana and Alice in Chains resonate for Generation X" (Reynolds/Press 2000). In fact, Kurt Cobain's lyrics on *Heart Shaped Box* from the conveniently titled album *In Utero* (Geffen Records 1993) demonstrate the basic opposition in the way they

> oscillate [...] between a nostalgia for the womb and a sort of castration-anxiety: one minute he's begging a woman to let down her "umbilical noose" so he can climb back inside, the next he's recoiling from her "magnet tar-pit." The female figure in "Heart-Shaped Box" seems to be a conflation of Cobain's mother, his wife Courtney Love, and heroin. This phantasmic woman signifies both sanctuary and death; in fact, on another song on the [...] album, he wails "I'm married, buried." (Reynolds/Press 2000)

"Bad Guys"

But Grunge is not the only phenomenon in 1990s music that sheds some light on the gender debate. One of the most radical of these is at the same time predominantly racial: HipHop. Created as a form of modern protest music for black underdogs, it has spread significantly across racial and national boundaries (and most recently also stylistic boundaries, as the number of crossover mixes of other styles with HipHop shows). During the course of this spread many influences have been taken over and thus changed the original concept. This was – and in many cases still is – a radical statement of male physical aggressiveness (cf. Ice-T's infamous track *Cop Killer*) which could be used to define a true identity within the group. Violence and aggression thus serve as distinguishing factors within society, and the music is a vehicle to state this distinction. Of course, as in other musical styles, the music is just one aspect of the whole. Especially the black heralds of HipHop culture often endorse violence and a gangster attitude as a vital part of their image. Consequently, they act and present themselves accordingly, and conflicts with the law are considered an achievement. Interestingly enough, even though HipHop used to be an almost exclusively "black" phenomenon at first it quickly became co-opted by "white" mainstream cultural forces – regardless of the urge of many "original" HipHoppers to withhold non-blacks from adapting a musical style which they felt was thoroughly "theirs".

As far as the issue of masculinity is concerned, one may speculate about the motivation here. It must be remembered in this context that the combination of images and stereotypes which is presented as black masculinity is highly and at least partly consciously constructed. This can be seen from the sheer degree to which male and female bodies in Rap/HipHop videos are obviously and aggressively constructed. The concentration on the body goes through the music as well – the beat is omnipresent, dancable, and further emphasized by the absence of a melody. The exact interpretations of the manifestations of black masculinity in HipHop music and culture are very much subject to an ongoing debate, though, and it is not the aim here to reflect on the implications. Furthermore, it is debatable whether black masculinity can by definition be hegemonic, because it always contains a subversive element in that it challenges the ethnic presumptions of hegemonic white masculinity. But generally speaking, it can be maintained that one of the major concerns of the black phenomenon HipHop was (and still is) the need to regain ground as men, to fortify racial and cultural awarenesses and identities in the face of radically changing perceptions of gender and ethnic roles. It also comes as no surprise that this programme appeals to non-black men as well. In a sense, it seems as if the non-blacks do not want to leave this territory of archaic maleness and this distinct opportunity for recuperation to the blacks. Moreover, the ostentatious display of manly vigour and self-confidence inherent in HipHop must look like a relief to men who feel challenged in the very basis of their gender identity. They are offered a construct that promises a possibility of self-fashioning and a redesign of codes to the effect that they can take parts out of the stereotypical model of aggressive masculinity in order to modify their own identity. Thus, paradoxically, an example of an appropriation of extreme hegemonic masculinity may turn into a socially subversive statement (while remaining the former through the participation in the perpetuation of hegemonic codes). From the point of view of the non-blacks, it can be seen as an appropriation of a stereotypical construct of supposedly "black" masculinity used to differentiate themselves from the effeminate glamour types who dominated the 80s Rock scene and the gay Disco bands.

"Pretty Boys"

A completely different, though no less vital, phenomenon is constituted by the emergence of the "boy groups", bands that are, as the term implies, chiefly characterised by the sexual attractiveness of their members. Prominent examples would be the Backstreet Boys or New Kids on the Block; interestingly both band names seem to stress the attribute of "boyness" instead of a possible masculinity. This may serve as a hint to how far the self-realization and conscious commodification on part of the music industry extends. Of course the concept as such is known since the mass hysteria at Elvis or The Beatles gigs, only that the later 20th century accounts for the further commodification of groups that are specifically formed to meet – and shape – what are imagined to be the sexual desires of pubescent girls. Thus, they are constituted of stereotypes, or at least men who are designed to represent those types. In this context the stage appearance and the choreography have become more important than the actual music. This new functionality of men as sex objects for young girls is likely to put additional pressure on them, since they would have to conform to the constructed representations of female desires. In a sense, it becomes possible to get a glimpse of the strains and problems that women are exposed to if they try to conform to the assumed standards of men, to attract them and their gaze. Therefore, the boy groups are characteristic of a general trend of a reversal of gaze. It is longer only the women who are subject to men's gaze and all the implications entailed, but men are increasingly conceptualized as objects of desire as well.

Another related instance of the male adoption of a traditionally female role as sex object is the emergence of the Latin singers, in a manner combining the good looks and overt sexual attraction of the boy groups, the inherent eroticism of the Latin rhythms, and the singability of the music in general. It is easily conceivable that the overall effect of all this is a profound disorientation – and perhaps even alienation – experienced by many men with regard to their self-concept as men. The commodification of sexuality in the music industry is thus not limited to women anymore, and the symptoms of alienation are roughly the same.

Something which is worth mention in this context is the interesting case of what can be designated "Teenage bands" (examples would be the group Hanson or the German band Echt). On the one hand, they clearly counter the tendency to commodify male sex appeal in that they tend rather to de-sexualize the boys/men. But on the other hand, significantly enough, they sing about the difficulties they experience in the process of becoming men and in this way appeal to both boys their age and older men likewise. The former are intrigued by the idea that they are not alone with their anxieties and problems while the latter can reminisce about their own puberty and the difficulties they had to deal with.

What's a Man now?

All in all, the situation in the contemporary music business can be described as a mirror of the concerns about gender issues that are characteristic for our society. It is easy to unmask the modern Rock scene in particular as a spectacle of what one may call gender hysteria – and this hysteria is predominantly male, since the business is dominated by men. All the well-known characteristics of manhood can easily be traced in different manifestations. As psychologist Robert Brannon has aptly summarized (quoted in Kimmel 1994: 125-126), traditional features of hegemonic manhood as it is popularly understood include the following premisses:

1) 'No sissy stuff!'": The repudiation of all that is considered feminine or connected with femininity is a marker of the ultimate homophobia that is located at the very basis of hegemonic masculinity

2) "Be a big wheel!"": Wealth and status are prime attributes through which men establish a hierarchy. Status is closely connected to wealth, of course, but it does also include the boast of sexual prowess.

3) "Be a sturdy oak!"": Emotions are not to be shown, especially not to other men.

4) "Give 'em Hell!'": Aggression and violence have always been an integral part of hegemonic masculinity and a more or less legitimate means to increase one's influence in a group. The aggression may also be directed against women (both in substantial and discursive form) or subordinate masculine discourses, thus pointing again to the importance of hierarchy: "the justifying ideology for the patriarchal core complex and the overall subordination of women requires the creation of a gender-based hierarchy among men" (Connell 1987: 110). It must be kept in mind that the above characteristics are constructed interpretations that are largely (and also in the music business) employed to mask the discursive strategies that are instrumental in the definition of gender codes, especially the codes that seem to underscore alleged innate behavioral differences between men and women. Given the potential for commodification of such popular definitions, it is not surprising that they are of relevance for the music business as a means to attract consumers.

Especially the modern Rock and the HipHop scene seem to conform almost completely to the pattern (although it appears to be, one might add, constructed by a very different group of men, namely white, presumably middle-aged American males). Given the conclusion drawn by Kimmel, namely that the single most important factor is the fear of being reduced to an effeminate figure before other men (Kimmel 1994: 126), the desire to appear as manly as possible becomes understandable. The derogatory terms for such weak men are legion: "wimp", "sissy", "mama's boy", to name but a few. In this sense the gaze of the other (man) becomes the ultimate source of self-esteem for men. Manifestations of masculinity are produced and modified in the discourse between men, thus masculinity is a much more discursive phenomenon than sex roles research pretends it to be. In this context, it can be hardly surprising that the homophobic element is by far the strongest aspect in the whole concept of being a man. It is of prime importance within the hegemonic discourses of masculinity to repudiate the discourse of feminity, and even the questioning of male hegemonic discourse that threatens the identity as a man; and of course self-confident homoeroticism is in itself a vehement threat to this identity. Therefore it has to be combatted, this has always been a common ground between heterosexual men, but notably the late 20th century has rendered things more complicated. Gay liberation has led to a heightened awareness even among conservative heterosexual men of the fact that the assumption that many homosexuals could be distinguished by certain attributes of their appearance or behaviour, which had been a commonplace in the hegemonic patriarchal concept, is obviously false; the realisation that gays can use macho codes as well has deeply disturbed the heterosexist male psyche. In addition, the very word "gay" (just like the word "queer") underwent a process which Judith Butler, following Foucault, has called "affirmative resignification" (1993: 223). The term designates the appropriation of a former derogaratory term by the targeted group themselves and the subversive act of initiating a semantic change and spreading it throughout society, thereby turning an instance of hegemonic discourse against itself. Accordingly, the need for dominant heterosexist masculinity to differentiate itself from a homosexual masculinity has become more urgent, and different ways of expressing "real" manhood have to be found. In this fashion, popular music can be read as a vehicle for heterosexual male concerns, and, more importantly, for the recuperation of hegemonic masculinity. Consequently it is no wonder that especially Rock music fans on the whole have been very reluctant to accept female musicians (although there are quite a few notable exceptions like Heart in the 1980s and Courtney Love in the 90s), whereas this has never been a matter of debate in Disco and Dancefloor music. If they manage to break through these invisible barriers, however, their impact is not to be underestimated. In a way, as Reynolds and Press have observed, women artists have the opportunity to challenge the whole concept of Rock by confronting it with female experience (Reynolds/Press 2000), thereby, of course, confronting masculinity as well – especially in the form of overt machismo, which is at the same time envied and loathed by women artists for its unblemished confidence.

The Struggle for a new Masculine Identity

In the following, I am going to look at a few examples of self-conscious songs about the problematic issue of masculinity and the difficulties brought about by the ongoing changes in the characteristics of what is to be considered "masculine". It is obvious that the more direct of these examples would stem from genres which traditionally put a lot of emphasis on the lyrics, while the more indirect ones are from the heavier Rock genres, or even the Dancefloor style where the lyrics are mostly very simple and elliptical. Thus, these styles have to be treated differently in that the analysis must incorporate the visual presentation on stage and in videos and the respective image as well as the music. It must be stated, therefore, that of course the members of the music business who consciously and explicitly take up the topic of masculinity are a minority, and they appeal to a minority of potential listeners. This is not to say that their voices are not heard at all, but they are certainly not in the focus of public attention. Nevertheless, it makes sense to include a analysis of examples from this particular field, since it is there where the underlying concerns are articulated most clearly.

Perhaps one of the most interesting voices in the context of musicians writing self-consciously about masculinity is that of Joe Jackson, the British singer-songwriter mentioned above who had a couple of top-ten hits in the US in the 1980s and 1990s. Jackson frequently takes up the topic of masculinity and gives voice to the anxieties and frustrations connected with this concept and its diverse manifestations in real life.

Real Men (Joe Jackson, *Night and Day*, A&M 1984)

Take your mind back – I don't know when
Sometime when it always seemed
To be just us and them
Girls that wore pink
And boys that wore blue   5
Boys that always grew up better men
Than me and you

What's a man now – what's a man mean
Is he rough or is he rugged
Is he cultural and clean   10
Now it's all change – it's got to change more
'Cause we think it's getting better
But nobody's really sure

Chorus: And so it goes – go round again

But now and then we wonder   15
who the real men are

See the nice boys – dancing in pairs
Golden earring golden tan
Blow-wave in the hair
Sure they're all straight – straight as a line   20
All the gays are macho
Can't you see their leather shine

You don't want to sound dumb – don't want to offend
So don't call me a faggot
Not unless you are a friend   25
Then if you're tall and handsome and strong
You can wear the uniform and I could play along

Time to get scared – time to change plan
Don't know how to treat a lady
Don't know how to be a man   30
Time to admit – what you call defeat
'Cause there's women running past you now
And you just drag your feet

Man makes a gun – man goes to war
Man can kill and man can drink   35
And man can take a whore
Kill all the blacks – kill all the reds
And if there's war between the sexes
Then there'll be no people left

In *Real Men*, as in several others of his songs, Jackson – or rather what could, on a superficial level, be interpreted as his speaking persona – gives the impression that he is feeling very uneasy with respect to his identity as a man. It is no longer clear what is expected of a man, and this gives rise to a quaint nostalgia for the "old times" when the gender definitions and boundaries were still reliable. What has remained is merely a feeling of despair and "defeat" (31), since it is by no means clear how one should "treat a lady" (29), let alone "be a man" (30). The result is a problem-laden and insecure subject/object (the "you" is ambiguous here) who can do nothing but "drag *your* feet" (33, my emphasis) in the presence of women. Thus, it is indeed high "time to get scared" (28), and the conclusion seems to be that some generations ago, boys could easily become "better" men than they can today in the face of changing values and gender roles. As a result, the changing of gender roles, though advocated and even wished for by many men, has led to a total flux of identities to the effect that nobody can be really sure if it is really something worth achieving (11-13). All that is left seems to be an obscure fear of an imminent "war between the sexes" (38) mainly caused by male violence, a violence that is in itself a result of frustration and helplessness, instead of a fruitful discussion. An interesting question is raised by the line that "it's got to change more" (11). It is left to debate whether this is intended as an imperative or whether it is simply an expression of agony – and by whom it is meant to be spoken (is it the one who perceives the need to change himself?). This realisation leads to the insight that the speaker need not be a person or a coherent subject in the first place, and thus the polysemy and impact of the text is emphasised. While it is still possible, on a superficial level, to understand Jackson's text as an example of male anxiety that is representative of many of his potential listeners, the text implies, at least in written form, further significations. In this way, Jackson manages to launch an effective attack against hegemonic masculinity. His aim is not so much men's anxiety and fears but the whole construct of the male subject, central to Western "phallogocentrism". Even the identity of the speaker is far from being clear. In fact, the song seems to incorporate multiple visions and voices of manhood. In the wake of Foucauldian poststructuralist thought any idea of essentialism has been banished from gender studies (although this can still not be taken for granted as the debate about Robert Bly's pseudo-Jungian mythopoetic concept of masculinity shows – see Petersen 1998: 7). Therefore it comes as no surprise that the actual experience of masculinity is a shattered and fractured one. Masculinity has always been intrinsically connected with power, and it is in itself a discursive phenomenon, shaping the power relations and at the same time being shaped by them. Thus, Jackson's text can be read against the grain as a manifestation of a male anxiety of being removed from a privileged position in society and reduced to a gendered object susceptible to infinite changes. The traditional male subjectivity is under threat from the fractured subjectivities that present themselves in the text. Notably the speaker changes during the description of the homosexual machos (23 ff). In the next lines, it is obviously the homosexual person who speaks, in turn initiating a further speaker change that is marked by the exclamation that it is "time to get scared" (28). What Jackson's first speaker longs for is, significantly enough, a time with clearly established gender demarcations, and thus an essential masculinity. It is, on a higher level, essentialism in general, an attempt to escape from the insecurities of poststructuralist or constructivist thought.

It is not surprising as well to find a reference to the ambiguous impression of the overt display of gay self-confidence and, first of all, the fact that gays are not recognizable, that they even appropriate typical macho poses (17 ff.). Even if they are clearly recognizable as other, the present situation leads to helpless aggression at the discovery of the homoerotic elements that form the hidden basis of hegemonic masculinity, as in the celebrated American songwriter Randy Newman's 1979 song *Half a Man* (from the album *Born Again* on Warner Bros. Records):

This big old queen was standing on the corner of the street.
He waved his hanky at me as I went rolling by. I pulled the truck
up on the sidewalk and I climbed down from the cab
With my tire-chain and my knife. As I approached him he was
trembling like a bird. I raised the chain above my head   5
He said, "Please, before you kill me Might I have one final word?"
And this is what he said: "I am but Half A Man, Half A Man
I'd like to be a dancer, but I'm much too large Half A Man, Half
A man I'm an object for your pity, not your rage."
Oh, the strangest feeling's sweeping over me. Both my speech and manner 10
have become much more refined I said,
"Oh, what is this feeling? What is wrong with me?"
She said, "Girl, it happens all the time
"And you are Half A Man, Half A Man Look,
you're walking and you're talking like a fag."   15
Half A Man, I am Half
A Man Holy Jesus, what a drag

Here, in Newman's typical sarcastic style, the initial aggression (that is also ironically heightened to an extreme) results in the ultimate discovery of that which is the real object and target of the aggression – one's own homophobia unmasked, the threat to any traditional concept of masculinity. The man is turned, or rather turns himself, into a desperate drag figure – "half a man", and that would be, as has been shown above, the worst nightmare for most men. This transformation is even marked by the identification of the speaker as "girl" (13). Especially in the light of what has been said earlier about the subversive potential of the crossing of gender boundaries and the essential role of homophobia for the definition of heterosexual normative masculinity it becomes evident that this example really constitutes a challenge of hegemonic masculinity. The drag pose is more than an attempt to adopt female codes, it is a basic challenge to gender identity. The disruptive quality of this experience is underscored by the application of the abusive term "fag" in combination with the disturbing fact that it is not at all clear who speaks at that point; significantly the pronoun shifts between "I" and "you". Thus, the text can be seen as an example of a radical demasking of the shaping powers of gender identity. The homosexual object functions as a mirror in which the attacker's homophobia becomes visible, and even aggression and open violence – the last resort and answer of hegemonic masculinity – fail and give way to a curious experience of gender switching or rather oscillation.

An experience of a different kind, though no less devastating, is the conflict of traditional and alternative masculine concepts in the course of courtship for women. Unfortunately, from the point of view of men, women are equally puzzled and insecure about whether to support one version or the other. Rather, one often gets the impression that men should be both extremes at the same time, macho and strong and weak and emotional at the same time. But it is obvious that nobody can possibly conform to this alleged "ideal" (which would indeed be undermined by the premise of the impossibility of a monolithic "masculinity"). It is again Joe Jackson who has put the frustration about this into the song *Is she really going out with him?* (from *Look Sharp!*, A&M 1979), where one line goes as follows: "Pretty women are walking with gorillas down my street". One aspect here is, of course, that of the envious loser who is ignored by the women he admires. But another aspect is certainly that of frustration about the exploits and successes of men who fail to obey the new ideal (if there is any such thing), but who just keep on being "rough and rugged". Still, they are preferred by at least some women to the ones who try to be "cultural and clean", to use the opposition from *Real Men*.

Interestingly enough, recent developments also include an appropriation of another specifically black – and usually very traditional though less aggressive – music style, R'n'B, in order to undermine claims of aggressive male sexuality. It was made by Beck, one of the heroes of the post-Grunge era, both musically and ideologically, who made himself known to a larger audience with the memorable lines "I'm a loser, baby, so why don't you kill me?" (from *Loser,* 1994). Thus, as Beck says: "In the rock world, you're not really allowed to explore that more vulnerable side of masculinity, so I got really interested in that [...]." Consequently, he states his fascination with R'n'B because of its depiction of sensuality: "I love the cheesiness [...], and the sexuality is so uninhibited and has a playfulness and a humour to it. It's so straight out but it's also coupled with little bits of sincerity [...] These guys are crying [...]" (Dalton 1999). Consequently, Beck included a song called *Sexxlaws* on his recent album *Midnite Vultures* (1999) that contains the telling line "I'm a full grown man but I'm not afraid to cry".

It is important to keep in mind, though, that the primary concern for most men is typically the judgment of other men. The judgment of women is important, of course, but only as a supplement to that of other men. It would seem that many men would desperately like to end the debate by defining a more or less monolithic new standard, but they are unable to do so (aside from the fact that it would hardly be desirable since it would mean oppression of alternatives instead of expanding horizons). Secondly, no man can possibly escape the spectacle of gender hysteria, for even the most radical assertions of traditional hegemonic masculinity are evidences of precisely this hysteria, the fear of an unstable gender identity in the face of uncontrollable changes. The symptoms include the ostentatious display of heterosexist and misogynist codes, the construction of male bodies through body building and the appropriation of technology as in Heavy Rock. Moreover, the hysteria manifests itself through the distinct stylizing of masculinity and the male body that is characteristic of many Rock and Rap lyrics. The media play their part in this, too, since gender hysteria offers diverse possibilities for commercial use. Different concepts of masculinity can be presented and sold according to a segmentation of the consumers, and it has to kept in mind that this entails a co-optation which is very difficult to resist and which in the end serves to perpetuate existing power relations, although it would, of course, not be a valid alternative to stop producing subversive discursive acts (see Mayer 1996).

In conclusion, it can be maintained that the contemporary popular music scene incorporates (and is in turn incorporated by) several conflicting discourses of masculine identity and thus caters for diverse needs in the audience. Masculinity in direct and indirect manifestations is both a way of expressing genuine anxiety about the artists' own respective masculine identity and a means of appealing to target groups. Even if Rock has generally changed from a straightforward and openly misogynist position to a more ambivalent one, an aggressive hegemonic masculinity is still unequivocally endorsed by many Rappers, where the homophobic basis of hegemonic masculinity clearly shows itself (although this black masculinity may also contain an attack on the ethnicity of hegemonic masculinity). Additionally, it is still present in Grunge, though in a somewhat more disguised and problematized form. But apart from this there are different and at least potentially subversive undercurrents which can be glimpsed in the works of artists like Joe Jackson or Beck, who voice the concerns and frustrations experienced by themselves and many members of their audience alike. There is undoubtedly an important truth in the assertion that

> [l]istening to rock bands today, it seems that the men have little new to say: the same old preoccupations, postures and scenarios are repeated with slight variations and diminishing returns. Having exhausted the psychosexual dynamic of male rebellion, rock culture is confronting the possibility that the only new frontier is female experience. (Reynolds/Press 2000).

But this seems to be only half of the matter. It turns out that there is much more to say for men, about their status and identity and their experience of masculinity as well their sometimes desperate search for new models and expressions. And it is not only in the interest of men alone that this search proves to be fruitful. While it is necessary for women to find an adequate expression for their experience, men have to cope with the legacy of that past and modify it according to their reshaped reality. The result could be an integral musical vision that embraces new masculinities and femininities alike. Such an instance of artistic expression could offer many possibilities for subversive discursive acts that could be employed to challenge the "asymmetrical binary of masculinity and femininity" (Butler 1990: 31). Perhaps this is something that can ultimately be achieved together.

Works cited

Attig, R. Brian 1991. "The gay voice in popular music: A social value model analysis of 'Don't Leave Me This Way'." *Journal of Homosexuality*, 21 (1/2, 1991), 185.

Brod, Harry and Michael Kaufman (eds.) 1994. *Theorizing Masculinities.* Thousand Oaks, CA: Sage.

Butler, Judith 1990. *Gender Trouble: Feminism and the Subversion of Identity.* New York: Routledge.

———— 1993. *Bodies that Matter: On the Discursive Limits of "Sex".* New York: Routledge.

Connell, Robert W. 1987. *Gender and Power: Society, the Person and sexual Politics.* Cambridge: Polity Press.

———— 1995. *Masculinities: Knowledge, Power, and Social Change.* Berkeley: University of California Press.

Craig, Steve (ed.) 1992. *Men, Masculinity, and the Media.* Newbury Park, CA: Sage.

Dalton, Stephen 1999. "Postmodern Irony is like a Bad Smell in the Bathroom: Has he who smelt it dealt it? Beck answers some burning Questions." *NME* 16 October 1999.

Denski, Stan and David Sholle 1992. "Metal Men and Glamour Boys: Gender Performance in Heavy Metal" in Steve Craig (ed.). *Men, Masculinity, and the Media.* Newbury Park, CA: Sage, 41-60.

Fiske, Eliot 1987. "British Cultural Studies and Television" in R. C. Allen (ed.). *Channels of Discourse: TV and Contemporary Criticism.* Chapel Hill, NC & London: University of North Carolina Press, 254-290.

Hall, Stuart 1993. "Encoding – Decoding" in *The Cultural Studies Reader.* Ed. Simon During. London: Routledge, 90-103.

Kimmel, Michael. (1994). "Masculinity as Homophobia: Fear, Shame, and Silence in the Construction of Gender Indentity" in Brod and Kaufman (eds.). *Theorizing Masculinities.* Thousand Oaks, CA: Sage, 119-141.

Mayer, Ruth 1996. "Schmutzige Fakten: Wie sich Differenz verkauft" in Tom Holert and Mark Terkessidis (eds.). *Mainstream der Minderheiten: Pop in der Kontrollgesellschaft.* Berlin: Edition ID-Archiv, 153-168.

Middleton, Jason 1999. "Heroin Use, Gender, and Affect in Rock Subcultures." *Echo* 1.1. URL: http://www.humnet.ucla.edu/ech/Volume1-Issue1/middleton/middleton - article.html.

Peterson, Alan 1998. *Unmasking the Masculine: 'Men' and 'Identity' in a Sceptical Age.* Newbury Park, CA: Sage.

Reynolds, Simon and Joy Press 2000. *The Sex Revolts.* Cambridge, MA: Harvard University Press. URL: http://members.aol.com/blissout/tsr.htm.

Wahl, Greg 1995. *Narrating Punk: Masculinity, Genealogy, Patriarchy.* URL: http://otal.nmd.edu/~jpaolett/grad/punk.html.

The White Hunter: Edgar Rice Burroughs, Ernest Hemingway, Clint Eastwood, and the Art of Acting Male in Africa

Ruth Mayer

Shortly after the turn of century, the white male became an endangered species in the United States. That is, if one is to believe popular magazines, pamphlets and a huge machinery of political propaganda, relishing as never before in horror scenarios of a country inundated by a flood of foreigners, and smothered in the sticky sweetness of a "feminized" culture of sentimentality. As different as the individual approaches and insights were, in one respect everybody seemed to agree: It was time to act. And acting – in both senses of the word – became indeed a means of dealing with the alleged crisis. In the early twentieth century, being male and being white turned into an achievement, an agenda to be acted out over and over again. And if the ethnified and feminized city spaces in the States stood in the way of the aspired goal of becoming truly male and truly white, there was always Africa.

In this paper I will approach two iconic images of the white man in Africa – the ape-man and the white hunter – and reflect upon some of the transitions these images have undergone since the turn of the century. Edgar Rice Burroughs' Tarzan and Ernest Hemingway's Macomber will thus be confronted with a contemporary representative of white masculinity on foreign ground – Clint Eastwood's fictional film maker John Wilson, the hero of the 1990 film *White Hunter, Black Heart*. All of these narratives, I argue, are so much more concerned with the role of white men in the Western world than with the African set-up they figure forth. Mapped out against the backdrop of exotic otherness, the scenarios of white male self-fashioning in the wilderness give scope to Western preoccupations about autonomy and authenticity in a modern world.

Work your Body! Tarzan and Tautology

Tarzan of the Apes, Edgar Rice Burroughs' pulp novel around a white British aristocrat growing up as an ape in the jungle and falling in love with an American girl, is obsessed with the issues of civilization, nationality, gender, and race. And where novelists of colonialism like H. Rider Haggard or Rudyard Kipling – Burroughs' big models – time and again enacted cultural encounters as instances of (uneven) negotiation and communication, Burroughs stresses the clash and the conflict between different realms. To survive on foreign ground, his novel argues, you have to fight. The refinements of Western civilization may very well prove futile in this battle.

Two central scenes in *Tarzan*, one of them forming the dramatic exposition in Africa, are thus centered around firearms, the epitome of Western technological superiority, and both show women handling them. When Lady Greystoke, Tarzan's mother-to-be, intervenes with a gun to save her husband from an assaulting ape, she manages to kill the ape, but more or less accidentally. For a precarious moment before the ape collapses, the horrified Lord sees him turning around and charging at "the terrified girl vainly trying to fire another bullet into the animal's body; but she did not understand the mechanism of the firearm, and the hammer fell futily upon an empty cartridge" (Burroughs 1990: 39). Later on a similar scenario of physical helplessness and technical futility evolves around Jane Porter who when confronted with an assaulting lion can think of no better use of the pistol in her hand but to kill her servant and herself to forego the terrible fate – and even there she fails... Putting pistols in the hands of women who do not know how to use them properly points to a trenchant skepticism against the achievements of civilization in this novel, a provision equally illustrated by the intellectual figures, Jane's father, the Professor, and his assistant – "impractical theorists" (Burroughs 1990: 134; cf. Bederman 1995: 226). It is no surprise that Tarzan, this "personification [...] of the primitive man, the hunter, the warrior" (Burroughs 199: 122) prefers the knife or bow and arrow to the mechanical weapons the Europeans and Americans brought along.

This preference for more "physical" weapons goes along with a focalization on the male body, which becomes Tarzan's ultimate weapon in the course of the novel. By dint of this process it might seem that eventually *Tarzan* recuperates another stock figure of nineteenth century adventure fiction – the "white warrior", exemplarily embodied by Sir Henry Curtis in Haggard's *King Solomon's Mines* (1885). But Tarzan's strength is not a product of archaic masculinity, even if it is time and again described in terms of classical heroism and ancient grandeur. Significantly enough, Edgar Rice Burroughs criticized the makers of the early Tarzan-films for casting Elmo Lincoln, the hulky muscle man, for the part:

> Tarzan was not beefy but was light and graceful and well-muscled. [...] Tarzan must be young and handsome with an extremely masculine face and manner. [...] It may be difficult to get such a man but please do not try to get a giant or a man with over-developed muscles. It is true that in the stories I often speak of Tarzan as the "giant Apeman" but that is because I am rather prone to use superlatives. (Letter of January 28, 1919, cited in Porges 1975: 315-316)

The Tarzan of the novels is not a freak of nature, his body is the result of highly modern planning, not biologically but culturally extraordinary. Reflecting on the imagery of the "white man's muscles" Richard Dyer differentiated between the "natural" and the "trained" body along the lines of biological disposition and cultural work. Reading the *Tarzan* films in their obsessive enactment of the perfect body, he concludes that within the figure of the built body tradition and modernity interfuse. The body builder draws upon allegedly long-standing aesthetic principles and techniques, yet the product of this work is markedly up-to-date:

> The built white body is not the body that white men are born with, it is the body made possible by their natural mental superiority. The point after all is that it is built, a product of the application of thought and planning, an achievement. It is the sense of the mind at work behind the production of this body that most defines its whiteness. (Dyer 1997: 164; see also Easthope 1990: 35-58; Brown 1993; Kimmel 1994)

The very same reconceptualization of body/mind constellations suffuses *Tarzan of the Apes*. The novel's ideological framework could be said to rest upon Tarzan's well-trained shoulders: his built body makes him equal to the apes and the natives, without qualifying his difference.

Situating this display of work and discipline in the African jungle, Burroughs manages to reenact the lines of differentiation between Europe, Africa, and America: the English Lord who grows up wild in the African wilderness manages to find himself by way of training, or rather, body building. And while the self Tarzan eventually finds for once clearly attests to his "aristocratic birth" and "many generations of fine breeding" (Burroughs 1990: 202) – and thus to the "old world" of Anglo-Saxon tradition – his disregard for status and over-refinement, the traditional markers of prestige in the old world, clearly discloses a new frame of reference for this particular self-fashioning: Tarzan the body builder is Tarzan the new (world) man.

Yet rendering body building the epitome of cultural self-fashioning is not unproblematic, as there is a structural deficit inscribed into the practice itself: its "uselessness". The implication of self-referentiality, of a lack of purpose, has haunted modern sport from its beginnings in the nineteenth century on. Both the new sport clubs established around the turn of the century and the paramilitary youth groups of the time could not altogether deny their "lack of any clear goals. Activity was an end in itself; the only commitment was to the idea of commitment," as T. J. Jackson Lears pointed out. "Formed in opposition to modern moral flaccidity," he concludes, "paramilitary youth groups unknowingly exacerbated it" (Lears 1981: 110). The very rhetoric of cultural masculinization and re-invigoration which these organizations enthusiastically embraced, alongside the Rooseveltian notion of a "strenuous life," thus always ran the risk of flipping over into its counterpart, the endorsement of decadent self-indulgence.

At first glance, Tarzan's body building seems to be unaffected by the stigma of unpractical narcissism, as it is justified time and again in countless fights against various beasts of the jungle. And yet, at a closer look it turns out that Tarzan's lifestyle is far from practical – his special status as a "white ape" can be seen to depend upon this very quality of body building which its American proponents around the turn of the century were so anxious to downplay: tautology. After all, apart from demarcating his equality with the "fierce brutes of the jungle" (Burroughs 1990: 62), Tarzan's body always also demarcates his fundamental difference, his exceptionality. Let me give an example: At one point in the novel, Tarzan escapes from his arch-enemy Sabor, the lioness, at almost the last moment. He reacts on the grounds of his "quickness of mental action" (Burroughs 1990: 55), jumps into the river and then works out how to swim, thus giving one more prove of his superior intellect and his bodily fitness (the ape on his side is killed). Yet at the same time Tarzan also discovers the "feeling of freshness and exhilaration which the cool waters had imparted to him" and discovers sport as a leisure activity: "ever after he lost no opportunity to take a daily plunge in lake or stream or ocean when it was possible to do so" (Burroughs 1990: 56). Here, both the concept of work (training) and the concomitant concept of "workout" (leisure) delineate the borderlines of Tarzan's exceptional situation in the jungle, setting him off from the apes who "did not like to enter water, and never did so voluntarily" (Burroughs 1990: 56).

Body-building turns into an end in itself at times, a ritualistic performance devoid of use value, acted out without any clear idea about its purpose and its consequences – an instinctive act of distinction. Indeed, Tarzan's entire behavior is made out as instinctive, determined by both his highly trained body and a high-bred ancestry which can be actualized whenever needed with "utter unconsciousness of self," constituting a "hereditary instinct of graciousness" (Burroughs 1990: 202). Insofar as heredity and training function as equivalents, even if they are put into explicit opposition – "heredity spoke louder than training" (Burroughs 1990: 202). Throughout the novel the two extremes in Tarzan's personality, his aristocratic blood and his primeval training, seem to confirm rather than contradict each other, suggesting a concept of identity as procedural quality – the instinctive body knowledge and the genealogical archive which form the backdrop for never-ending processes of self-fashioning in the wilderness – which becomes in turn the blueprint for any new and alienating environment (see Yurca 1996; Mayer 1995).

Eric Cheyfitz has reflected upon the "irony of redundancy" in *Tarzan*, coming to the fore in the notion "that a man must be civilized in order to be civilized" (Cheyfitz 1991: 13). And indeed, where earlier enactments of the colonial encounter from H. Rider Haggard to Rudyard Kipling stylized civilization as a gift to be handed over to the unknowing natives, Edgar

Rice Burroughs makes it out as a complicated mixture of heredity and training that has to be protected and cultivated, and is much too unique to be passed on. Walter Benn Michaels has shown how such a notion of civilization as precarious heritage rather than disposable achievement goes very well together with the "culturalization" of identity in the twentieth century: "Culture, put forward as a way of preserving the primacy of identity while avoiding the embarrassments of blood, would turn out to be much more effective [...] as a way of reconceptualizing and thereby preserving the essential contours of racial identity" (Michaels 1995: 13).

Tarzan of the Apes can be seen as located at the outset of this development: obviously, the rhetoric of race and blood still prevails, yet it is increasingly by way of cultural practices – training, body building, sport – that it comes to be expressed. In the course of this subtle substitution – or hybridization – categories like race are not discarded but translated into the vocabulary of modernity, while the cultural practice of body-building is drained of any clear functionality or reference and thus essentialized in turn. The trained white body documents superiority (actively overcoming the animalesque and primitive) and demarcates difference. By dint of this development, identity comes to be conceptualized as a highly performative quality, suggesting an underlying matrix which has to be acted out time and again in order to be sustained. If instincts, intimations and unconscious reflexes bring about the true self, then the traditional means of self-reflection – meditation and communication – have to figure as detours and deflections at best. To paraphrase Walter Benn Michaels: To be a white male you have to do white male things, but you can't really count on doing white male things unless you are already a white male (Michaels 1995: 125).

Hence, Tarzan's obsessive enactments of white male identity are necessarily as self-referential as they are: instead of imposing himself on others like colonial bearers of civilization, he fences himself off markedly from his environment – be that primitive wildlife or effeminate civilization. As this differentiation is an end in itself, tautology becomes the trope of the day.

From *Tarzan* to the White Hunter

Tarzan of the Apes turns white male identity into a performance piece, thus indirectly – and certainly unintentionally – drawing upon contemporary models of ethnicity in order to conceptualize whiteness and masculinity. But of course, Burroughs' most spectacular move vis à vis an ethnified and feminized modern US-American culture consists in his choice of location: to become truly white and truly male, his novel argues, you have to go to Africa and become an ape. This is an extreme move with extreme implications. Not to forget its comic appeal. After all, the Tarzan figure has quickly gained a dubious reputation – there is undeniably something embarrassing about a man yodling in the treetops. By contrast, Burroughs' big idol Theodore Roosevelt found a mode of endorsing wildness and animality without the extreme implication of turning into a wildman, or an ape. Associating wildness with Native Americans and animality with big game Roosevelt promoted fighting and hunting as means of acquiring these attributes of masculinity, without losing the refined status of whiteness. As Gail Bederman noted about Roosevelt's careful self-stylization in the frontispiece of his *Hunting Trips of a Ranchman* (1885): "Sans eyeglasses, [...] TR stands in a woodland setting, wearing a fringed buckskin suit. [...] although he bears the weapons, and manly demeanor of civilized man, he wears the clothing of savages. [...] he is at once like the Indians and superior to them" (Bederman 1995: 176; see also Slotkin 1996). In a way, Roosevelt anticipates the moves of mimicry so popular in contemporary enactments of white men – his ranchman is, after all, almost, but not quite, like an Indian. If this Western frontier act was successful, Roosevelt would later become even more famous for another white hunter performance – this one set in East Africa.

The gestures of masquerade and mimicry permeate twentieth century white hunter narratives, and even if most of them are less open about their performative agenda than Burroughs' *Tarzan*, enacting ranchmen, cowboys, and white hunters instead of an ape-man, they conceive of white male identity along exactly the same lines as Burroughs: as a category that has to be acted out incessantly in order to be maintained. However, while ape-man stories were getting more and more fantastic throughout this century, white hunter stories were becoming more and more nostalgic. This development is already pertinent in the work of a writer who would literally come to embody the white hunter figure, following hard on Roosevelt's heels in his performative interlinkage of life and work. Ernest Hemingway's "public image [...] as the white hunter of the safari, overtook and, some would argue, overshadowed the private artist," as Paul Smith pointed out in a reflection on the intersecting functions of self-stylization and writing in Hemingway's life (Smith 1998: 11).

Even if, as will see, Hemingway's project differs considerably from Roosevelt's – or Burroughs' at that – there are some commonalities between these Americans' approaches to Africa that should be briefly considered. From Roosevelt's *African Game Trails* (1910) to Burroughs' *Tarzan of the Apes* and Hemingway's *Green Hills of Africa*, the experience of Africa is time and again enacted via a strange oscillation between an almost aggressive claim for authenticity ("this is what life is really like") and an emphasis on the experience's fantastic exceptionality ("this is no way like ordinary life"). Africa, as Toni Morrison put it with reference to Hemingway's posthumously published *The Garden of Eden*, figures as "a blank, empty space into which [the writer] asserts himself, an uncreated void ready, waiting, and offering itself up for his artistic imagination, his work, his fiction" (Morrison 1992: 88-89). By this token, Africa becomes the epitome of authenticity – the uninscribed, primeval continent – *and* at the same time a fantasy space: the perfect setting for a daydream.

Of course, on a basic level every adventure narrative revolves around just that – daydreams. Not accidentally the genre has been described as giving vent to a very specific kind of identification: "Its purpose is not to confront motives and experiences in myself that I might prefer to ignore but to take me out of myself by confirming an idealized self-image" (Cawelti 1976: 19). And indeed, even more than Roosevelt or Burroughs, Hemingway seems to be obsessed with leaving behind the mundane routines of modern urban life, so much so that his African writing at times involuntarily calls to mind the vagaries of one of the most proficient daydreamers ever – James Thurber's Walter Mitty. This character, so popular in the United States of the 1940s, could be seen to dream himself time and again out of his middle-class urban white male existence into stereotypical set-ups that paradoxically promised agency and authenticity by way of blotting out everyday experiences: most notably the experience of an overpowering wife, cast as a "predatory female, spawned – like the perplexing machines around her – by an industrialized and advanced culture" (Kenney 1984: 49).

But as striking as the analogies between Walter Mitty on the one hand, and Hemingway's protagonists in "The Short Happy Life of Francis Macomber" and "The Snows of Kilimanjaro" on the other, might be – all of these men desperately striving to escape the stranglehold of modernity and femininity – Hemingway's implementation of the daydream mode is too complex to be explained in terms of escapism. Or rather, it is too complex to be explained in terms of escaping Western modernity alone. In a way, as we will see, Hemingway's protagonists not only try to get away from the West: eventually they will escape from Africa as well, and in that respect they certainly top both Roosevelt's white hunter and Burroughs' ape-man, not to mention James Thurber's Walter Mitty. Totalizing the very aspects of withdrawal and isolation which his predecessors took such great pain to downplay, Hemingway manages to contain the paradoxical insight that the notion of authenticity – being a true man – came to be intricately conjoined with the logic of escapism and the daydream – leaving the real world behind.

What Hemingway kept at bay, however, takes center stage in contemporary white hunter narratives. It seems that for several years now, popular narratives could not stress enough that authenticity is a mere construct, and that the quest for self-authentication a fantasy. Yet that is not to say that the white hunter is finished. We will see that this cultural icon is tougher than it seems.

Hemingway's Hunt

Large parts of early twentieth century cultural history could be written in terms of a desperate struggle for authenticity and truth in the face of technological overrefinement and alienation. Donna Haraway has shown how in the course of this struggle African "unspoiled nature" came to function as the counterpart for notions of civilization as a "germ" (Haraway 1989: 53). While the desires for an unchanged and unchanging order were to some extent projected onto African natives, the full force of the Western desire came to bear on another object: big game. Big game hunting presented itself as the cure for the diseases of civilization, and, by extension, as the reinvigorating potion for white men.

As we have seen with regard to Burroughs' *Tarzan,* the imperialist formula of true manhood drew on the components of hunting and sportsmanship likewise, figuring forth the white man's being equal to but never identical with the jungle population. Reflecting upon Ernest Hemingway's African writing, Peter Messent paraphrases Donna Haraway's description of Rooseveltian sportsmanship to suggest Hemingway's adherance to the self-same imagery: "Africa functions as an unspoiled territory where 'decadence [...] decay's contagion, the germ of civilization' can be combated by a narrator who 'restor[es] manhood in the healthy activity of sportsmanlike hunting' " (Messent 1992: 148).

Yet while for Theodore Roosevelt and Edgar Rice Burroughs sportsmanship and hunting were indeed tightly conjoined, matters are different with Hemingway, let alone with later writers, filmmakers and artists grapling with the icon of the white hunter. If in *Tarzan* sport, training, and body building figured as the civilizing elements in a savage setting, in Hemingway's "The Short Happy Life of Francis Macomber" (1936), published more than twenty years after Burroughs' first *Tarzan* volume, it is precisely by way of the differentiation between the sportsman and big game hunter that masculinity will be mapped out. This shift goes along with another, no less consequential reevaluation: where *Tarzan of the Apes* focused on the spectacularly trained white male body, Hemingway's short story seems curiously unimpressed with the trained, well-muscled, built body and its display:

> Francis Macomber was very tall, very well built if you did not mind that length of bone, dark, his hair cropped like an oarsman, rather thin-lipped, and was considered handsome. He was dressed in the same sort of safari clothes that Wilson wore except that his were new, he was thirty-five years old, kept himself very fit, was good at court games, had a number of big-game fishing records, and had just shown himself, very publicly, to be a coward. (Hemingway 1995: 4)

Francis Macomber, the man whose cathartic "coming of age" we witness in Hemingway's short story is indubitably a sportsman, a member of the "international, fast, sporting set" (Hemingway 1995: 26). But sportsmanship is no proof of manhood here. While Macomber's entire appearance calls to mind Tarzan's well-muscled but not disproportionate body, it is Robert Wilson, the white hunter, who comes to demarcate the model here. And Wilson is not "handsome":

> He was about middle height, with sandy hair, a stubby mustache, a very red face and extremely cold eyes, with faint white wrinkles at the corners that grooved merrily when he smiled. [...] she looked away from his face at the way his shoulders sloped in the loose tunic he wore with the four big cartridges held in loops where the left breast pocket should have been, at his big brown hands, his old slacks, his very dirty boots and back to his red face again. [...] the baked red of his face stopped in a white line that marked the circle left by his Stetson hat that hung now from one of the pegs of the tent pole. (Hemingway 1995: 4)

Wilson is dirty, ungroomed, weatherworn, a far cry from Macomber's neat and fit appearance. Both descriptions are given from the point of view of a woman, Macomber's wife, Margot, who looks the men over, "as though she had never seen them before" (Hemingway 1995: 4) and in the following tries to come to terms with the fact that it is not the handsome sportsman she is attracted to: "Wilson, the white hunter, she knew she had never truly seen before" (Hemingway 1995: 4).

This experience of the suddenly changed perspective, the "never before seen", will inform the entire story, a story which has after all been canonized for its intricate techniques of focalization, continually switching points of view, so that we obtain a multitude of insights into what is going on – and a highly fractured picture. If Margot is introduced in the process of reorientation, it is her husband's much more pervasive transformation that forms the core of the narrative. The story builds slowly up to relate the circumstances of his embarrassment, his cowardice at a lion hunt, and then reiterates and refashions this experience in positive terms, tracing the sportsman's transformation into a white hunter. This process takes the guise of replacing one framework with another, the frameworks themselves being described in terms of useful and useless knowledge. Macomber came to Africa knowing a lot of useless things:

> He knew about [...] motor cycles – that was earliest – about motor cars, about duck-shooting, about fishing, trout, salmon and big-sea, about sex in books, many books, too many books, about all court games, about dogs, not much about horses, about hanging on to his money, about most of the other things his world dealt in, and about his wife not leaving him. (Hemingway 1995: 21)

Macomber's American "knowledge" comprises a well-balanced mixture of athletic (sports and hunting), educational (books), business (money) and social skills, in which the wife figures as just another calculable asset – in other words, this knowledge demarcates the framework of modern upper-class masculinity. The monotonous list of banal entertainments and skills emphasizes the predictability of this framework, in which sport functions as a regular and superficial practice among others, a leisure activity which is very much part of the workday.

Africa, however, appears to call for a completely different kind of knowledge, if knowledge is the right word for what is needed here. In a recapitulation of the lion hunt Macomber's predicament is summed up as a lack of "knowing":

> Macomber did not know how the lion had felt before he started his rush, nor during it when the unbelievable smash of the .505 with a muzzle velocity of two tons had hit him in the mouth, nor what kept him coming after that, when the second ripping crash had smashed his hind quarters and he had come crawling on toward the crashing, blasting thing that had destroyed him. Wilson knew something about it and only expressed it by saying, "Damned fine lion," but Macomber did not know how Wilson felt about things either. He did not know how his wife felt except that she was through with him. (Hemingway 1995: 21)

What Macomber does not know is precisely what gets the narrative going – an insight into other beings' innermost life, their feeling. The fantasy of knowing what others feel seems to infuse the very narrative strategy of multiple focalization, which is after all just another way of getting in on other modes of perception in order to relate the "never before seen." And on the plot level it is this kind of knowledge, or rather "knowingness" as Hugh Kenner called it (Kenner 1975: 136), that will turn Macomber from a member of the "international sporting set" into an African white hunter. "Knowingness," the mindframe of the bullfighter and the white hunter, entails a peculiar mode of action, not rationalized, regular and standardized as in the American way of life, but deeply corporeal, instinctive, animalesque: "action in which you had something to do, in which you can kill and come out of it, doing something you are ignorant about and so not scared, no one to worry about and no responsibility except to perform something you feel sure you can perform," as Hemingway described the same phenomenon in *Green Hills of Africa* (Hemingway 1996: 116).

Seen that way, knowing comes to merge with this other key term of Hemingway's story: feeling. However, the skill of entering the other mindframe is not to be confused with compassion: getting a feel for the lion's predicament does not bring about communion, but ensures "the compressed act of shooting a lion" (Kenner 1975: 138). This kind of identification eschews communication or exchange, the contact imagined is strictly unidirectional, demarcating an extreme form of takeover or intake, and thus an endeavour much less self-transcending and expansive than might seem at first glance.

The impression of withdrawal or isolation is further enhanced by what Walter Benn Michaels called Hemingway's "aesthetics of untranslateability" (Michaels 1995: 74), the insistence that what Macomber experiences is beyond words, pure feeling, to be cast in negative terms, vague allusions or tautologies at best: "For the first time in his life he really felt wholly without fear. Instead of fear he had a feeling of definite elation" (Hemingway 1995: 31). "I've never felt any such feeling", "I feel absolutely different" (Hemingway 1995: 32). Talking about this feeling will not do, not even among the initiate, between white hunters:

> "Do you have that feeling of happiness about what's going to happen?" Macomber asked, still exploring his new wealth. "You're not supposed to mention it," Wilson said, looking in the other's face. "[...] Doesn't do to talk too much about all this. Talk the whole thing away. No pleasure in anything if you mouth it up too much." (Hemingway 1995: 33)

Talking about an extraordinary experience means getting a grip on it or holding it at bay, and this is the last thing Hemingway means to achieve in this story. The strange must never be familiarized, difference never collapsed into sameness – a logic which pertains to the very effort at translation as Michaels has shown, and which pertains to the convention of omniscient narration just as well. The practice of multiple focalization, by contrast, allows for momentary glimpses at the "never before seen" without compromising its difference, the very transgression of boundaries bringing about their stabilization. By the same token, the white hunter's transgression into the animal world ultimately reinforces the autonomous male subject, precisely because it elides communication and reflection, as Macomber's very last confrontation with this different realm underscores:

> [...] they saw [...] the bull coming, nose out, mouth tight closed, blood dripping, massive head straight out, coming in a charge, his little pig eyes bloodshot as he looked at them. [...] Macomber, as he fired, unhearing his shot in the roaring of Wilson's gun, saw fragments like slate burst from the huge boss of the horns, and the head jerked, he shot again at the wide nostrils and saw the horns jolt again and fragments fly, and he did not see Wilson now and, aiming carefully, shot again with the buffalo's huge bulk almost on him and his rifle almost level with the on-coming head, nose out, and he could see the wicked little eyes and the head started to lower and he felt a sudden white-hot, blinding flash explode inside his head and that is all he ever felt. (Hemingway 1995: 36)

This passage conveys an impression of utter concentration or focalization, a narrowing down of vision (from "they" to "he", from an overall view to chaotic details) suggestive of a series of extreme close-ups or the fragmented density of a cubist painting: the nose, the mouth, the horns, the head, the nostrils, the horns, the huge bulk, head, nose, eyes, the head. The delineation of short descriptive nouns and concise paratactical sentence structures communicates a breathtaking closeness, but forgoes contact – both in the sense of a devastating clash and in the form of merging. Instead, the intense awareness of the other's presence brings about an extraordinary self-awareness or self-feeling, further accentuated in the ulterior transmutation of vision into feeling: the "sudden white-hot, blinding flash" is felt, not seen. This last turn culminates the story's strange logic of internalization, its privileging of daydreamlike seclusion (Zapf 1990), as it demarcates that most precarious, most private and uncommunicating of moments: dying – it is, after all, the moment when the bullet, not the bull, hits home; his wife having shot Macomber from behind.

The real adventure of "Macomber" does not take place on African ground, but deep within the white male mind. In its marked disregard for contact or exchange this story at times comes across like an inverted version of *Tarzan of the Apes*, the celebration of masculine body-feeling replacing and aggrandizing the earlier celebration of the trained male body. In their dismissal of the appearances and exteriorities of US-American middle class life, Hemingway's heroes figure forth another stage for performing masculinity: the male psyche.

White Hunter, Black Heart, or, Elephantasias

> You ask how this was discussed, worked out and understood with the bar of language, and I say it was as freely discussed and clearly understood as though we were a cavalry patrol all speaking the same language. We were all hunters [...] and the whole thing could be worked out, understood and agreed to without using anything but a forefinger to signal and a hand to caution. (Hemingway 1996: 251)

In Africa, Hemingway suggests time and again, instinctive and immediate insights supersede calculation, reflection and ultimately language itself. What has rightfully been called an "aesthetics of untranslateability" is intricately entwined with an "aesthetics of action" – both systems eliding communication and exchange and both indulging in the isolated and totalized experience of selfhood, an experience best brought about by hunting.

Yet the aesthetics of action and the theme of hunting present themselves in stark contrast to this other big project of representing "Africa" in the first half of our century: primitivism. In Hemingway's autobiographical reflections, *Green Hills of Africa*, this oppositionality is brought to the fore when he relates an absurd encounter in the wilderness: the semi-celebrity Ernest Hemingway coming across the semi-celebrity Vassily Kandinsky, a European who evidently adheres to an entirely different set of values than his American peers:

"I kill nothing, you understand," Kandinsky told us. "Why are you not more interested in the natives?"

"We are," my wife assured him.

"They are really interesting. Listen –" Kandinsky said, and he spoke on to her.

Hemingway would rather discuss the results of the outing of the day with his white hunter, and leaves Kandinsky to his wife, the latter's remarks then forming the comical backdrop to the manly debates around tracking, shooting and skinning wild game: " 'So,' Kandinsky was saying to my wife. 'That is what you should see. The big ngomas. The big native dance festivals. The real ones' " (Hemingway 1996: 16). If the Hemingways did ever go to see one of these dance events, it certainly did not make its way into *Green Hills*. Kandinsky, however, would himself make good use of the "real" Africa that he encountered. But that is another story.

In *Green Hills*, the anecdotal encounter is meant to differentiate Hemingway's project unequivocally from what is presented as a sentimental fantasy: while Kandinsky's "interest for the natives" appears as trite exoticism, hunting is made to demarcate a much more concrete, realistic and direct approach to the foreign space. Instead of seeking contact to the natives, Hemingway chooses to go native himself, mapping out a quest not for knowledge but for knowing, not for cultural inspiration but for sensual focalization – self-feeling (see Moddelmog 1998). At the same time, his plea for sincerity against trite clichés inaugurated the dichotomy of the sentimental glance and the unflinching gaze which was to experience a dramatic revival in the rhetorics of travel writing, journalism and their fictional outcrops from the 1980s onward.

Yet if Hemingway's rhetorical tirade against sentimentalists and romantics in Africa became a standard device, the conceptual grounds for his distanciation to Kandinsky did not hold out for long. Being interested in the natives and being interested in wild game turned out to be compatible concerns, as white hunters and African natives came to be paired in countless narratives of hunting and traveling in the following decades, and the more the figure of the white tough guy was discredited, the more credit the African native would gain. Or, to be more precise, the symbolic systems of blackness and Africanicity. Countless contemporary narratives, literary and filmic, invert the categories of whiteness and Africanicity, turning the white man into the exemplary African, while bringing the old paradigms of white huntership up to date with current cultural values and incentives.

Obviously, Clint Eastwood's film *White Hunter, Black Heart* (Warner Bros., 1990) is one such narrative. Indeed, here the very contact with the African native brings about the demise of the white hunter. Or so it seems. At any rate, Clint Eastwood's white hunter will never kill big game. Instead, he will come to face the fact that the classical white hunter model has outlived itself, and the film will eventually vehemently disclaim

Hemingway's collation of the white hunter with the realistic perspective and consign the figure to the realm of fantasy. But then reality and fantasy have always been hard to separate when it came to Africa, so that this relegation demarcates not so much the final disassembly of the established imagery as its reconfiguration in the face of different circumstances.

From the outset, *White Hunter, Black Heart* is stranded between the real and the fictional – the film relates the familiar story of coming to terms with the self on foreign ground, which is stratified on two levels here: first, there is the traditional – Hemingwayeske – plot line of self-authentication by way of shooting wild game. And then there is another plot line of self-authentication by way of shooting a film. Negotiating these two narrative realms involves the inevitable insight that the very boundaries of reality and fiction are hard to make out these days, as they are certainly no longer to be equated linearly with the practices of hunting and filmmaking. In a thinly veiled allusion to the events around John Huston's making of *The African Queen* in 1952, Eastwood's film traces the trials of an American director in Africa, who instead of concentrating on the film to be shot works himself into an obsession about hunting an elephant. Hence for the most part of *White Hunter, Black Heart* the film project is used as a cover for the "real" project of elephant hunting. It is only at the end that the error of this preference for hunting over filmmaking becomes evident. The times of hunting, this self-fashioning by violence, are over. Now self-fashioning is to be achieved by representation. The camera has replaced the gun as the main instrument of control.

In line with this reconfiguration, the dichotomy of hunter and sportsman seems to undergo a profound reevaluation in *White Hunter, Black Heart*. While filmmaker John Wilson (Clint Eastwood) clearly represents the hunter; his best friend, script writer Pete Varrell (Jeff Fahey) just as clearly stands for the sportsman. When the film begins Varrell has just arrived from a skiing trip; in Africa he plays tennis in an immaculate white outfit and soon joins the local soccer team. Representing the voice of reason and moderation as opposed to Wilson's egomania, Varrell is, not surprisingly, vehemently opposed to the project of shooting an elephant, endorsing Kandinsky's provisos when he calls elephant hunting a "crime" against a species which is "part of a world which no longer exists." This kind of logic is lost on his friend though, who, Ahab-like, seeks the absolute encounter and victorious conquest: when Wilson finally confronts the elephant, an extreme close-up of the animal's eye quotes an earlier, much similar shot: the vicious eye of the white whale in John Huston's *Moby Dick*, produced four years after *The African Queen* (Benayoun 1990). The outcome of the 1990 confrontation with the wild beast deviates from the established pattern, however. Wilson refrains from his destructive quest and lowers his gun.

But his conversion comes too late, the elephant charges after all, and the white man's life is saved only because the African guide Kivu (Boy Mathias Chuma) steps in and dies in his stead. This turn of events is even more devastating, as Kivu came to represent everything truly important to Wilson before: the epitome of silent, dignified, authentic manhood. Kivu figured forth the ideal partner, so much more attractive than the foolish and self-centered blond women the film lines up in unabashed misogyny and so much more authentic than the white men behaving like "dames" and "old ladies." The fact that this partnership precluded communication – none of them spoke the other's language – only enhanced the impression of "an instant bond that transcends language and culture," as one reviewer put it (Knapp 1996: 152).

The film's last scene seems to give the lie to this idyll, though. Tough masculinity, we are told, brings about death, as the quest for the primeval confrontation ends up revealing nothing but its futility and meaninglessness. Eventually, Wilson returns to Kivu's village, the place where his film is to be shot, and sits down to do what he is there for. *White Hunter, Black Heart* ends upon a close-up of his tired face, his voice cracks: "Action". Fade to African landscapes, the drums mourning Kivu's death merging with the Africanized musical score.

"The ending turns the entire film upside down, or rather, right side up," enthused film critic Verena Lueken:

> For after Eastwood up to then enacted at length more than familiar rituals of masculinity, in the course of which John Wilson may come across somewhat exaggeratedly at times, yet remains "intact" as a sympathetic figure despite some flaws [...], this John Wilson is mercilessly dismantled in the last scenes and together with him all the rituals he and the film celebrated before. (Lueken 1990: 32).

But can an ending turn an entire film around? Can images be taken back? Impressions simply blotted out? While it is certainly interesting to note that the film's ending seems to see a need to distanciate itself from the preceding action, to turn around and disclaim everything that has been presented up to then, I doubt whether this deconstruction works. Or whether it was meant to work in the first place. Thus, Susan Jeffords' reflections on another Eastwood film, the western *Unforgiven* (1992), seem much more to the point here: "it simultaneously presents and critiques a version of hard-bodied masculinity that verges on machismo, while debunking the myth of Hollywood westerns" (Jeffords, 186). Of course, Clint Eastwood's work lends itself exemplarily well to such "renarrations" as it was he himself who once set the status quo now to be revised and reassembled: "What [...] is most fascinating about [...] *White Hunter, Black Heart* is that Eastwood still seems to be working through a self-critical agenda: about himself, about performing, about the egoism and vulnerability of the artist," another critic noted (Combs 1990: 279). Eastwood is a master at the game of self-reflection and self-referentiality, a game which is also played in virtually all action-adventure films of the period – variously inflected with irony or skepticism. But Eastwood adds a characteristic note to the generic trend. His film transmutes the symbolic system of action into the symbolic system of acting. In *White Hunter, Black Heart* the quest for truth and authenticity entails masquerade and make-belief, until these strategies finally take over.

Seen that way, the film does not problematize Wilson's belief that filmmaking and life are basically conjoined and subject to the same laws, but his definition of these basic laws: sincerity and simplicity. When discussing the screenplay with Pete Verrill in Africa, he rejects an episode on the grounds of its being too complicated. In one of his many pompous monologues he then continues to lay out his concept of art:

> That's what creates truly important art. It's simplicity. [...] Hemingway understood that. That's why he always reduced life to its simplest terms. Whether it's courage, fear, impotence, death. People's lives just sort of unfolded, things just happened to them, one thing after another. They were never bogged down with that nonsense of subplot that we sweated over in the past.

He gives this speech first reclining in a chair in the open air, in safari gear, balancing his gun, and then posing on the edge of a terrace, aiming his gun at obviously no particular goal. This strangely out of place white hunter act – this is a script session after all – makes the passionate plea for simplicity and sincerity ring false. But then Wilson's entire lifestyle deviates radically from his own maxims – he lives a masquerade of masculinity. Thus his outings in African safari gear echo the scenes in England with which the film began: the American on horseback clothed in a classy red coat – fox hunting – and then made up in aristocratic garb in the impressive mansion he got to live in during the production phase. He played the aristocrat just as he will play the white hunter, a filmmaker having thoroughly, but also quite self-defeatingly absorbed the principles of his profession. Hence the unnerved request his producer Paul Landers (George Dzundza) voices in Africa seems very well to the point: "Can you dip that phoney English accent and, for God's sake, abandon your role of the great white hunter and become a movie director again?" But Wilson can't and won't at this point, getting sharply back at Landers to the embarrassment of the dinner company around:

> My role of the great hunter, as you put it, is strictly my own business. It has nothing to do with you. It's a sacred subject. [...] Why, I'd have to explain to you the sound of the wind and the smell of the woods. I'd have to create you all over again and stamp out all those years you spend on the dirty pavement in cramped shoes.

This arrogant retort contains a logical twist that is crucial for the entire logic of the film: if Wilson can embrace a "role" as his true identity, turning the masquerade into the epitome of self-fashioning, why shouldn't the same logic work for Paul Landers? Why indeed can't he be "created all over again"? The answer, of course, is that such self-fashioning from scratch is a precarious undertaking in the first place, always at the risk of clashing with the harsh facts of everyday life, the cramped shoes, if you will. This is what Farrell tries to tell Wilson when his aged body gives out during one of the safari outings: "Come on let's face it, this country is too tough for us [...]. We're not two heroes out of one of your films." Just like Hemingway's "Macomber," it seems, Eastwood's film turns against the Tarzanian myth of the well-trained body. But where Hemingway turned to body-feeling, Eastwood stays firmly on the grounds of looks, or rather, images.

It takes some time, but eventually Wilson will accept that the white hunter is a creature not of real life but of fiction, an artificial image (see for this logic Smith 1995: 94). And still, his final turn away from hunting and back to his film project comes across less as an act of fundamental reorientation – Wilson's finally being "able to sit down and be himself" (Knapp 1996: 152, 154) – but as a continuation of his former masquerades by other, more appropriate means. Where Macomber's defeat, his failure to shoot the lion, called for a cathartic reiteration of the hunt, now in daydreamlike control, Wilson's defeat, his failure to shoot the elephant and to safe Kivu's life, brings about the white hunter's transformation into the filmmaker. And indeed having control over images seems to be so much more crucial than having control over wild game in the late twentieth century, in a time which has discovered the "joy of receiving from the external world images that are usually internal, images that are familiar or not very far from familiar, of seeing them inscribed in a physical location (the screen)," as Christian Metz defined the age of the cinema, in which "fiction film enters into a functional competition with the daydream" (Metz 1982: 135-137).

Turning the white hunter figure into nothing but an act, the film takes a peculiar stance vis à vis established concepts of masculinity and whiteness. To come to self-expression, Eastwood's persona imitates other, earlier versions of itself. Where Burroughs' *Tarzan* endorsed tautology ("the white male doing white male things"), this film totalizes mimicry ("the white male being almost, but not quite, like other white males"). With this the film seems to visualize what Eric Lott called practices of "self-mimicry" in white male self-fashioning, giving evidence of the fact that "whiteness itself ultimately becomes an impersonation" (Lott 1993: 491) or, to cite Judith Butler, that gender is "a *corporeal style*, an 'act,' as it were, which is both intentional and performative" (Butler 1990: 139). In the representational framework of our days, the act is all there is – there is nothing underneath it any longer but other images, different acts. *White Hunter, Black Heart* evokes a concept of self-fashioning which almost unnoticeably moves away from long-standing notions of originality, independence and autonomy, toward the idea of life as an enactment. By this token, to turn from actor to director might be the ultimate self-assertion. As Hemingway's aesthetics of action moves into the background, an aesthetics of acting, masquerade and make-belief takes over, which paradoxically enough manages to consolidate and stabilize the imagery of white male self-authentication on foreign ground once more, and this time seemingly against all odds.

Works Cited

Baym, Nina 1990. " 'Actually, I Felt Sorry for the Lion' ", in Jackson J. Benson (ed.). *New Critical Approaches to the Short Stories of Ernest Hemingway*. Durham: Duke University Press,112-120.

Bederman, Gail 1995. *Manliness & Civilization. A Cultural History of Gender and Race in the United States, 1881-1917*. Chicago: The University of Chicago Press.

Benayoun, Robert 1990. "Clint et John: une saison infernale (*Chasseur blanc, chasseur noir*)." *Positif* 351 (March 1990), 2-4.

Benson, Jackson J. (ed.) 1990. *New Critical Approaches to the Short Stories of Ernest Hemingway*. Durham: Duke University Press.

Brown, Bill 1993. "Science Fiction, the World's Fair, and the Prosthetics of Empire" in Amy Kaplan and Donald E. Pease (eds.) 1993. *Cultures of United States Imperialism*. Durham: Duke University Press, 129-163.

Burroughs, Edgar Rice 1990. *Tarzan of the Apes*. Ed. Gore Vidal. New York: Signet.

Butler, Judith 1990. *Gender Trouble. Feminism and the Subversion of Identity*. New York: Routledge.

Cawelti, John G. 1976. *Adventure, Mystery, and Romance: Formula Stories as Art and Popular Culture*. Chicago: University of Chicago Press.

Cheyfitz, Eric 1991. *The Poetics of Imperialism. Translation and Colonization from The Tempest to Tarzan*. New York: Oxford University Press.

Combs, Richard 1990. "Do the Wrong Thing. *White Hunter, Black Heart*." *Sight & Sound* 59: 4 (Autumn 1990), 278-279.

Dyer, Richard 1997. *White*. London: Routledge.

Easthope, Antony 1986. *What a Man's Gotta Do. The Masculine Myth in Popular Culture*. Boston: Unwyn Hyman.

Haraway, Donna 1989. *Primate Visions. Gender, Race, and Nature in the World of Modern Science*. New York: Routledge.

Hemingway, Ernest 1995. *The Short Stories*. New York: Simon & Shuster.

Hemingway, Ernest 1996. *Green Hills of Africa*. New York: Simon & Schuster.

Jeffords, Susan 1994. *Hard Bodies. Hollywood Masculinity in the Reagan Era*. New Brunswick: Rutgers University Press.

Kaplan, Amy and Donald E. Pease (eds.) 1993. *Cultures of United States Imperialism*. Durham: Duke University Press.

Kenner, Hugh 1975. *A Homemade World. The American Modernist Writers*. New York: Alfred A. Knopf.

Kenney, Catherine McGehee 1984. *Thurber's Anatomy of Confusion*. Hamden: Archon Books.

Kimmel, Michael S. 1994. "Consuming Manhood. The Feminization of American Culture and the Recreation of the Male Body, 1832-1920" in Laurence Goldstein (ed.). *The Male Body. Features, Destinies, Exposures*. Ann Arbor: The University of Michigan Press, 12-42.

Knapp, Laurence F. 1996. *Directed by Clint Eastwood*. Jefferson: McFarland.

Lears, T.J. Jackson 1981. *No Place of Grace. Antimodernism and the Transformation of American Culture, 1880-1920*. New York: Pantheon.

Lott, Eric 1993. "White Like Me. Racial Cross-Dressing and the Construction of American Whiteness" in Amy Kaplan and Donald E. Pease (eds.) 1993. *Cultures of United States Imperialism*. Durham: Duke University Press, 474-495.

Lueken, Verena 1990. "Weißer Jäger, schwarzes Herz". *epd Film* 7: 6 (Juni 1990), 32.

Mayer, Ruth 1995. " 'Ther's somethin' in blood after all.' Late Nineteenth-Century Fiction and the Rhetoric of Race." *Real: Yearbook of Research in English and American Literature* 11 (1995), 119-138.

Messent, Peter 1992. *Ernest Hemingway*. New York: St. Martin's Press.

Metz, Christian 1982. *The Imaginary Signifyer. Psychoanalysis and the Cinema*. Trans. Alfred Guzzetti et. al. Bloomington: Indiana University Press.

Michaels, Walter Benn 1995. *Our America*. Durham: Duke University Press.

Moddelmog, Debra A. 1998. "Re-Placing Africa in 'The Snows of Kilimanjaro': The Intersecting Economies of Capitalist-Imperialism and Hemingway's Biography" in Paul Smith (ed.). *New Essays on Hemingway's Short Fiction*. Cambridge: Cambridge University Press, 111-136.

Morrison, Toni 1992. *Playing in the Dark: Whiteness and the Literary Imagination*. Cambridge, MA: Harvard University Press.

Porges, Irwin 1975. *Edgar Rice Burroughs: The Man Who Created Tarzan*. Provo: Brigham & Young University Press.

Slotkin, Richard 1996. *Regeneration through Violence: The Mythology of the American Frontier, 1600-1860*. New York: Harper Perennial.

Smith, Paul 1995. "Eastwood Bound" in Maurice Berger, Brian Wallis, Simon Watson (eds.). *Constructing Masculinity*. New York: Routledge, 77-97.

Smith, Paul 1998. "Introduction" in Smith (ed.). *New Essays on Hemingway's Short Fiction*, ed. Paul Smith. Cambridge: Cambridge University Press, 1-18.

Yurca, Catherine 1996. "Tarzan, Lord of the Suburbs." *Modern Language Quarterly* 57:3 (September 1996), 479-504.

Zapf, Hubert 1990. "Reflection vs. Daydream: Two Types of the Implied Reader in Hemingway's Fiction" in Jackson J. Benson (ed.). *New Critical Approaches to the Short Stories of Ernest Hemingway*. Durham: Duke University Press, 96-111.

Notes on Contributors

Neil Badmington lectures at the Centre for Critical and Cultural Theory, Cardiff University, UK.

Stefan Brandt is Assistant Professor of American Studies at the Free University of Berlin, Germany.

Rainer Emig is Professor of Modern British Literature at the University of Regensburg, Germany.

Madalena Gonzalez is Lecturer in English at the University of Avignon, France.

Stefan Herbrechter is Senior Lecturer in Cultural Studies at Trinity and All Saints College, University of Leeds, UK.

Eleanor Hogan is Senior Policy Officer in the Social Justice Unit, Office of the Aboriginal and Torres Strait Islander Commissioner at the Human Rights and Equal Opportunity Commission, Sydney, Australia.

Elisabeth Krimmer is Professor of German Studies at Mount Holyoke College, USA.

Frank Lay is a musician and doctoral candidate in Cultural Studies at the University of Cologne, Germany.

Ruth Mayer is Visiting Professor of American Studies at the University of Hannover, Germany

Peter Middleton is Senior Lecturer in English at the University of Southampton, UK.

Monika Müller is Assistant Professor of American Studies at the University of Cologne, Germany.

Russell West is Professor of British and American Studies at the University of Applied Sciences, Magdeburg, Germany.